MAHOGANY HIGHBOY, 18TH CENTURY

An
ENCYCLOPEDIA
of
ANTIQUES

by
HAROLD LEWIS BOND

Fully Illustrated

HALE, CUSHMAN & FLINT—BOSTON
1937

First printing, September 1937

This book is dedicated to the memory of the early craftsmen both here and abroad who by their skill, labor, and good taste produced work of lasting merit.

PREFACE

The purpose of this book is to give concise information regarding a multitude of objects made by the craftsmen of earlier days, and included within the term Antiques. These objects, naturally, fall into different classifications, and for the sake of clarity and easy reference the arrangement of the contents is in sections, each in alphabetical order, taking into account these differences. The principal subjects in each section have been treated at some length, with numerous references for further reading appended. The attempt has been made to include here only the essential facts for quickly available information, in other words, to make this book an encyclopedia. It is not intended for use as a textbook.

We are, in this country, a composite of an ancestry mingling many generations with many nationalities. We have, unconsciously perhaps, retained to some extent the likes and dislikes of our forbears and their talents and their shortcomings. In this, to them a New World, they worked hard, played but little, and feared only God and the Indians. As time passed and they became prosperous, they desired those home comforts they had left behind them when they came here. Their craftsmen became expert in the various trades, devoting their efforts to supplying a steadily increasing demand for their products, and the work done reflected the influence of their native origins. The early furniture was made by the carpenter and joiner, glass and pottery works were started, the women spun, wove and dyed the fabrics needed for clothing and other household purposes. Truly remarkable was the work of the silversmiths, who, before the end of the seventeenth century, were making those beautiful pieces that today attract so much admiration. Seeking to know, find and to preserve worthily the work of these pioneers is more than a pastime; it is a matter for serious study. This is recognized by the numerous clubs, organized in recent years, for the exchange of ideas and the promulgation of newly discovered information.

It has been said that the birth of interest in the products of these early craftsmen took place in the New England Cottage at the Centennial Exposition in Philadelphia in 1876. Be that as it may, it is certain that but little was known at that time concerning the men themselves. With a few notable exceptions, this was also true regarding the foreign craftsmen of the period, and even at this time good authorities differ as to the date of birth and the birthplace of Thomas Chippendale. Although there has been considerable progress made in the past few years in obtaining and printing biographical information this, is a field that has not yet received sufficient attention. With the thought that interest in this direction may be stimulated, brief accounts of the lives of some of the leading craftsmen of early times, those whose names and accomplishments have been in some measure recorded, are included in a separate section of this book. Besides these comparatively few names, there were literally thousands of others at work, furniture- and clock-makers, pottery and glass workers, pewterers and silversmiths of whom little or nothing is known at present, excepting the name. Because of their number no attempt has been made to list those names here. They should, however, receive their share of recognition for their part in helping to maintain a high level of excellence in their respective trades, and it is to be hoped that, as time passes, more of those sturdy craftsmen may emerge from the obscurity which now surrounds them.

IT IS only necessary to add that the apparent need for a book of this character inspired its preparation, but credit for the material contained therein must go to the men and women whose books, the result sometimes of years of patient study and research, have been the source of its information. Those books and many others will be found in the Bibliographical section (Part 7) arranged for ready reference for further reading, as none of the subjects included here could be exhaustively treated within the scope of the work. The pages of ANTIQUES and other magazines have also supplied valuable materials. The author has been favored with expert advice and criticism of the manuscript by Mr. William Germain Dooley, Antiques editor of the BOSTON TRANSCRIPT. His services in that respect are gratefully acknowledged.

HAROLD LEWIS BOND.

Boston, 1937.

Table of Contents

LIST OF ILLUSTRATIONS

PART I

FURNITURE AND PERIODS

Definitions unless otherwise stated are from the standpoint of the American antiques collector.

WALNUT VENEER SLANT-FRONT DESK, WILLIAM AND MARY
PERIOD, CIRCA 1690

MAHOGANY VENEER BOW FRONT CHEST OF DRAWERS SHERATON STYLE,
EARLY 19TH CENTURY

Courtesy of the Pennsylvania Museum of Art, Philadelphia

SERPENTINE FRONT CHEST OF DRAWERS BEARING LABEL OF JONATHAN GOSTELOWE

MASSACHUSETTS BLOCK FRONT CHEST OF DRAWERS, 18TH CENTURY

PART I

FURNITURE AND PERIODS

A

ACACIA

A wood of dull yellow color with brown veins used in 18th-century English country furniture for inlay and banding as a substitute for tulipwood. It is stronger, harder and more elastic than oak and it ranks next to ash and oak for durability. It is the locust wood of America.

ACANTHUS

A Greek conventionalized leaf used in carving. It is to be found on English furniture of the 17th and 18th centuries and is also notable on the knees of the Philadelphia Chippendale chairs.

ACORN TURNING

A term applied to turned ornaments resembling the acorn and used chiefly on the backs of Jacobean chairs.

ADAM STYLE

Takes its name from the four Adam brothers of whom Robert Adam was the leading spirit, the "Adelphi" of London, architects and designers of furniture during the last half of the 18th century. The style is distinguished by its rich and delicate ornamentation in classical form, slender straight lines,

small tapering legs, small and narrow moldings. Under-bracing was used occasionally and delicate carving, sparingly. The wide, flat urn and vase were favored embellishments, and plaques of Wedgwood ware were used as inserts. Inlay, painting and gilding were the popular decorations, and French brocades were used for upholstering. Mahogany was the principal wood used and the designs were executed by Chippendale, Hepplewhite, Sheraton and other cabinet-makers of the Period. See ROBERT ADAM, PART 6.

ADELPHI

Greek word meaning brothers.

3

Adopted by the Brothers Adam as a trade mark.

ALMERY

The name long used in medieval times for an inclosed niche or cupboard near the altar of churches, built to contain the requisites for conducting worship. Also a receptacle for that portion of provisions reserved for alms. Known also as aumbry. The name is also applied to the dole cupboard (q.v.).

AMBOYNA

A wood obtained in the Spice Islands, East Indies, and much used in the 18th century for inlaying, veneering, and fine panel work. It is very hard and durable, not unlike bird's-eye maple, but it is of a somewhat browner color.

AMERICAN FURNITURE

The furniture of the 17th century was of the plainest character, rugged and home-made. The design followed the Elizabethan and Jacobean styles of the English furniture with which the Colonists were familiar before coming to this country, yet it has a distinctive character of its own. Certain furniture forms which fitted closely the needs of the Colonists became particularly popular and were frequently reproduced. In New York the Dutch influence was felt also. Oak, pine, maple, cherry, and other local woods were used. Joints were fitted with mortise and tenon or dovetailed into each other, and wooden pins, usually square in form, fastened pieces together. There were no screws for use in those days, and glue was seldom used. The methods of decoration included chamfering, molding and turning, and carving of a simple type. The furniture included chests, chairs, cupboards, forms (benches), stools, settles and tables. Some of this furniture was stained or painted black or a bright red. In the 18th century, foreign models were followed but the construction is plainer and more sturdy during the first half of the century. By the middle of the century, the work of some of the American cabinet-makers rivaled that of the English. The block-front pieces of John Goddard of Newport and of Aaron Chapin of Hartford and the productions of William Savery, and other cabinet-makers, notably in the Chippendale style, have never been excelled by the cabinet-makers here or abroad. The work of these craftsmen, together with that of several others prominent in the various parts of the country, concluding with Duncan Phyfe in New York, kept the standard of American furniture very high to the end of the century. The American Eagle inlaid on various kinds of furniture was an important feature in decoration at this period.

REFERENCES

Colonial Furniture of New England, DR. IRVING W. LYON; Construction of Early American Furniture, AN-

TIQUES Sept. 1922; *Furniture Treasury*, 3 vols., WALLACE NUTTING; *Turnings on Early American Furniture*, ANTIQUES, May and June 1923; *Colonial Furniture in America*, LUKE V. LOCKWOOD; *French Influence in American Furniture*, ANTIQUARIAN, Oct. 1931, *Early American Furniture*, CHARLES OVER CORNELIUS; *Art in Primitive Americana*, FINE ARTS, Jan. 1932; *The Story of American Furniture*, THOMAS H. ORMSBEE; *Southern Antiques*, PAUL H. BURROUGHS, 1931; *Queen Anne Chairs of Colonial Days*, ANTIQUES, Dec. 1932; *Pine Furniture of Early New England*, R. H. KETTELL; *Blue Book, Philadelphia Furniture*, W. M. HORNOR, JR.

AMORINI

The Italian name for the cupids or cherubs seen upon furniture painted or carved. This motif figured prominently in Renaissance decoration and was used in England following the Restoration.

ANTHEMION

The Greek honeysuckle, conventionalized.

APPLE WOOD

A fruit wood used for country furniture in England in the 17th and 18th centuries and in this country to some extent.

APPLIED ORNAMENT

One which is carved or sawed separately and fastened upon the surface. Applied moldings originated in Spain in the 16th century. They came thence to the Netherlands and later to England.

APRON

The strip of wood beneath the table top or chair seat extending between the legs. The lower edge may be straight or shaped.

ARABESQUE

A species of ornament used on English furniture in Tudor days for enriching flat surfaces. It was either painted, inlaid or carved in low relief. It was derived from the Moors in Spain who made much use of it.

ARCADING

A form of ornament which reproduced in flat relief, arches, singly or in series, on panels and friezes. In use in the 16th and 17th centuries in England and on the Continent of Europe.

ARCHITECTS' FURNITURE

A name given to some of the furniture of the early Georgian period, designed by William Kent and some other of the cabinet-makers of that time. It was in favor between 1714 and 1730 in houses which were entirely planned, including furnishings, by architects. Later in the century the Adam brothers became famous for work of the same character but the furniture designed was much lighter in type and of classical form. Examples of architects' furniture are among the products of the American craftsman also.

ARKWRIGHT

See JOINER.

ARM-CHAIR (French, *Fauteuil*)

See CHAIRS, ARM-.

ARM SUPPORT

Either an extension of the front leg of a chair or sofa, or a separate piece rising from the seat rail supporting the front end of the arm.

ARMOIRE

Indicative of a cupboard in which armor was formerly stored. When armor was discarded it then became a wardrobe or cupboard for apparel. Armoire is the French name for cupboard.

ASH

This wood is white, tough and hard and ranks next in value to oak for strength and durability. It was much used by early craftsmen in this country especially for Windsor chairs. Ash has a long fibrous grain and will not turn without splitting.

ASTRAGAL

A small convex, beaded molding, usually placed at the junction of a pair of doors on cabinets and book-cases to exclude the dust.

AUMBRY

See ALMERY.

AVENTURINE

A term applied to the minute clippings of gold wire sometimes sprinkled over the surface during the lacquering of furniture.

B

BALBOA MIRRORS

See MIRRORS, *Balboa*.

BALL-AND-CLAW FOOT

See CLAW-AND-BALL FOOT.

BALL FOOT

See BUN FOOT.

BALUSTER (or Banister)

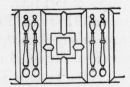

A small, slender turned column, usually swelled outward at some point between base and top. Sometimes split vertically, it is used for the uprights of a chair back or for ornament on chests and cupboards. A characteristic of the Elizabethan and Jacobean periods.

BANDING

An inlay contrasting either in color or grain with the surface of the wood it is intended to decorate. In the second half of the 18th century banding became very

Courtesy of the Museum of Fine Arts, Boston

McIntire Chamber from the Derby House, Salem, Early 19th Century

Courtesy of the Museum of Fine Arts, Boston

Room from Orme House in Marblehead about 1730

CHIPPENDALE STYLE EASY CHAIR, TRIPOD TABLE WITH CARVED RIM, TEA SET AND SHEFFIELD U

PHILADELPHIA CHIPPENDALE CHAIR,
18TH CENTURY

Courtesy of the Museum of Fine Arts, Boston
AMERICAN HEPPLEWHITE CHAIR

decorative, a great variety of exotic woods being employed. See STRINGING.

BANDY LEG

Another name for CABRIOLE LEG (q.v.).

BANISTER

See BALUSTER.

BANISTER-BACK

Chair back made of vertical pieces of baluster shape. See CHAIRS, Banister-Back.

BANJO CLOCKS

See CLOCKS, Banjo.

BAROMETER

An instrument for measuring the weight or pressure of the atmosphere, indicating changes of the weather and altitude of any place. The first barometer was made by Torricelli, an Italian, about the middle of the 17th century. The wheel or dial barometer, now most often seen, became popular second half of 18th century.

BAROQUE

A style of Italian origin, characterized by conspicuous curves, scrolls and highly ornate decoration. In general terms it exhibits an over-emphasis on detail. English furniture of the transitional late 17th-century period displays a tendency to baroque ornament, and it is to be seen in the carving of Philadelphia Chippendale furniture. Baroque is the Italian antecedent to the French Rococo (q.v.).

BASIN STANDS

See WASHSTANDS.

BAS-RELIEF (BASSO-RELIEVO)

Carved work, the figures of which project less than half of their true proportions from the surface on which they are placed.

BAYBERRY CANDLES

See CANDLES.

BEAD

A small molding of nearly semi-circular section, sometimes with rounds and ovals, used either flush with the adjacent surface or raised above it. Also called cockle bead.

BEAUFAIT

Variously spelled: beaufat, buffet, beaufett. In this country a corner cupboard extending to the floor and finished to correspond with the paneling of the room was usually called beaufait. They were usually built-in. See CUPBOARDS, Corner.

BEDS

The bedstead, sometimes in England called bedstock, is the frame upon which the bedding is placed. Rooms set apart for sleeping were unknown in medieval times. Beds with their heavy framework and concealing curtains were, in effect, separate sleeping chambers. They were the most striking feature of the furniture of the Middle Ages. The tester, or roof, and the back were of paneled wood. The tester was supported in the front by two posts and the curtains depended from the tester. Beds of this description were succeeded by the four-post kind in the time of Henry VIII, which continued to be the vogue until the end of the 18th century. The four-poster beds of the Queen Anne period were all upholstered, posts, tester, headboard and base, with velvet or other textiles so that little of the woodwork was shown. In the Georgian period, the back posts were usually plain as they were concealed by the curtains. The front posts were ornamented by carving. In the 18th century the standard width of the bed was four feet and an extra charge was made for beds wider than that. Bedsteads in use in this country in the 17th century were usually made of oak, but in the 18th century maple, cherry, walnut, and mahogany were all used. The surest indications of an early style in bedposts are great height and slenderness.

REFERENCES

Dictionary of English Furniture, MACQUOID and EDWARDS; Bedsteads of Former Days, ANTIQUES, Jan. 1923.

Day Beds. The day bed came into use in England in the days of the Stuarts and it was the forerunner of the present-day reclining couch or lounge. The day bed corresponds to the French chaise-longue and was also known as settee and stretcher bed. They were usually made of walnut with carved stretchers and six or eight scroll or turned legs, and the head-rest was frequently adjustable. They were both caned and made for cushions. See COUCHES.

Field Beds. An American bed with light, curving bars overhead in place of heavy tester. This was called a sweep and when covered with draperies produced somewhat the effect of a tent. The posts were about six feet high, of a graceful design, made of native hard woods or mahogany. They came into use about the middle of the 18th century and were popular for a long time.

Folding Beds. In use in this country in Colonial times. The side rails were fitted with a hinged joint, and by this means the main part of the bed was folded up against the head and covered by curtains attached to the top of the head.

Great Bed of Ware. Presumed to have been made about 1570 for the Earl of Huntington of Ware Park. It is an example of monumental English Renaissance construction and it is now in the Victoria and Albert Museum in London. It is about twelve feet square and it figures frequently in the literature of the last three centuries.

Press Beds. Also a folding bed but designed so as to fold up into a closet made to fit the bed. The door was then closed or curtains drawn over it during the day. Sometimes called "Cupboard" beds.

Sleigh Beds. These beds of the Empire period had rolling curved head and foot boards and no posts. They were massive and plain and patterned after the French style.

Stump Beds. A bed without a footboard.

Tent Beds. See *Field Beds.*

Truckle (or Trundle) Beds. A small low bed, which could be pushed under the larger bed when not in use. A relic of the days when every nobleman needed a faithful and armed guard to sleep at his feet all night.

BEECH

A hard wood used in Tudor days for chairs. It was also used to some extent in this country in Windsor chairs. Sheraton and his contemporaries made use of it for chairs which were to be painted or gilded. It is comparatively soft, the color varying from white to pale brown.

BELLOWS

For creating a blast of air. The two boards and handles were often elaborately carved and gilded and the metal nozzle cast in various designs.

BENCH

In England known as "form." Here it was, in Colonial days, simply an elongation of the stool and used for seating at table. See FORMS.

BERGÈRE

A French arm-chair with a very wide seat, upholstered sides and solid upholstered back. It was a feature of the Louis XV period. See FAUTEUIL.

BIBLE-BOX

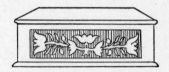

The Bible-box was common in cottage and farm in the days of oak and when the Bible was the only book owned. These boxes were usually about 28 inches long, 16 inches wide, and 10 inches deep, with a flat lid, although smaller ones are frequently seen. They were often carved and fastened with a strong lock with a large piped key. The so-called desk of the period was similar, although somewhat larger and made with a sloping lid.

BIEDERMEIER FURNITURE

A type of German furniture modeled after the styles of the Empire Period and in fashion from about 1815 to 1850. The materials used were inexpensive fruit woods with gilt and embossed metal decorations. Black horsehair upholstery was common.

BILBAO MIRRORS (BALBOA)
See MIRRORS, *Balboa.*

Billiard Tables

See Tables, *Billiard*.

Bilsted

The name given to the wood of the red sweet-gum tree, used in cabinet-making, sometimes as a substitute for mahogany. It was much used in early New York furniture.

Birch

Birch wood is close-grained, generally hard, susceptible of high polish, and it was much used by early cabinet-makers in this country and in England. It was also sometimes used as a substitute for satinwood.

Bird-Cage Clocks

See Clocks, *Bird-Cage*.

Block Foot

A square vertical-sided foot at base of straight, tapered leg.

Block Front

Swelling projections on drawer fronts and doors, the "block" and the surrounding lower parts being cut usually from one solid piece of wood. Although the block front is claimed as an American invention, there is evidence of its earlier use in Holland, but its perfection came at the hands of American craftsmen. The best and more ornate examples were made in the 18th century in Rhode Island and Connecticut.

References

John Goddard and His Block Front, ANTIQUES, May 1922; *More Light on the Block Front*, ANTIQUES, Feb. 1923; *Editorial*, ANTIQUES, April 1929; *Furniture Treasury*, Vol. 3, Nutting.

Bog Oak

Oak preserved in peat bogs. Used as inlay with holly and other woods in Tudor times. See Oak.

Bolection

That portion of a group of moldings which projects beyond the general surface of a panel.

Bombé

(French, to bulge, to jut out). Kettle-shaped contour in furniture, frequently to be seen in Dutch furniture and English furniture of the William and Mary period.

Bonnet Top

A curved or scroll top or pediment which made its appearance in England in the Queen Anne period. See Broken Arch and Pediment.

Book-Cases

As a piece of domestic furniture their history cannot be carried back beyond the time of Charles II. The book-cases of Queen Anne's reign are marked by extreme simplicity, excellent in proportion. Chippendale and Adam, Hepplewhite and Sheraton gave particular attention to their style and construction.

The later ones were usually in three sections, sometimes quite large, and with a desk arranged in the center section, known here as a break-front secretary book-case.

REFERENCE
Dictionary of English Furniture, Macquoid and Edwards.

Books of Furniture Design
See Furniture Design, Books of.

Boss
A circular or oval protuberance for surface ornament. It came into use in England by way of the Low Countries.

Boston Rocker
It is derived from the Windsor chair and it was one of the most popular chairs ever made. See Chairs, Rocking.

Boulle
(Also spelled, sometimes, Buhl). Tortoise-shell and metal inlay much used in France during 18th century, said to have been invented by André Charles Boulle (q.v., Part 6). That this form of decoration originated in Italy is claimed by some authorities.

Bow Front

A front that curves outward from side to side. Also called swell front.

Bow Top
Unbroken curve across the top rail

of a chair. This cresting of the early Georgian period turns upward at the outer ends and rests upon the back posts of chairs.

Box
One of the most primitive forms of furniture, coeval with the chest and differing from it in size only. The early boxes were made with a flat lid, and with a sloping lid, and they were used for a variety of purposes such as a Bible-box (q.v.) and for writing purposes (see Desk). The plain box eventually became the somewhat elaborate casket of the 17th century and the work-box of the 18th.

REFERENCE
Dictionary of English Furniture, Macquoid and Edwards.

Boxwood
A yellowish-orange wood used for inlay and marquetry. It has a fine uniform grain.

Bracket
The piece of wood, of bracket shape, used in the angle made by the top and the leg of a piece of furniture.

Bracket Clocks
See Clocks, Bracket.

Bracket Cornice
A cornice molding supported by brackets attached to the frieze, a feature of the Elizabethan and Jacobean periods.

BRACKET FOOT

A two-way foot in bracket or ogee form succeeding the Bun Foot about 1690.

BRACKETS

Designed for supporting busts, candelabra or vases. These came into use in the 17th and continued throughout the 18th century, and many of them were elaborately carved and gilded. In this country they were often seen supporting the so-called Banjo clock. See CONSOLE.

BREAK FRONT

The term denotes the front line of a sideboard or other piece of furniture, broken by the center portion's being advanced or recessed. It is also applied to a broken pediment.

BROKEN ARCH

An arch in which the cornice is not complete but lacks the central section. It was very popular in England and in this country from about 1715 to 1800. The swan-neck form consists of opposed S curves, scrolling over at the top and finishing in patera (q.v.). See PEDIMENT.

BUFFET

A heavy English table of the 17th century placed against the wall for the display of plate and for convenience in serving. It was evolved from the hutch and was probably also known as a cupboard. It usually had three open shelves supported by columns in front and at the back and some of the older ones contain small drawers. See SIDEBOARD.

REFERENCE

Dictionary of English Furniture, MAC-QUOID and EDWARDS.

BUHL

See BOULLE.

BUN FOOT

Sometimes called ball foot. A flattened ball used last half of 17th century and replaced in England about 1690 by the bracket foot.

BUREAU

English and French term for the Desk (q.v.). In this country it is used to indicate a chest of drawers, usually for the bedroom. See CHESTS, Bureaus.

REFERENCE
Dictionary of English Furniture, Mac-
QUOID and EDWARDS.

BURL
Name given to a veneer formed of transverse slices of the roots or excres-
cences on trees, caused by abnormal growth, such as large knots.

BUTTERFLY TABLES
See TABLES, Butterfly.

C

CABINET-MAKERS
(French, Ébéniste). Until the end of the 17th century the craft of the wood-worker had been vested in the carpenter and joiner, who were responsible both for design and workmanship. The influx of new workmen into England from the Continent, following the Revocation of the Edict of Nantes, caused the crafts-men in wood to organize as cabinet-makers. They were no longer to be joiners and carpenters; they were to make furniture only. Early in the 18th century cabinet-making had become a distinct industry.

CABINETS
A development of the enclosed cup-board known in England at an early date, and in general use throughout Eu-rope during the 16th and 17th centuries. These were nearly always in two parts. The upper was usually with doors, which, being opened, disclosed tiers of drawers sometimes built about a central cupboard or pigeon-hole recesses. The lower part was in the form of a table or lowboy. The "press" cabinet had drawers in the lower part, also, and was virtually a cabinet set on a low chest of drawers. Some of the cabinets of the 17th century were ornate speci-mens of workmanship with inlay or marquetry the leading feature of deco-ration. Some were of Oriental make imported from the East.

CABINETS, CHINA
The china cabinet or cupboard for the display of Oriental china came into use during the William and Mary pe-riod. The top portion was fitted with shelves and glazed doors. Doors also enclosed the lower part but had no glass. This type of cabinet was also used as a book-case.

REFERENCE
Dictionary of English Furniture, Mac-
QUOID and EDWARDS.

CABOCHON

A plain round or oval surface, convex

or concave, enclosed within ornamentation. The cabochon-and-leaf style in England was in vogue from 1735 to the time of Chippendale's prominence.

CABRIOLE LEG

This form of leg on furniture introduced into England from Holland became a feature in the reign of William and Mary and continued a distinctive mark through the Queen Anne period. It was in use in France and Italy prior to its appearance in England. It is the generic name for furniture made with a knee leg and concaved ankle. It was at first made with stretchers between the legs of chairs but these were gradually abandoned. It originally had the "hoof" foot, in time becoming the "club" foot, the "duck-bill" or "pad" foot as it was variously known. The cabriole leg was used on furniture in all positions where previously the turned leg had occurred.

CAMEL-BACK

Name given to the back of chairs of the Hepplewhite style with the raised curve in the center of the shield.

CANAPÉ

A French settee or a divan. Originally a couch with canopy of mosquito curtains.

CANDELABRUM

See PART 5.

CANDLES

In England in the 17th and 18th centuries, candles were made both of tallow and of wax. In this country early candles were made of mutton tallow, usually, but there were candles made from the wax of the bayberry, a pale green in color, giving a soft light and a pleasant odor. Candles were made by molding or dipping. For the former process, tin or pewter molds, two, four or more together were used. Dipping was a much slower process. Spermaceti candles were introduced in 1748 at Boston. Candles were mounted in either plain candlesticks or by sconces (wall brackets) for wall lighting, candle stands of wood or of wrought iron, or by hook pendants of iron. The elaborate chandeliers of the 18th century were fitted for use with candles. There were many variations of all of these methods of early lighting. See LIGHTS, PART 5.

CANDLE STANDS

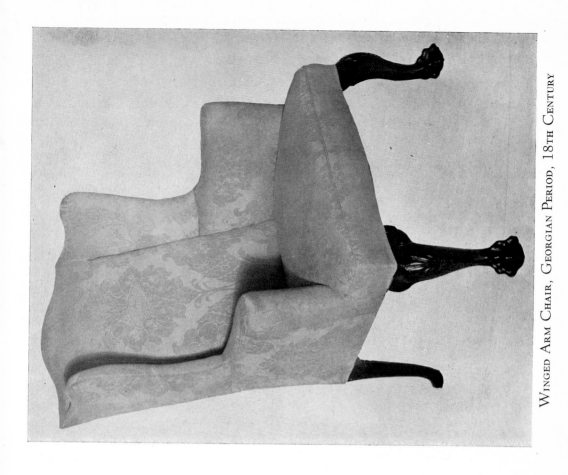

WINGED ARM CHAIR, GEORGIAN PERIOD, 18TH CENTURY

AMERICAN CHIPPENDALE WING CHAIR, CIRCA 1775

Room from Fiskdale, Mass., about 1740

Room with Pine Paneling, Essex County, Massachusetts, about 1700

In the 17th century these were made of wood or of wrought iron fitted with holders for one or more candles. In the 18th century, walnut or mahogany was used and some of them in latter part of the century were elaborately carved and called Torchères. They were 3½ to 4½ feet high with a tripod base and a circular flat top, designed to hold the candlestick. In this country three-legged stands of the Windsor design came between the other mentioned forms.

REFERENCE

Rare Windsor Candlestands, ANTIQUES, Oct. 1924.

CANDLEWOOD

The pine-knot used by early colonists in America for lighting.

CANE

The use of cane for chair seats and backs came through Portugal from the Orient and was first used in England in the reign of Charles I. It was at first very coarse in quality, but was much improved in that respect by the end of the century. See RUSH BOTTOMS.

CANTERBURY

A supper tray, latter part of 18th century, with partitions to hold knives, forks and plates.

CAPITAL

The upper part of a column or pillar.

CARCASE

The main body of a piece of furniture.

CARD-CUT ORNAMENT

A feature of Chinese Chippendale. A shallow flat-relief ornament, usually applied. See same topic, PART 5.

CARD TABLES

See TABLES, *Card.*

CARE OF ANTIQUE FURNITURE

This is a subject that has had too little attention. Wood, unless it receives an occasional treatment of oil and wax (q.v.), is apt to be injured by the dry air of the average home. Cracks will appear, the veneer will loosen, the drawers will stick and the surface will lose its lustre and become dull; the piece is starved for lack of care. If the furniture is rubbed and polished with wax at regular intervals, it may be kept in good condition indefinitely. "Elbow grease" is still one of the best polishes in existence. Supplement this with either oil or wax (or both) and you will not have to worry about the condition of the surface of your furniture.

CAROLEAN PERIOD

(Late Stuart) 1660-1688. See JACOBEAN PERIOD.

CARTOUCHE

An ornamental form of irregular shape, enclosing a plain central surface, often used as field for painted device or inscription.

CARVER CHAIRS

See CHAIRS, *Carver*.

CARVING

Carving was usually done by one of three processes. Incised or "scratch" in which the design is sharply cut in the surface; flat, the groundwork cut out, leaving flat surfaces outward; and modeled, where the design stands out in well-molded relief.

CARYATID

A conventionalized human figure serving as the top member of a pedestal or leg and used as a support.

CASKET

A small chest, with lid and lock for safe keeping of trinkets.

CASSONE

Also called coffer. The marriage coffer of the Italian Renaissance often lavishly decorated by carving or by inlay, and by painting on gesso. The rise and fall of the Renaissance can be traced in its decoration. It was never made in England.

CELLARET

Made of mahogany, sometimes bound with brass and lined with zinc, to hold the ice-cooled wine. It was of a size to place under the sideboard. See WINE COOLERS.

CERTOSINA

A kind of inlay work of light or dark woods, composed of small pieces put together in geometrical forms. See INLAY.

CHAIRS

(French, *Chaises*). Of ancient chairs, ordinarily used for domestic purposes, a variety have been discovered in excavations, or represented in ancient frescoes. The spread of Greek and Roman culture westward introduced the chair to the lesser advanced European nations. Very little is known of the intermediate stages of the evolution of the chair until about the close of the 15th century. Chairs of Gothic design were made in Germany, and, in Italy, velvet-covered chairs were made at the beginning of the 16th century, and the curule-shaped chair was introduced into England by Italian workmen during the reign of Henry VIII. Hardly anything so fully reflects the manners and customs of an age as furniture, and the chair is by far the most sensitive to new and foreign influences.

The medieval chair as distinct from the clerical "throne" or stall is the rarest of all early furniture. They were often made entirely of turned members and were known as "thrown" chairs. Chairs were at first seats of great dignity, and, for a long time, reserved for the head of the family. Benches and stools were for the use of the others. In Elizabeth's reign chairs were square, ugly and uncomfortable and it was not until nearly the close of the 16th century that domestic chairs were in use. The backs and seats of these were sometimes padded and covered with damask or velvet upholstery. They were not the usual seat at the table for meals, until after the Restoration in 1660. During the reign of Charles II, the use of the chair increased very rapidly, although it retained its function as a seat of honor, and from that time until the present the chair has continued to be one of the chief articles of domestic furniture. In this country chairs were very scarce in early Colonial times, but by the end of the 17th century chairs with leather backs and seats, turned chairs, and the slat-back chairs were comparatively common. The craft of the chairmaker, beginning with the Restoration, was quite separate from that of the cabinet-maker, and for honesty of workmanship and beauty combined with utility, the chairs of the 18th century, both in England and in this country, have not been surpassed.

REFERENCE
English Chairs of the Period 1600-1688, ANTIQUARIAN, Oct. 1930.

Arm-Chairs. Chairs with arms, an "easy" chair. The "bergère" was a French arm-chair with upholstered sides, the "fauteuil" one open under the arms. See *Wing Chairs.*

Banister-Back Chairs. Early 18th century. Made with arms or without arms and with upright spindles in the back, usually four in number, either flat or half round on the back side. The seats were of rush or splint, combining both the Flemish and Spanish styles in legs,

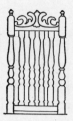

and with cresting at the top and a large bulb stretcher across the front. The banister-back chair is characteristically American.

REFERENCE
The Banister Back Chair, ANTIQUARIAN, Aug. 1930.

Brewster Chairs. See Carver Chairs.

Caned Chairs. Often called Jacobean although more definitely connected with Carolean furniture, as caning of seats and backs was not introduced into England from Holland before the reign of Charles II. There were two distinct types of these chairs; one the scroll-foot chair, called Flemish, the other with the well-known Spanish foot. Lines were straight and the under-bracing carved. Cushioned seats were often used on these chairs. Cane-work was re-introduced and applied to furniture about 1770, Robert Adam using it in his designs quite extensively.

Carver Chairs. So-called from the one in Pilgrim Hall, Plymouth, said to have been owned by Governor Carver. It was a heavy chair made entirely from turnings fitted into each other horizon-

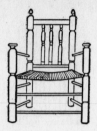

tally and vertically. Side chairs of this type were made here. The Brewster chair is an elaboration of the Carver chair by the addition of spindles under the arms and the seat.

Chippendale Chairs. See CHIPPENDALE STYLE.

Comb-Back Chairs. See *Corner* and *Windsor Chairs.*

Corner or Roundabout Chairs. An arm-chair, the back of which extends around two sides, leaving two sides and a cor-ner in front. Those of the Queen Anne period usually had upright spindles in the back, or solid splats. Chippendale's

chisel cut through this splat, and it be-came ornamental. Seats were of rush or of wood. Sometimes a head piece was placed above the back, also with spin-

dles, giving the appearance of a comb, hence the name comb-back chair.

REFERENCE

English Roundabout Chairs, AN-TIQUES, Nov. 1936.

Cromwellian Chairs. The low back of the Cromwellian chair has a deep top rail with the seat and back usually up-holstered in leather in the Spanish style, fastened to the frame by rows of brass-headed nails. Legs and stretchers were in the style of the Wainscot chair (q.v.).

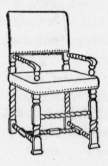

The Cromwellian chair was also made with bead or sausage turnings and with Turkey-work covering in place of leath-er. These chairs are frequently men-tioned in inventories of estates in this country, last half of 17th century. These chairs must not be confounded with the so-called Spanish leather chairs which came after the Restoration.

Fancy Chairs. An outgrowth of Shera-ton and Phyfe designs, delicate in form and usually painted black, with gold and flower decorations. They were made of soft wood, light in weight, and

English Walnut Side Chair with
Original Mortlake Tapestry,
17th Century

Louis XVI Carved and Parcel-gilded Side
Chair, 17th Century

Chippendale Carved Mahogany Side Chair
English, 18th Century

Italian Curule Chair, 16th Century

GRANDFATHER'S
CLOCK WITH
CASE MADE BY
JOHN GODDARD,
NEWPORT, CIRCA
1760-1770

BANJO CLOCK,
WILLARD
TYPE, CIRCA
1810

Courtesy of the Museum of Fine Arts, Boston

ENGLISH BRACKET CLOCK WITH TORTOISE-SHELL

had cane or rush seats. During the first quarter of the 19th century, these chairs

and sofas were made and sold in large numbers.

Farthingale Chairs. A type of English chair without arms. A seat of the Tudor

period and later, when hooped petticoats of enormous size were worn.

Hepplewhite Chairs. See HEPPLEWHITE STYLE.

Hitchcock Chairs. The name given to a type of chair made by Lambert Hitchcock and others in Connecticut about 1826, and thereafter for many years. Hitchcock's early chairs were stenciled on the back edge of the seat with his name, and were decorated with stenciled designs. They were generally made of birch or maple and with cane or rush seats. Whether he originated the style is open to question. That he made some of the finest is admitted, and

the name Hitchcock became a generic term for the so-called "fancy chairs" of the period. Hitchcock also made the so-called Boston Rocker (see *Rocking-Chairs*). Several of his competitors imitated his chairs, and chairs of his design are still being made.

REFERENCE
   Hitchcock of Hitchcocksville, AN-TIQUES, Aug. 1923.

Hogarth Chairs. A chair of the Queen Anne period made of walnut, with cabriole legs, a wide seat and a solid, central supporting vase-shaped (also called "fiddle-back") splat from the frame of the seat to the top of the back.

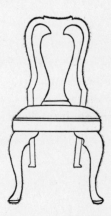

This chair was very comfortable and popular because it is said to have been the first chair in which the furniture maker had considered human anatomy in his design. The back is slightly dished.

Ladder-Back Chairs. See CHIPPENDALE STYLE.

Lancashire Chairs. A variation of the *Yorkshire Chair* (q.v.). Instead of hav-

ing an open back it had a solid panel with a semi-circular carved cresting at top.

REFERENCE

> *Chair Types from the English Provinces,* ANTIQUARIAN, June 1930.

Martha Washington Chairs. An upholstered chair with high, canted back and with arms usually without upholstery, made here, late 18th century. It has tapered square legs and in its design shows Hepplewhite influence.

Phyfe Chairs. See PHYFE, DUNCAN, STYLE.

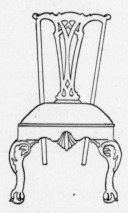

RIBBAND-BACK CHAIR

Ribband-Back Chairs. Chairs of the Chippendale style, with pierced or scrolled splats and carved ribbon forms. Usually with cabriole legs.

Rocking-Chairs. They seem to have had their origin in this country, probably not earlier than the Revolutionary War. Many of the existing old rockers had the rockers added long after the chair itself was made. The Boston Rocker, which in the opinion of Wallace Nutting is probably the most popular chair ever made, is an adaptation of the Windsor design. It was usually made with arms, rounded top and rolling seat. The earliest date for these is about 1825.

REFERENCES

> *The American Rocking Chair,* ANTIQUES, Feb. 1928; *The Boston Rocker,* ANTIQUES, May 1928.

Roundabout Chairs. See *Corner Chairs.*

Savonarola Chairs. See *X-Shaped Chairs.*

Sedan Chairs. A portable chair, or covered vehicle with side windows and an entrance through an opening in the front. It was carried by means of poles on each side passing through rings set in the body of the chair.

Sheraton Chairs. See SHERATON STYLE.

Side Chairs. Chairs without arms.

Slat-Back Chairs. Chairs, usually of turned stock, of native hard woods, made with and without arms and with two to five and sometimes, although seldom, six horizontal slats usually of ash across the back, and usually curved outward. The slats are graduated in width, the narrowest at the bottom. The upper slat in the 17th century was sometimes five inches wide and the upper and lower edges of all the slats were flat. In the 18th century they ranged

from three to four inches in width and the edges were curved slightly. The seats were of rush or splint. Some of these chairs, with large turned posts, date well back into the 17th century, and they were among the most popular of the early types of chairs. Simple slat-back chairs, following the early form, but lightened in their elements, were made throughout the 18th century and well into the 19th century, the Shaker chairs of modern manufacture being a continuation of the form.

Spanish Chairs. A chair of the Carolean period, with the Spanish foot, turned legs and carved under-brace. The seat and tall narrow back are covered with Spanish leather. It is of a type

similar to the caned chairs (q.v.) of the same period.

REFERENCE
Spanish Chairs of the 17th and 18th Centuries, ANTIQUES, Aug. and Oct. 1927.

Table Chairs. This was a combination of a chair (settle) and table, the top (or back) turning on a pin at the point where the arms join the back posts, and forming the table top, when turned down flat. They were at first made with a

square top, later with round top, and sometimes were made with a chest beneath the seat. Oak, pine and maple were the woods used. They were in use in England in the 16th century and were quite common in this country during the 17th century.

Turned Chairs. Medieval chairs were often made entirely of turned members and were known as "thrown" chairs. Also, chairs of the Colonial period, probably of English origin, usually made of ash although maple and hickory were also used, in which turned pieces only were used in the construction, with more or less elaborated spindles. Seats were of rush or flag. The so-called Carver chair (q.v.), at Plymouth, is an example. The spiral turned chair of the Jacobean period was of Eastern origin and came into England through Portugal and Holland. The backs of these chairs, and the stretchers, were often elaborately carved, and they were upholstered in leather or with Turkey-work.

Wainscot Chairs. A chair usually of oak, characteristic of the 16th and 17th centuries. In the Tudor period always a box bottom. When made with legs it is of the Jacobean period. It had arms, and seat and back were of solid panels. The back was vertical and carved in the same pattern, usually, as

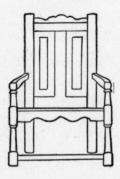

the chests and cupboards of the period. The seat was often made more comfort-

able by the use of cushions. American Wainscot chairs are seldom encountered. The earlier or Elizabethan chairs had a cresting between the stiles of the back and a finial at the summit of the stiles, horizontal arms, square seats. In the Jacobean period the cresting consisted of the Flemish scroll across the entire top, the arms began to slope downward and to spread outward, and the seat was wider at the front than at the back. The back of the American Wainscot chair was slightly "canted" instead of being vertical as the English chairs were.

Windsor Chairs. The Windsor chair was probably of English peasant origin,

ENGLISH

in a little town north of Windsor where they were made before the time of Queen Anne, and they remained popular in England throughout the 18th century. A solid or pierced splat in the center of the back, with spindles on each side, is a characteristic of the English chair. The English Windsor chair was made sometimes with the cabriole leg but never made so in this country. Windsor chairs of the American design have the shaved, upright spindles only. Of the

AMERICAN

two, the American Windsor is more graceful and more harmonious in proportion and design. Both chairs are made with and without arms, and in this country, the "comb-back," the "fan-back," the "hoop-back" and the "low-back" are all familiar types. It is thought that the first Windsor chairs in this country were made at or near Philadelphia about 1725, and soon after spread to other of the northern colonies, becoming the most common and popular chairs of the 18th century. Hickory, ash, beech and maple were used in the construction of the legs and backs. The seats were of pine or other soft woods. A Windsor chair made of but one kind of wood is seldom found. They were usually painted green or black.

REFERENCES

A *Windsor Handbook*, WALLACE NUTTING; *The American Windsor Chair*, ANTIQUES, April 1926; *Windsor Chairs*, ANTIQUES Feb. 1922; *The Windsor Chair in Eng-*

land *and Its Ancestors*, FINE ARTS, June 1932.

Wing Chairs. This type of chair appeared first about the middle of the reign of Charles II, and because of its comfort soon became very popular, remaining in vogue for more than a century. It was graceful in design, with high back and wings projecting forward

at the sides, extending down to the arms which were made with a scroll or straight turnover. Feet and legs were of varied design, and sometimes stretchers were used. The Wing chair, late 17th century, was the progenitor of everything that claims to be an easy-chair.

Writing Arm-Chairs. An adaptation of the Windsor chair by the addition of a large desk arm, usually with a drawer underneath the arm for paper, etc., and sometimes with a drawer beneath the seat. It is believed to have been of Philadelphia origin, fairly early in the Windsor chair period. The arm was, roughly speaking, pear-shaped, but the chairs made differ so greatly in detail of design that it is evident they were produced by the makers to suit the individual ideas of the purchaser. There was even a slide for a candlestick to rest upon, sometimes placed in front of the arm.

X-Shaped Chairs. A frame of wood in X shape, with a fabric seat and back. They were of the Tudor period in Eng-

land, derived from the Italian, and sometimes called "curule" after an early Roman chair.

Yorkshire Chairs. An English chair of Puritan design, with turned legs and an

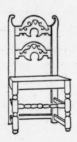

open back, with carved crescent-shaped cross rails, linking the vertical members of the back.

REFERENCE
    North of England Chairs, AN-
    TIQUES, Nov. 1929.

CHAISE-LONGUE
    French reclining chair or day bed, with elongated seat and an upholstered back supported by extra legs. It was a feature of the French Empire furniture.

CHAMFER

A beveled cutting away of a corner angle.

CHANNELING
    A system of paralleled, vertical or horizontal grooves or channels, cut into the surface of a frieze or other woodwork.

CHECKER OR CHEQUER
    A favorite motif in 16th- and 17th-century inlay in dark and light woods.

CHERRY
    A firm, strong, close-grained wood suitable for cabinet-making purposes. It takes on a good polish and colors well with age. About the middle of the 18th century it competed with maple for preference with many American cabinet-makers, especially in the Connecticut River Valley.

CHERUB MOTIF
    See AMORINI.

CHESTNUT
    A very durable white wood and suitable for high-class cabinet work. Sometimes used in England in the 18th century as a substitute for satinwood, as the grain is similar.

CHESTS

(French, *Coffre*) The earliest piece of furniture, associated with the life history of all civilized nations, is the chest. The accumulation of property necessitated a place for storing what had been accumulated, and the chest provided the place. In very early times, they were huge oak boxes, bound with iron and furnished with strong locks and with iron handles or rings through which a pole could be passed and the chest, then slung from the pole, was borne on men's shoulders. They served also for seats and for tables. In England, they were usually made of oak but some of the later ones were made of West Indian cedar or cypress for the storage of clothes, to prevent damage from moths. During the Tudor and early Jacobean periods, they were paneled and carved. Ornament consisted of carved linenfold or heads within medallions. The chest became a chest with a drawer and raised on low legs in Cromwellian days, then a chest with drawers but retaining the hinged lid, and a chest of drawers in the Restoration, mounted on legs, joined by stretchers. The simple chest is, therefore, the parent of many pieces of furniture. Chests of drawers with a fixed top were in use in this country during the 17th century, although not common. Examples of these early chests of drawers are rarely seen. They were usually made of oak and were decorated with carving, paneling and (or) applied ornaments.

Late in the 17th century, chests of drawers mounted on legs were introduced into New England. These eventually became known as highboys (q.v.), a relatively modern term. Chests of drawers with cupboard tops were much in use in England during the latter half of the 18th century. Until about 1750 walnut was chiefly used for these. Later mahogany was favored. Many chests were brought to this country from England and Holland by the early settlers and others were made here very soon after their arrival. These early chests were at first made of plain boards, dovetailed or pegged, usually without ornament. Later, they were framed or joined together with mortise and tenon and paneled and carved or painted. Usually, the top, the back and the bottoms of both chest and drawers were made of pine. The size varied from 18 inches in height, when without drawers, to 48 inches, when with three drawers. The length, from 30 inches to 60 inches. The earliest carved chests found here are with panels in arched designs, identical with patterns seen in England during same period. The carving is usually very shallow.

REFERENCES
> Dictionary of English Furniture, MAC-QUOID and EDWARDS; The American Chest, ANTIQUARIAN, Oct., Nov. 1931.

Bureaus. What is known in this country as a bureau is simply a chest of drawers called by another name. (In England and in France the bureau is what is known here as a desk.) Those made earlier than 1750 are very scarce, but many of the last half of the century have survived, mostly made of mahogany, with plain and inlaid surfaces, and

with flat, swell and serpentine fronts, usually with bracket feet, four drawers, and the so-called "willow" brasses. Following these were the bureaus of Sheraton design with oval brasses and later the heavy Empire designs with glass or wooden knobs for drawers.

Connecticut Chests. Made by Nicholas Disbrowe (q.v. PART 6) and others of Hartford, Connecticut, late 17th century. They were ornamented with flat-carved all-over design of tulips and sun-

flowers on the front, with two drawers at bottom.

REFERENCE
> The Sunflower Chest, ANTIQUARIAN, July 1930.

Dowry Chests, also called *Dower Chests.* The name given generally to the chests of the German settlers in America, although it is applicable to similar chests of other of the early settlers, such as the Connecticut and Hadley chests. The German chests were made with two or three small drawers across the bottom and usually mounted on ball or bracket feet. They had arched or square panels, with painted decoration in various designs, and most of them bear the initials of the bride and the date.

REFERENCES
> Pennsylvania Bride Boxes and Dower Chests, ANTIQUES, Vol. 8, pp. 20-23, 79-84, Vol. 11, pp. 119, 280, 475; The Bridal Furniture of the Pennsylvania Germans, ANTIQUARIAN, May 1930.

Hadley Chests. So-called because of the considerable number of chests of similar size, construction and design that have been found near Hadley, Massachusetts. They were probably made from 1675 to 1710, by a group of joiners led by John Allis of Hadley, a grand-nephew of Nicholas Disbrowe of Hartford, who designed and made so-called Connecticut chests. The top, the back and the bottom, also the drawer frames of the

Hadley chest are made of pine. The front is of oak, carved and painted. The ends are paneled but not carved, and the center front panel almost invariably has initials, which add to its human interest. No two of the Hadley chests are just alike.

REFERENCES

The Hadley Chest, C. F. LUTHER; *The Secret of the Hadley Chest*, ANTIQUARIAN, Feb. 1930.

Nonesuch Chests. With marquetry designs in colored woods, of architectural form, a style of Italian origin, introduced into England in the 16th century and continuing in vogue until well into the Jacobean period. The name is derived from the palace of Nonesuch, built by Henry VIII, which the outlines of the ornamentation are supposed to represent.

Taunton Chests. A type of early American painted chests previously ascribed to Connecticut, but made in Taunton, Massachusetts, probably by Robert Crossman, first half of 18th century. They were decorated by painted design.

REFERENCE

The Tantalizing Chests of Taunton, ANTIQUES, April 1933.

CHEST-ON-CHEST. Two chests, both with drawers, set one above the other. It never enjoyed as much popularity in America as in England. There it was a favorite device of the Chippendale era. It differed from the highboy (q.v.) in that the latter was set up on a frame with legs, while the chest-on-chest had drawers reaching nearly to the floor, at times with one of the drawer fronts let down at a suitable height for writing. The upper section was usually slightly smaller in width and depth than the lower. The earlier flat top was followed by the scroll top. Dr. Irving W. Lyon, pioneer collector and author of one of the first books on early American furniture in 1891, includes the highboy in his descriptions and illustrations of chests-on-chests. Among authors of later date the two are classified separately.

REFERENCE

The American Chest-on-Chest, FINE ARTS, March 1932.

CHEVAL MIRRORS
See MIRRORS, *Cheval.*

CHIP CARVING
Shallow faceted ornament executed with chisel and gouge and common in England in the 16th and 17th centuries.

CHIPPENDALE STYLE

The Chippendale style is a generic term. It includes not only the work of

Chippendale, but also the work of his contemporaries and some of the work which was done before he attained distinction himself. Nevertheless, Chippendale was the dominant figure in English furniture design from 1745 to 1770 and about 1750 his influence began to be felt, too, in this country. Chippendale went to London before 1749, and in 1754 he published the *Director* containing designs not only for chairs in great variety, but for bookcases, mirror frames, tables and stands, fire screens and numerous other pieces of household furniture, which established his leadership as a cabinet-maker. It is said that he originated tripod furniture. His chair patterns are particularly notable. They consisted of chairs with square-topped backs and with upright center splat pierced and scrolled in never ending variety (the so-called "ribband-back"), usually with cabriole legs, and claw-and-ball feet; the Gothic and Chinese types, with all-over patterns, square legs, often with stretchers, and the "ladder-back" chair with three or four wavy horizontal rails across the back carved to match the top rail, and with square legs. The arms joined the uprights at an angle on all of these styles. Fret-work in the Chinese style was popular with him and is to be seen on a great variety of his furniture. The English Gothic cluster column leg is an actual innovation of the Chippendale school.

Chippendale worked in mahogany almost altogether and relied upon carving for decorative effects, until, in his later years, he was employed to produce designs by Adam. His style may be described as having strength and solidity without heaviness, grace, wonderful craftsmanship and adaptability to the use for which the piece was made. See THOMAS CHIPPENDALE, PART 6.

CLAVICHORD

Obsolete keyed stringed instrument, the forerunner of the old square pianoforte. It was first made in the 15th century. It never became as popular in England as the virginal or spinet.

CLAW-AND-BALL FOOT

This style of foot was of Chinese origin, referring to the legend of the dragon's foot holding a pearl. In England, where the style was introduced about 1715, the eagle's claw or the lion's paw was substituted for the dragon's foot. The style remained popular throughout the Chippendale era.

Clock Reel

A reel for winding flax in skeins, designed to record the amount wound so as to be uniform in quantity.

Clocks

(French, *Cloche*, a bell). The origin of the time-keeping device is shrouded in the mists of antiquity. The sundial (q.v.), the sand glass (q.v.), and the water-clock have each had their uses in recording the passage of the hours. Candles made exactly twelve inches long and burning one inch in every twenty minutes was another simple way of marking time. The water-clock, the first mechanical device for keeping time, was first used by Eastern nations, and was introduced into Greece by Plato. Among the first of the clocks, composed of an assemblage of wheels, is that of St. Paul's Cathedral in London which was put up in 1286. The famous clock at Rouen, France, was made in 1289, and it is still the chief clock of the city. By the end of the 16th century, clocks for domestic use, with but one hand and with a balance or fly-wheel escapement, were made at a moderate price. In the middle of the 17th century, the short "bob" pendulum and the minute hand were introduced, followed soon by the long pendulum introduced into England from Holland by Fromanteel, and the anchor escapement, invented by Dr. Hooke in 1658, insuring accuracy of time. The dials of these early clocks

were usually ten inches in diameter. After 1720, twelve-inch dials were usual. The earliest English tall-case clocks are said to have been those of William Clement, made in London about 1680, although the long-case is said to be of Dutch origin. Many of the early long-cases were decorated with marquetry, and later lacquer was also used for the same purpose. This was before the use of mahogany for cases, although lacquer continued to be used until the last half of the 18th century. Clocks were made with wooden and with brass works at about the same time. The "Clock-makers Company" was founded in 1631 and the most important work which this company accomplished was training men for the art. Each apprentice had to make his masterpiece before he was admitted as a workmaster. There were two general styles of clocks in use, one which was run with weights, the other with a spiral spring. The first variety was the older.

Owners of "ancient clocks" are sometimes anxious to know if they are by good makers. On general principles, any clock which has been going more than a hundred years is a good clock, no matter who made it. Prior to 1777, at which time Parliament passed a law that English clocks must have the name and abode of the maker engraved on them, the name inscribed was often that of the owner. The earliest clocks in America were made in Boston. Clock-makers in New York and in Philadelphia before 1700 and in Connecticut about 1712 followed, and clock-making became one of the really early American crafts. A very large list of names of American and English clock-makers is to be found in Mrs. Moore's *Old Clock Book*, and in Volume 3 of *Furniture Treasury* by Wallace Nutting.

REFERENCES

A Century of English Clocks, ANTIQUES, Nov. 1926; *Chats on Old Clocks*, Arthur Hayden; *English Domestic Clocks*, Cescinsky and Webster; *Old Clocks and Watches and Their Makers*, Britten; *Dictionary of English Furniture*, Macquoid and Edwards.

Banjo Clocks. The so-called banjo

clocks were invented by Simon Willard and called by him his "improved timepiece." They were intended by him to replace the long-case "Grandfather's" clock. He applied for and received a patent in 1801, but he did not restrain imitations of the clock by other makers, including Aaron Willard, Lemuel Curtis and others, and as a consequence the pattern became well known and had a wide sale, the benefits of which Willard received in but a moderate degree. In its simplicity, grace and adequacy of design, the banjo clock is little short of a masterpiece. The works were of brass and the dead-beat escapement gave it great accuracy. Sometimes the case below is made in the form of the lyre, giving it the name of "lyre" clock. This was a variation originated by Aaron Willard, Jr. Genuine Simon Willard clocks of this type (or any other that he made) command high prices, and some of those made by other makers are very highly regarded.

REFERENCES

Clocks of Simon Willard, ANTIQUES, Feb. 1922; *Clocks of Lemuel Curtis*, ANTIQUES, Dec. 1923.

Bird-Cage Clocks. The bird-cage or so-called "lantern" clocks of the 16th and 17th centuries were among the earliest clocks in use in England for domestic purposes. They were made of brass, about ten inches high and were set upon a bracket on the wall, with the weights hung upon cord or chain passing through openings in the shelf. The dial, at first, had but one hand with the hour spaces divided into fifths. About the middle of the 17th century the "bob" (short) pendulum superseded the crown-wheel escapement controlled

by a spring, which was a decided improvement. The clocks ran for not more than thirty hours. The dials were usually of engraved brass and stood out beyond the frame which was surmounted by a bell. These clocks were of English design and all of the makers of clocks of that early period followed identically the one design. They continued in use for more than a century and some of them were brought to this country by the early settlers.

Bracket Clocks. The bracket clock, spring-driven, is a development of the bird-cage clock. The clock was placed in a wooden case, often carved and ornamented with ormolu or other decoration in quite a luxurious manner. A

handle on top, or one on each side, made removal easy. This style of clock continued in use for more than one hundred years, and many of them are still in good running order. These clocks are among the things that make the greatest appeal to the lovers of the antique.

REFERENCE

The English Bracket Clock, ANTI-QUARIAN, April 1931.

French Clocks. Portable clocks in a variety of forms, following the styles of the period, were made in France in the 17th and 18th centuries. They were usually supported by a pedestal, a bracket, or were in a tall case. There were but few mantel clocks before the time of Louis XV. From about 1760 these clocks were made in marble and bronze or with wood cases, and the works, as a rule, were excellent. Many of these were imported to this country in the late 18th and early 19th centuries.

Grandfather's Clocks—Long-Case Clocks. The long pendulum coming into use in the latter half of the 17th century, at first swinging below the shelf on which the bird-cage clock was placed, gave the name of wag-on-the-wall to the clock although the real wag-on-the-wall was of Dutch origin, sometimes called Friesland clocks, also. Someone conceived the idea of making a case to enclose the whole (William Clement of London is said to have made the first in England in 1680) and in that manner the long-case clock had its origin.

The early clocks had thirty-hour movements but Tompion and other clockmakers of the period perfected the eight-day movements which have continued in use since. The earliest cases were very plain, made mostly of oak, walnut or pine, and at first the dials were square with frosted center, silvered dial ring, steel hands and cast brass spandrel ornaments at the corners.

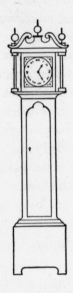

About 1730, the half circle over the dial appeared and the flat top gave place to the hood with arched top. Brass works were used. In 1773, the engraved brass dial without frosting or ring was introduced, and about 1790 white painted or enameled dials appeared. The cases were usually made by some cabinet-maker, although some makers of the works made the cases also. Long-case clocks by American clock-

makers of the 18th and 19th centuries rank very high in workmanship and in timekeeping qualities. Much of this work was confined to New England, and clocks from that section were sent to all parts of the then settled country.

REFERENCE

Connecticut Clockmakers of the 18th Century, PENROSE R. HOOPES.

Grandmother's Clocks. A clock of the same general appearance as the grandfather's, but not so tall. One of the early Simon Willard clocks was of this type, four feet high.

REFERENCE

ANTIQUES, May 1937.

Lantern Clocks. See Bird-Cage Clocks.

Lighthouse Clocks. A clock with a glass hood covering the works and standing on a wooden case about twenty inches high.

Lyre Clocks. See Banjo Clocks.

Mantel Clocks. See Shelf Clocks.

Shelf Clocks. These were first made

by Eli Terry in 1814. They were made with both wood and brass works and ran thirty hours. This style of clocks is one of the first, if not the first, articles of manufacture in this country to benefit by "quantity production." Chauncey Jerome, a clock-maker of the period, in his book on american clock-making published 1860, says that "these clocks completely revolutionized the whole business." The clocks of this pattern supplied the American market for twenty-five years or more and they were exported to foreign countries in large numbers. The Terry "pillar-and-scroll" case is regarded as the best of this style of clocks, and the sharp Gothic pattern designed by Elias Ingraham of Bristol was one of the most widely known.

Wag-on-the-Wall Clocks. See Grand-father's Clocks.

CLUB FOOT

A plain flat foot not unlike the Dutch foot. It is known also as the duck-bill or pad foot, and is less graceful than the hoof foot which was originally the termination of the cabriole leg. It first appeared on English furniture about 1705 and continued to be used throughout the 18th century.

COASTERS

Devices of various forms for circulating food and bottles on a dining table. Sometimes called "Lazy Susan."

COCK-BEADING

A narrow raised beading used to surround the edges of drawers, first introduced about 1730 and continued to be used throughout the 18th century.

COFFER (French, *Coffre*)

In medieval times a strongly made chest with a lid and with lock for the safe keeping of valuables, often carved and otherwise ornamented.

COLONIAL FURNITURE-MAKERS

In Colonial days every town, however small, had its joiners and chair-makers, and judging from their work, many of them must have been skilled craftsmen. Many of them settled in and about Boston and the other New England Colonies, and most of the American furniture of the 17th century was of New England origin. These early makers used oak, ash, elm, walnut, maple, cedar and pine. Although New England retained its leadership in the 18th century, Philadelphia rose to prominence through the splendid work of Savery, Gillingham and Gostelowe, and others, and before the end of the century, furniture made in this country compared favorably with that of the best English cabinet-makers. Besides the native woods, mahogany was imported and its use in this country preceded that in England.

COLONIAL PERIOD (American) 1620-1775

The early settlers in this country

brought with them into New England
and the other colonies only a few pieces
of furniture. The ships were small, the
space was limited and furniture was
quite bulky. The carpenters and joiners
among the immigrants found occupation
at once, and in providing the needed
furniture they, quite naturally, followed
the construction and designs with which
they were familiar, with no thought of
producing anything distinctive. Certain furniture forms became particularly
popular and were frequently reproduced.

In the decoration of the earlier work
the carving was crude, and some of the
tables, chairs and chests were painted.
Their materials were air-dried, and in
all of the 17th-century furniture the presence of American pine, white and yellow, maple, local fruit and nut woods,
Virginia walnut, or oak, which is
generally lighter in color than the English, is an important clue to its origin.
Furthermore, it was made to endure,
with mortise and tenon joints and pins
to hold them tight. Later, as settlers
continued to arrive from England and
from Holland, bringing with them furniture of a changing style or period, the
designs here were slowly adapted to
those changes. The joiners became
more expert in the use of their tools,
their carving was better, they began to
show evidences of originality in designing new and useful pieces.

Early in the 18th century many so-called transition pieces were made,
combining features of the Jacobean, perhaps, with the William and Mary or
Queen Anne design. The usual banister-back chair of that time, characteristically
American, is an example. The highboy,
although it had its origin in England,
received much more attention here than
there. Toward the middle of the century the genius of some of the New
England cabinet-makers and of those of
Philadelphia resulted in the production
of furniture forms of the highest order.
The use of mahogany had become general during the second quarter of the
century, and the carving done on some
of these later pieces approaches and
often equals that done by the best
cabinet-makers abroad. During all the
period of about one hundred and fifty
years, however closely the work done
by local craftsmen may resemble European models, there are variations in certain parts due not only to the lack of
models to follow exactly but to the
ideas regarding improvements, by the
craftsmen themselves. During the later
years of this period the Philadelphia
craftsmen assumed increasing importance. See REVOLUTIONARY PERIOD.

REFERENCES
Colonial Furniture in America, LOCKWOOD; Story of American Furniture,
ORMSBEE; Furniture of Our Forefathers, 2 vols., SINGLETON.

COMMODE
The name borrowed from France for

CORNER CUPBOARDS, 18TH CENTURY

McIntire Carved American Sheraton Sofa, Early 19th Century

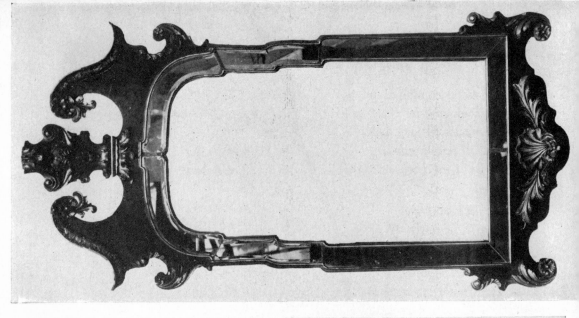

AMERICAN CONVEX MIRROR, CIRCA 1800

a chest of drawers, similar to our bureau, designed chiefly in the French style. It is ornamental and decorative and in England it displaced the tallboy (highboy) early in the 18th century.

REFERENCE
Dictionary of English Furniture, MAC-QUOID and EDWARDS.

CONSOLE
A French word, meaning a bracket, also indicates a table standing or leaning against a wall. See TABLES, *Console*.

CONSTITUTION MIRRORS
See MIRRORS, *Constitution*.

CORBEL
A supporting projection, often ornamented with flowers, fruit or figures. A bracket.

CORDOVAN LEATHER
See LEATHER.

CORNER CUPBOARD
See CUPBOARDS, *Corner*.

CORNICE

The highest projection at the top of chests, cupboards and other furniture. Also the top or finished molding of a column. See LOCKWOOD's *Colonial Furniture in America* for detailed analysis of case furniture.

COUCHES
Early couches were really long chairs, without back on the long side, but instead attached to one end. They were Flemish in style with scroll feet and carved under-braces, followed by those in the Queen Anne and Chippendale styles. The French chaise-longue (q.v.) was in the same general style. See BEDS, *Day*, also SOFAS.

COURT CUPBOARD
See CUPBOARDS, *Court*.

COURTING GLASS

A mirror found in New England seaport towns, presumed to be of Chinese origin. They varied in size from eight by ten inches, to twelve by fourteen inches, and they were usually fastened with removable pegs into a small flat box. The mirrors were framed with strips of painted glass and they were usually hung on the wall, in the box.

CRADLES
There were two varieties of cradles in use in Colonial times, one swinging between uprights, the other mounted on short rockers, with hood. Some of the cradles of the Pennsylvania Germans of the 18th century were decorated.

CREDENCE

A kind of cupboard or buffet on legs of the Renaissance period. The back was solid, the front supported by two or four legs, resting on a base. Often used as a serving table, but chiefly as a repository for valuable plate or vessels.

CRESTING

Carving on the top rail of a chair or settee back. It became the salient feature of the type of chair introduced into England at the Restoration.

CROMWELLIAN PERIOD

1649 to 1660. See JACOBEAN PERIOD.

CROSS BANDING

A border banding of veneer, placed so that the grain runs across that of the main surface. It was used throughout the 18th century.

CROSS RAIL

The horizontal bar or splat in a chair back.

CUPBOARDS

At first but a single shelf, literally a "borde" on which to set cups, then other shelves added, then a door covering the contents, at first plain, then paneled, then carved, until it became the piece of furniture that collectors today value and admire. In its development, it was called by various names (see ALMERY) and it served for various purposes. The word began to acquire its modern significance in the second

DOLE CUPBOARD

quarter of the 16th century. It ranged in size from the early small lowly structure made to sit on a table to the later stately press cupboard. Cupboards were fastened together, mortise and tenon fashion, with wooden pegs. No nails were used in them and almost all the designs carved on them were those of the room panels of the period to which the furniture belonged. They were in use in all of the colonies in the 17th century, with the same variations as in England; the court, livery and press cupboards. They were superseded by the high chests of drawers which came into use in the last quarter of the 17th century.

REFERENCES

Dictionary of English Furniture, MACQUOID and EDWARDS; The Early English Cupboards, FINE ARTS, July 1933.

Corner Cupboards. Also called, in this country, beaufait. The upper part was semi-domed in shape and a carved shell was frequently the decoration. This part was sometimes with doors, frequently without. The lower part was usually closed in with paneled doors, corresponding to the room paneling. They made their appearance in the first quarter of the 18th century. Later, a hanging corner cupboard was designed, from thirty inches to four feet high, with enclosed shelves. These hanging corner cupboards were quite common in England where they made their appearance in the 17th century.

Court Cupboards. A development of the chest, it was originally a low cupboard set on a side table, taking its name from the French word, *court*, meaning low or short. Later the two were combined and the lower part was fitted sometimes with shelves, sometimes with doors making a lower cupboard. In England this piece of furniture was used for the display and keeping of plate and other table furnishings. It corresponded in a measure to the modern sideboard. Strictly speaking, it was open below the main shelf, and when closed should be called a press cupboard (q.v.). Early in the 17th century it became a tall carved piece of furniture with the cupboard of the upper part set back so that there was a ledge in front of it. The top projected like a roof and was supported by two turned columns, often of the melon bulb pattern. In England they were made all of oak. Of those made in this country the backs were usually of pine. The court cupboards were designed to contain the wines, food and candles for the lord and lady of the manor of the early days, while the livery cupboard (q.v.) was for the servants' use.

REFERENCE

The American Press and Court Cupboards, FINE ARTS, Dec. 1932.

Dole Cupboards. These contained meat and bread for distribution to the poor. They were placed, not only in the churches, but in the homes of the wealthy as well, for pensioners and for family retainers. See ALMERY.

Hanging Cupboards. For clothing, about five feet in height or even less, with openings in the doors to ventilate the clothing hanging within.

Livery Cupboards. A receptacle for food, wine or candles for servants, common in Tudor and early Jacobean periods. They were made both with doors and without and were hung on the wall

or set on a table. American-made pieces of this type are rare although they are mentioned frequently in inventories of estates in the 17th century. Presumably, they were brought from England.

Press Cupboards. Resembling the *Court Cupboard* (q.v.) above the shelf dividing the upper from the lower section, but below, instead of shelves, the press cupboard is fitted either with compartments with doors, or with drawers, used for linen or for clothing. In England it was also generally larger than the court cupboard. In this country these early cupboards, of which there are very few remaining examples, are usually about five feet high and four feet wide and they were made of native oak. They were primarily a place for storage, and no two are exactly alike. In Connecticut the decoration on them resembles the "Sunflower" chest of Nicholas Disbrowe. The applied ornaments and the carving are virtually identical. The use of these cupboards declined toward the end of the 17th century, being displaced by the high chest of drawers or by the highboy.

REFERENCE
The Tulip and Sunflower Press Cupboard, ANTIQUES, April 1935.

Cupboard Cloths

All kinds of cupboards here as in England were furnished with cupboard cloths of various materials and colors. Cupboard cushions are also frequently mentioned in the inventories in this country of estates of the 17th century.

Cupid's Bow

A variety of compound or serpentine curves much used in the top rails on Chippendale's chairs.

Curule

The name given to the shape of the chair derived from a chair of the early Romans. Very popular in Italian and Spanish chairs of the Renaissance period. It had a square seat with a loose cushion and X-shaped legs.

Cyma Curve

A wave curve, a double or compounded S curve called cyma recta, convex below and concave above, and cyma reversa, convex above and concave below. It is characteristic of the familiar cabriole leg and chair backs of the Queen Anne period.

Cypress

A hard, very durable, close grained wood of reddish color. A native of Persia and the Levant, it was used in England because of its moth- and worm-resisting properties.

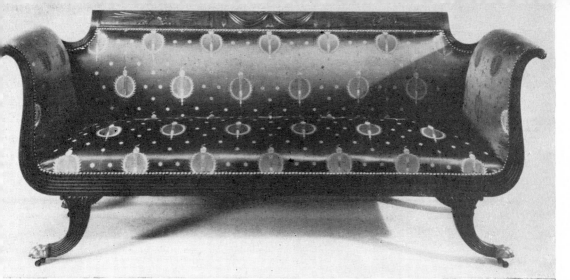

Duncan Phyfe Mahogany Sofa, New York, 1810-1815

Courtesy of the Museum of Fine Arts, Boston

American Hepplewhite Sofa, circa 1790

English Chippendale Sofa, Needlepoint Covering, 18th Century

AMERICAN PINE SETTLE WITH HINGED SEAT AND FIREPLACE ACCESSORIES, 17TH CENTURY

CONNECTICUT BUTTERFLY TABLE, CIRCA 1700

NEW ENGLAND SLAT-BACK CHAIR, C
1700

D

Dado

An ornamental border around the lower part of a room, usually with a plain or paneled surface. The dado came into use when paneling to the top of the room was discontinued.

Day Bed

See Beds, Day.

Deal

A timber used in England in the 16th and 17th centuries for furniture-making. It is the wood of the North European pine with hard and soft fibers alternating. Red deal is the wood of the Scotch pine.

Decorated Queen Anne Style

See Georgian Period.

Dentil

A form of molding ornamentation made by small oblong blocks, set at equal distances from each other, placed usually on cornices.

Desk

A piece of furniture, an early distinctive feature being a sloping front lid. It originally meant in England a box with a slant top, usually plain, sometimes carved, set on a table, for holding writing materials. In this form it was in use in the Elizabethan and Jacobean periods. Some of them had the owner's name and a date carved upon them, perhaps with a lock for safe keeping of money, wills, etc. Later, the box and table were combined in one piece and often referred to in the 17th century as a scrutoir. The desk in its present form came into use in the William and Mary period. The space below the desk box had been filled with drawers, and behind the lid, small drawers and pigeon-holes were arranged, many of the desks having secret drawers for the safety of valuable papers. Pine, maple, cherry, walnut, and later mahogany were used. The desk in its present form is known in England and in France as bureau. See Secretary.

Knee-Hole Desks. A desk with a flat top and a recessed space below, between drawers at each side. While seated at it one may have the whole resources of it at hand. With the fall-front desk when the lid is down it is difficult to get at the drawers beneath it. It belongs to the 18th century almost exclusively and the best examples of these desks have the block front. The knee-hole desk is similar to the smaller dressing table with which it is often confused.

REFERENCE

Dictionary of English Furniture, Macquoid and Edwards.

Diaperwork

A method of surface decoration, consisting of a design, usually geometrical, made up of regular repeats, and generally used in friezes.

Dipped Seat
See Dropped Seat.

Dished Corner
A table corner, usually a card table, slightly hollowed out, to hold a candle-stick, or for counters.

Dish-Top
A table top with plain raised rim.

Divan
A low cushioned seat, similar to the seats provided for the council chamber in Eastern palaces.

Dole Cupboards
See Cupboards, Dole.

Dolphin
A marine animal, whose head and body, or head alone, is seen on Renaissance furniture for conventionalized decorative purposes. It was also in use frequently in 18th-century work.

Dovetail

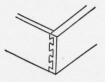

A manner of joining wood by inter-locking wedge-shaped tenons and spaces.

In Colonial times, the spacing was greater than on modern work.

Dowel
A wooden pin fastening two pieces of cabinet work. In old pieces these were made by hand, and seldom round, often octagonal or square.

Dowry (Dower) Chests
See Chests, Dowry.

Dragon's Claw
A name sometimes given to the claw-and-ball foot.

Draw-Bore Pin
A method employed in Colonial times to tighten a mortise and tenon joint. The tenon hole was about one-sixteenth inch nearer the shoulder than in the mortised piece.

Draw-Runner
See Runner.

Dresser (French, Dressoir)
Not unlike the cupboard in its development in the Gothic period, the dresser retained its simplicity of plain open shelves, on which were placed the fla-gons and cups. Sometimes the lower shelves were enclosed with a door or doors, the open shelves being used for displaying pewter or pottery. Toward the end of the 17th century in the more opulent families, its place was taken by the handsomer press or court cupboard. Dressers made in this country in the 17th century were usually of pine with a cornice of moldings at the top. In Eng-

land in the country districts, a dresser was made of oak in the 17th century, similar in form to the sideboard of the late 18th century. It had drawers immediately below the top, and sometimes shelves were arranged at the back with a canopy top. With variations this form of dresser persisted until well into the 18th century.

DRESSING-GLASS OR MIRROR

See MIRRORS.

DROP ORNAMENT

A turned ornament used on Jacobean work, also a decoration resembling a husk to be seen on late 18th-century furniture.

DROPPED SEAT

A seat concaved so that the middle and front are lower than the sides.

DUMB WAITERS

An English invention of the 18th century, consisting of tiers of trays affixed to a central stem. There were generally three trays revolving on the stand, mounted on tripod feet for floor use.

DUTCH FOOT

A foot which spreads from the leg in a circular termination. Frequently used as a terminal of cabriole legs. See CLUB FOOT.

DUTCH FURNITURE

The furniture designs of both Dutch and Flemish furniture were influenced strongly by the French styles of the Huguenot refugees, who fled from France following the Revocation of the Edict of Nantes. Marquetry was much used for ornamentation and the variety of furniture was greatly increased. Ball feet as a support for cabinets, bureaus (desks), etc. is typically Dutch. The "bombé" or swell front, also Dutch, was used extensively on such pieces as chests of drawers, bureaus, wardrobes and cabinets. Another feature is that of hanging drawers on runners attached to the carcase, the runners sliding in grooves cut in the drawer sides. The interiors of cabinets were usually painted, and the carving on Dutch chairs is very elaborate. Examples of genuine Dutch furniture of the late 17th and early 18th centuries are rare. During the William and Mary period the influence of Dutch styles on English furniture was very pronounced.

REFERENCES

Dutch and Flemish Furniture, SINGLETON; English and Dutch Furniture Compared, ANTIQUES, Jan., Feb., Mar. 1926.

E

EBONY

A close-grained black and very heavy wood. Not used much for furniture except for veneering and inlaying. In Italy, Spain and France it was used to some extent for furniture in the 16th century.

EGG-AND-DART

A form of molding, derived from Greek design, made of egg-shaped pieces with dart-shaped pieces between. This design was frequently carved on furniture from the 16th century onward.

ELIZABETHAN PERIOD 1558-1603

There are few genuine dated pieces before the time of Elizabeth, and most of those are in museums, but of her reign there are more. The wood carvers were more skilled than those of earlier periods and they introduced new designs, derived from the Renaissance of Italy and France. A strong Flemish influence is also seen. The furniture was massive, straight in line, elaborately carved, and they utilized the round arch, conventional flowers, the interlaced strap decoration, the Tudor rose, the linen-fold panel, and grotesque terminal figures were used as supports. The few chairs were of the wainscot type, with finials on the back uprights. The development of the court cupboard is a feature of this period, in that the upper part was recessed with a canopy at the top. The jeweled bulbs of the balusters supporting the canopy were especially bold and pleasing. The favorite wood used was oak.

REFERENCES

Practical Book of Period Furniture, EBERLEIN and McCLURE; Period Furniture Handbook, GOULD.

EMPIRE PERIOD 1793-1830

The chief material for furniture of this period was mahogany, both solid and in veneer. The types of design are of two kinds, one the Egyptian, the other the Classical. Both motives are so intermixed as to be difficult to distinguish from each other. The lines were mostly straight. It has frankly been said by one critic that "the style of the Empire period is least interesting and least French of all of the styles developed in France." Strictly speaking, the Empire period means Napoleon. In construction it was heavy by comparison with other styles. Its influence, however, spread to other parts of Europe and to America. In 1808 a book was published in England, containing designs mostly copied from French Empire patterns, which did much to popularize the style there. However, it lacks every one of the qualities that give charm to the French Empire Period. The furniture of the French depended largely for its excellent effect upon the beautifully chased, classic ormolu mounts with which it was lavishly decorated, and by the rich and vivid colorings in upholstery, contrasted with the mahogany and ormolu. Deep green, red, royal blue and purple were the colors used. The chairs were of simple construction and small; tables were usually round with marble tops and with a central carved pillar with three carved feet on the floor. The beds of the period approach more nearly the modern type. Simplicity of style and rather heavy design were characteristic of this period.

In this country Duncan Phyfe utilized the Empire period with charming effect at first, and the cornucopia motif with paw foot was used by him and by others quite extensively. The styles of the Empire period were very popular in New York. Later developments of the period in this country were heavy and clumsy furniture and the use of black walnut and rosewood in construction. The work of John H. Belter of New York is a conspicuous example of this later period. He supplied many New York families with this type of furniture.

REFERENCES
  Practical Book of Period Furniture, EBERLEIN and McCLURE; Period Furniture Handbook, GOULD; Decorative Styles and Periods in the Home, HELEN C. CANDEE.

ENDIVE SCROLL
  A carved ornament seen on furniture of the Chippendale style.

ENGLISH FURNITURE
  This subject is treated under the headings of the periods from Tudor to Empire and of the styles of the four master craftsmen of the 18th century, Adam, Chippendale, Hepplewhite and Sheraton, to which the reader is referred for details.

ENGRAILING
  Cutting the edge of a board to design.

ESCALLOP SHELL

Ornament in use first half of 18th century, derived from the badge of the

Crusaders who had been on a pilgrimage to the Holy Land.

Escritoire

French name for writing desk or bureau. See Secretary.

Escutcheon

A shield and crest carved ornament, frequently seen on furniture. Also it is applied to the brass fitting for a keyhole. See Part 5.

F

Fakes

The collector of antique furniture must be on his guard against frauds and the fraudulent dealer. While there is no general rule that will apply in all cases, there is one method by means of which one can often avoid making mistakes, and that is to buy antique furniture only in the original condition, unrestored and from reputable dealers. Repairing and restoration that may be required, within reasonable limits, should not prevent one from purchasing if the piece shall then be serviceable and in harmony with your other furnishings. There are so many pitfalls for the inexperienced buyer that to attempt to catalogue them would require more space than is available here. Until one gains experience through study of good examples the best advice is to rely upon a good dealer.

    REFERENCES

    Genuine Antique Furniture, Arthur de Bles; *Antiques, Genuine and Spurious*, Frederick Litchfield.

Faldstool

A folding stool not unlike a camp stool. A common type of early seat.

Fall Front

The falling front of a desk or bureau.

Fan Back

The back of a Windsor chair with the spindles flaring like an open fan.

Fan Motif

Its use was similar to the shell ornament and popular at the same time. It was sometimes made in rosette form but this was merely doubling the fan, producing a sunburst effect.

Fancy Chairs

See Chairs, *Fancy*.

Farthingale Chairs.

See Chairs, *Farthingale*.

Fauteuil

An arm-chair of French origin, open under the arms, in contradistinction to the bergère.

Feather Banding

A feather pattern of veneering. See Herringbone.

Federal Period (American) 1789-1812

In this period the work of the American cabinet-maker continued on a high plane of excellence. The styles of Adam and Sheraton and later the influence of the French Empire styles are all reflected in the production of the craftsmen of Boston, Salem, New York and Philadelphia, and some of the smaller towns. Duncan Phyfe in New York rose to leadership in not only his designs, which were a combination of the best of Sheraton and of the French, but in the careful selection of the wood he used and in his masterly carving. Much furniture in this period was made at Salem and other places in New England for shipment to southern states and foreign ports, an enterprise which began in the preceding period.

REFERENCES

Blue Book, Philadelphia Furniture, HORNOR; Furniture Masterpieces of Duncan Phyfe, CORNELIUS; The Wood-Carver of Salem. Samuel McIntyre, His Life and Work, COUSINS & RILEY.

FESTOON

A decorative series of scallops, forming a rope, flower chain or draperies.

FIDDLE-BACK

The name given in this country to the shape of the splat on the chairs of the Queen Anne period. The shape was derived, however, from the oviform Chinese vases then so popular in Europe. See VASE MOTIF.

FIELD BEDS

See BEDS, Field.

FILIGREE PAPER DECORATION

Rolled paper or mosaic work, a favorite recreation for ladies in the 18th century. The patterns employed were used for fire screens, tea caddies, frames, etc.

FINIAL

An architectural term for an ornamental pinnacle on the pediments of furniture. A finishing device.

FINISH

A method of finishing restored or repaired pieces of old furniture, recommended by a good authority (H. H. Taylor), consists of what he calls general purpose finish, using a brown shade of orange shellac as the base, mixed with an equal part of wood, or denatured, alcohol, which makes a thin mixture to be applied three or four times in succession, as each coat dries, producing a fine, smooth surface. Soft, porous woods such as pine absorb more than the harder woods. Maple or mahogany may require but two coats. These shellac coats dry very quickly. After this, the piece is ready for its wax finish. This may be prepared as follows: take a can of yellow floor wax and mix with it a small quantity of burnt umber to give it the desired color. This wax is known as a paraffin-base wax and it is very in-flammable. Apply a fairly heavy coat of the wax over the shellacked surfaces, rub it well with a soft woolen cloth, and repeat three or four times, setting the piece aside in a warm room for twenty-four hours between each appli-cation. This finish will not mar, chip or bruise. See OIL FINISH and WAX FINISH.

FIRE SCREENS

To protect the face from the heat of the fire. They were made from designs by Chippendale, Hepplewhite, Shera-ton and other cabinet-makers from the middle to the end of the 18th century. They were made in two patterns: the pole screen and the horse (cheval) screen. The pole, four to five feet in height, is set in a tripod stand and the screen, usually oblong, slides up and down the pole. The horse screen was in the form of two uprights, supporting a good-sized rectangular panel of needle-work. Some of the screens were painted or decorated with bead work design.

Fire screens are distinctly English and most of those used in this country were imported.

REFERENCE

Variants of the Fire Guard, ANTI-QUARIAN, Sept. 1930.

FLAT CARVING

Carving in which the background is cut or taken out, leaving the design itself flat. It is a feature of 17th-century chests made in England and in this country.

FLAX WHEEL

See SPINNING WHEELS.

FLEMISH FOOT

Used on Jacobean furniture, with one scroll turning in, the other turning out.

FLEMISH FURNITURE

Until the middle of the 17th century the style of Dutch and Flemish furniture was similar. After that, while Holland developed a style of her own, Flemish furniture followed French fashions. The wood chiefly used was oak and the dis-tinguishing feature was a profusion of elaborate carving. The furniture was often heavy and bulky and more clumsy than graceful. The so-called Flemish scroll was prominent.

Mahogany Three-part Dining Table with Drop-leaf Center, Late 18th Century

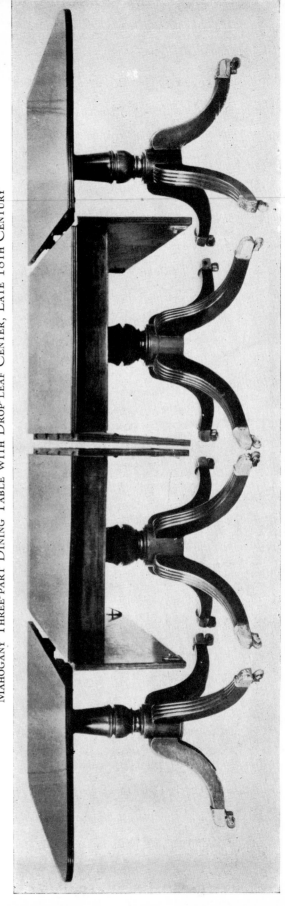

English Sheraton Mahogany Four-part Dining Table, 1800-1810

DUNCAN PHYFE CARD TABLE, CIRCA 1810

MAHOGANY CARVED DUNCAN PHYFE DROP-LEAF TABLE, EARLY 19TH CENTURY

FLEMISH SCROLL

A baroque form of the 16th and 17th centuries with the curve broken by an angle.

FLORENTINE MIRRORS

See MIRRORS, *Florentine*.

FLUTING

Channeling or grooving on a flat surface.

FOOT STOOLS

See STOOLS, *Foot*.

FORMS

The name given in England to the bench in use in the 17th century and earlier in the place of chairs. Two varieties of bench, portable and fixed, were common in medieval days. The fixed seat usually had a back and it was attached to the wall. Short forms, or joint stool (q.v.), were placed at the ends of the table and the long forms along-side.

FRAME

This was a separate four-legged support to several different pieces of furniture, in Colonial days, as evidenced by many inventories of estates of that time.

FRENCH CLOCKS

See CLOCKS, *French*.

FRENCH FURNITURE

In France during the Renaissance, the furniture was solid and carved elaborately. Walnut was the most used wood. There was but little French furniture of note previous to the days of Louis XIV, and French provincial furniture bears the same relation to period styles that American Colonial furniture does to the styles of the Mother Country. It was generally made of local woods. The long enduring Louis Quatorze (XIV) and Louis Quinze (XV) periods (q.v.), rich in furniture development, wrought a strong influence on both English and other European cabinet-makers. Chippendale and Sheraton borrowed heavily from French designs. Usually the French bias was partially disguised under a shell of English adaptation but the French leaven was there and working.

REFERENCES

French and English Furniture, SINGLETON; *The Source of the Label*, ANTIQUARIAN, April 1930.

FRET-WORK

Interlaced, ornamental work, sometimes applied on a solid background and sometimes perforated. It was a popular form of ornament with Chippendale. Also called lattice-work.

FRIEZE

The middle division of an entablature, usually carved, inlaid or painted.

FURNITURE DESIGN, BOOKS OF

Published in England in the 18th century.

The Gentleman's or Builder's Companion, WILLIAM JONES, 1739; *Original Designs for Furniture*, LOCK and COPELAND, 1740; *Some Designs of Mr. Inigo Jones and Mr. William Kent*, 1744; *Treasury of Designs*, BATTY LONGLEY, 1745; *Six Tables*, MATTHIAS LOCK, 1746; *Book of Ornament*, MATTHIAS LOCK, 1765; *The Gentleman's and Cabinet Maker's Directory*, THOMAS CHIPPENDALE, 1754, 1759, 1762; *A New Book of Chinese, Gothic and Modern Chairs*, MATTHIAS DARLY, 1754; *Cabinet and Chairmaker's Friend and Companion*, ROBERT MANWARING, 1765; *Universal System of Household Furniture*, INCE & MAYHEW, 1748; *Household Furniture*, SOCIETY OF UPHOLSTERERS, 1760; *The Cabinet Maker's and Upholsterer's Guide*, HEPPLEWHITE, 1788, 1789, 1794; *Cabinet Maker's Book of Prices*, LONDON SOCIETY, 1788, 1793, 1803; *Cabinet Maker's and Upholsterer's Drawing Book*, THOMAS SHERATON, 1793, 1796, 1802.

REFERENCE

Old English Books of Furniture, ANTIQUES, Sept., 1929, compiled by FISKE KIMBALL.

G

GADROON

A carved and curved fluted or ruffle ornament for edges, both concave and convex, characteristic of the Elizabethan and Jacobean periods.

GALLERY

A raised rim of fret-work or metal for surrounding table tops, or at the back of sideboard tops.

GARLAND

A wreath of leaves, flowers or fruit, used as a decorative detail.

GATE-LEGGED TABLE

See TABLES, Gate-Legged.

GEORGIAN PERIOD (1714-1793)

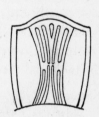

For thirty or more years after the death of Queen Anne in 1714, furniture exhibited no radical changes in form, but was rather an elaboration of patterns already well recognized. There was the "Decorated Queen Anne" style, 1714-1725, the "lion" style, 1720-1735, the "satyr-mask" style, 1730-1740, and the "cabochon-and-leaf" style from 1735 to the rise of Chippendale to recognition. The first was a greater elaboration of carving and gilding than was formerly the fashion, resulting in the most highly ornamental furniture ever produced in England. The lion style brought lion's heads on the knees, backs and seat rails of furniture; the satyr-mask had grotesque heads instead of the lion's heads. These in turn gave way to the cabochon-and-leaf motif which Chippendale afterwards used as an important factor in the design basis of his earliest manner. From the time of Chippendale onward through the Hepplewhite and Sheraton styles, refer to the respective names of each in this section. Their styles together with that of Robert Adam (q.v.) dominate the remainder of the period.

REFERENCES

Practical Book of Period Furniture, Eberlein and McClure; *Period Furniture Handbook,* Gould.

GERMAN FURNITURE
See BIEDERMEIER FURNITURE.

GESSO

A fine plaster, generally composed of gypsum, resin and glue which, while soft, was molded or pressed into the desired form of ornament or bas-relief and when hard and dry was painted or gilded. It could also be carved after it was dry. Although it had its origin in Italy in the 15th century, gesso was first used in England early in the 18th century.

GILDING

Gilding is done by one of two processes, either water or oil gilding. For water gilding, which was in use on furniture and frames in the 18th century, the ground is prepared whiting and size and brought forward in preparations of lead for the burnishing of the gold. Oil gilding is laid on a varnish called "gold size" to which the gold adheres. It makes the surface partly water-proof but the gold cannot be burnished or toned. See PARCEL GILT.

GIRANDOLE
See CANDELABRUM, PART 5.

GIRANDOLE MIRRORS
See MIRRORS, *Girandole.*

GOTHIC PERIOD (1100-1453)

This period of about 350 years covers a wide range of development in the decorative arts from early crude simplicity to later luxurious elaboration. During the whole of this period French artists preferred to express themselves in stone. Exquisitely wrought tracery was the special glory of every church and Cathedral. The English, however, excelled the French in the development of ecclesiastical wood carving. At this period the same forms appeared in both secular and religious work. The pointed arch, carved, foliated ornament and tracery are the signs manual of the style. Comparatively few examples of this period have survived. The medieval chair, distinct from the clerical throne or stall, is the rarest of all early furniture and until nearly the close of the 16th century a domestic chair was unknown. Benches and stools were the only seats in common use. Gothic furniture followed closely upon the architectural mode in vogue during the period. Simplicity and portability were the main characteristics of that furniture. Chests were a principal item, made of oak, heavy and cumbersome. In the later part of the period, the highback chair and various types of cupboards appear, also some tables with fixed legs. The carving on some of this furniture was very elaborate.

REFERENCES

Period Furniture Handbook, GOULD; The Gothic Craftsmen, ANTIQUES, Nov. 1924.

GRAINING

A process of painting furniture and wood-work by which the color and figure of a more costly wood is imitated.

First used in England, end of 16th century and continued since.

GRANDFATHER'S CLOCKS

See CLOCKS, Grandfather's.

GRANDMOTHER'S CLOCKS

See CLOCKS, Grandmother's.

GREAT BED OF WARE

See BEDS, Great Bed of Ware.

GUERIDON

A small pedestal table or stand for candelabra.

GUILLOCHE

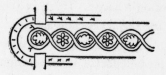

An ornament in the form of two or more bands or strings, twisted in a continued series, which produce circular openings, which openings are usually filled with round ornament. It was either carved, painted or inlaid and it was used intermittently from the middle of the 16th century to end of the 18th.

GUMWOOD

A wood obtained in New South Wales and resembling mahogany in appearance.

H

HADLEY CHESTS

See CHESTS, Hadley.

HANGING CUPBOARDS

See CUPBOARDS, Hanging.

HAREWOOD

Sycamore, stained a greenish yellow color. Much used by English cabinetmakers for inlay, late 18th century.

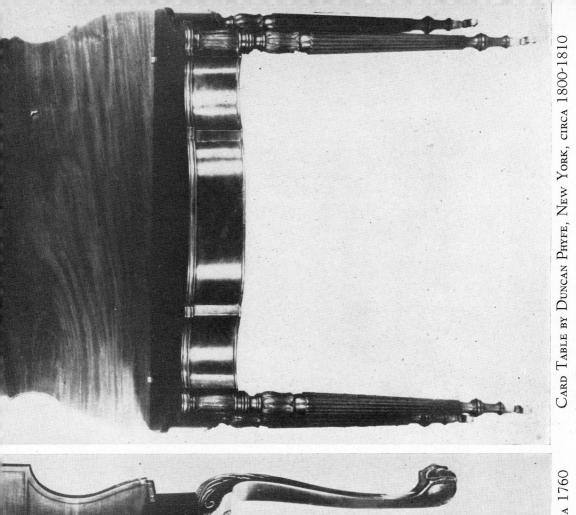

CARD TABLE BY DUNCAN PHYFE, NEW YORK, CIRCA 1800-1810

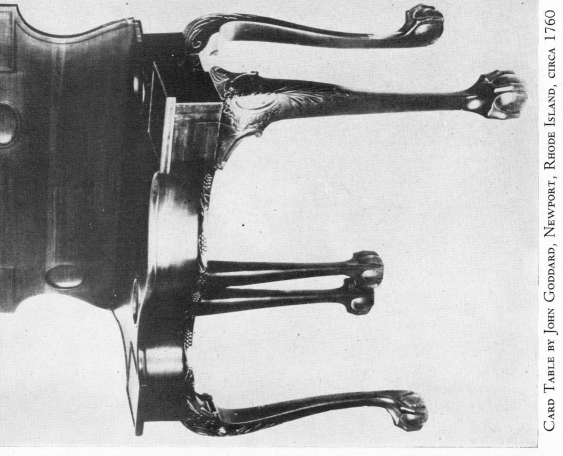

CARD TABLE BY JOHN GODDARD, NEWPORT, RHODE ISLAND, CIRCA 1760

PHILADELPHIA LOWBOY BY THOMAS TUFFT, 18TH CENTURY

LOWBOY LABELED THOMAS TUFFT, PHILADELPHIA, 18TH CENTURY

HARPSICHORD

A keyed musical instrument sometimes with two or three banks of keys, which differed from the virginal (q.v.) and spinet (q.v.) by the addition of extra strings which could be brought into use by means of extra stops. It preceded the piano and was formerly in extensive use, but is now little known. It was made in three shapes; one resembled the "grand" piano of later days, upright in form and very rare. It produced a brilliant but somewhat metallic sound, and after the invention of the pianoforte the harpsichord was gradually superseded by it. See PIANO.

HEPPLEWHITE STYLE

George Hepplewhite was the second of the great English cabinet-makers to make a distinct impression upon the furniture styles of the Georgian period. Most of his work was confined to the smaller items of furniture and he represented the simplest, most graceful and most delicate type form in England of that period. Much of this classic feeling was derived from the designs of the brothers Adam. His style was also in-fluenced by French designs. It was in making chairs that he struck out on new lines. His chairs are lighter and more graceful than those of Chippendale, but they are lacking in strength and durability. The backs are in shield, oval or heart shape, the top rails and side posts are fluted, the legs are straight or tapering, square or round, often fluted, with collared or spade feet, and he enriched his chairs with veneers and inlay. Mahogany was used for carved work and satinwood where painting or inlay was employed. The Prince of Wales feathers, the honeysuckle and the husk were favorite Hepplewhite motives. Also, the plain, elongated urn. He was partial to curved lines, using them wherever possible, while Sheraton, who followed him, preferred straight lines. In spite of this, some of their designs are so much alike it is very difficult to differentiate between them. The tambour front for small writing tables, the pouch work-table and sideboard with drawers and cupboards are characteristic pieces of Hepplewhite design, although Shearer shares with Hepplewhite the credit for the sideboard of the period. For up-holstering he preferred silks and satins and was fond of narrow stripes and French designs. This was generally brought down over the frame of the chair all around. The furniture of Hepplewhite was practical, designed in the workshop, and the designs after his death were published by A. Hepplewhite & Company in a book called *The Cabinet Maker's and Upholsterer's Guide*, which went into several editions. It is, by far, the best exposition of Adam's style, adapted to the use of cabinet-makers. See GEORGE HEPPLEWHITE, PART 6.

HERRINGBONE

An inlay much used in walnut and mahogany furniture in the Georgian period. It first came into use in the 17th century. It is composed of two strips with the grain of each running diagonally.

HICKORY

The hickory is exclusively American, unlike many other of the woods used for cabinet-making. The wood is heavy, strong and tenacious, but decays speedily when exposed to heat and moisture. For this reason, probably, it was not made use of freely by Colonial cabinet-makers, although the delicate spindles of the Windsor chair were usually made of hickory.

HIGHBOY

The form, a chest-on-chest, though of English origin, late 17th century, and designed in English period styles, never had much vogue in England, and is notably an American development. In England they were known as tallboys.

They were superseded there by the commode. The highboy consists of two parts; a chest of drawers above and a stand with from one to three drawers below. The early stand, or table, had six legs, four in front and two at the back, united by stretchers running all the way around, just above the floor. Later they were made with four cabriole legs, without stretchers. The earliest highboys had flat tops, with a light molded cornice. The ornamental cornice, with broken arch pediment and finials, formed a decorative finish on the later designs. The highboy remained in use in this country for more than a century and reached its highest development here. The highboys (and lowboys) in the Chippendale style made by Philadelphia cabinet-makers from 1762 to 1776 are among the noteworthy furniture creations of all time.

REFERENCE
The American Highboy, ANTIQUARIAN, June and July, 1931.

HITCHCOCK CHAIRS
See CHAIRS, *Hitchcock*.

HOLLY
A wood used for inlaying and for marquetry. It is a hard white wood with a speckled grain.

HONEYSUCKLE
A form of ornament used both by Adam and by Hepplewhite.

Hood

A shaped top to cabinet work. A bonnet or arch.

Hoof-Foot

A style of foot often found with the cabriole leg, introduced into England at end of 17th century.

Hoop-Back

A back of chairs whose uprights and top rail continue in one unbroken arch.

Horologe

Early name given to clocks, derived from the Greek.

Hourglass

Used for telling time in both ancient and more modern times. The quantity of sand used required just one hour in passing from one chamber to the other.

Hunt Sideboard
See Sideboard.

Husk Motif

A form of ornament, taken from nature, generally used in a pendent manner, or in the form of a festoon. A favorite with Adam and with Hepplewhite. First introduced into England in the reign of Charles II.

Hutch (French, Huche)

A coffer or chest, standing on legs with doors opening in front, instead of a lid on top. In England in the Gothic period it was the dole cupboard or almery, and in Tudor times it was used for storing clothes.

I

Inlay

Decorating surfaces with wood and other materials of contrasting colors or pattern, let into a solid base. Broad inlay is called banding, narrow inlay, stringing. See Boulle and Marquetry.

Intarsia

Inlaying by incising or cutting away the groundwork and inserting other substances. It was a favorite Italian ornament of the Renaissance period and is older than marquetry (q.v.). Strictly speaking, the term intarsia should apply to inlay representing landscapes, still life or other scenes. It was also a popular inlay in Germany in the 16th and 17th centuries.

IRISH FURNITURE

Early oak and walnut Irish furniture of the 17th century is almost non-existent. Furniture of the 18th century was mostly of San Domingo mahogany and although some of it precedes Chippendale, it displays some of the features found in Chippendale's designs. It is probable that examples imported from England were copied by native Irish craftsmen. Irish furniture of the latter half of the 18th century shows little to distinguish it from contemporary English work.

REFERENCES

Old English Furniture, G. OWEN WHEELER; Irish Furniture of the Chippendale Period, ANTIQUARIAN, Dec. 1930.

ITALIAN FURNITURE

During the 13th and 14th centuries, the furniture of the home consisted mainly of chests, tables, benches, stools and low bench-beds. The style was Gothic. Late in the 14th century and early in the 15th, there sprang into existence a new era and craftsmen were not slow to catch the new spirit. Dropping the Gothic, they launched into the classic of the Renaissance, drawing their inspiration from Greek models. The furniture was at first elaborately carved, then exquisitely painted or gilded. The closer the Greek detail and motive was adhered to, the more exquisite the work. Siena and Florence were centers of activities in furniture-making during the whole of the Renaissance period. This lasted almost two hundred years and eventually declined with the exaggerations of the Baroque and the Rococo, into the ugliness of our present industrial age. Walnut was used for the best work, but pine, chestnut, elm, cypress and other woods were employed.

REFERENCES

Practical Book of Italian, Spanish and Portuguese Furniture, EBERLEIN and RAMSDELL; Renaissance Period, ANTIQUES, April 1925.

J

JACOBEAN PERIOD (1603-1688)

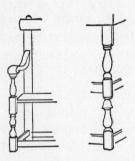

Includes Jacobean Period (proper) from 1603 to 1649, Cromwellian period 1649 to 1660, and the Carolean period 1660 to 1688. The furniture of the early Jacobean period retained the general characteristics of the preceding periods, but Flemish and Dutch arts and manufactures were influential in forming what is known as the Jacobean style. The term is derived from *Jacobus*, the Latin for James. Furniture was stout and staunch, even to clumsiness, severe in form and line and replete with ornament, much of which was discontinued during the Cromwellian days. As a rule it was put together with mortise and tenon, and held in place with dowels. Chairs were comparatively scarce. They usually had arms and they were seats of great dignity. The characteristic chair of early 17th century was the wainscot chair with a cresting across the top. Oak was still the favored wood. At the time of the Commonwealth, chairs with spirally turned legs and low, open backs appeared with either caning or vertical balusters or slats. Bun or ball feet with under-bracing generally used. It was not until after the Restoration in 1660 that chairs became the usual seat at the table for meals. At the end of the Carolean period, chairs with Flemish "C" and "S" scrolled legs, stretchers and top rail were common. Tables in considerable variety appeared, notably the gate-legged type; the cupboard in different sizes, and for a variety of purposes, was a favorite piece of furniture during the last half of the century. It was an article of both convenience and ceremony.

From 1660 onward, Restoration influences, essentially foreign, wrought a vast change in the fashion and forms of English furniture. At first, oak was the staple material used, superseded by walnut after 1660. This last was a more suitable medium for the scrolls, twists and curves then coming into fashion. Other native woods were also used occasionally. Glass began to be used for mirrors, doors of book-cases and other furniture. Carving, inlay, veneer, turning, painting, gilding, paneling, applied ornament and upholstering in brocades, velvets and needle-point were all used in processes of decoration during the progress of the period. The furniture of the American Colonies reflected many of the styles of the mother country.

REFERENCES

Practical Book of Period Furniture, Eberlein and McClure; *Period Furniture Handbook,* Gould.

Japanned Furniture

Japanned or lacquered furniture was popular in this country first half of 18th century, although seldom found at the present time. Presumably the japanned surface has either been removed or it has worn off with the passage of time. This method of decorating furniture was popular in England latter part of the 17th century and continued in vogue intermittently throughout the 18th century. Amateur japanning was a veritable rage in early Georgian times.

Japanning

The name given to imitation lacquer work in the early days of its use in England. Its derivation is obvious. Lacquered furniture from the East had become very popular and English craftsmen took this method of supplying the demand. In late 18th century it meant applying a ground coat of paint on which the decoration was laid and treated with a coat of thin varnish. The japanned surface was then rubbed with pumice and the final polish given to it by the palm of the hand. A very brilliant polish may be thus secured which is more durable than ordinary painted or varnish work. See Lacquer.

Joiner

The early craftsman who became the cabinet-maker (q.v.) of more modern times. In the 16th century he was known as arkwright. The joiner's work of the 17th century stands unequaled for solidity and for adherence to sound principles. The mortise and tenon joint is an example of his work.

Joints

The early joiners made use of various methods in joining together parts of furniture. Screws were unknown to them and nails and glue were seldom used. Wooden pins and dowels were common. For corners, posts and rails, mortise-and-tenon and dovetailing made firm joints. For joining boards for chests, paneling, etc., the tongue-and-groove, the rabbet, the mortise-and-tenon and doweling were all used at times when a plain butt joint would not answer.

Joint Stools

See Stools.

K

Kas or Kasse

The Dutch name for cupboard, although it was really more of a wardrobe than a cupboard. Many of those in this country were made by the Dutch descendants of the early settlers of New York. Some of them are very large and usually are mounted on bun feet. Some were fitted with shelves, usually with doors and some of them had a drawer or drawers beneath the cupboard. They were usually painted or carved on the front, or decorated in marquetry in the Dutch style.

KETTLE FRONT

A swelling or bulging form of Dutch inspiration of earlier date and sharper curves than the "bombé" (q.v.) front.

KNEE

The uppermost curve of the cabriole leg, where it is thickest.

KNEE-HOLE DESKS

See DESKS, *Knee-Hole.*

KNIFE BOXES or CASES

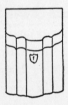

Made usually in pairs to contain knives and forks and sometimes spoons, to be set on ends of early sideboards. They were usually of mahogany or of soft wood, lacquered, about twelve inches high and with lid sloping down in front, which was either flat or serpentine in form. The knives and forks were inserted with their handles upwards and spoons with the bowls upwards. They were most popular from middle to end of 18th century and it was in England that the knife case appeared most widely and in greatest variety.

REFERENCE
Knife Cases, ANTIQUES, Nov. 1934.

KNIFE URNS

These were in common use in England during last half of 18th century but were seldom seen in this country. At first they were placed on pedestals made especially for them, but with the development of the sideboard by Shearer, they were made lighter in form and placed at each end of the sideboard. The partitions in these were arranged concentrically about the central stem to which the lid was secured and kept up by a spring when required. They were contemporary with knife boxes, served a similar purpose, and like them were usually made of mahogany, although metal urns, lacquered or japanned, were made.

REFERENCE
Knife Cases, Part II, ANTIQUES, Dec. 1934.

L

LACQUER

This is a varnish-like covering for furniture and ornamental woodwork, which in the process of drying and hardening is peculiarly suited to the application of other decorative ornament. It is treated as a solid body, built up stage by stage and polished, not varnished, at every stage. It is a natural gum-lac of the *Rhus vernicifera*, a variety of the sumac, a tree growing in Central and Southern China and cultivated for its valuable sap, and the lac is virtually ready made when extracted. Modern scientists have not yet been able, but are trying, to rival the Chinese product. In the production of the Oriental lacquers some twenty colorings were employed, but the remarkable white lacquer of the 15th century became a lost art. Although the invention of lacquer is credited to China, Japan has more highly perfected the art. Today, recent scientific attention to lacquer holds much promise.

There are four important types of decorated lacquer work: painted, carved, encrusted and incised. The commoner form of ornament was the ordinary black lacquer combined with gold and a brilliant vermilion red, finely penciled with gold. Mother of pearl, ivory, lapis lazuli and jade were also used for decorative effect, upon lacquered work. The time required to finish a lacquered surface by the Oriental method insured its durability. Never less than three and sometimes as many as eighteen thin layers were applied to the surface of the wood before the actual decoration by the artist commenced. English lacquer work of the 18th century, called japanning, never approached either the Chinese or Japanese work, decoratively or technically, even at its best. See JAPANNING.

REFERENCES
The A B C of Japanese Art, BLACKER; *The Art of Lacquering*, ANTIQUES, Nov. 1932.

LACQUERED FURNITURE

This furniture came into use in England last half of 17th century through importations from the Orient. Most of it came through Holland. All of the furniture forms of the William and Mary and Queen Anne periods, made of walnut, are also found in lacquered work. The degree of rarity on the basis of color is as follows: black, comparatively common; less common in the order given are red, yellow, buff, green and blue. The last named color is rarely seen. The interior of a lacquered cabinet should be of the same color as the exterior.

REFERENCE
Lacquer Furniture in England 1660-1780, ANTIQUARIAN, May 1931.

LADDER-BACK

A back of chairs, in which horizontal

cross rails are used instead of a vertical splat. It was a favorite design of Chippendale.

LANCASHIRE CHAIRS
See CHAIRS, *Lancashire.*

LANTERN CLOCKS
See CLOCKS, *Bird-Cage.*

LATTICE-WORK
See FRET-WORK.

LAURELING

Derived from the laurel leaf, it was a common motif for carving on rails, friezes and posts in cabinet work, in the 17th century.

LEATHER
Leather for chair backs was introduced into England about 1645. It had been much used in Spain and other parts of Europe before that time for wall covering as well as for furniture. Spanish leather was embossed and polychromed by an art brought into Spain by the Moors. Cordovan leather, famous in all parts of Europe, was a flourishing industry in Spain during the 17th century.

REFERENCE
Cordovan Leather, ANTIQUARIAN, Jan. 1930.

LETTER RACKS
See RACKS, *Letter.*

LIGHT FIXTURES
See PART 5.

LIGHTHOUSE CLOCKS
See CLOCKS, *Lighthouse.*

LIGHTS
See CANDLES and RUSH LIGHTS. Also LIGHTS, PART 5.

LIGNUM VITAE
A hard, greenish brown wood, from the West Indies, used to some extent in England in the 17th century for cabinet work.

LIME
A wood used in England in Tudor days for carved work. It is white and soft, without cross grain, and it is free from knots. In this country it is known as white wood or bass wood.

LINEN-FOLD

The linen-fold or linen scroll is of Gothic origin and is thought to have been introduced into England from Flanders about 1470 and its use continued there for about one hundred years. It is a form of carving used on the fronts of chests and cupboards, the backs of chairs, and on wall panels of rooms. It is said to be a semblance of the veil covering the chalice at the consecration of the Host in the Catholic

Mass. Of the same period is the so-called curved rib or vine panel and the parchemin fold.

Lion's-Head Mask

Used on the knee of the cabriole leg of tables and chairs in England from 1720 to 1735. There is nothing quite like it in furniture elsewhere. It was followed by the satyr-mask (q.v.). The lion's-paw foot is contemporary with this feature.

Livery Cupboards

See Cupboards, *Livery*.

Locust Wood

See Acacia

Long-Case Clocks

See Clocks, *Grandfather's*.

Looking-Glasses

See Mirrors.

Looms

The loom on which the flax and wool of Colonial times was woven was the same in principle as that used by the nations of antiquity, and the process of weaving was the same also. In the early days of this country, the loom for home weaving was quite as familiar an object as the spinning wheel. It consisted, usually, of four posts joined together by side and cross pieces, and between the upright posts were two wooden rollers, one at the back and one at the front. Between these was stretched the warp threads. The woof threads were "shuttled" through these from the side. This

form of loom was known as the "low warp" (horizontal) loom. The upright form where the warp threads are perpendicular is known as the "high-warp" loom. This form of the loom was that used in weaving the magnificent tapestries of the Middle Ages. Modern looms are, of course, power looms.

Lopers

The sliders supporting the fall front of a desk or bureau.

Louis XIV (Quatorze) Period (1643-1715)

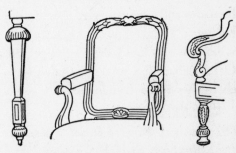

Charles Le Brun, the great master of decorative art, gave to France not only the style of Louis XIV but all the essential elements of the styles to come under the succeeding periods. Boulle was made "*ébéniste*" and devoted himself to designing furniture for the king and his courtiers. The greatest artists and craftsmen were employed, quartered in the Louvre, and the furniture they made was sumptuous in the extreme. All of the chairs of this period were instinct with dignity. The same may be said of the canapés or sofas. Legs of tables were straight and tapering or with cabriole curve and they were connected with saltire stretchers. Bedsteads were imposing pieces of furniture, with highly ornate posts, testers and curtains. The structural lines of consoles, cabinets, bureaus and other furniture were almost invariably rectilinear. Much carving and gilding was in vogue, and tortoise-shell veneer with metal inlay (said to have been an invention of Boulle) added to the enrichment. Lacquering was extensively practised, also painting, inlaying and marquetry were favorite forms of decoration. Lyons velvets, brocades and tapestry were used for upholstery. The shell motif is found everywhere on the furniture of this period. Oak, walnut and mahogany, also some ebony, were the woods used.

REFERENCES

Practical Book of Period Furniture, EBERLEIN and McCLURE; Period Furniture Handbook, GOULD; Decorative Styles and Periods in the Home, HELEN C. CANDEE.

Louis XV (Quinze) PERIOD (1715-1774)

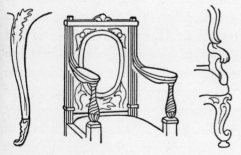

During this period the cabinet-makers

use the curved line more freely, the Rococo influence increases, no classic motifs are found. Cabriole legs assume stronger curves, the arms, seat rails and framing of the backs of chairs are curved and elaborately carved. Tables are fancifully shaped and the legs, like the chair legs, exhibit more pronounced curves. Under-bracing disappeared. Bedsteads were less ponderous, with draped and towering canopies over the head. It was almost impossible to find straight lines in the form of consoles, cabinets and cupboards, as well as in bureaus. The richest materials were used for upholstering. Mahogany was used more than heretofore. Gilding, painting, lacquer (Vernis-Martin, q.v.), Boulle inlay and marquetry continued favorite forms of decoration. Further, ormolu and other metal mounts were employed extensively for purely decorative purposes. It has been said that the period of Louis XV was the most gorgeous of the world in its rich and luxurious creations of decorative furniture, a style which belongs exclusively to France, and to her artists the honor.

REFERENCES

Practical Book of Period Furniture, EBERLEIN and McCLURE; Period Furniture Handbook, GOULD; Decorative Styles and Periods in the Home, HELEN C. CANDEE.

Louis XVI (Seize) PERIOD (1774-1793)

During the twenty years previous to

the Revolution the style of French furniture reached a high standard of artistic

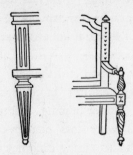

excellence, both in design and execution, although it is a direct reaction from the Rococo ornamentation and the excessive curves of the previous reign. One of the results was the influence it exerted upon Thomas Sheraton in producing one of the most graceful and beautiful phases of furniture development in England and, through Duncan Phyfe, the "American Sheraton," in America. In the Louis Seize period vertical and horizontal lines were emphasized. Legs of tables and of chairs were straight and tapered, generally fluted. Rectangular tables occur more frequently than round or oval forms. The woods consisted of mahogany, satinwood and other ornamental kinds. Brocades and exquisite tapestries, damask and velvet, were used in upholstery. Carving, painting, lacquer, marquetry, ormolu, fluting, reeding and beading were some of the many types of decoration used. Revival of classical taste marks the period.

REFERENCES
Practical Book of Period Furniture, Eberlein and McClure; Period Furniture Handbook, Gould; Decorative Styles and Periods in the Home, Helen C. Candee.

LOUNGE
See Couches.

LOVE SEAT
A chair with a double back and with two arms was so-called. The seat was just wide enough for two. See Settee.

LOWBOY

The lowboy (a modern term), as a distinct piece of furniture, followed the introduction of the highboy and was frequently made as a companion piece to the highboy. It was used as a dressing or toilet table. It was seldom seen in England.

REFERENCE
The American Lowboy, ANTIQUARIAN, Aug. and Sept. 1931.

LOZENGE

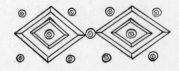

A diamond-shaped decorative motif.

introduced about 1600, and continuing in favor throughout the 17th century.

LUNETTE

A half-round- or half-moon-shaped motif, often repeated in a long line, and more or less elaborated.

LYRE-BACK

The lyre was used in the design of chair backs, notably by Duncan Phyfe and to some extent by Adam and Sheraton. It is also to be found in the pedestals for tables. It resembles the musical instrument of same name.

M

MAHOGANY

The use of mahogany for furniture, displacing walnut, in England came about 1715; in this country, somewhat earlier. It is said that Jonathan Dickinson of Philadelphia imported mahogany in 1699 and that he had some furniture made from it at that time. By 1720 it came into common use. It was strong, tough, and admitted of methods of treatment that were before impossible. Mahogany is a native of the West Indies and Central America. The best comes from San Domingo and Cuba and is known also as Spanish mahogany. That from Honduras is straighter grained, softer, lighter in color and much lighter in weight. The years from 1720 to 1810 may well be called the Age of Mahogany for furniture.

MANTEL CLOCKS
See CLOCKS, *Shelf.*

MANTEL MIRRORS
See MIRRORS, *Mantel.*

MANTELS
Mantels of wood are a development of the elaborately carved stone chimney breasts of the 15th and 16th centuries. Wood was first employed late in the 16th century, and early in the next century the influence of Inigo Jones began to show itself, continued by Sir Christopher Wren and Grinling Gibbons. In this country it was not until about the middle of the 18th century that the mantel was given prominence. By 1800 it had become one of the chief features of the room. The wood used was pine, painted white, ornamented with carved

or molded design in relief and supported by classic columns or pilasters. The mantels by Samuel McIntire at Salem, Massachusetts, are outstanding examples of the work of one of the leading craftsmen of that period.

REFERENCES

> Types of American Chimney Pieces, ANTIQUES, Sept. 1927; American Mantels, and the Source of their Design, ANTIQUARIAN, March, 1930.

MAPLE

Maple was one of the most popular woods used by joiners and chair-makers during Colonial times, and won increasing appreciation throughout the 18th century. It is distinctly an American development. The wood of the common maple is compact, fine grained and takes a high polish; that of the sugar or rock maple, sometimes marked with undulations of fiber and known as curly maple, was used a great deal for veneering. It is, however, hard, brittle and of a grain almost impossible to carve successfully. From the knotty parts of these trees the bird's-eye maple is also obtained.

REFERENCE

> Maple Furniture, ANTIQUARIAN, April 1930.

MARBLE

Slabs for table tops were not used until the 18th century in England. They were usually imported. Rare varieties of marble were obtained from ancient Italian palaces. See SCAGLIOLA.

MARQUETRY

This is an inlaying of veneer on furniture surfaces by patterning and cutting to design two layers of rare woods, and inserting the design, one into the other. It is a development of the Italian intarsia (q.v.). In Western Europe, during the 17th century marquetry became the leading feature of furniture decoration. It was introduced into England from Holland about 1615 although it did not become popular until the reign of William and Mary under the influence of Dutch and Huguenot craftsmen. The older designs represent flowers, foliage, birds and animals. Later, so-called seaweed and arabesque marquetry became popular.

REFERENCE

> Dictionary of English Furniture, MACQUOID and EDWARDS.

MARTHA WASHINGTON CHAIRS
See CHAIRS, Martha Washington.

MASK OR MASQUE MOTIF

A full face, human, animal or grotesque used as a form of carved ornament, of great antiquity and common to many countries. The lion's head and the satyr-mask are examples of its use in England first half of 18th century, on both walnut and mahogany furniture. The mask is also seen on English furniture of the 16th century.

MAZER BOWLS
Of maple. See PART 5.

MEDALLION

Carved, painted or applied, circular, oval or square ornament, much used latter part of 18th century.

MIRRORS

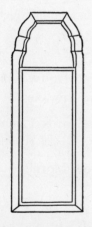

Called also LOOKING-GLASSES. In their earliest form, mirrors consisted only of well-polished pieces of metal and they continued in that form for many centuries. The amalgam of mercury and tin which produces a silvered surface on glass was not discovered until the 16th century, although mirrors of glass backed by tin, lead, etc., in various crude forms, were produced in Europe as early as the 13th century. In 1670 workmen from Venice were brought to England and in 1673 mirrors were produced at the Lambeth glass works. Soon after the use of mirrors in England became quite common. Until late in the 18th century, mirrors there were made from blown cylinders of glass, split open, flattened and polished, the backs being silvered by mercury floated over tin foil. The glass was very thin and the sheets were small, shaped to conform to the intended frame, and the edges were slightly beveled. One can distinguish an old bevel by rubbing one's finger over it. It is so slight it can hardly be felt, where the modern bevel is sharp and distinct. Until the Queen Anne period, mirrors were attached to the walls securely instead of being hung on them. These early mirrors were made in two parts, joined by simply lapping the glass.

Mirrors were imported into this country from England and from Italy during the Colonial period, although because of their cost they were to be found only in the homes of the wealthy. The frames of many mirrors of the late 18th century follow the pattern of frames of the Queen Anne period very closely, and are often mistaken for each other. Mirror frames reached their final expression of originality in the first quarter of the 19th century. To the 18th century belongs the convex or distorting mirror, an idea borrowed from Venice where they were made in the 17th century.

REFERENCES

Dictionary of English Furniture, MacQUOID and EDWARDS; A Brief Dictionary of English Mirrors, FINE ARTS, April 1932.

Balboa or Bilbao Mirrors. These mirrors were brought to New England ports, presumably from Bilbao, Spain, but their style suggests Italian origin. The frames were of marble with gilt ornaments, and double scroll at the top. Late 18th and early 19th centuries.

Cheval Mirrors. Toilet mirrors, sufficiently large to reflect the entire person. Candle branches were often fixed to the standards supporting the glass.

Constitution Mirrors. The frame embellished with gilt ornaments on wires at the side, and with gilt eagle of carved wood or plaster in the broken arch at the top. The frames were flat, of solid or veneered mahogany, resembling the style of Queen Anne period. Late 18th century.

Courting Mirror. See COURTING GLASS.

Dressing Mirror. Also called *Toilet Mirror.* A small mirror in use during late 18th century, usually oval or rectangular in form, attached to uprights

above a small cabinet with drawers to contain toilet articles. These mirrors were probably introduced into England from France.

Florentine Mirrors. Frames of pine, elaborately carved and gilded, oval, square, or irregular in shape. Very popular in this country early 19th century.

Girandole Mirrors. This name was used during the 17th and 18th centuries to designate circular glasses, sometimes flat or concave, but usually convex. They always had a pair of metal candle branches affixed to the frame.

Mantel Mirrors, also called *Overmantel.* Oblong in shape, in three sections separated by molding, the two end sections

American Sheraton Card Table Salem, Mass., circa 1790

American Hepplewhite Inlaid Mahogany Sideboard and Knife Boxes, circa 1790

Irish Chippendale Tripod Table, Gallery Top, 18th Century

narrower than the center. Cornice top with acorns beneath and light pillars, often fluted at the sides, was the usual frame, 1780-1800. After 1800 heavier pilasters divided the sections.

Pier Mirrors. In use over pier or console tables.

Tabernacle Mirrors. This name was given to the Empire mirrors common to both England and America of the early decades of the 19th century. They were vertical in shape, in two sections, the upper with a painted glass or modeled stucco panel in bas-relief, and they are usually found with balls beneath the cornice, varying in number, although occasionally acorn pendants were used. The frames are in gold or black and gold and sometimes in mahogany.

REFERENCE

Tabernacle Mirrors, ANTIQUES, July 1922.

Toilet Mirrors. See *Dressing Mirrors.*

MIRROR KNOBS

The vertical mirrors frequently rested on knobs, usually of brass, with glass or enameled copper medallion, decorated.

MITRE

The mitre is employed in the moldings of paneled and other work in furniture. It is cut obliquely to form an angle and first came into use about 1600.

MIXING TABLES

See TABLES, *Mixing.*

MOLDINGS

Ornamental or shaped strips either carved or applied on furniture. Those of early times were cut by hand labor.

MORTISE

A space hollowed out to receive a tenon. Almost all chair jointing is by this method. A dowel driven through holes bored in the mortise and tenon prevented the joint from working loose. In general use in this country in Colonial days.

MOTIF, MOTIVE

The controlling idea or leading feature in a piece of work.

MOUNTS

The handles, escutcheons and other ornamental metal work, decorating a piece of furniture. See BRASSES, PART 5.

MUNTIN

A vertical member of framework, similar to a stile but occupying a central or intermediate position between panels.

N

Neo-Classic (New Classic)

Designating the revival in classic taste in art. 18th century.

Niddy-Noddy

A reel on which yarn from the spin-ning wheel was wound with a wobbly motion of the worker's left hand.

Nulling

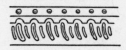

Ornament applied to the bulbous legs of Jacobean furniture, made up chiefly of beading, cabling and hollows. It was also in use to some extent in the early Georgian period.

O

Oak

The material of which the furniture of England of the 15th, 16th and 17th centuries was constructed was almost without exception good oak. It was of two varieties: live-oak of a rich brown color and fine grain, and swamp-oak with a long grain, much like the American ash. There was also the bog-oak found in peat bogs and used as an inlay. The oak timbers were riven or split with the wedge and beetle. The riving iron follows the grain of the wood and riven oak endures better than if sawed. Adzes and planes were used for dressing the surfaces. In the 16th century two-handled saws were first used for cutting purposes. Oak can be carved and joined but it is difficult to turn it, and it was never used as a veneer. The stretchering of legs of furniture was general during the "Age of Oak"—1450 to 1685. No wood persists like oak throughout the history of English furniture. The American oak is more easily worked than English oak, but it never attained to the prominence here for furniture that it did in England.

Ogee

A form obtained from the use of the cyma curve, a double curve as of a molding. Convex above and concave below is called the cyma reversa, the reverse of which is the cyma recta.

Ogee Foot

A foot of the bracket type using the cyma curve.

Oil Finish

This consists of applying thin coats of boiled linseed oil, to pieces that have been cleaned and carefully smoothed, and thoroughly rubbing in each coat with a soft woolen cloth. After each treatment, the piece should be left in a warm room for twenty-four hours. The success of this oil finish depends upon much rubbing and little oil, each time, until the desired finish is attained. This is satisfactory only on furniture made of hard, close-grained wood such as maple, beech, cherry and mahogany. Smoothing of the surface, in preparation for the oil, may be done by fine sandpaper and steel wool. In the preservation of old mahogany furniture it will be helpful if it is rubbed regularly with a soft, oily woolen cloth.

Olive Wood

A hard close-grained wood of greenish-yellow color with dark cloudy markings. In use for veneering in the 18th century.

Organs

Although organs had been in use in the churches of Europe by the opening of the 16th century, their first use in this country was not until after the beginning of the 18th century. An imported organ was presented to King's Chapel in Boston in 1713. The first church organ built in New England was one for Christ Church in Boston in 1752.

Ornament

Carved or applied decoration in great variety of design. See Applied Ornament.

Orrery

A mechanical device for representing the movements of the heavenly bodies. It derived its name from the Earl of Orrery in England in the early 18th century. David Rittenhouse of Philadelphia made one of these for the University of Pennsylvania and another for Princeton College in 1768, and Joseph Pope made one for Harvard College in 1786.

REFERENCE
ANTIQUES, May 1932 and March 1937.

Ottoman

A stuffed seat without a back, first used in Turkey.

Ovolo Molding

A molding in which the chief member is of oval or convex contour. Sometimes decorated by egg-and-dart ornament.

Oystered Veneer

Made from transverse slices of small limbs, showing cross section of grain. It was used on Carolean and William and Mary furniture and was of Dutch or Flemish origin.

P

Pad Foot

A club foot on a disc or pad.

Pagoda Top

A type of ornament used in the Chinese Chippendale style.

Painted Furniture

This form of decoration was in use in England and on the Continent even in medieval times, and through all of the periods since, it has been employed to some extent for decorative purposes. It was customary in Colonial times in this country to paint chairs and tables in black, dull red or dark green, and in New England chests and cupboards were both painted and carved. In Pennsylvania the German settlers painted the chest particularly, quite lavishly. The Windsor chair and the gate-legged table were usually painted. Late in the 18th century, Sheraton and Adam made painted furniture popular, employing celebrated artists for the purpose, and the fashion was adopted in this country early in the 19th century. About 1820, stenciling began to be used in connection with painting, and chairs, tables, clocks, trays and other furniture were decorated in this manner. Gold leaf was used with the various colors of the design and this furniture became very popular. See Stenciled Furniture.

REFERENCE
Painted Furniture in America, ANTIQUES, June and Sept. 1924, Jan. 1925.

Panel

A surface set above or below the general surface of a wall or of a piece of furniture, or effected by means of applied moldings, grooved to receive it. In the 16th and 17th centuries it was customary to carve the surface of the panel.

Paneling

In the medieval house, the private apartments had either bare stone or plastered walls, or these were hung with

ROOM FROM HAMPTON, NEW HAMPSHIRE WITH PANELING—FOLDING BED WITH CREWEL EMBROIDERED LINEN SPREAD, TURNED JOINT STOOL AND TRANSITIONAL COUNTRY CHAIR OF THE QUEEN ANNE PERIOD

CHARACTERISTIC NEW ENGLAND GROUPING, 17TH TO 19TH CENTURIES

INTERIOR FROM IPSWICH, MASSACHUSETTS HOUSE CIRCA 1675

ROOM FROM WEST BOXFORD, MASSACHUSETTS ABOUT 1700

arras (tapestry). Wainscot or wall paneling appears only at the close of the 15th century. Oak was the timber generally used up to the end of the 17th century, and the panels were small. Dutch and Flemish cabinet-makers made frequent use of paneling on furniture and such work became popular in England in the early 17th century.

Papier-Mâché

A revival of an art long practised in Persia came into England from France. It was paper pulp mixed with glue, chalk, and sometimes fine sand. It was then pressed, molded and baked so hard that it could be sawed. It took a high polish readily and was often japanned.

REFERENCE
Papier-Mâché, ANTIQUES, March 1929.

Parcel Gilt

A method of applying decorative detail in colors or relief by the use of a varnish that will not take gilding. After the varnish is removed the desired color is added, or it is left plain. In effect it is similar to the "resist" work on pottery.

Parchemin

An old form of wainscot carving, made in imitation of rows of parchment upon rods.

Parquetry

Wood mosaic used for floors, generally in different colors and in geometric designs.

Partridge Wood

A close, straight-grained wood of a reddish-brown color, imported from Brazil and used in England for inlay and veneering in the 17th and 18th centuries.

Patera

A small disk, oval, round or square, as a base for ornamental detail, in decorating furniture.

Patina

The surface or finish resulting on wood or metal from wear, polishing, or oxidation, with age.

Pear Wood

The finest-grained of all of our native fruit woods, tinged with red, used here to some extent in Colonial times, and in England for inlay, and from a very early period for the construction of simple, provincial furniture.

Pedestal

The support to the column of a tripod table or stand.

Pediment

An architectural term applied to furniture, indicating an ornament surmounting the piece, usually low at the sides and higher in the middle. It was used in unbroken form from 1675 to 1760 and the broken arch (q.v.) form from 1715 to 1800.

PEMBROKE TABLE

See TABLES, Pembroke.

PENDANTS

A hanging form of ornament, generally used in the Jacobean period to embellish posts or stiles. It was derived from the Moors in Spain. In this country, the split baluster with the larger pear-shaped part at the bottom was much in use in the 17th century for decorating chests and cupboards.

PERIODS

AMERICAN

A tribute to early American Craftsmen

Colonial Period	1620-1775
Revolutionary Period	1775-1789
Federal Period	1789-1812
Empire Period	1812-1850

ENGLISH

Gothic Period	1100-1485
Tudor Period	1485-1558
Elizabethan Period	1558-1603

This period may be, also, considered a STYLE *of the Tudor period.*

Jacobean Period, Early	
Stuart	1603-1649
Cromwellian Period	1649-1660
Carolean Period, Late	
Stuart	1660-1688
William and Mary Period	1688-1702
Queen Anne Period	1702-1714
Georgian Period	1714-1793
Empire Period	1793-1830

FRENCH

Louis XIV Period	1643-1715
Louis XV Period	1715-1774
Louis XVI Period	1774-1793
Empire Period	1793-1830

Each of these periods will be found described, briefly, under their respective alphabetical headings.

PHYFE, DUNCAN, STYLE

The distinguishing characteristics of Duncan Phyfe's furniture resulted from his ability to combine the best elements of the Georgian designers with the simplicity of those of France without sacrificing one to the other. It was excellent in proportion and classic in outline. It is essentially domestic, strongly constructed and well finished, and the best of his work equals anything produced by Sheraton or Hepplewhite. His adaptation of French models contributed the best and truest element in the work of the American Empire period. He was master of the curve. His pedestal tables with the lyre and curule-shaped legs, terminating in brass paw casters, represent a distinct type of design, and in quality of workmanship have never been excelled. Chairs, sofas and other pieces show similar characteristics of good design and good workmanship. Nearly all of his work was done in mahogany of the best quality. In his later years Phyfe's work deteriorated. See PART 6.

REFERENCES
Furniture Masterpieces of Duncan Phyfe, CORNELIUS; The Distinctiveness of Duncan Phyfe, ANTIQUES, Nov. 1922.

PIANO

The piano, an improvement over the harpsichord, is largely due to the work of an Italian, Cristofori, early in the 18th century. His first instrument is now in the Metropolitan Museum in New York. Up to 1760, at which time the square piano was first made, pianos were made in the wing shape. The compass of the early piano, like that of the harpsichord, was only four, or at most five, octaves, but it has gradually increased to seven octaves or more. Its great difference from the harpsichord is a mechanism that enables the player to modify, at will, the intensity of the sounds.

REFERENCE
History of the Pianoforte by BRINSMEAD.

PIE-CRUST TABLE
See TABLES, Pie-Crust.

PIER GLASS
A large looking-glass. See MIRRORS, Pier.

PIER TABLES
See TABLES, Console.

PILASTER

A portion of a rectangular pillar set flush against its background, slightly projecting from the surfaces. Uusally carved. Mainly used as a support for an arch, cornice or other superstructure.

PINE
A soft wood used freely for all kinds of furniture during the Colonial period. It is straight in grain, quite free from knots, and it is easy to work. In England, little appears to have been used prior to the Restoration, oak having been the staple and cheaper material.

PINEAPPLE
A pattern in carving much used in the Empire period, chiefly as a finial.

PIPE RACKS
See RACKS, Pipe.

PLANE WOOD

A very white wood, close in grain and tough, used in the 18th century in England for painted chairs, instead of beech.

PLATEAU

An ornamental stand used in England on a low plinth, or on feet, for the center of a dining table, constructed usually in parts so that it could be lengthened.

PLINTH

The projecting base of a pillar. In furniture the term is applied to low stands for figures, or escutcheons on pediments.

PLUM WOOD

A yellowish wood with a heart of deep brownish-red very like West Indian mahogany, hard and heavy and used in England in the 16th and 17th centuries by country joiners.

PLUMES

An English design of feathers, usually three or five, used principally on chair backs. See PRINCE OF WALES FEATHERS.

POLYCHROME

A form of painted decoration of furniture much used by Italy in the 16th century.

POPLAR

A wood, yellow to gray in color, with fine grain used in England in the 18th century for inlay and for marquetry.

POSTS

The upright corner pieces of any article of furniture.

PRESS CUPBOARDS

See CUPBOARDS, Press.

PRESS BED

See BEDS, Press.

PRINCE OF WALES FEATHERS

A decorative design used by Hepplewhite in chair backs.

Q

QUARREL

The square or diamond-shaped pane of a door. It also denotes the traceries of the 18th-century bookcases and cabinets; square-headed tools and weapons; and lozenge-shaped tiles.

QUATREFOIL

Conventional adaptation of the four-leaved clover.

QUEEN ANNE PERIOD (1702-1714)

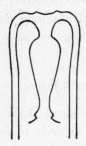

Queen Anne furniture has certain clearly defined characteristics of form, that enable one to distinguish it at once from antecedent types. A truly English style was established in this period. The cyma curve is characteristic on all Queen Anne furniture. Shell carving was the most popular ornament. The chairs are graceful and comfortable, with cabriole legs and solid-splat back. The tables are of a drop-leaf type usually, with a swinging leg. Stretchers are no longer seen on chairs, tables and other furniture. The bedsteads had tall, slender, round, square or octagonal posts that supported a high tester. The scroll top is to be found on secretaries and cupboards, and it was essentially the age of graceful tallboys with their broken pediment. Kettle-front chests of drawers were occasionally seen and drawer fronts were finished with a quarter round lap which concealed the space between drawer and frame. The claw-and-ball foot came into use during this period. Walnut was the wood chiefly used, both solid and in veneering, although oak was still used to some extent. The importation of lacquered furniture from the East during the last half of the 17th century resulted in efforts by English craftsmen to imitate it and many pieces of this period are decorated in that manner. Needlework in wool was extensively used for upholstery purposes, also damask, brocades and velvets.

REFERENCES

Practical Book of Period Furniture, EBERLEIN and MCCLURE; *Period Furniture Handbook,* GOULD.

QUILTING FRAMES

Long pieces of wood held together at the corners with wooden pegs, used in lining and padding patchwork and quilted quilts.

R

RABBETTING

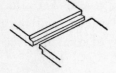

A term in carpentry for the recess or rebate in or near the edge of one piece to receive the edge of another piece cut to fit it.

Racks

Letter Racks. First appeared in England about the middle of the 18th century, sometimes quite decorative in form.

Pipe Racks. Various styles were made in England for the accommodation of the clay pipes with long stems in vogue in the 17th and 18th centuries. Some were vertical in form, others horizontal —all with spaces for several pipes and for the spill holders.

Spoon Racks. Racks for holding metal spoons date from the Elizabethan period. The common form was of oak, sometimes painted or carved, with two or three narrow shelves pierced or slotted for spoons, and a box, with or without a lid, at the bottom for knives and forks. They are considered as being of Dutch origin.

REFERENCE

Spoon Racks Carved, ANTIQUES, June 1925.

Rail

A horizontal member of the frame of chairs or other cabinet work. The ends were formed as tenons to slide into mortises cut in vertical members.

Rake

The angle or slant of chair or settee back.

Recessed Stretcher

See Stretchers.

Reeding

Wood carved in convex relief in parallel lines. Resembling the reverse of fluting, which is sunk or grooved.

Refectory Table

See Tables, *Refectory*.

Renaissance Period (1450-1650)

A change in style of furniture followed the revival of classic form in architecture. The Renaissance had its birth in Italy and all Europe took its artistic inspiration from Italy. This period saw a tremendous increase in the art of comfort. In France, the styles from the beginning of the 16th century to the middle of the 17th (Louis XIV) show a rapid assimilation of Italian design coupled with French ideas. England followed the lead of Italy and France more slowly, producing cruder and simpler but sound designs and the style was well established during the reign of Elizabeth. Construction was generally solid and massive, allowing bold carving and elaborate inlays. The honeysuckle, acanthus, bead molding, rosettes, medallions, etc., were used in place of the characteristic details of the Gothic period. There was a great increase in the quantity and variety of furniture. Chairs were more commonly used; the four-posted bedstead took the place of the paneled recess. The principal wood used was walnut, and the upholstery was largely of crimson velvet with gold fringe.

REFERENCES

Genuine Antique Furniture, DE BLES; *Italian Furniture*, ANTIQUES, April 1925.

REPAIRS AND RESTORATION

The problem of deciding whether to purchase a piece of old furniture, in a condition requiring more or less repairing or restoration, may usually be solved if one gives consideration to three important principles: first, if the piece is of a rare or of a good, representative type, will it warrant making substantial repairs or restoration; second, if when restored, if it is not of an unusual or rare type, will it then become a useful piece for your home and third, if it will also fit in with your general scheme of furnishing. If it would not be useful or if it would be incongruous, it should be rejected. A piece of furniture is not always desirable simply because it is old. To combine the French or Italian styles in the same room with early American would be distinctly inharmonious. English and American furniture usually combine pleasantly.

REFERENCE

Restoration of Early American Furniture, ANTIQUES, May, July, and Sept. 1927.

REVOLUTIONARY PERIOD (American) (1775-1789)

During the Revolutionary War, the production of the cabinet-makers was very much limited, but following 1780 their efforts were again directed to meeting the needs of the American people, whose supplies of furniture from England had been cut off by the war. The eagle was adopted as a national emblem, long before the eagle of the Empire period, and it began to appear as a design feature. Furniture of the Chippendale style was still popular, and the designs of Hepplewhite and Adam were treated with characteristic simplicity and with careful attention to structural details. The Philadelphia cabinet-makers, perhaps, were the leaders during this era.

REFERENCES

Blue Book, Philadelphia Furniture, HORNOR; *Furniture Treasury*, 3 vols., NUTTING.

RIBBAND-BACK

A chair back with ribbon motif, having its origin early in the 18th century and a favorite with Chippendale and cabinet-makers of his time. See CHAIRS, *Ribband-back*.

RISING STRETCHER

See STRETCHERS.

ROCKING-CHAIRS

See CHAIRS, *Rocking-*.

Rococo

French, *Rocaille* (rock) *Coquille* (shell). A florid style of ornamentation common from 1740, designed from rocks and shells and of Chinese origin. It followed the Baroque style and was much used by the French and by Chippendale in his adaptation of the French style in his furniture. It had its best expression in the work of the French *ébénistes*.

ROMAYNE WORK

A method of ornamentation, chiefly 16th century, in which heads in medallion are introduced. It was an early Tudor adaptation of Renaissance details.

ROSETTE

A rose-shaped pattern used on the opposing curves of a bonnet top, etc. The rosette with a foliated decoration above the rosette is found on some of the best Philadelphia highboys, secretaries and clock cases.

ROSEWOOD

A native of various tropical countries, of different species, but all having the same weight, depth of color and worm-resisting qualities. It was popular during the Empire period and was first used in this country about 1825. It was too hard for the cabinet-maker to work readily, it was brittle, and it was difficult to repair because of its resistance to glue.

ROUNDABOUT CHAIRS

See CHAIRS, *Corner*.

ROUNDEL

A small circular ground for ornamentation.

RUNNER

A member of rectangular section, sliding in a groove or slot, also applied to the narrow strips added along the bottom edge of drawer sides. The fall fronts of desks are supported on runners, called by cabinet-makers, "lopers."

RUSH BOTTOMS OR SEATS

These were used extensively in England and in this country in Colonial times, as a cheap and durable seating for chairs. Made from dried rushes, the weaving to cover a required space called for considerable skill and experience.

RUSH LIGHTS

Used by pioneers in America, made by braiding or binding together the cat-o'-nine-tails and soaking them in tallow or oil. They were held on either wooden or iron stands. Such lights were also used in remote districts in England. They preceded candles. See LIGHTS, PART 5.

PENNSYLVANIA PINE DRESSER, EARLY 18TH CENTURY. SPATTERWARE DECORATED WITH AN
IDENTICAL TULIP IN BLUE AND RED.

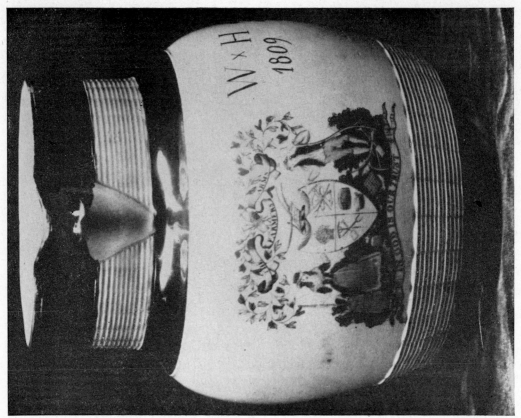

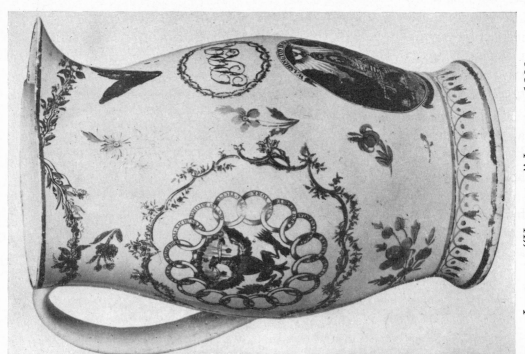

Liverpool "Historical" Jug, circa 1800

S

SALTIRE, SALTIER

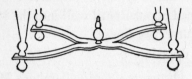

Stretchers in X-form of Italian origin, sometimes scrolled or in serpentine form with a finial in the center. Introduced into England toward the end of the 17th century.

SANDALWOOD

Yellow-brown in color, mostly used for making small pieces.

SANDGLASS

See HOURGLASS.

SATINWOOD

A hard, very close-grained light-colored wood obtained from both the East and West Indies. It takes a fine polish and was much used for inlaying by cabinet-makers from 1770 to 1820. Next to mahogany, it was a favorite wood in the designs of Robert Adam.

SATYR-MASK

The head or face of a satyr, much used in ornament of furniture, especially in England from 1730 to 1740.

SCAGLIOLA

An imitation of marble made in Italy from calcined gypsum, isinglass and glue. It was colored in red and white and black and gold and took a high pol-

ish. It was popular in England in the early 18th century.

SCALLOP

A carved design resembling the escallop shell, for edges or borders.

SCONCES

The earliest type of wooden sconce as a support for candles dates from the middle of the 17th century, followed by carved and gilded patterns in early 18th century. See PART 5 for metal sconces.

SCREENS

Folding screens with two to six panels, the space within the frame of each leaf in panels of decorated wood, embroidered or painted textiles. See FIRE SCREENS.

SCROLL FOOT

A foot in the form of a double scroll. See FLEMISH FOOT.

SCROLL TOP

See BONNET TOP.

SCRUTOIRE

French name for desk in 17th century, which later was called escritoire, and bureau. See SECRETARY, and ESCRITOIRE.

SEAT RAILS

The frame on which the seat is built.

SECRETARY

The form is evidently derived from the French *escritoire*. The secretary is a desk with a book-case or cabinet with shelves and doors sitting on top. It was one of the developments of the William and Mary period. The top of the earlier pieces was flat. Later, the broken arch came into fashion. The doors covering the upper section were either of paneled wood or were fitted with glass and the space behind was devoted to various purposes.

REFERENCE

The American Scrutoire, FINE ARTS, June and Nov., 1932.

SEDAN CHAIR

A portable vehicle or covered chair, with side windows and an entrance through a doorway in front. Instead of being mounted on wheels, it was carried by means of poles on each side, passing through rings set in the body of the chair.

SERPENTINE FRONT

A front shaped with two concave curves with convex curve between, or vice versa.

SETTEE

Settees were in use from Carolean times onward. In the 18th century they usually took the form of a double chair back and were often referred to as a "love seat." They were also made to be upholstered on the back, the seat and the arms. In this country the settee of the Windsor type was produced and remained popular until well into the 19th century. See SOFAS.

REFERENCE

Dictionary of English Furniture, MACQUOID and EDWARDS.

SETTLE

Settles with arms and paneled backs were in general use all during Jacobean days. They seem to have been an evolution from the chest, and they were frequently carved in the same manner and design as the chests of the period. Early American settles were made with a high back and wing pieces at ends to ward off drafts, a drawer or locker underneath the seat, and sometimes with a shelf at the back for a candle. Occasionally they were carved, following the example of those made in England, but these carved American settles are rare.

SEWING TABLES

See TABLES, Work.

SHAGREEN

A sharkskin of fine granular texture, but originally a species of untanned leather from the hide of a horse. Shagreen was fashionable in England in the 18th century.

SHAKER FURNITURE

The Shaker sect was founded in England and the founder and some followers settled near Albany, New York, in 1774, since which time they have spread into various states of the eastern part of this country. Wherever they settled, they carried with them the doctrine of simplicity in their household furnishings. All of their furniture is plain, but substantially made, with little or no attempt at decoration, but well adapted to the purpose for which it was intended. As time passed, chair- and cabinet-making became an industry, and much of their product was in use in other than Shaker homes.

REFERENCE
   Shaker Furniture, ANDREWS.

SHAVING MIRRORS
   See MIRRORS, *Dressing*.

SHELF CLOCKS
   See CLOCKS, *Shelf*.

SHELL ORNAMENT
   A carved design in the form of a shell, either convex or concave. The shell was a favorite ornament in the Queen Anne period and with John Goddard on his block-front furniture. The scallop style of shell is to be preferred to the cockle shell.

SHERATON STYLE
   While the styles of Sheraton and Hepplewhite overlap, and it is sometimes difficult to tell the styles apart, it must be conceded that Sheraton was the greater man of the two. His early furniture is distinguished by elegance of design, fine construction and graceful orna-

ment. He was doubtless influenced by the designs of French cabinet-makers of the Louis XVI period, adapting them to English taste. Sheraton, in contrast with Hepplewhite, eliminated curves, working along straight lines almost en-

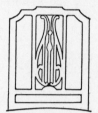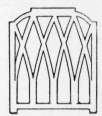

tirely. Sheraton's chairs are the most original and most characteristic of all of his designs, the central panel usually rising slightly above the top rail. His arm-chairs have curved arms that flow into the back without a break. All of his chairs were very carefully planned to give strength where needed. He discarded the cabriole leg and used instead

tapering or reeded legs. He employed the urn motive freely. His carving is generally applied in low relief. His sideboards are identified by the convex corner, while those of Hepplewhite are concave. He used mahogany and satinwood, delicate inlay and painted decoration. His preference was for inlay. The beauty of his style is its chasteness and the perfection of craftsmanship lavished upon it, and during the last decade of the 18th century and the earlier years of the 19th, Sheraton's influence dominated the style of English, and of course, of American furniture of the best type. His time is frequently referred to as the "Age of Satinwood." See THOMAS SHERATON, PART 6.

SHIELD-BACK

A feature of Hepplewhite style of chair backs.

SIDE TABLES

See TABLES, *Side*.

SIDEBOARD

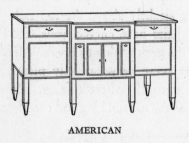

AMERICAN

The sideboard at first was literally a board fixed against a wall for convenience: a shelf. To give it strength it had front legs; in time back legs were added and it became independent. It was then often called buffet. Sideboards as we know them are of comparatively recent origin, belonging to the latter half of the 18th century. The design is credited to Thomas Shearer, a contemporary of Hepplewhite. Both Hepplewhite and Sheraton followed his lead, but Sheraton carried the sideboard to fuller develop-

ment than did Hepplewhite. Sheraton used the convex curve at the corners, while Hepplewhite's were concave. In other points they are often precisely alike. The sideboard with a straight front is usually of American make, as they were seldom made of that design in England. What is known as the hunters' sideboard, of plain construction and rather smaller in size than the usual sideboard, was characteristic of the southern part of this country early in the 19th century.

REFERENCE

The American Sideboard, FINE ARTS, July 1933.

SKIRT

See APRON.

SLAT-BACK

FINIALS ON SLAT-BACK CHAIRS

A type of chair back much used in Colonial times with from three to five horizontal slats between the posts. It bears a strong resemblance to the ladderback of the 18th century. See CHAIRS, *Slat-back*.

SLATE

Slate had a limited use for mixing-table tops.

LIVERPOOL HISTORICAL JUGS AND OTHER WARE, EARLY 19TH CENTURY

ORIENTAL LOWESTOFT BOWL, 18TH CENTURY

ENGLISH TABLEWARE WITH ORIENTAL MOTIVE, EARLY 19TH CENTURY

ORIENTAL PORCELAIN CUP AND SAUCER, LATE
18TH OR EARLY 19TH CENTURY

Courtesy of the Museum of Fine Arts, Bo
MENNECY PORCELAIN COVERED CUP

ORIENTAL PORCELAIN PUNCH BOWL, 18TH CENTURY

SLEIGH BEDS
See BEDS, *Sleigh.*

SNAKE FOOT

A foot of a tripod table or stand, elongated to resemble a snake's head.

SNAKEWOOD

An extremely hard wood growing in Brazil, used for inlaying and veneering. It is reddish in color with black spots and marks.

SOFAS

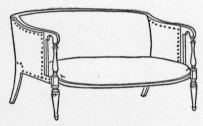

SHERATON STYLE

The sofa differs from the settee (q.v.) and double chair. It is longer and it is entirely covered with upholstery, and did not appear in England until early in the 18th century. Those designed by Sheraton were in his usual good taste. After 1800, sofas, together with furniture of all kinds, followed the Empire style. The word "sofa" is derived from the Arabian word "suffah," meaning a couch.

REFERENCE
Dictionary of English Furniture, MAC-QUOID and EDWARDS.

SPADE FOOT

A four-sided tapering block-like foot in which the leg terminates. Used by Hepplewhite and Sheraton.

SPANDREL

The irregular triangular space between the shoulder of an arch and the rectangular figure formed by the moldings over it. See SPANDRELS, PART 5.

SPANISH FOOT

A broad, hoof-like foot, turning slightly outward at the base and usually grooved. It dates from the 17th century and it retained its popularity for a long time.

SPANISH FURNITURE

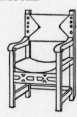

The furniture builders of Spain never developed an exclusively national style.

Roman, French and Moorish art fashioned Spanish furniture from the 11th to the 16th centuries, and in the 16th century Italian art provided the key note. Later, France and England were the dominating influences upon the Spanish craftsmen. Heaviness, massiveness and simplicity were the characteristics of Spanish furniture of the 17th and 18th centuries; walnut and oak were the woods used, and metal mounts were common. The upholstery was of velvets, heavily embroidered in gold. Leather was also much used for chair coverings, often finely tooled, gilded or painted. Cabinets, elaborately inlaid with ivory, bone, ebony or other colored woods, are typically Spanish.

REFERENCES
Practical Book of Italian, Spanish and Portuguese Furniture, EBERLEIN and RAMSDELL; Spanish Furniture of the 18th Century, ANTIQUARIAN, Nov. 1929.

SPINDLE
A slender turned vertical baluster or rod.

SPINDLE-BACK
Slender rods used on Windsor chairs.

SPINET
A stringed musical instrument, smaller than the harpsichord, which succeeded the virginal (q.v.). The general outline of the spinet nearly resembled a harp laid in a horizontal position, that is, wing-shaped, with the keys occupying the position of the sounding board. It was small, compact and portable. The oldest known specimen is dated 1490.

SPINNING WHEEL
The spinning wheel had its origin in the Orient. It was brought to Europe about the time that Columbus discovered America. By use of it, wool, cotton and flax are converted into threads prepared for weaving. It was in early use in this country with the flax wheel. The wool-spinning wheel is larger in circumference than the wheel used for flax; it had no treadle and the spinner stood at her work. The flax wheel was an invention of the 16th century.

REFERENCE
Some Rare Spinning Wheels, ANTIQUES, Oct. 1929.

SPIRAL TURNING

A twisted form of lathe turning for legs in the Carolean period. There was also a hand carved spiral twist used at about the same time.

SPLAT

The central portion of the chair back, connecting the top and seat rail. It succeeded the carved wood and cane filling of the late 17th century. During the Queen Anne period it was plain and unpierced. Later, under Chippendale's designs, the splat became very elaborate.

SPLINT SEATS

This was a form of seating used extensively in Colonial times and later with slat-back chairs. They comprised thin strips of ash, woven basket-fashion and turned over the seat rails, as were the rush seats. The splint seat was cheaper but less durable.

SPOOL TURNING

Continuous turning of spool-like pattern.

SPOON-BACK

The shaping of the chair back to fit the contour of the occupant. This was a development of the Queen Anne period.

SPOON RACK

See RACKS, *Spoon.*

SQUAB CUSHIONS

Movable cushions for chairs and settees.

STANDISH

A dish or tray for a desk made of wood, sometimes of metal, in which were set boxes or stands for ink and sand.

STANDS

See CANDLE STANDS.

STENCILED FURNITURE

Just who discovered that stencils could be used for the speedy decoration of furniture we do not know. Stenciled wall papers were produced from 1760 to 1785 and stenciling had been in use on cloth, plaster walls, pottery, wood and glass before its adoption for furniture, early in the 19th century. It soon became very popular, and not only chairs were decorated in this manner, but tables, clocks, beds and trays were included, and its use resulted in lower labor costs. Gold leaf was used with the various colors in the designs. Stenciled chairs were to the 19th century what Windsor chairs had been to the 18th. Modern stenciled work is made comparatively easy through use of stencils made of metal or of oiled cardboard.

REFERENCE
The Golden Age of Stenciling, ANTIQUES, April 1922.

STILES

The vertical members of frames of furniture or paneling. Upper and lower rails of furniture are set into the stiles with mortise and tenon joint, usually.

STITCHED-UP SEATS

The upholstery on these seats comes down to the lower edge of the seat frame, concealing it.

STOOLS

The stool was in common use throughout medieval times, and until the Carolean period it served the purpose in conjunction with the bench (form) for seats around the table. This stool was

known as the joint (joyned) stool, indicating that it was put together with mortise and tenon joints, and made fast with dowel pins. They were made with three or four legs and were made in England of oak; in this country, where they were much used in Colonial times, they were made of oak, maple or birch. These stools were gradually displaced by chairs during late 17th century. In England, in the 18th century, stools in

form and decoration follow the same evolution as in chairs, many of them being carved and upholstered in a most attractive manner. They were much used for seats at dressing tables. Robert Adam designed long stools to stand against the wall or in window recesses, richly upholstered.

Foot Stools. These lowly stools first came into use in Queen Elizabeth's time, to keep the feet off the cold and dirty floor. They were then made of oak, but since that time various other woods have been used in their construction. Their frame followed the styles of the successive periods and early in the 18th century they were covered with brocade or needlework, and since that time have usually been upholstered.

REFERENCE
Dictionary of English Furniture, MacQUOID and EDWARDS.

STRAP-WORK CARVING

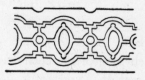

A type of ornament consisting of a narrow fillet or band, folded, crossed or interlaced, generally in repeated patterns. It is of the Elizabethan period and later.

STRAW MARQUETRY

A process of decorating objects of various materials, such as wood, papiermâché, glass, metal or bone, employed by the Italians and French in the 15th and 16th and 17th centuries. The invention of this straw work is credited to the Chinese.

STRETCHERS

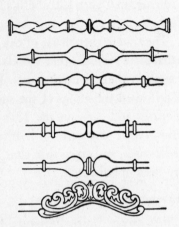

This name is given to the under-braces connecting the legs of chairs, tables and other furniture. They were in general use through all the periods up to the time of Queen Anne. The adoption of the cabriole leg of that time gradually displaced stretchers, and they disappeared almost altogether about 1730. Later in the century they were revived by Hepplewhite and other cabinet-makers of that period. Sometimes the front stretcher was set back or "recessed," between the two side stretchers. Another form known as saltire (q.v.) was connected with the four legs in X-shape. Doubtless, one important use of the stretcher in early times was to rest the feet upon, to keep them from the cold and often dirty floors.

STRINGING

A narrow band of light-colored wood used as inlay to contrast with the surrounding veneer. During the Empire period stringing of brass lines is seen.

STUMP BEDS
See BEDS, *Stump.*

SUNBURST MOTIF
See FAN MOTIF.

SUNDIAL

For many centuries the sundial was mankind's only means of telling the time of day, but useful only when the sun shone. They were made both in stationary and portable form; some of the latter, in size for the pocket, were very ornamental.

SWAG

A festoon of drapery, leaves or flowers, used as a carved, painted or inlaid decoration on furniture. It became prominent in the 18th century.

SWAN NECK
Opposed S curves, scrolling over at the top and finishing in patera. It was a favorite with Chippendale.

SWEDISH FURNITURE
A few years ago, considerable quantities of old Swedish furniture were sent to this country, where it met with

ready sale because of its resemblance to early American furniture. This was in part due to the woods used, and in part to the unsophisticated style common to both countries. Swedish authorities have since forbidden any further export of native antiques.

Swell Front

A convexly curved front, sometimes called bow front (q.v.).

Sycamore

A variety of maple used as a base for decorative surfaces. See Harewood.

T

Tables (Latin, *tabula*, a board).

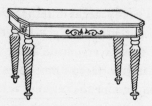

AMERICAN EMPIRE TABLE

Tables in early times in England were called "bordes," literally a plank or board. They were placed on trestles or frames when in use and taken apart and placed out of the way after being used. (See *Trestle Tables*, below.) It was not until late in the 16th century that "joined" and "framed" tables became common. One early form of these was the so-called *Drawing Table* (q.v.).

The rectangular tables of the Jacobean period had heavy legs, turned in vase or

baluster forms with stretchers at the bottom and skirting beneath the top. There was considerable overhang to the top. From that time, the development in tables was rapid and in great variety.

Billiard Tables. A French invention of the 14th century. In use in England in the 16th century and from that time onward. Billiard-table-making was usually a branch by itself, although sometimes done by regular cabinet-makers.

Butterfly Tables. A small table with turned legs and stretchers, with drop leaves which are held up by swinging

brackets, with the outer edge curved like a butterfly wing. They were made with square, oval and rectangular tops. Round tops are rare. The butterfly table is essentially American, perhaps with

Connecticut origin, and made its appearance about 1670. The type was unknown in England.

REFERENCE

The Butterfly Table, ANTIQUARIAN, April 1931.

Card Tables. Card tables were an innovation of the late 17th century, and made with a double top of same size and shape, hinged in the center. They were at first circular in form, succeeded by the square or rectangular top. At first walnut was chiefly used for these tables, followed by mahogany. Cabriole legs were common and many of these tables were elaborately carved. Some were made with cylindrical corners to hold candlesticks, and wells for counters and money were provided. When opened for use, the leaf is supported by one of the legs, which swings out for the purpose. Later in the Empire period, the top swiveled in the middle and swung around in such a manner that the top of the table base supplied the support.

Chair Tables. See CHAIRS, Table.

Console Tables. Console and pier tables of the 18th century were similar to side and card tables, except that they were made without the double top, and sometimes, when semi-circular in form, they were without rear legs. Console tables were designed to be placed against the wall and they were often fitted with marble tops, although many were painted or richly inlaid. Pier tables were usually placed between the windows of a room. Many were of satinwood.

Credence Table. The Credence table was usually a small stand placed near the altar of a church, on which remained the bread and wine until consecration. The name was given also to a table and cupboard combination for domestic use and used as a serving table. See CREDENCE.

Dining Table. The table most commonly used in the 18th century as a dining table, was of the drop-leaf type, with cabriole or square legs, two of which were hinged to pull out to support the leaves when open. Later, sectional dining tables, which could be fastened together, made by Hepplewhite with square legs, and by Sheraton with round reeded legs, were used by those who did much entertaining. The extension or telescopic form of dining table was invented by Richard Gillow in 1800. The pedestal dining table was a favorite design of Duncan Phyfe and was made so that it might be extended with extra leaves.

Dish-Top Tables. A round tripod tip-table with a rim or gallery around the edge of the top to keep the dishes from falling off. This is one of Chippendale's designs, similar to the Pie-Crust Tables (q.v.).

Dough Table. An early form of table for storing flour and dough. The top served as a dough board. These tables were oblong in shape and from three to five feet long. Turned legs which spread outward supported the bin at each corner, which was made with sloping sides. The top lifted off, which gave access to the bin.

Draw or Drawing Tables. One of the earliest tables of the Tudor period,—made of oak with heavy plank top and four bulbous legs connected with a square stretcher at the bottom. Extended by means of two shelves sliding under the central top, but so arranged that, drawn out, the upper top falls into their place, thus forming a level surface. Its principal was long retained and Sheraton, as late as the beginning of the 19th century, recommended its use for certain purposes. Another form of table in use in early days was made with a leaf, hinged to fold on top or beneath the table, and supported by wooden braces when in use,—the forerunner of the drop-leaf table.

Dressing Tables. About the middle of the 18th century a table was required for the complicated toilet apparatus of the day, and the result was a dressing chest on four tapered legs, with a top fitted sometimes with a disappearing mirror, or with a fixed mirror, and supplied with various small drawers and compartments. Before that time the lowboy (q.v.) was in general use for a dressing table.

Extension Table. See Dining Table.

Gate-Legged Tables. Also, "hundred-leg" tables, although the number of the legs never exceeds twelve. This table dates from the Jacobean period and it was the first table to have the drop-leaf. It was made, usually, of oak and the early tables had spiral twisted legs, of which there were usually six stationary upon the middle section of the table and one or two on each side which swung

out to hold up the drop-leaves. Tops were square, round, oblong or oval. In this country, maple was used mainly in New England; walnut was preferred south of New York. The gate-legged table held its popularity from about the middle of the 17th century through the Queen Anne period and during the long period of its history it had as great a vogue as the styles of Chippendale chairs at a later date. The gate-legged table is always regarded with veneration by collectors. Early English oak tables with spiral twisted legs are very rare.

Kidney Tables. A design of Sheraton, so-called because it resembles a kidney in form. The kidney desk table with tiers of drawers on each side sprang from the same design.

Library Tables. Large library tables of pedestal form with drawers came into use in England about 1725, although there are examples of earlier date. Smaller tables of the same type were in use by ladies for correspondence and for dressing tables also.

Mixing Tables. A table with compartments for bottles and the other necessaries for making punch, which often accompanied the sideboard in the dining room in England, and also over here.

Pembroke Tables. A small table with drop-leaves, with or without a drawer,

used as a breakfast table, introduced about the middle of the 18th century.

Pie-Crust Tables. One of the dish-top tripod tip-tables with a scalloped rim. It preceded the carved or fretted gallery in the Chippendale style. With its carved supporting column, carved knees of the tripod and claw-and-ball foot, the pie-crust table is much sought after by collectors.

Pier Tables. See *Console Tables.*

Refectory Tables. The old tables such

as were used in monasteries. They were of heavy construction, rather narrow, with four or six stout turned legs, a heavy stretcher around the base, and a carved apron below the top. They were commonly used in England up to the time of the gate-legged table during the Cromwellian period.

Sewing Tables. See *Work Tables.*

Side Tables. In no kind of furniture is there greater variety of treatment than in the side table dating from the first half of the 18th century. In the hands of William Kent and other architect-designers of furniture, such tables in England assumed a monumental character. They remained in use until superseded by the sideboard.

Sideboard Tables. These tables were in use before the regular sideboard took their place. They were oblong in shape and made oftentimes of a length to fit into a recess in the room. At first without drawers, these were subsequently added. Cabriole legs with claw-and-ball feet were usual and the top was sometimes of marble instead of wood.

Sofa Tables. Oblong tables with small drop-leaf at each end and with one or two drawers. The end supports were generally connected with a stretcher.

Sunk-Top Tables. Another name for *Dish-Top Tables* (q.v.).

Tavern Tables. An 18th-century table commonly used in taverns. The top was either rectangular or oval, made of maple or of pine; the turned legs and stretchers were of maple. Some of the

later tables were made with cabriole legs and without stretchers.

Tea Tables. Tea tables were first mentioned early in the 18th century. They were made with a plain top either round, oval, square or octagonal, tripod legs with snake or claw-and-ball foot, and were usually lower than other tables. In common with other tripod tip-tables, these tables were also made with a secondary platform beneath the

top, resting on a collar around the central column, with four small uprights at the corners attached to the top, which enabled one to revolve the top without moving the table. This contrivance was given the name of "bird-cage." It is a desirable feature in any tripod table.

Toilet Tables. See *Dressing Tables.*

Trestle Tables. The "borde," resting on trestles at each end, is the oldest form of table known. They were simple in design and very strong. The top was usually of a soft wood, the trestles of oak. Much used in the 15th and 16th centuries in England, and a similar table

was made and used in this country in the early period of settlement. The stretcher between the trestles was held firmly by keyed mortise and tenon joints. They were supplanted by the solid table about the middle of the 16th century.

Windsor Tables. In the 18th century, tables with four raking legs and candle stands with three legs, with the familiar Windsor turnings, were made in New England and in Pennsylvania. They are now very rare.

Wine Tables. A table fitted with revolving top and with recesses turned out to a slight depth for glasses to stand in. They were made last half 18th century, usually of mahogany. Examples are now quite rare.

Work Tables. Small tables, late 18th century, with the top arranged to lift, disclosing a cabinet with compartments for sewing materials. They were also made with folding flaps to allow for their use as a writing table or for cards or chess. Another design has drawers, often fitted with a frame beneath, to which is attached a silk or velvet bag. The frame pulls out like a drawer, exposing the open top of the bag. Those of Sheraton design are of superior excellence. The so-called Martha Washington table is probably an American innovation on the English work tables.

TABOURET
An ornamental cushioned stool.

TALLBOY
An English name for highboy (q.v.).

TALL-CASE CLOCKS
See CLOCKS, *Grandfather's.*

TAMBOUR FRONT
This consisted of small strips of wood pasted on heavy cloth, so as to be flexible. Hepplewhite is given credit for the invention. It was the forerunner, in a delicate and attractive fashion, of the modern roll-top desk.

TAUNTON CHESTS
See CHESTS, *Taunton.*

TEA CADDIES

These are relics of the times when tea was a luxury and expensive, and the early term was chest. Called caddy last part of 18th century. They were made frequently of choice woods with inlay or other decoration, and fitted with a lock. In shape, they were square, oblong or hexagonal. Inside there were usually two pewter containers, called canisters, for the tea, one for the black tea, the other for the green. Tea caddies were also made of porcelain and of silver.

TEA POY
A small low table with three legs and a receptacle beneath, in use middle of 18th century, sometimes referred to as a tea chest on legs.

TEA TABLES
See TABLES, *Tea.*

TEAK WOOD
Dark brown in color and obtained in India. It is easily worked and was in use in England to some extent in the 18th century, but is little used now.

TENON

The end of a timber cut for inserting in a mortise.

TESTER (French, *Testière*)
The frame for holding the canopy of a high-post bedstead.

THROWING
Medieval term for turning. "Thrown" chairs mean turned chairs. Chairs of

that type are of 16th-century origin in design.

TINDER LIGHTING EQUIPMENT

See PART 5.

TOP RAIL

The top member of a chair back. It is made in a variety of forms; straight, curved, serpentine, pillow, etc.

TORCHÈRE

A candle stand (q.v.).

TOWEL HORSES

Wooden frames mounted on feet with two or more cross bars, in use about middle of 18th century and onward following the introduction of the specially designed wash stands (q.v.) of the period.

TRAYS

Few trays survive dating from before the middle of the 18th century, but from that time a considerable number are found designed in successive styles for the service of the dinner table and for tea equipage. Some of these were mounted on legs or folding stands. Wooden trays were gradually superseded by those of other materials, papier-mâchè, silver or japanned ware.

TRENCHERS (French, Tranche, meaning slice)

Wooden platters used in the 16th and 17th centuries. The name was also given to pewter plates.

TREEN WARE

Name given in England to early wooden household utensils, commonly made of sycamore, such as bowls, trenchers, etc. They were also made and used in this country during Colonial times. They preceded pewter, as pewter preceded silver and china, for table use. An excellent account of "treen" appears in ANTIQUES, Volume 18, Page 504.

REFERENCE

Domestic Utensils of Wood, 16th to 19th century, EVAN-THOMAS.

TRESTLE

An early heavy frame support for tables, with the termination extending in opposite directions so as to form a two-way foot.

TRIPOD

A support with three feet. Stools of that kind were in use from early times but tripod forms for tables, stands, etc., did not become general until the 18th century.

TRUCKLE BED

Also called Trundle. See BEDS, Truckle.

TUDOR PERIOD (1485-1558)

This was truly the "Age of Oak." English oak cut from the heart of the tree was the principal wood at that time both for furniture and for buildings, although some of the other native woods were used to some extent. Strength and solidity were characteristics of the period, and furniture of great magnificence was made to furnish the important houses in England. Nearly all of that furniture was lost during the Civil

War of the 17th century. There was a very limited amount of variety in furniture. The refectory table, chests, cupboards, bedsteads, stools, an occasional wainscot chair comprise the principal items. The so-called bulbous leg is to be found on tables, bedsteads and other pieces, and much carving was done on all kinds of furniture. The Tudor rose and linen-fold paneling are characteristic of this period. The influence of the Renaissance was felt in England during the latter part of the period, resulting in more luxurious surroundings in the homes of the wealthier class. Tudor furniture retains the Gothic structure but adds much Renaissance carving and some inlay.

REFERENCES
Practical Book of Period Furniture, EBERLEIN and McCLURE; Period Furniture Handbook, GOULD.

TULIPWOOD
A wood obtained in the West Indies with stripes of pinkish color and used for inlaying and veneering. In this country it is often called "white wood."

TURNED CHAIRS
See CHAIRS, Turned.

TURNINGS

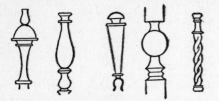

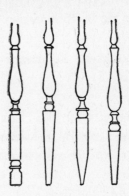

WINDSOR CHAIR LEGS

Pieces of wood that have been turned on a lathe. The vase and spiral turnings of the 17th century were followed by the inverted cup, the bell and the trumpet turnings. Turned wood was used in great variety on all kinds of furniture from the 16th to 18th centuries. Medieval chairs were often made entirely of turned members and known as "thrown" chairs.

REFERENCE
Turnings on Early American Furniture, ANTIQUES, May, June 1923.

TURNIP FOOT

A truncated ball or bun foot (q.v.).

U

Under-brace

Another name for stretcher (q.v.) on furniture.

Urn

Ornament used in the 18th century as a finish to a pediment, with the broken arch, or for inlay on surface of furniture.

Knife boxes in urn form were also made. It is a characteristic of the Adam style.

Urn Stand

A small tea table of the 18th century, usually on four tapering legs. Some were made with a small slide beneath the top, on which to rest the tea-pot when the slide is drawn out.

V

Varnish

A resinous solution of certain gums or resins in alcohol, linseed oil or the like, used by cabinet-makers to produce a shining, transparent hard coat on a surface. A receipt for making an antique varnish is given in a book entitled *Art Recreations*, published in 1860: "Take one ounce pure Venice turpentine; mix with two ounces spirits of turpentine and warm in a large bottle. In another bottle put four ounces best fir balsam and two ounces of 95% alcohol. Shake each bottle well at frequent intervals for six hours or more, then mix both preparations in the large bottle. The whole should stand several days in a warm place before using."

Varnish Remover

Marketed under a number of different names, but all with practically the same base, it is the best solvent for old varnish and paint. It is very inflammable so that it must not be used near a fire. It does not injure the wood, raise the grain, or

harm the glue. It is the only solvent suitable for use on veneered furniture. It is rather slow in action and expensive compared with lye, but a more satisfactory result is obtained and it is less harmful to use.

Vase Motif

A favorite form of decoration on furniture, carved, painted or inlaid. Vase-shaped members were also introduced into the structure. In the reign of Queen Anne, splats of vase outline were common on chairs.

Veneer

Veneering is a process of achieving ornamental results that would be impossible if solid panels of wood were used. It was first commonly used in England for that purpose in the William and Mary period, before which time only furniture of solid wood, with few exceptions, had been made. It consists of a thin layer of wood showing a rich grain, overlaid upon a body of plain, solid wood. The walnut veneer of 1700 cut with a hand saw was from a sixteenth to an eighth of an inch thick, while the mahogany veneer of modern times has been reduced in some instances to one-fiftieth of an inch in thickness. Veneering at the time of its adoption was used for sound decorative purposes and not solely for purposes of gain, as is too often the case in modern furniture. What is known as three-ply veneer is a modern invention. Crotch veneering is obtained from planks cut from joints on the tree from which the branches spring.

REFERENCE

Veneers and Their Preservation, ANTIQUARIAN, Sept. 1931.

VERNIS-MARTIN

A French imitation of Chinese lacquer which was much used in France and in England in the 18th century. A Dutch inventor named Huygens made a varnish very like the Oriental in finish, and Simon-Étienne Martin, one of his workmen, learned the secret of making it. Together with two of his brothers, he established a factory in France which became very successful and the manufacture was carried on until about 1765. It was a fine transparent lac-polish, susceptible of taking on a beautiful surface. It has been said that the secret of the formula was lost with the death of Simon-Étienne Martin, but his successors continued to do similar work for some time afterwards.

VIRGINAL

A keyed instrument, resembling in form a small pianoforte with a compass of four octaves and with a single string to each note. It followed the clavichord and preceded the spinet. The case was often elaborately ornamented. At first the virginal was in the form of a recumbent harp, but in the middle of the 17th century the name was restricted to the rectangular shape and the spinet became the title of the wing-shaped form. Their peculiar mechanisms are identical. The invention of the piano early in the 18th century displaced it.

W

WAG-ON-THE-WALL CLOCKS

These were of Dutch origin, sometimes called Friesland clocks. See CLOCKS, *Grandfather's*.

WAINSCOT

The name derives from the Danish "*Wagenschot*" and it was originally a plain wall boarding, which was later paneled. In England, it was customary to use oak, much of which was imported from Norway and Denmark, hence the name, and in this country in Colonial times pine was generally used.

WAINSCOT CHAIRS
See CHAIRS, *Wainscot*.

WALL BRACKETS
See BRACKETS.

WALL PAPER
Paper was used for wall covering in England even before the importations from China and Japan in the 17th century. During the 18th century paper, both printed and painted, competed with woven fabrics for wall coverings. In this country paper for the purpose was obtained from England as early as 1700, and most of the wall paper used here, prior to the 19th century, was imported. The earliest process of manufacture in America was that accomplished by hand-block printing.

REFERENCE
Wall Papers of Early England, ANTIQUARIAN, Mar. and Dec. 1932.

WALNUT
The use of walnut as a wood for furniture may be said to have begun during the Cromwellian period and much extended in the reign of Charles II. Before that time oak was usually chosen for both furniture and paneling. The replacement of oak by walnut revolutionized both design and processes. For sheer refinement, furniture made of wal-

nut in the Queen Anne period has never been excelled. It was much used for veneering and, except for chairs, furniture of solid walnut is very rare. In America the walnut used for furniture was either the black walnut of New England or the curly figured walnut of a deep rich color found on the banks of the Schuylkill River in Pennsylvania. This last seems never to have been found elsewhere, and it was much used by the Philadelphia cabinet-makers of the 18th century. The supply was long ago exhausted. Beside the English walnut, there are the French, Dutch, Spanish and Italian, each variety possessing marked differences in texture, color and figure.

WARDROBE
An English piece of furniture of the Queen Anne period, derived from the Dutch kas (q.v.) and used for the storage of clothing. The lower part consisted of three or four drawers and the upper part was fitted with shelves and hooks for hanging clothing, with double doors in front covering the shelves. They were usually made of oak and pine veneered and frequently inlaid with marquetry. They were about seven feet in height and five feet in width and nearly two feet in depth.

WASH STANDS
Also called basin stands. These were of middle 18th-century design, to hold the bowl and pitcher, in chambers.

ORIENTAL LOWESTOFT SERVICE, CIRCA 1760

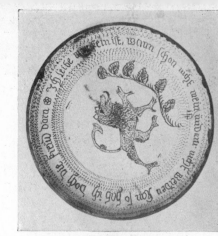

GUBBIO LUSTRE PLAQUE AND BOWL, 16TH CENTURY

Courtesy of the Pennsylvania Museum of Art
PENNSYLVANIA SGRAFFIATO PLATE,
ABOUT 1830

Courtesy of the Pennsylvania Museum of Art
PENNSYLVANIA SLIP DISH, ABOUT 1830

URBINO BOWL (RIGHT) AND PLATE, 16TH CENTURY

Courtesy of the Pennsylvania Museum of Art
PENNSYLVANIA SLIP-DECORATED DISH,
ABOUT 1760

Courtesy of the Pennsylvania Museum of Art
PENNSYLVANIA SLIP-ENGRAVED DISH,
1760

They were either square in form or triangular with a rounded front, to stand in the corner. They were supported by three or four square tapering legs, splayed out at bottom, or sometimes with turned legs, and they were usually fitted with a drawer. They followed the wig stands (q.v.).

REFERENCE

Washstands and Basin Stands, ANTIQUARIAN, Jan. 1931.

WAX FINISH

A satisfactory wax may be made by using one-half pound of yellow beeswax, one-half pint of turpentine and one-half pint boiled linseed oil, mixing together in a double boiler. In heating, be careful, as the ingredients are inflammable. Add a small quantity of burnt umber to give the desired brown tone. Three or four well-rubbed coats of this wax, with intervals to dry in a warm room, will give a soft dull finish. Avoid applying too much wax at one time.

WEB FOOT

A style of foot following the club-foot and preceding the claw-and-ball foot.

WIG STANDS

These were not stands for wigs, but basin stands with a glass attached, before which wigs could be adjusted and powdered in the 18th century.

WILLIAM AND MARY PERIOD (1688-1702)

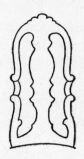

This period is important as marking, on the one hand, an almost complete revolution from the forms and principles of preceding times, and on the other, a crystallization into forms that endured through much of the 18th century. There came into England foreign influences from France and Italy, Holland and Spain, China and India. Daniel Marot (q.v., PART 6) was the leading spirit in the change in styles during this period. Dutch and French styles were everywhere in vogue, and lacquer, marquetry, painting, gilding and upholstery stuffs were gorgeous in color. Greater simplicity of form, grace of proportion and comfort were held to be of more account than dexterity of carving. The inverted cup leg is a distinguishing feature of this period, although the cabriole leg originated before the end of the period. Chair backs were "spooned" to fit the contour of the body or slanted backward slightly; and tables were made for cards, tea, writing, etc., for the first time. Two-section chests of drawers with bracket or bun feet became "tallboys" with flat tops, and the lowboys were used for small dressing tables. The beds were exceedingly tall, with slender posts and elaborate hangings. The knee-hole desk, and the secretary or book-case desk with hooded top made their appearance, also china cabinets with glass doors. The use of brass mounts began in this period. Walnut was the favorite wood, although oak and other woods continued to be used to some extent. Burl or crotch walnut veneer was in favor for decorative fronts. Needlework upholstery became popular for chair seats, settees and stools, and damasks, brocades and velvets were also used. These marked changes in style, design and purposes for which furniture was used persisted throughout the Queen Anne period, and reached America in due time and appear in the work of the craftsmen of the period, here.

REFERENCES
Practical Book of Period Furniture, EBERLEIN and McCLURE; *Period Furniture Handbook,* GOULD.

WINDSOR CHAIRS
See CHAIRS, *Windsor.*

WINE COOLERS
In the 18th century before the sideboard of Shearer was designed, the sideboard table was flanked at each end by square pedestals, with compartments for wine bottles and ice, zinc-lined and with a faucet at bottom for drawing off water from melted ice. The pedestals were surmounted by the knife boxes. Another style, called cellaret, was made to be set beneath the table or early sideboard.

WING CHAIRS
See CHAIRS, *Wing.*

WOODEN DOMESTIC UTENSILS
See TREEN.

WORK TABLES
See TABLES, *Work.*

WRITING ARM-CHAIRS
See CHAIRS, *Writing Arm-.*

Y

YARN WINDERS
A contrivance for winding yarn, usually in windlass form, with six spokes and mounted on a platform with short legs.

YEW
A wood of very ancient use in England. It is hard, elastic and of a reddish brown tone. In the 16th century it was used for country-made pieces of furni-

ture, and for veneer work in the 17th and 18th centuries.

YORKSHIRE CHAIRS
See CHAIRS, *Yorkshire*.

Z

ZEBRA WOOD

A wood of light brown color, strongly marked with deep brown. It was imported from Guiana and employed for veneering, late 18th century. Beautiful in markings, but infrequently seen.

WORCESTER PORCELAIN, DR. WALL PERIOD, CIRCA 1760-1780

ORIENTAL LOWESTOFT PORCELAIN, 18TH CENTURY

CHELSEA PORCELAIN—THE MUSIC LESSON; ONE OF THE MOST DISTINGUISHED FIGURE PIECES
EXISTENCE, CIRCA 1760

PART II

POTTERY AND PORCELAIN

Because of the tardy development of fine earthenware products in the United States many
late 19th-century potteries are here included.

PART II

POTTERY AND PORCELAIN

A

ABORIGINAL POTTERY

There were, roughly, three groups of pre-Columbian pottery produced in this country; that of the Atlantic Slope, Indian, that of the Mississippi Valley, the Mound Builders, and that of the house building tribes of the far West.

REFERENCE

Pottery and Porcelain of the United States, BARBER.

ABRUZZI WARE

The kind of majolica which is known as Abruzzi is not the production of any particular factory, but the term is applied to specimens which it is difficult to assign to any of the more distinguished Italian factories.

ADAMS WARE

ADAMS

One of the oldest names in the Staffordshire potteries is that of Adams. William Adams (1745-1805) of Tunstall (Greenfield) was perhaps the best potter of that family. The foundation of the firm dates from 1657. Their product has always been of excellent quality. Their specialties have been Adams jasper, Egyptian black, Imperial stoneware, Etruscan ware and vitreous stoneware. In the first half of the 19th century they produced blue-printed ware with American and English views which are much sought for by collectors. The firm of William Adams & Co. is still in existence making earthenware of a high grade of excellence.

REFERENCE

William Adams, An Old English Potter, TURNER; A B C of 19th Century English Ceramic Art, BLACKER.

AGATE WARE

Earthenware made either solid or in surface decoration to resemble the veinings of agate or other natural stones. If solid, it is produced by layers of different colored clays twisted together and then cut transversely with wire. Pieces of a small size only were made of these mixed bodies. The surface ware is splashed and grained on an ordinary cream body. The former method was never made to the same extent as marbling on the surface.

105

ALCOCK (S.) & COMPANY

A pottery established in Burslem in works formerly operated by Ralph Wood. Molded figures in relief were a notable product. The company was succeeded by the Hill Top Pottery in 1867. Samuel Alcock had been a figure painter at Copeland's.

ALCORA WARE

A Spanish factory established in 1727 and continuing through the 18th century, producing at first a fine faience and later a soft porcelain. Experienced workmen from France, Italy and Holland were at first employed and they taught the Spanish potters the latest methods in modeling and decorating.

REFERENCES

Pottery and Porcelain, FREDERICK LITCHFIELD; Alcora Ware, ANTIQUARIAN, Feb. 1930.

AMERICAN ENCAUSTIC TILING Co.

Factory at Zanesville, Ohio, began making glazed flooring tiles in 1880. They also made relief tiles, imitation mosaic tiles, embossed damask-finished tiles and an unglazed floor tiling by the name of "Alhambra," by means of which soft, beautiful effects in carpet patterns have been obtained on a vitreous body of great hardness.

AMERICAN PORCELAIN

See PORCELAIN, American.

AMERICAN PORCELAIN COMPANY

Name given to a company succeeding the American China Manufactory at Philadelphia, but it does not appear to have operated under that name.

AMERICAN POTTERY

See POTTERY, American.

AMERICAN POTTERY MANUFACTURING Co.

Jersey City, N. J. See JERSEY CITY POTTERY.

AMPHORA

The name of a vase with two handles used by the ancient Greeks for wine and for domestic purposes.

AMSTEL PORCELAIN

Factory near Amsterdam, the first in Holland, began producing a hard-paste porcelain in 1764. It had a fine white body closely resembling the body of Dresden china with landscape and figure decorations. Factory was discontinued in 1810.

ANGOULÊME PORCELAIN

A French hard-paste porcelain of excellent quality made at Paris from 1780 to 1829 in one of the smaller factories. It successfully reproduced all the underglaze colored grounds used at Sèvres and all the colors for on-glaze painting.

ARRAS PORCELAIN

Pas-de-Calais, France. Although this factory was in existence from 1770 to 1790, there were but four years (1782-1786) when the soft-paste porcelain was of excellent quality, rivaling Sèvres. The ordinary production was inferior and of little importance.

ASHFIELD (Mass.) POTTERY

Stoneware of ordinary quality made from clay brought from Perth Amboy, New Jersey, was made at Ashfield about the middle of the 19th century.

ASTBURY WARE

ASTBURY

A generic term applying to stoneware pottery with raised floral decoration of white on a colored, unglazed body, then glazed. It derives its name from John Astbury and Thomas, his son, potters in Staffordshire in the 18th century, and it was imitated by other potters in Staffordshire as well as those of Liverpool. The ware is of red, black, chocolate and fawn in color and similar to the Elers ware (q.v.) although not so sharp in its details. Devon pipe clay was used for ornamentation. Astbury first introduced ground flint into pottery about 1720, and he was constantly making experiments in methods of improving his product.

B

BARBOTINE WARE

Biscuit, decorated with a kaolin clay thinly mixed and molded separately and attached to the surface of vases, etc.

BASALT WARE

A solid black stoneware of great hardness, unglazed, which takes its name from a black Egyptian rock. It was one of the earliest products of the English potter's art, although Wedgwood's basalt is regarded as superior to others. He made his from native clay, ground ironstone, ocher and oxide of manganese. Black basalt has not been reproduced to any extent by modern potters and when a piece of this ware is found it is quite likely to be an antique. Wedgwood made a number of fine busts in this ware.

BASSANO PORCELAIN

At this Italian factory established in 1728, a soft-paste porcelain was made, decorated in deep blue in the Oriental manner, similar to that of Doccia and Venice.

BAT

A slab of coarse clay used for the building up of the ware in the kiln or oven during firing.

BAT PRINTING

This method of printing on glazed pottery was in use towards the close of the 18th century. The design was first engraved on a copper plate and then given a coat of linseed oil, which was rubbed off, leaving the oil only in the lines of the design. Instead of paper, "bats" of gelatin or glue were used to take the impression from the plate to place it upon the surface of the ware. It was then dusted with the color desired in such a manner that no superfluous color remained and the pottery was then placed in the kiln. It is a more difficult process than printing with paper but many of the larger potteries still make use of this method. Much of the early 19th-century work was decorated by this process. Because it is on the surface of the glaze, it is easily distinguished from other methods.

BATTERSEA ENAMELS

The origin of these was the factory of Stephen Janssen, established at Battersea near London about 1750 and lasting only six years. He did much to popularize enamel work and to bring it within reach of the average purse. Almost all of the output was in small pieces, and the designs were painted by hand in colors or by the transfer-print process. Later, imitations were produced at Bilston (q.v.) in Staffordshire, and at other places. See ENAMEL.

REFERENCE
Battersea Enamel Knobs, ANTIQUES, Aug. 1922.

BEAVER FALLS ART TILE CO.

Factory at Beaver Falls, Pennsylvania, was organized in 1886 and at first made plain enamel, embossed and intaglio tiles. These works have always employed the best designers that could be obtained. They made a specialty of artistic tile designs suitable for solid wall decorations of libraries, dining rooms and bath rooms.

BELLARMINE JUGS

Also called Greybeard Jugs. The name is derived from Cardinal Bellarmine, 16th century, whose writings were obnoxious to the "Reformed Church." The jugs are a species of stoneware, of a mottled red-brown color, salt-glazed, and they were made in pint, quart, two-quart and one-gallon sizes, both in Germany where they originated and in England.

BELLEEK PORCELAIN

This Irish china is thin and light of body, highly translucent, and has a cream-like surface in ivory tone. It is noted for its lustre, resembling the iridescent surface inside a mother-of-pearl shell. The designs are mostly of a marine character. The factory was founded in 1857, near the borders of Donegal in Ireland, and much of the product was sent to America. Belleek china of excellent quality is now made in this country.

REFERENCE
An Appreciation of Belleek, ANTIQUES, Oct. 1922.

BENNETT (EDWIN) POTTERY CO.

Established in 1846 at Baltimore, Maryland, by Edwin Bennett, an English potter who came to this country in 1841 to work for his brother James at Liverpool, Ohio. The products at Baltimore were Rockingham and yellow ware, sage and blue hard-body wares. The manufacture of white ware began in 1869, and shortly after a decorating department was added. The so-called "Rebekah" teapot was one of their best known products. In 1890 the business was incorporated under the name above, and at the same time they began making porcelain of good quality.

BENNINGTON (Vermont) POTTERY

A pottery was first started there in 1793 by John and William Norton for making earthenware and in 1800 they began to make salt-glazed and lead-glazed stoneware. This was known as the Norton Stoneware Co. and it continued more or less active for many years. John Norton retired in 1823 and the business was continued by his sons Luman and John, Jr., and in the succeeding years until 1894 one or more of the descendants of John Norton were active in the business.

In 1846 Julius Norton, a grandson, formed a partnership with Fenton and Hall. In 1848, this was dissolved and a new firm of Lyman and Fenton took its place. In 1849 the name was changed to The United States Pottery Co., and a new factory was erected and conducted as a separate enterprise from the Norton Stoneware Co. The variety of the wares turned out was formidable. Rockingham, yellow and white wares continued to be made and some creditable work in Parian ware was turned out. The pitchers alone offer a wide field for the collector. The range of coloring include olive, green, brown, yellow and various shadings and mixtures. Bennington figures were carefully modeled and the glaze was uniform and evenly applied with a rich velvety sheen. A small amount of porcelain was also made. Daniel Greatbach, a noted English potter, joined the company in 1852 and modeled some of their best pieces.

The business ability and energy of Christopher Webber Fenton were largely responsible for the success of the company, but to Decius W. Clark, a potter from New York State, more than to Fenton or to anybody else the notable advancement of American pottery at Bennington was due. Fine Bennington ware is now nearly as rare and as valuable as Lowestoft. The factory closed in 1858.

REFERENCES

Potters and Potteries of Bennington by JOHN SPARGO; The Fentons, Pioneer American Potters, ANTIQUES, Oct. 1923; The Facts about Bennington Pottery, ANTIQUES, Vol. 5.

BERLIN PORCELAIN

This German factory was established in 1752 by Frederick the Great. The models and molds were taken from Dresden as a consequence of war with Saxony and the early production was a porcelain of hard paste with decoration of a classical type and rivaling Meissen (Dresden, q.v.). The most attractive examples are the finely painted service pieces decorated with German garden and landscape scenery. The later work is coarse in modeling and not refined or delicate in color.

REFERENCE

Porcelain Table Ware of Old Royal Berlin, ANTIQUARIAN, Nov. 1930.

BILSTON ENAMELS

Made at Bilston in Staffordshire by Thomas Perry, Mary Bickley and Isaac Becket. It is the Bickley and Becket enamels among Bilston types that are most liable to confusion with Battersea productions. In general Bilston colors are less refined than those of Battersea.

REFERENCE

Battersea & Bilston Enamels, ANTIQUES, July 1929.

BISCUIT

The term applied to earthenware and porcelain when it has been fired once. It is after the biscuit stage that decorations in color are applied and the specimen goes to the oven a second time.

BLUE

In the Orient blue had a religious and mythological as well as a historical significance, but to the Occident potter it was used for its durability and cheapness in imitation of Oriental china and Dutch delft. William Littler of Longton is credited with being the first potter in England to use oxide of cobalt as a ground for salt-glazed ware. Cobalt blue, alone, of all the colors known to the 18th century could withstand, without alteration, the high temperatures needed for the running of most glazes. Chemistry of the 19th century has made other colors of the same durability. See MAZARINE BLUE.

BODY

The body of a piece of earthenware is the clay of which it is composed.

BOLOGNA

Italy. A factory of majolica was established in 1849 and it is principally known for its fine reproductions of the old ware, Luca della Robbia and Urbino.

BONE CHINA

Since about 1800, the manufacture of porcelain has been altered by the mixture of bone ash with kaolin and feldspar and the product has been called "bone" china by some writers. This product holds a middle ground between soft-paste and hard-paste porcelains. It is more white than the soft-paste and harder but it is not so white generally as the hard-paste nor quite as hard.

BOOTE (T. & R.)

This firm took over the Waterloo Potteries at Burslem in 1850 and in the ensuing years produced Parian ware of great excellence, also encaustic tiles and earthenware.

BORDEAUX

France. A hard-paste porcelain of fine quality and faience have been produced

Chelsea Porcelain Shepherd and Shepherdess, circa 1765

Chelsea Porcelain Figures, circa 1765

WORCESTER PORCELAIN, DR. WALL PERIOD, CIRCA 1760

DECORATED CHINESE GINGER JAR ON TEAK-WOOD
STAND, YUNG-CHING PERIOD (1723-1736)

WORCESTER VASE, CIRCA 1760

at the factory here established about 1784.

BOSTON EARTHENWARE MANUFACTURING Co.

A small pottery operated by Frederick Mear (1822-1876) from Burslem, England, was making brown-mottled yellow ware at East Boston, Massachusetts, in 1853-4.

REFERENCE
Boston Earthenware, ANTIQUES, June 1924.

Bow PORCELAIN WORKS

At Stratford-le-Bow, East London, was founded a factory in 1744, at first called New Canton, where the first soft-paste porcelain in England was made from a white clay (kaolin) brought from North Carolina. No specimens of this earliest Bow china can be positively identified. Many pieces of china classed as Chelsea belong to Bow. The paste of Bow is of different kinds, that of which the groups and figures are generally composed being of a soft artificial porcelain similar to Chelsea, but coarser, heavier and more vitreous in appearance. A much harder paste was also made, sometimes white and sometimes having a blue-grey tint, with a thick greenish glaze. The factory output largely consisted of tableware. A very large part of the Bow production was unmarked. Of the marked pieces, the anchor and dagger in red are characteristic. The productions from 1752 to 1760 include

some of the most charming porcelain ever made in England.

A remarkably soft and delicate style of flower painting is quite peculiar to Bow and printed decoration was also used here to some extent. Blue and white ware painted in under-glaze blue in the Chinese manner was produced in large quantities. The "Old Japan" pattern of polychrome decoration was also very popular, and decoration in the styles of Dresden, Sèvres and other Continental factories were included. The later productions of the factory are not of the same excellence. Bow figure pieces with plain bases were made prior to 1755, those with scroll bases afterwards. These figures are frequently attributed to Chelsea or Worcester, owing to the similarity of the marks. In 1776, William Duesbury of Derby bought the works and removed them to Derby as he had previously done with Chelsea.

REFERENCES
Pottery and Porcelain, FREDERICK LITCHFIELD; *Bow Porcelain*, FRANK HURLBUTT; *Old English Porcelain*, W. B. HONEY; *Old Bow China*, EGAN MEW.

BRADWELL WARE
See ELERS WARE.

BRAMELD WARE
See ROCKINGHAM.

BRAMPTON WARE
A brown ware also known as Chester-

field ware. Posset-pots, puzzle jugs, bear mugs and other vessels having grey-hound handles were made during the 18th century.

BRISTOL PORCELAIN

Bristoll 1750

Porcelain of soft paste was made at Bristol probably as early as 1750, and a factory operated there by William Lowdin was some time after transferred to Worcester. About 1766 under Rich-ard Champion they began to make hard-paste porcelain from Dresden models. They also imitated Chinese ware in color and design. Technical short-comings mark much of this work. Warping and fire cracks are common; handles are often askew and the glaze is often pitted. In 1773, porcelain was made from the formula of William Cookworthy, who had previously operated a factory at Plymouth. In 1778, the works were closed, and in 1781 Champion sold his patent rights to a company of Stafford-shire potters who had works at New Hall (q.v.). It is very difficult to dis-tinguish Bristol china from that of Ply-mouth (q.v.).

Every piece of true Bristol china is rare and of value, owing to the brief time the works were in operation. Some of the Bristol figures rank with the finest ever made in England. Standing apart from the other Bristol productions are the biscuit plaques with modeled and applied decoration in relief, which Champion made for presentation to his friends.

REFERENCES
Bristol Porcelain, FRANK HURLBUTT; Pottery and Porcelain, FREDERICK LITCHFIELD.

BRISTOL WARE

Early in the 18th century several firms were engaged in making delft, frequently inscribed with dates. The earliest-existing example is dated 1703. The blue in the decoration is of a darker and more pronounced tone than that used at Lambeth (q.v.). The decora-tions were frequently in the Oriental or Dutch style. In addition to blue other colors were also used. Excellent tiles of a decorative character were made, difficult to distinguish from Dutch tiles, unless the subject is English or unless identified by initials or a date. Suc-ceeding the delftwares, Joseph Ring in 1786 began to make cream ware, of a warm cream color due to the glaze and not to the body of the ware itself. This ware was decorated in finely painted flower patterns in enamel colors. Dur-ing the 19th century the pottery has been carried on by different owners.

REFERENCE
Old Bristol Potteries, W. J. POUNT-NEY.

BUEN RETIRO (Madrid) PORCELAIN

The factory was established by King Charles III of Spain in 1759 and carried on until the works were destroyed by the French, when Napoleon invaded Spain. The ware is a soft paste, of a delicate white and more than usually translucent. It is very much like that of Capo-di-Monte at Naples, also established by Charles III, while King of Sicily, but excels that in delicacy and thinness of body. It was probably the most costly and most technically perfect of any 18th-century porcelain. Even in Spain this ware is exceedingly rare. Outside of Spain it is scarcely known.

BURLINGTON (Vermont) POTTERY

A pottery was started here in 1806 by Norman L. Judd, who learned his trade at Norton's pottery at Bennington.

Soon after starting work here the pottery was destroyed by fire and Mr. Judd went to Rome, New York, where he carried on a pottery business for more than twenty years. The Burlington pottery was afterwards rebuilt and operated by Nichols and Alford, and they made ware which was, at that time, very popular in Northern New England. Much of it closely resembled Bennington ware of the same type. Ballard Bros. afterwards ran the plant until into the Seventies.

REFERENCE
Burlington Pottery, ANTIQUES, Nov. 1924.

BURSLEM

Known as "The Mother of the Potteries." In the 17th century it was the largest pottery center in England. See STAFFORDSHIRE.

C

CAMAIEU

A method of painting porcelain, usually in pink or green in deeper and lighter tones of a single color.

CAMBRIAN POTTERIES

CAMBRIAN

The factory established at Swansea in Wales about 1750 produced salt-glaze, cream and other wares. These wares are decorated with birds, butterflies and flowers and are well painted.

Black basalt figures and vases and Etruscan ware, exceedingly well decorated, were also made at this factory, at a later period. Specimens marked Cambrian are rare. See SWANSEA WARE.

CANISTER

See TEA CADDY.

CANTA GALLI

A modern factory of faience, located at Florence, produces excellent reproductions of old Urbino majolica, lustred Gubbio ware and della Robbia.

CAPO-DI-MONTE PORCELAIN

This famous Italian factory was established near Naples in 1736 by Charles III and later transferred to Naples. The productions of this factory are very beautiful. The soft paste has a delicate texture and is soft in appearance, and the hard paste made early in the 19th century is generally of excellent quality. Old Capo-di-Monte is usually unmarked and it is hard to find genuine pieces. About the middle of the 19th century a factory was started on the site of the old one and reproductions are made there, but not equal to the original. A majolica ware is also made there at the present time, of good quality.

CASTEL DURANTE

An Italian center of majolica manufacture, 16th century.

CASTING

The method of making articles by means of pouring the clay, reduced by water to a "slip" condition, into plaster molds, which molds absorb the water. When the clay has dried or hardened to the right degree to hold its shape the mold is removed.

CASTLEFORD WARE

DD & C°
CASTLEFORD

This factory, about twelve miles from Leeds in Yorkshire, was established about 1790 by David Dunderdale. Cream ware, black basalt and white porcelain tea services with ornaments in relief were made there. The ware is seldom found with any color on it. Castleford ware was to some extent made for the American trade, soon to be overwhelmed by Staffordshire ware. Factory was discontinued in 1820. Reopened later, a pottery is still in operation there.

CAUGHLEY (or SALOPIAN) WARE

SALOPIAN

Earthenware made at this Shropshire factory, from 1750 to 1785, was finely modeled and equal to the finest work of the Staffordshire potters. It is, however, eclipsed by the soft-paste porcelain which Thomas Turner (who had previously been with the Worcester factory) began to make at Caughley in 1772. In 1780 he introduced the "willow pattern" designed by Thomas Minton, one of his decorators, from Oriental models. Whole dinner services were made with this design in under-glaze, blue-transfer print, and became very popular. Porcelain with under-glaze blue painted decoration was also one of their products, and Caughley, at that time, rivaled Worcester in production. The mark on the later productions is "Salopian" impressed in the paste. Salopian porcelain commonly gives a warm yellowish tone to transmitted light. The Caughley works were sold

Bennington Parian Ware, circa 1850

Bennington Rockingham Ware, circa 1850

AMERICAN BLOWN GLASS FLASKS, 19TH CENTURY

to Coalport (q.v.) about 1799 and in 1821 the works were demolished.

REFERENCE

Caughley, FINE ARTS, Feb. 1932.

CAULDON POTTERY

Established at Cauldon Place, Stoke-on-Trent, by Job Ridgway in 1802, and after 1830 and until 1855, carried on by his son John Ridgway. Table and toilet services in fine earthenware and excellent porcelain were made at this factory. Ridgway produced "The Beauties of America" series. In the last half of the 19th century, their porcelain work was of a high grade of excellence, and other products of the factory include almost every description of ceramics.

REFERENCE

A B C of 19th Century English Ceramic Art, BLACKER.

CELADON WARE

One of the earliest kinds of decorative pottery made by the Chinese, dating from the Sung dynasty, 960-1279, of a peculiar pale, watery-green color in the southern provinces, owing its origin to an attempt to copy the much-prized green jade, and brownish-green or dark Celadon in the northern provinces. The body is heavy and thick. Some of the ware is decorated under the glaze with floral designs or figures in relief, or stamped into the paste before the pieces were glazed and fired. The term was originally applied only to Oriental porcelain but some of the English and

French factories have adopted it. Celadon green is but one color of a large group of Chinese self-colored porcelains, that is, where the color is applied with the glaze and subjected to but one firing. In other words the term is used to describe both a special class and a special color.

CERAMIC

Generic term, which comprises all objects made of clay, and derived from the Greek word *Keramos*.

CERAMIC ART COMPANY

Trenton, New Jersey, established in 1889. This factory has produced Belleek ware of exceptional beauty, both in design and decoration. Their carved ware in Belleek body, with decoration in porcelain bisque in relief, possesses a high order of artistic merit.

CERAMIC ART IN THE UNITED STATES

Up to 1876, the year of the Centennial Exposition in Philadelphia, comparatively little had been accomplished in this country of a really artistic nature, and the existence of a true ceramic art here may be said to have dated from that year, because greater progress has been made since that time than during the two centuries that preceded it. See CHELSEA KERAMIC ART WORKS, ROOKWOOD POTTERY, DEDHAM POTTERY, LOW ART TILE CO.

CHAFFERS PORCELAIN

Made at Liverpool by Richard Chaffers and Co. in 1756 and for several years thereafter. The better known examples are characterized by a Worcester-like body, painted in enamel colors with subjects of a Chinese character or with transfer-printed subjects. See LIVERPOOL PORCELAIN.

CHAMPLEVÉ
See ENAMEL.

CHANTILLY PORCELAIN

An important French factory making soft-paste porcelain, established about 1725 by the Prince de Condé. In the earlier period an opaque tin glaze was used and the forms and decoration were in the Oriental manner. The later productions have a clear lead glaze and consist largely of table services. Two of the workmen of Chantilly initiated the factory at Vincennes. The Chantilly factory was closed in 1789.

REFERENCE
Pottery and Porcelain, FREDERICK LITCHFIELD.

CHELSEA KERAMIC ART WORKS
This factory at Chelsea, Massachusetts, was started in 1866 by A. W. Robertson and produced in the succeeding years ware of a quality which entitles it to a prominent place in collec-

tor's interest. In 1867, Hugh C. Robertson, a brother who was to become so prominently identified with ceramics here and later at Dedham, joined the company, and in 1872, his father, James Robertson, experienced Scotch potter.

A red bisque ware in imitation of antique Grecian terra cotta was produced in 1875, of a remarkably fine texture and smooth finish in the manner of the old originals, and in 1877 Chelsea faience attracted the attention of connoisseurs. It was characterized by floral decorations and a beautiful soft glaze. James Robertson died in 1880, and four years later Alexander went to California, leaving his brother, Hugh, to carry on alone.

The world owes a debt to the memory of Hugh Robertson for, at great personal sacrifice, he devoted the rest of his active life to an endeavor to rediscover many lost processes of ceramics. Experiments in reproducing the famous Chinese sang-de-boeuf were successful and vases were made with no other decoration than this wonderful surface color, which in the light glistens with all the varying hues of a sunset sky. Imitations of the Chinese crackle ware, with blue under-glaze decoration, were made which compare favorably with Oriental examples. Owing to lack of financial support by the buying public, the factory was closed in 1889 and in 1891 Hugh Robertson joined the Dedham Pottery Co. (q.v.).

CHELSEA (England) PORCELAIN

Chelsea

△

ςƀ Lι

Factory here began making very soft-paste porcelain about 1745, requiring all decoration to be done at one time as it could not withstand a second firing. The well-known "goat and bee" cream jugs are marked Chelsea 1745, a proof of the early date of this factory. In body, it is uneven, and the glaze on the earliest pieces is thick and was applied unevenly. The glaze of the later periods was much better. In decoration, Oriental, particularly Japanese, Dresden and Sèvres patterns were closely followed. Every conceivable thing that could be made of porcelain was made at Chelsea under the direction of Nicholas Sprimont, who joined the company about 1750, and who later became owner of the works. He gave especial attention to the decoration of the product and remained at the head of the company until 1769.

In 1758 the composition of the paste was altered by the addition of calcined bone ash, and about 1759-60 we find the gorgeous costumes and handsome gilding, so rich and decorative. Its dark blue ground was never equaled by any other English factory, and the rich claret color was never produced anywhere else. Nearly all pieces of Chelsea porcelain exhibit stilt marks. The unique objects known as Chelsea "toys" are among the most valued of all Chelsea productions. In 1769 the factory was sold to William Duesbury, proprietor of the Derby factory (q.v.), and from 1770 to 1784, when the works were removed to Derby, is known as the Chelsea-Derby period, in which period some very beautiful products were made. A good specimen, by the softness of its paste, fine glaze and refined coloring may be said to resemble closely fine Sèvres china. The marks are distinct.

REFERENCES

Chelsea and Chelsea-Derby China, EGAN MEW; *Chelsea Porcelain,* WILLIAM KING; *Old English Porcelain,* W. B. HONEY; *Pottery and Porcelain,* FREDERICK LITCHFIELD; *Why Chelsea,* ANTIQUARIAN, Jan., 1931; *Chelsea Porcelain Toys,* G. E. BRYANT; *Cheyne Book of Chelsea China and Pottery,* REGINALD BLUNT.

CHESAPEAKE POTTERY

Of Baltimore, Maryland, was started in 1881 by D. F. Haynes & Co., and it has achieved a high reputation for the variety of excellent bodies and glazes it has produced, and still greater distinction by the beauty and originality of its designs, both in form and decoration. The most original and perhaps the most refined and beautiful was the so-called Severn ware, first made in 1885. It marked "an era in the history of American ceramics." It was a fine body of a subtle, greyish-olive tint. Parian ware was also produced in the same year. In 1886, the manufacture of a fine semi-porcelain in a great variety of articles, both useful and ornamental, was commenced.

CHINA

This term, derived, of course, from China, where porcelain was first made, is applied to porcelain of all classes, whether true porcelain of hard paste, or artificial porcelain of soft paste. Examples of the former are the Oriental porcelains, Meissen (Dresden), Plymouth, Bristol. Of the soft-paste porcelains are Worcester, Chelsea, Bow, Lowestoft and other English porcelains.

CHINA COLLECTING

"However small the collection, let it be good and perfect as far as it goes. Every specimen should be examined carefully as to the quality of its paste, modeling, shape, color and special characteristics as a specimen of its particular factory. It is a mistake for a collector to buy second and third-rate pieces because they are cheap. In the same way imperfect and restored specimens should be avoided, unless needed solely for decorative purposes. By taking every opportunity of seeing collections and making comparisons one's judgment and knowledge is improved. Beware of imitations"—LITCHFIELD. Since 1891, all pottery made in foreign countries has been subject to a law of the United States that requires importations to be stamped with the name of the country of their origin. This serves to identify some of the imitations of the early products. A fertile field for the collector is in gathering representative pieces of the wares of the American potteries, some of which equal those of the best European works.

CHINA STONE (See PETUNTSE.)

Known also as Cornish stone, used in conjunction with kaolin (q.v.) for porcelain and light-colored stoneware.

CHINESE LOWESTOFT

See LOWESTOFT.

CHINESE PORCELAIN

See PORCELAIN, *Chinese.*

CHINESE POTTERY

See POTTERY, *Chinese.*

CHURCH-GRESLEY PORCELAIN

This ware was made in Church-Gresley in Derbyshire in a factory started by Sir Nigel Gresley in 1795. No authentic piece of this china is known. The factory was closed in 1808.

CINCINNATI ART POTTERY Co.

Established in 1880 by T. J. Wheatley & Co., its early under-glaze work is remarkable for beauty and originality of form and excellence in workmanship. The most distinctive of the products in style was the ivory-colored faience decorated with gold scroll work and flowers in natural colors. The pottery was discontinued after a few years of activity.

CLAY

The clay used in pottery is a plastic soil owing its origin to decomposition of various rocks, and consists chiefly of aluminum silicate. The blue clay used in this country for making stoneware, although very strong, will not stand intense heat unless mixed with other substances. Kaolin or china clay is used in making porcelain. It is a product of the decomposition of aluminous materials, especially feldspar, and it is white both before and after it is fired. This clay was early found in China, later in Saxony, and about 1765 in Cornwall, England. It is also found in several of the states in this country. It was by the discovery of this clay in Europe and here that the porcelains in imitation of those of China were made possible. Kaolin is not fusible, even at the highest temperatures to which the kiln can be brought.

CLEWS WARE

See JAMES CLEWS, PART 6.

CLOBBERED WARE

Porcelain and pottery originally decorated in blue and later redecorated in other colors and refired.

CLOISONNÉ

See ENAMEL.

COALPORT PORCELAIN

Situated in Shropshire in the Severn Valley, the factory was established about 1780 by John Rose who had been an apprentice of Thomas Turner of Caughley. The chief production was

Coalport

tableware. The body was white and translucent, similar to the Caughley paste, and the glazing was excellent. Coalport at first made imitations of Dresden, Chelsea, Sèvres and other wares, counterfeiting their marks with the avowed purpose, it is said, to deceive buyers. The gilding on these productions, however, was usually thin and burnished, quite unlike the dull, soft-looking gold on the originals. Later, Rose bought the Caughley works in 1799, the Swansea factory in 1820, and in 1828 Nantgarw and Jackfield also. At Coalport the marks of these various factories were used on the production, causing great confusion.

In 1819 William Billingsley, a decorator who previously had been employed by Derby, Worcester, Swansea and Nantgarw, joined Rose, and he died at Coalport in 1828. Specimens of later Coalport, not in imitation of other factories, are good in color and design and command a fair price. Under-glaze blue-printing and painting were the chief modes of decoration. The works are still in existence.

REFERENCES

Coalport Porcelain Works, L. JEWITT; *A B C of 19th Century English Ceramic Art*, BLACKER.

COBALT BLUE

See BLUE.

COLOGNE STONEWARE or GRÈS DE FLAN-
DRES

A German stoneware of the 16th and
17th centuries, consisting of jugs, pots
and tankards, with an incised or molded
pattern, picked out in colors and then
covered with salt-glaze. Many of these
pieces have hinged covers of pewter and
their decorative effect is pleasing. See
GERMAN STONEWARE.

COMBING

An effect obtained by splashing slip
of another color on the object to be
decorated and then dragging a flexible
toothed instrument over the surface.

COPELAND PORCELAIN

See SPODE.

COPENHAGEN PORCELAIN

The present factory was started in
1772, although a previous factory was
in operation from 1756 to 1768, in
which a soft-paste porcelain of good
quality was made. Since 1779 the factory has been under Royal direction and
very creditable work in hard-paste porcelain has been turned out. It ranks
among the best produced in Europe and
strikingly reflects the influence of Japanese ceramics, more so than any other of
the European porcelains.

REFERENCE

Chats on Royal Copenhagen Porcelain,
ARTHUR HAYDEN.

COPPER LUSTRE

See LUSTRE WARE.

COREAN WARE

See KOREAN WARE.

CRACKLE

Crackle is produced by making the
body of the piece of a mixture more sensitive to heat and expansion than the
coating or glaze. When it occurs accidentally it is called crazing (q.v.). The
Chinese made of it a regular form of
decoration, producing crackle of various
sizes, and they sometimes rubbed red
coloring matter into the tiny cracks to
make the crackle more marked.

CRAZING

The accidental fire-cracks in the glaze
somewhat resembling crackle, due to
the china's being withdrawn from the
kiln before it is cooled, or by a defect
in the firing.

CREAM WARE

The term applies to all light-colored
English earthenware from about 1750
to the present time, although since the
beginning of the 19th century the body
has itself been white, due to the invention of so-called ironstone china by
Mason. Cream ware was perfected by
Wedgwood by the use of Cornwall clay
and adopted as the standard earthenware of Staffordshire, until the perfection of the white body about fifty years
later.

CROLIUS WARE

Stoneware made in New York, in the

18th century, at first by William Crolius and his partner, John Remmey. They eventually dissolved and each continued under his own name, both factories being near each other just north of the present City Hall. The business of William Crolius was carried on by several succeeding generations, and the regular product of this pottery was jugs, jars and dishes for table use. Some "specials" made were artistic in form, finish and decoration. The ware, in general, is lighter than that of Remmey.

REFERENCE
Unmarked New York Pottery, ANTIQUARIAN, Jan. 1930.

CROUCH WARE
This ware of dense body made from a whitish clay and salt-glazed, in the late 17th and early 18th century, represents the transitional stage between the ordinary brown earthenware and the later drab or greyish-white examples.

CROWN DERBY
See DERBY PORCELAIN.

CROWN STAFFORDSHIRE PORCELAIN CO.
This company operates the Minerva Works at Fenton formerly occupied by Mason & Co., makers of the well-known

ironstone china. The Crown company has successfully reproduced the exact shades of the enamels which the Chinese brought to perfection, also their powder blue. They have copied, too, old English work with equal success. Of their production one authority is of the opinion that "nothing of finer quality has ever been made in England, nothing with such an Oriental tone." They use the Crown mark on these reproductions.

CUP PLATES
Plates, three to five inches in diameter, occasioned by the custom of drinking tea from the saucer, which arose early in the 19th century. They were made at Staffordshire in great variety and their attractiveness served, probably, to prolong their use. The deep-blue examples date from 1815 to about 1835. The later pieces, printed in light colors, appeared about 1828 and continued until about 1860. These cup plates were in constant competition with the glass cup plates (q.v.) but the demand for both varieties gradually ceased.

REFERENCE
China Cup Plates, ANTIQUES, April 1927.

D

DAVENPORT WARE

In a factory established in 1793 at Longport in Staffordshire, John Davenport made both earthenware and porcelain domestic ware of excellent quality with colors and designs following the Derby style. Great use was made of ground colors for rich decorations, an apple-green being particularly favored. The factory was in operation until 1886 and much porcelain with their mark has survived, and fine examples are now much sought after.

DEDHAM POTTERY

To Hugh Robertson is given the credit by French and German ceramists of note for producing ware at the Dedham potteries "forty to sixty years ahead of public appreciation," after he had spent more than twenty years in such work at the Chelsea Keramic Art Works (q.v.). In 1895 a new pottery was built at Dedham where Chinese "crackle" ware and high-fired vases were produced. These vases were self-colored red, green, yellow and slate, all simple and heavy to withstand the strain of high-firing. They equaled any of the finer Oriental wares.

REFERENCE

The Dedham Pottery, ANTIQUES, Aug. 1926.

DELFTWARE

A pottery made first in Delft, Holland, early in the 17th century of a soft reddish clay, containing an unusual quantity of lime, after a method of the Italian majolicists of the 15th and 16th centuries. In the biscuit form delft was coated with an opaque white tin-enamel slip, and then while the enamel was still

wet the colors were applied and the enamel was liquefied and the colors fixed at one firing. Blue was the earliest color used in imitation of the more costly porcelain which had been brought from the Far East, followed by the polychrome colors. A great variety of ware was made including tiles. Later delft is glazed with lead.

English delft was first made at the Lambeth potteries about the middle of the 17th century, followed later by those at Bristol and Liverpool. In Liverpool it was the principal industry of the town for many years. English delft is of a much harder body base and the painting is more coarse than the Dutch examples, and is mostly under the glaze in blue, yellow or dull purple.

REFERENCES

Dutch Pottery and Porcelain, W. P. KNOWLES; Delftware, Dutch and English, N. HUDSON MOORE; Old English Delft, ANTIQUES, Oct. 1934; English Delft Pottery, R. G. MUNDY.

DERBY PORCELAIN

$$\mathcal{D}$$
1750

Although the factory was established about 1750, little is known at the present time of the early production before the time of William Duesbury in 1756. The porcelain made after that is white, fine and soft and the "biscuit" is worthy of special notice, rivaling in many respects the biscuit of Sèvres. Bisque figures were often modeled from drawings by Angelica Kauffmann. Its finest work is regarded as that done in the Chelsea-Derby period 1770-75 and the Crown-Derby period 1785-90. The paste and decorations of these periods may be compared in every way to good Sèvres china. Crown Derby is lighter in weight than any other ceramic, and although very thin, it is strong. After about 1811 the product of the factory deteriorated rapidly and the works were closed in 1848. The present Royal Crown Derby Porcelain Company was formed about 1875. It is not a lineal descendant of the earlier company. Although the products of this company are very decorative, but little attempt is made to copy the old models. Beauty of form, purity of body, excellence of gilding and delicacy of painting distinguish the work of the present company.

REFERENCES

Old Derby Porcelain and Its Artist-Workmen, FRANK HURLBUTT; Old English Porcelain, W. B. HONEY; Chelsea and Chelsea-Derby China, EGAN MEW; Pottery and Porcelain, FREDERICK LITCHFIELD.

DERBY WARE

Derby earthenware is worth considering from a collector's point of view. Slip ware was made in the earlier days, also delft. Later, cream ware was produced, although not equal to the Staffordshire products. The Cock Pit Hill pottery made a slip ware with the design raised from the surface, and, between, slips of several colors were poured, a distinctive style of decoration.

DERUTA WARE

The monumental decorative style of early Renaissance majolica was crowned with the achievement reached by the Deruta ware early in the 16th century. The product is equaled only by the Hispano-Moresque lustre plates.

REFERENCE

A History and Description of Italian Majolica, M. L. SOLON.

DOCCIA PORCELAIN

Made at a factory near Florence, Italy, where it was established in 1735 by the Marchese Carlo Ginori and is still in operation. Doccia china is generally found in parts of table services, rarely in vases. The earlier productions are well worth acquiring. Of the early production the body was of semi-hard paste and the glaze soft, sometimes with a tendency to run. In the later production both the body and glaze are perfect. The decoration followed Oriental and European motifs. Capo-di-Monte molds were obtained by the Doccia factory in 1834 and copies of that porcelain were made, also majolica, of good quality.

REFERENCE

Practical Book of Chinaware, EBERLEIN and RAMSDELL.

Don Ware

The factory at Swinton, Yorkshire, founded in 1790 by John Green made ware similar to Leeds, and when unmarked it is difficult to distinguish between them. The pottery passed through various vicissitudes of fortune and in 1834 was purchased by Samuel Barker, and it remained in the Barker family for about fifty years. They made the usual varieties of the common classes of earthenware, some of it decorated with enamel colors, gilt or lustre.

Doulton Ware

John Doulton established a stoneware factory first at Vauxhall, afterwards transferred to Lambeth, early in the 19th century, and under the name of Doulton a large variety of wares were made differing greatly in design and decoration, as well as in the material itself. The works are still in existence producing Doulton ware, Lambeth faience and Impasto. The first is decorated while in the "biscuit" state and then placed in the kiln, receiving but one firing. The appearance of this ware is very similar to Grès de Flandres (Cologne) of which its production is really a revival. It is a salt-glazed stoneware impervious to the action of acids and when made thin it is semi-translucent.

The faience is hand-painted and requires more than one firing. It is entirely different from the Doulton ware in body and decoration. The glaze of this class is somewhat duller, too. Impasto consists of an application of colored clays to the surface, leaving the design in slight relief and very effective. One peculiarity of this production is that they do not print their designs and so rarely, if ever, repeat the pattern of even the most inexpensive articles.

REFERENCE
A B C of 19th Century English Ceramic Art, Blacker.

Dresden Porcelain

A factory was established at Dresden, Saxony, in 1709, under the patronage of August II, Elector, where a hard stoneware resembling porcelain was produced by a process discovered by Johann Friedrich Böttger. Later the factory was removed to Meissen, near Dresden, where it has flourished since under state control. Really fine porcelain was produced about 1715 by means of using kaolin (white clay). The early productions (prior to 1720) were made in white in imitation of blanc-de-Chine. Gradually, the secret for making this porcelain spread to France and England and the models of Meissen were copied by Sèvres, Worcester, Bow, Chelsea and Derby.

After the Death of Böttger in 1719

Herold became the master painter, and in 1731 Kändler the modeler, who became famous. Painted figure subjects were introduced and relief ornament became a leading feature. Figures were also made for mounting in ormolu, then fashionable in Europe. It was previous to 1740 that the beautiful ground colors in canary yellow, apple green, lilac, maroon or claret and blue were introduced. Vases, table services and other ware of this period command the admiration of collectors. During the so-called King's period, 1778-1796, the reputation of Dresden porcelain became world-wide. The true Meissen is strong and serviceable, the glaze is even and brilliant, the colors are sharp and bright, while the painting is for fineness and finish unsurpassed. Owing to the high value of old Dresden (Meissen) ware, many imitations have been made to impose on inexperienced collectors. During the 19th century Dresden ware has not equaled its earlier product.

REFERENCES

Dresden China, W. B. Honey; Dresden China, Egan Mew; Practical Book of Chinaware, Eberlein and Ramsdell; Old Dresden China, ANTIQUES, Feb. 1929.

E

EARTHENWARE

The ware usually designated earthenware is of soft body, fired at low heats, made of clays selected for plasticity, hardening qualities, fusibility or color. When in the biscuit stage it is too porous for domestic use and requires a coating of glaze. As a rule it is opaque and lighter than porcelain. Earthenware may be divided into four kinds: unglazed, simply baked clay; lustrous, selected clay baked and coated with a slight vitreous glaze; glazed, ordinary ware such as household crockery, with a lead glaze; enameled, glazed with vitreous or glass compound, owing its coloring properties to mineral oxides or sulfates. The use of china clay in earthenware has resulted in the disappearance of the once popular cream ware for general use. See POTTERY.

REFERENCES

The Art of the Old English Potter, Solon; The Earthenware Collector, Rhead; English Earthenware and Stoneware, Church; History and Description of English Earthenware and Stoneware, Burton.

ELERS WARE

This ware was made by John Philip and David Elers, brothers, who came from Holland at the time of William and Mary and established a factory at Bradwell Wood, Staffordshire, about 1690. They made black and red unglazed ware of very dense, hard body, some of it turned on a lathe and perfectly finished with stamped ornament in relief, the first of such in Staffordshire. The later potters making such ware called it "Elers" ware. The spouts on turned tea-pots were plain and molded by hand. Elers ware was of a quality superior to anything before produced in England and authentic pieces of their product are very rare, although imitations are numerous and are constantly mistaken for real specimens. The early black ware made here may have been the prototype of Wedgwood basalt of later days. Their pottery was in existence about twenty years.

ENAMEL

This is an opaque, semi-transparent or colored substance, used in coating the surface of metals or porcelain, and afterwards fired. The basis of all enamels is an easily fusible colorless glass to which the desired color and opacity are imparted by mixtures of metallic oxides. The art of enameling has been practised in almost all countries where art has flourished and it is very ancient in its origin.

The enamels of Limoges (q.v.) in France of the 12th to the 16th century have attained great fame and long before that time the Greeks and Romans produced beautiful enamels. The Chinese made early use of enamels on their pottery and in England over-glaze colors

with enamel effect were applied on pottery early in the 18th century. The painted enamels of France were superior to the English product, but the Battersea factory (q.v.) and its English contemporaries in the middle of the 18th century helped to restore the balance. The characteristic of these is a copper base, covered with soft white enamel, the surface of which is decorated by painting by hand or by the transfer-printing process.

Other processes of enameling are the Cloisonné, in which the design is outlined by wires soldered to the surface of the body, much in use by the Chinese and Japanese, and the Champlevé, a process of cutting the design into the metal itself. The hollow spaces of both methods are then filled with the enamel paste, rubbed down smooth or heated until they run smoothly over the surface to which they adhere by fusion with the metal.

REFERENCE
Clay Glazes and Enamel, GRIFFIN.

ENAMELED POTTERY
Known also as stanniferous faience from *stannum*, the Latin word for tin. It is a coarse ware covered with a heavy, opaque, white enamel. See DELFTWARE.

ENAMEL KNOBS
Designed for the express purpose of use with looking-glasses and much in vogue in the last half of the 18th century. They were made round and oval and

rarely exceeded three and one-half inches in diameter. They took the name of Battersea, having been made there first, but they were produced elsewhere, also, in characteristic Battersea style of decoration.

ENCAUSTIC
Pertaining to the burning in of colors on a ground of another color.

ENGLISH PORCELAIN
See PORCELAIN, *English.*

ENGLISH POTTERY
See POTTERY, *English.*

ETRURIA POTTERY (Trenton, New Jersey)
This factory, under the operation of Ott & Brewer Co., was noted for the production of "Belleek" china, entirely from American materials, regarded as being equal to the Irish Belleek. Its extreme lightness of body and its lustrous glaze has served to make it widely known. In addition the factory produced granite ware and opaque china, both print-decorated and hand-painted, and its Parian ware was soft and mellow in texture and a close imitation of the finest statuary marble.

ETRUSCAN MAJOLICA
This name is marked on earthenware produced by Griffen & Smith at Phoenixville, Pennsylvania, late 19th century.

ETRUSCAN WARE
An ancient product of Etruria of black clay without painted decoration, but with repoussé ornaments. The forms were copied from Greek vases or from metal vases from Egypt and Carthage.

EXETER POTTERY WORKS
Established at Exeter, New Hampshire, by J. Dodge in the 18th century and operated by succeeding members of his family until 1895, when the pottery was closed. The earthenware produced was red, and practically all of it was glazed. It consisted of all of the household types in use during the pottery's existence. Some of the pieces, especially the earlier ones, had variations in yellow, brown and greenish hues, owing to oxides used.

REFERENCE
The Exeter Pottery Works, ANTIQUES, July 1932.

F

FAENZA
The majolica of Faenza produced at the end of the 15th century is perhaps the most highly prized of all of the beautiful ceramic productions of the best period of the art of Italy. The pigments used are generally blue, red and yellow. A revival of the art of making this majolica took place here in 1850 and the old models and decorations were successfully reproduced. The municipal art gallery contains fine old pieces.

REFERENCE

A History & Description of Italian Majolica, M. L. Solon.

Faience

A greatly misused French term, properly applied to French tin-enameled wares. By many, it is now applied to every kind of glazed earthenware excepting porcelain. The name probably derived from Faenza in Italy, one of the many cities famous for medieval pottery, and still manufacturing it. See French Faience and Majolica.

Faience Manufacturing Co.

At Greenpoint, Long Island, started work in 1880. In 1884, Edward Lycett, formerly of Staffordshire, England, joined the company and under his able direction a fine grade of porcelain was produced, better glazes, new shapes and decorations. One of his discoveries was the method of making the reflecting glaze of the ancient Persian tiling.

Feldspar

A naturally occurring mineral, mostly a potassium aluminum silicate. It is fusible at a great heat, melting into a milky white, glass-like substance, and is used with kaolin to produce porcelain.

Fenton (Staffordshire)

This is a large district where pottery has been made from very early times and in the 18th century there were several factories there. Thomas Whieldon, Thomas Green and John Barker had potteries there, and the pottery of Felix Pratt produced an excellent cream-colored ware with a bluish glaze, known as Pratt's ware (q.v.) from 1775 to about 1820. C. J. Mason & Co. also established a factory here in 1825 for the production of their ironstone china (q.v.). See Staffordshire.

Figures

Both earthenware and porcelain were freely used in the production of figures. Figures in enameled earthenware had been made in Italy in Renaissance times and later in Holland. In China, porcelain had long been employed for this purpose. The Meissen factory at Dresden was the first in Europe to make figures of porcelain in the second quarter of the 18th century. To Kändler, the modeler, can be given the credit for most of the styles seen in all mid-century china figures. In England the potters of Bow, Chelsea and Derby, at first taking their examples from Meissen models, soon began to model subjects after English design.

In pottery, about the middle of the 18th century, English potters began to model figures of a higher artistic merit than the work of Astbury and Whieldon, and the figures of Ralph Wood, John Turner, Ralph Salt and many other of the Staffordshire (q.v.) potters are of marked interest for fine modeling and delicate coloring.

REFERENCES

Staffordshire Pottery Figures, Read;

English Porcelain Figures of the Eighteenth Century, KING; *A Footnote to Staffordshire Lore,* ANTIQUES, April 1935.

FLAMBÉ

The term is applied to pottery or porcelain which depends for its decorative effect upon the cloudy or shaded or splashed color of the glaze. The Chinese were the first to produce this decoration but it has been adopted by both English and French potteries.

FLINT

A form of silica used in the pottery industry. When calcined and ground, it produces a white infusible powder used for whitening the body. It was first used about 1720 by John Astbury and was the means of great improvement in earthenware.

FLORENCE (MEDICI) PORCELAIN

Towards the end of the 16th century the Medici princes made experiments in porcelain in imitation of that of China. The porcelain that was produced is of soft and creamy paste decorated in shaded under-glaze blues, with designs of Oriental motifs in Italian rendering. This was the first European porcelain of which we have certain knowledge. Specimens of this porcelain are exceedingly rare. There are said to be only forty specimens now remaining. The factory closed shortly after 1600.

REFERENCE
Pottery and Porcelain, FREDERICK LITCHFIELD.

FLUX

A chemical substance, for example, fluorspar, introduced into the color bases to enable them to fuse at comparatively low temperatures in enameling. Other materials used for fluxes are feldspar, borax, alkaline carbonates and preparations of bismuth.

FONTAINEBLEAU WARE

At Avon, near Fontainebleau, there was a considerable manufacture of faience as early as 1608. The production seems to have been mostly small figures and other pieces in imitation of Palissy. Another pottery was at Belleville where Dresden models and styles of decoration were copied.

REFERENCE
Pottery and Porcelain, FREDERICK LITCHFIELD.

FRANKENTHAL PORCELAIN

A hard-paste porcelain which ranked among the best of German porcelains was made at a factory established here in 1755. The paste is not so white or so hard looking as Meissen and the coloring is simpler. Rich dark blue as ground color was used, and sometimes the gilding was in two shades of gold. The factory was closed before 1800.

FRENCH FAIENCE

Decorative earthenware of this kind

was produced at various French potteries. That of Saint Porchaire (q.v.) is one of the earliest, about 1520, followed by the unique pieces of Bernard Palissy (q.v., PART 6). Lyons, Nevers, Rouen, Marseilles, Paris and other places produced admirable work, and for three centuries the industry commanded the skill and good taste of artists and sculptors. The standard is now lower.

REFERENCE
History and Description of the Old French Faience, M. L. SOLON.

FRENCH PORCELAIN
See PORCELAIN, *French*.

FRENCH POTTERY
See POTTERY, *French*.

FRIT PASTE
This was a paste used in old Worcester made by a mixture of sand, gypsum, soda, salt and niter, melted together in a mass. After cooling it was then broken and pulverized to be mixed with the clay which gave the paste its body. The frit gave it translucency.

FROG MUGS
Drinking mugs with a small model of a frog fixed to the inside, near the bottom. They were made at Leeds, Sunderland, Nottingham, and at other English potteries.

FUDDLING CUPS
Nests of three to six cups, cemented together with an opening in them so that the drinker must empty all or none of them. It was an early Staffordshire device.

FULHAM WARE
John Dwight produced (1671-1703) at Fulham, a suburb of London, white stoneware busts and figures, red unglazed ware, brown stoneware jugs and mugs. Some of this brown ware was salt-glazed, probably the earliest in England. Dwight also received a patent for transparent earthenware (porcelain) and for a stoneware which he called "Cologne" ware. He was one of the greatest of English potters and to him must be attributed the foundation of an important industry. His magnificent life-size bust of Prince Rupert, now in the British Museum, excites the wonder and admiration of modern potters. All specimens of his make are very rare. The pottery continued in existence long after Dwight's death.

REFERENCE
The Art of the Old English Potter, M. L. SOLON.

FÜRSTENBERG PORCELAIN
A factory for making a hard-paste porcelain was started here about 1750 and it is still in operation. The production was somewhat like Meissen but coarser. Some of the pieces were also modeled after Bow and Chelsea English china and the French Sèvres.

English Glass, 19th Century

American Flint Flip Glasses

Irish Cut Glass Decanters and Sugar Bowl, circa 1810

American Three-mold Blown Glass, Early 19th Century

G

GALENA

Sulfide of lead. In powdered form it was dusted on the ware and liquefied by the firing. See LEAD GLAZE.

GALLIPOT

A small earthenware jar. These are sometimes found of old delft, made for apothecary's use, about eight inches in height, round body, decorated in blue and usually with a spout and handle.

GERMAN PORCELAIN

See PORCELAIN, German.

GERMAN POTTERY

See POTTERY, German.

GERMAN STONEWARE

A ware of the Renaissance period, fired at a temperature so high as to vitrify the body and render it impervious to liquids, without a coating of glaze. The body was relatively coarse, the forms roughly "thrown" and the surface covered with molded pictorial ornament. Some of the earliest of this stoneware is ascribed to Cologne, where the so-called Bellarmine (q.v.) or grey-beard jugs are thought to have originated. Many pieces of this stoneware found their way into England early in the 16th century and were imitated in England by John Dwight at Fulham (q.v.). German stoneware was brought into this country by the German settlers in Pennsylvania in the 18th century. See COLOGNE STONEWARE.

REFERENCE

German Stoneware, ANTIQUES, Nov. 1932.

GILDING

The early method was to apply the gold by oil "sizing" without firing, which was liable to be rubbed off. This process was improved late in the 18th century by grinding the gold leaf with honey, which was painted on the ware and then "fixed" with a gentle firing. Later, this method was replaced with the present mercury process, which allows the gilding to be burnished.

GINORI PORCELAIN

See DOCCIA.

GLAZE

The coating applied to earthenware and porcelain when in its biscuit stage, usually composed of elements similar to those of glass. Liquid glaze into which the piece is dipped was introduced in 1750. Hard glaze is colorless and thin and feels cold to the hands. Soft glaze is a white cream color and has a wet, sticky feeling. In the earlier days tin was used for the opaque glaze peculiar to delftware, called tin-enameled, and in England lead in powder form was sprinkled over the biscuit and then fired. See LEAD GLAZE, SALT-GLAZE and SMEAR GLAZE.

GLOST OVEN

The chamber in which pottery is

placed for the purpose of firing the glaze. Saggers (q.v.) are used to protect the ware from the flames and gases of the oven. The heat of the earthenware biscuit oven ranges from 1200 to 1350 degrees centigrade, that of the china (porcelain) oven from 1300 to 1450 degrees. See OVEN.

GOLD LUSTRE
See LUSTRE WARE.

GRAFFITO
See SGRAFFIATO.

GREENPOINT (Long Island) POTTERY
Established in 1848 by Charles Cartlidge & Co., where a fine quality of decorated table china was produced, also portrait busts in biscuit porcelain. Factory was in operation only eight years.

GREENSBORO (Pennsylvania) POTTERY
Established early in the 19th century. It produced at first red ware, partially or wholly covered with brown or black slip. Later, a white clay was used for making a grey stoneware, with salt-glaze, consisting of jars, jugs, pitchers and other household ware. The best of this ware is decorated with blue. This pottery continued work until near the close of the century. Another pottery known as the Eagle Pottery was also located at Greensboro for some time. See NEW GENEVA.

REFERENCE
The Pottery of Greensboro, ANTI-QUARIAN, Sept. 1931.

GREENWICH (Connecticut) POTTERY
Salt-glazed grey stoneware was made there by Abraham Mead, during the last half of the 18th century.

REFERENCE
The Deacon Potter, ANTIQUARI-AN, March 1930.

GREENWOOD POTTERY CO.
Of Trenton, New Jersey, was established in 1861 by Stephen Tams & Co., and incorporated in 1868. Mr. Tams was from Staffordshire, England, where he had learned the pottery business in all of its branches. This pottery made a specialty of vitrified and translucent china for hotel, steamship and railway uses. They also produced a thin china tableware of superior quality for domestic uses.

GRÈS DE FLANDRES
See COLOGNE STONEWARE.

GREYBEARD JUGS
See BELLARMINE JUGS.

GRISAILLE
A method of painting in grey tints so as to represent a solid body in bas-relief. The effect of relief is given by varying the shades.

GRUEBY FAIENCE CO.
Boston. Organized in 1897. The ware produced is regarded as one of the best made in this country, and it is highly regarded abroad. The forms are delightful, the decorations are of the simplest

character in plain colors, and the glaze is soft and beautiful.

GUBBIO (Italy) WARE

Majolica was made there in the 15th and 16th centuries and is at the present time very rare. The collector who desires to possess genuine specimens of this ware should use great care, as very clever imitations are offered. Gubbio ware was noted for its beautiful gold and ruby lustre and the artistic designs of Giorgio Andreoli. The old majolica manufacture was recently revived.

REFERENCE

A History and Description of Italian Majolica, M. L. SOLON.

H

HAGUE PORCELAIN

The hard-paste porcelain made at a factory at the Hague, Holland, established in 1775, is a very desirable possession. Its table services were decorated with a beautiful bleu-de-roi color with rich gilding. The factory continued in operation for about ten years.

HAMPSHIRE POTTERY

Factory at Keene, New Hampshire, started work in 1871 producing red ware. Later, stoneware and majolica were added.

HANDLES

See KNOBS.

HAVILAND PORCELAIN

See LIMOGES.

HERCULANEUM WARE

This pottery became the largest and most successful in Liverpool. It was established in 1790 by Richard Abbey, who had formerly been an assistant of John Sadler of transfer-printing fame. Stoneware, black and red unglazed ware, cream ware, both painted and blue-printed, and after 1800, bone china, were made. There is no difficulty in identifying its wares as they are plainly marked with the full name of the place. The factory was operated by men from Staffordshire and, with Staffordshire traditions, they made a great range of under-glaze printed subjects in both brown and blue, also terra cotta vases of good design and small busts of celebrities in stoneware, basalt and white earthenware, the latter frequently painted in enamel colors. The factory was dismantled in 1841.

HILL TOP POTTERY

See ALCOCK (S.) & Co.

HISPANO-MORESQUE WARE

This pottery, dating from about the 14th century, was the successor to the much earlier Arabian pottery. Malaga,

Valencia and Talavera were identified with the production of this ware. The particular feature of the decoration is the ornament in lustre pigment of a rich, iridescent brown color, sometimes relieved in blue, which is highly effective. Those specimens which we see generally date from the 16th century and are usually unmarked. Of late years there has been a revival of its manufacture in various parts of Spain, but the modern productions are very inferior.

REFERENCE

Hispano-Moresque Ware of the 15th Century by A. VAN DE PUT.

HISTORICAL CHINA

This name was given to a group of Liverpool and Staffordshire products, late 18th and early 19th century, consisting of transfer-printed subjects relating particularly to American views, portraits of American statesmen, Army and Navy heroes and other events like the visit of Lafayette in 1824, the opening of the Erie Canal, etc. The names of the potters making this ware include Enoch Wood, the two Stevensons, Clews, Ridgway, Mayer, Adams, Jackson, Stubbs, Green and others. Some of the pieces are marked but many are unmarked and the makers unidentified, unless it be possible from the style of the border design on the front or surface of the piece. Nearly every potter customarily made use of one distinctive pattern. Until about 1830, blue was the only color used in the Staffordshire potteries. Later a variety of colors were in use. The Liverpool ware was mainly in the form of jugs, with portraits, maps and marine views in black transfer-print.

REFERENCES

The Blue-China Book, ADA W. CAMEHL; *American Historical Staffordshire*, ANTIQUARIAN, July 1930.

HÖCHST PORCELAIN

This was produced at a factory near Mayence, Germany, established about the middle of the 18th century, in which Ringler, a porcelain-maker from Vienna, assisted. The finest productions of the factory were made during the employment of Melchior, a modeler, from 1766 to 1779.

REFERENCE

Pottery and Porcelain, HANNOVER.

HUNTINGTON (Long Island) POTTERY

The earliest wares of this pottery, last half of 18th century, were made from local red brick clay in shapes of many sorts and sizes. Smudges of darker colorings of brown or black were applied irregularly for decoration. Later, the forms were dipped in a wash of fluid clay, containing red lead, and these came out of the kiln in rich, red shades. This ware was thick, rather soft, and easily broken. At the beginning of the 19th century grey salt-glazed stoneware of a flint-like hardness and often decorated in blue was produced, consisting largely of jugs and crocks. Work in this pottery ceased in 1904.

REFERENCE
The Pottery at Huntington, Long Island, ANTIQUES, April 1923.

I

IMARI WARE

This name is given to a ware made in the province of Hizen in Japan and exported from the port of Imari. The potters were originally Koreans brought from their own country in the 16th century by princes of Japan. The old Imari ware was an article of commerce with the Dutch traders of the 17th century, and imitations were made at Delft, and the later product was also copied at Meissen (Dresden) and Chantilly. Modern Imari ware is inferior to the earlier product.

INDIANA POTTERY Co.

At Troy, Indiana, organized in 1837. James Clews, the famous English potter, was one of those interested. Blue, yellow and Rockingham wares were made, but nothing of superior excellence. The venture was unsuccessful, attributed to the unsuitableness of the clays used and the incompetence of the workmen. Mr. Clews returned to England where he died in 1856, and the work at the pottery ended at about the same time.

INTERNATIONAL POTTERY Co.

This pottery at Trenton, New Jersey, was started in 1878 by James Carr and Edward Clark, for the manufacture of cream-colored and white granite wares. The following year they disposed of the plant to Burgess and Campbell, who have since produced there porcelain of excellent quality. Many of their pieces are characterized by elegance of form and a richness and depth of blue ground seldom surpassed in this country or abroad.

IRONSTONE CHINA

An earthenware made at a factory established in 1797 by Miles Mason (see MASON WARE) at Lane Delph, Staffordshire, for which Charles Mason, his son, took out a patent in 1813. The body contains a large proportion of flint and slag of ironstone, and it is heavier than porcelain. It was both cheap and durable, and soon secured a large market. A rich shade of blue was a feature of the decoration. In 1851, the manufacture of ironstone china was removed to Shelton and since that time it has continued to be one of the most successful of the Staffordshire products.

ISLEWORTH WARE

S & G

A small factory established in 1760

by Joseph Shore which produced some red unglazed earthenware of a highly artistic character. Some of the finer pieces have been mistaken for Elers ware. At first both pottery and porcelain were made here, but porcelain-making was discontinued in 1787. The works were closed in 1825.

ITALIAN FAIENCE AND MAJOLICA
See MAJOLICA.

ITALIAN PORCELAIN
See PORCELAIN, *Italian.*

J

JACKFIELD WARE

The known history of this factory located in Shropshire, on the Severn River, begins in 1713, although potting in this district was done as early as in the 16th century. Jackfield was noted for its black ware, made of red clay and covered with a lustrous black glaze and ornamented with oil colors or gilt. Its best work was done between 1760 and 1772 under Maurice Thursfield, son of the founder Richard Thursfield. In 1780 the works were sold and removed to Coalport.

REFERENCE
A *Note on Jackfield Ware,* ANTIQUES, March 1926.

JAPANESE PORCELAIN
See PORCELAIN, *Japanese.*

JAPANESE POTTERY
See POTTERY, *Japanese.*

JASPER WARE
This fine, hard, unglazed white bisque made by Wedgwood and other potters was perfected about 1775. It was made in various surface colors introduced

about 1777, known as dip jasper, and in blue, colored clear through, called

solid jasper, and white bas-relief was used in combination with the different colors. Jasper was used for making vases, medallions, plaques and many other articles. The points which mark excellence in the eyes of the collector are the smoothness and color of the background, the sharpness and translucency of the ornament, and the undercutting in which certain parts are relieved by cutting while the clay is soft.

JERSEY CITY POTTERY
Established in 1825 as the Jersey Porcelain and Earthenware Co. In 1833 the name was changed to the American Pottery Manufacturing Co., and again

about twenty years later to the Jersey City Pottery. Various kinds of pottery were made there of a buff or cream-colored body of excellent quality. For the first time in America the English method of transfer-printing in decoration was adopted before 1840. Many of the best potters of the old school in this country learned their trade at this factory. Although earthenware was the chief product, porcelain was produced to some extent. The factory was discontinued in 1892.

JIGGER

A machine used in potteries in making circular and swelled vessels such as jars, jugs, crocks, etc. It carries a revolving mold, in which the clay is shaped in a "former."

JOLLY

A contrivance somewhat similar to a jigger for making flat ware, consisting of a revolving disk or plate on which the mold is placed.

JUGS

An earthenware vessel with handle, used to carry liquids. The earlier jugs of the Staffordshire potters were nearly all molded. The Liverpool jug (q.v.) is that best known to collectors. The early pitchers were usually called jugs.

K

KAOLIN

Chinese name for clay. See CLAY.

KERAMIC ART WORKS

See CHELSEA KERAMIC ART WORKS.

KILN

The chamber used for firing pieces decorated in enamel colors and distinct from the oven (q.v.), a much larger chamber used for bringing the ware to the "biscuit" and "glost" state. The heat of the enamel oven varies from 700 to 900 degrees centigrade.

KNOBS

China and enamel set in brass were frequently used in knobs for furniture, first quarter of the 19th century. They were often decorated with painted designs.

KNOWLES, TAYLOR AND KNOWLES Co.

The factory by this name at East Liverpool, Ohio, was started in 1854 by Isaac W. Knowles, where at first Rockingham and yellow ware were made. In 1872 the manufacture of white granite ware (ironstone china) was begun and later bone china was made, on which especial attention was given to decorative work. This factory has been one of the most successful of any of the pottery enterprises in this country.

KOREAN WARE

Korea or Corea long produced porcelain attributed to both China and Japan. The decorations were conventional forms of either floral or animal subjects and the colors were limited to red, black, green, yellow and gold. Although the Koreans still make pottery the manufacture of porcelain ceased long ago.

L

LAMBETH WARE

The earliest work identified as Lambeth is of about the middle of the 17th century. The earliest dated known example is 1634. It has the general characteristics of Holland delftware with a thick opaque white enamel of a pinkish tinge on which is painted, generally in blue, the decoration. The painting is inferior to that on the Dutch delft. At the same time the delft of Lambeth is regarded as the best produced in England. At one time there were twenty potteries here active in making delftware, and drug jars and pots are among some of the most important pieces which have survived. See DOULTON WARE.

LANE DELPH WARE

See MASON WARE.

LANE END

In Staffordshire. At this place, now known as Longton, there have been many manufactories of pottery and porcelain, some of which are still in existence. John Turner was one of the best known and some of his work rivaled that of Wedgwood.

LEAD GLAZE

The earliest form used in England was the so-called "galena" glaze consisting of sulfide of lead in powder form dusted on the ware. About 1750, liquid lead, composed of ground flint and white lead into which the body was dipped, was first used. Body and glaze were then fired together, giving an appearance as though covered with a heavy coating of varnish.

LEEDS WARE

LEEDS * POTTERY

Although known to have been in operation in 1760, the best period of Leeds was from 1783 to 1800, when under the operation of Hartley Greens & Co. The ware then produced is noted for its lightness in weight, the fine finish, the peculiar color of the body and especially for the light green tinge in the glaze. Enameled salt-glaze ware preceded its cream ware, which rivaled the best production of Wedgwood. A characteristic feature of Leeds ware is the varied use of pierced work in the rims of plates, trays and other dishes. Each perforation of this work is done separately by hand and the edges are sharp and clean-cut. Transfer-printing in red, black, purple and lustre was also used in decoration.

REFERENCES
Leeds Old Pottery, KIDSON; Old Leeds Ware, WILSON.

LIMOGES (France) ENAMELS

The earliest of these famous enamels are of the Champlevé kind and are mostly ecclesiastical pieces. Examples of this work are very rare, although they may be seen in our leading museums. The painted enamels produced at the end of the 15th and during the 16th century are of a very high order of merit. The painting was done by some of the leading artists of the period. It is brilliant in color and the composition is strong. The Musée du Louvre and the Cluny Museum in Paris, the British Museum in London, The Metropolitan Museum in New York, and the Walters Art Gallery in Baltimore possess beautiful examples of the best of this work.

LIMOGES (France) PORCELAIN

Hard-paste porcelain was made here in 1783. The table services which were the chief production have an ivory-tinted body and decoration in rather dull colors of sprays of flowers. In 1840 David Haviland started a factory and a large trade was built up, especially for export to this country. Limoges is, at the present time, the center of a district containing several important porcelain factories.

LINTHORPE ART POTTERY

Made at a pottery in Middlesbrough, England, established in 1880 and continuing for about twenty years. The ware in great variety was made from common brick clay and it is noted for the beauty of its form, color and the brilliance of its glazes. In this respect it is only matched by the splendid wares of the East. Low-toned reds, mottled olives and browns, yellows of great variety of tone are found in this ware.

LIVERPOOL JUGS

Jugs made at Liverpool in the 18th century in a great variety of sizes, usually cylindrical in shape and decorated with a transfer design in black and white, often bearing the likeness of some prominent man or of a ship, sometimes both. Many American subjects are depicted upon them in the later period of their manufacture.

LIVERPOOL PORCELAIN

Richard Chaffers, William Reid and some other Liverpool potters made a soft-paste porcelain about the middle of the 18th century. But little is known of the history of those enterprises and the known specimens are very few. Some of these were decorated with cobalt blue on a white ground with copies of Oriental subjects. There are also existing examples of transfer-printing in brown and other colors.

LIVERPOOL WARE

Early in the 18th century, delft dishes decorated in the Chinese style were the principal trade of the city. It is characterized by a bluish tone of the enamel, which often contains small pinholes. The three principal potteries were those of Alderman Shaw, Seth Pennington and Zachariah Barnes. Astbury salt-glaze (q.v.), Whieldon (q.v.) and cream ware were subsequently made, the latter largely decorated with transfer-printing in black and white, a process perfected by John Sadler of Liverpool and much employed there. Potteries at Staffordshire and other places sent pottery to Liverpool for printing. The so-called Liverpool jug or pitcher is one of the most interesting pieces of this ware. See HERCULANEUM.

REFERENCE

Liverpool Wares and Their Identification, ANTIQUES, Nov. - Dec. 1925.

LONGPORT

Longport

In Staffordshire had, and has, many manufactories of both pottery and porcelain. Stoneware, salt-glaze and cream ware, also printed ware were produced here. Of all the factories that of John Davenport and his successors, perhaps, was most prominent. (See DAVENPORT WARE.) At the St. Mary's Works, Moore Brothers produced porcelain rivaling in color and enameling the finest Chinese ware.

REFERENCE

A B C of 19th Century English Ceramic Art, BLACKER.

LONGTON HALL PORCELAIN

Near Stoke-on-Trent, Staffordshire, William Littler, an important figure in the history of English ceramics, who previously had been successful in the manufacture of salt-glaze ware, started making salt-glazed porcelain in 1752, the first Staffordshire porcelain. This porcelain is the only one with a salt-glaze. Two different kinds of paste were used; the first is highly translucent and glossy, like very early Bow, and later the paste is notably heavy with a rather greyish glaze. The under-glaze blue of this ware is its most characteristic feature. No recognized mark is known to have been used at Longton Hall and because of the scarcity of identified pieces, the prices are higher than its artistic merit would warrant. Table service ware was the principal production although some figure pieces were also made. About 1759, William Duesbury purchased the plant and closed it.

REFERENCES

Longton Hall Porcelain, W. BEM-ROSE; *Old English Porcelain*, W. B. HONEY; *Longton Hall Porcelain*, FINE ARTS, May 1932.

Low Art Tile Co.

John G. Low, an art student who had studied in Paris, established a tile factory at Chelsea, Massachusetts, in 1877, and in little more than a year afterwards won a gold medal, over all the manufacturers in England, at an exhibition in Crewe, England. The product of this company is characterized by a marked originality both in style and designs, which has caused it to be extensively imitated at home and abroad. An interesting collection of these tiles is on public view at the Massachusetts Institute of Technology.

Lowesby Ware

This pottery in Leicestershire usually made small ware of red terra cotta, coated with dull black, upon which the design was painted in bright enamel colors. The decoration was probably done in London.

Lowestoft Porcelain

Lowestoft is a small town on the southeast coast of England. Here, in 1757 a factory for making porcelain was established which continued in operation for nearly fifty years. The factory was small; the number of workmen at no time exceeded seventy. The actual Lowestoft productions were chiefly tableware and small objects, sometimes called trifles. It was, at first, decorated mostly after Chinese patterns with blue and white under the glaze, which was of a bluish-green tinge. After 1770 the painting was usually over the glaze. Although the ware resembles old Bow and Worcester, it is inferior in quality to those early porcelains.

All the marked and dated pieces, definitely known as Lowestoft, in English collections are marked as part of the blue and white ornamentation or with numerals, and there are no Lowestoft pieces anywhere with makers' marks and stamps. All are of soft-paste porcelain. After the works were closed in 1803, Robert Allen bought undecorated china from other factories and decorated it at Lowestoft in the Lowestoft manner and continued that work for about thirty years.

Because so-called Lowestoft has been, is now, and probably will continue to be cherished by collectors of porcelain and for the reason that there has been so much controversy and confusion with regard to its provenance, the subject cannot be dismissed in a brief sentence or two. The origin of the controversy may be laid to Chaffers, who, in the first edition of *Marks and Monograms* in 1863, definitely claimed as Lowestoft the hard-paste porcelain table services which had been made to order for English families in the 18th century. It was not until more than thirty years afterwards, that his opinion was disputed.

In the meantime the assertion had been accepted as a fact, and has since been difficult to overcome. The argument has been going on ever since, supported by the fact that all of the so-called Lowestoft in England and here is of hard-paste porcelain, and in spite of the fact that no one has yet proved that hard-paste porcelain was ever made at Lowestoft. Those who deny the Lowestoft origin of this ware assert confidently that it was all made in China and exported from there to England at first, and later to this country, supported in their claims by copies of orders to Chinese manufacturers and invoices covering such orders, still in existence. One writer claims that there is so much of the so-called Lowestoft in existence in England and in this country, even now, that no factory in England was large enough in those days to have produced all of it, making allowance for what must in the meantime have been destroyed.

The Chinese Lowestoft was made at Ching-tê-Chên, and sent to Canton, a distance of nearly 450 miles, where it received its decoration by enamelers who catered to the European and American markets. The decoration on most of the early Lowestoft followed Chinese patterns.

The ware consisted chiefly of table services, much of it decorated with designs sent with the orders, some of it in characteristic Chinese manner. The first of this china arrived in America in 1784, although shipments to England and to other European countries were made much earlier.

REFERENCES

Oriental Lowestoft, J. A. Lloyd Hyde; *Lowestoft Porcelain*, ANTIQUES, June, 1922; *Lowestoft: What Is It?* ANTIQUES, Vols. 13-14-15; *Chinese Lowestoft*, ANTIQUES, Vol. 16, p. 381; *Chinese Lowestoft*, ANTIQUARIAN, Dec. 1930.

LUDWIGSBURG PORCELAIN

A factory was started in Württemberg in 1758 and Ringler, formerly of Vienna, became the active head and remained here for forty years. Well modeled figures and tableware, all finely decorated, were produced. The factory was closed in 1824. This ware is also known as Kronenberg.

REFERENCE

Pottery and Porcelain, HANNOVER.

LUSTRE WARE

This well-known ware was made at

all of the principal potteries in Staffordshire and elsewhere. It is not exactly known when this mode of decoration was first invented. It was introduced into Spain by the Moors in the 7th century, and became an established industry extending into the island of Majorca off the coast of Spain, thence into Italy and France. The ancient lustre pieces were ornamented, not covered, by the lustre as are specimens of more modern times. The composition of the pigment and of the enamel was long carefully guarded. English lustre ware, fine as some of it is, holds no comparison with the old Spanish and Italian wares. Lustrous effects are produced on pottery or porcelain by the application of an exceedingly thin glaze of metal oxides. Lustre ware of the English potteries may be divided into the following classes:

Canary Lustre. This is a ground shade, occasionally used with silver resist.

Copper or Bronze Lustre. The early brown copper lustre was first made about 1770 in Staffordshire, and was improved by Spode's factory, also in Staffordshire. The shade of copper lustre differs considerably, and it was made both plain and undecorated, then in combination with painted designs. It became very popular.

Gold Lustre was probably invented by Josiah Wedgwood about 1792. The effect varies from pink to purple and it was often used as a decoration around the rim of pottery. The term "pink" lustre includes rather generally all types of china that are decorated with any amount of precipitated rose-gold. It was mainly used to ornament tea sets, although it was employed in decorating other wares. This particular kind of lustre ware was manufactured only in England. The Sunderland and New Hall potteries produced the best of this ware, and much of it was made for the American trade.

Silver Lustre was first made in 1791 by applying a solution of platinum chloride, which is subsequently reduced to a metallic deposit on the surface of the pottery. Early ware was lustred inside and outside, but later the lustre was applied only to the outside. Silver lustre "resist" comes into this second period. This ware was made as an imitation of silver ware, and the models follow the designs of the silversmith frequently. The usual ground shade is white, but occasionally canary, buff or blue was the color used.

Silver lustre ranks first in value, followed by the pink lustre of Sunderland. Lustre ware of Leeds and Wedgwood is also highly regarded. The term "self ground" refers to pieces on which the whole or greater part of the surface is covered with the lustre. "Resist" is a term applying to the pattern painted on the surface of the ware in a medium easily soluble in water, such as glycerine. The whole is lustred over and when dry the piece is washed in water, the painted pattern washes off, leaving the pattern on the lustred ground. The ware is then fired to complete the process. "Resist" lustre is considered by many connoisseurs the most artistic type of this class of ware, although this may be disputed, as a matter of taste.

REFERENCES
Collecting Old Lustre Ware, W. BOSANKO; Collecting Old English Lustre, HODGDON; Pink Lustre, ANTIQUES, Dec., 1922; Lustre, ANTIQUARIAN, Aug. 1930.

LYNDEBORO POTTERY

A pottery at Lyndeboro, New Hampshire, founded by Peter Clark in 1775 and continued after his death by his sons. The product was jugs, jars and pots for various purposes. The body was red and the glaze usually of a dark brown color. Specimens of this pottery are rare.

REFERENCE
The Lyndeboro Pottery, ANTIQUES, Feb. 1928.

M

MAASTRICHT POTTERY

Holland pottery established in 1834 by P. Regout. As a potter, he followed English methods, probably employing skilled workmen from England and the production was designed to compete with English earthenware which had become very common in Holland.

REFERENCE
Maastricht Pottery, ANTIQUES, March and April, 1931.

MADELEY PORCELAIN

Made at a factory in Shropshire from about 1827 to 1840 by Thomas Martin Randall, who was a chemist and a good decorator of china. The body was of soft paste, closely resembling the best old Sèvres, creamy in tone and very translucent. Tableware and decorative accessories were the principal products.

The decoration was in the typical French 18th-century manner. The ware was not marked. This was the last soft-paste porcelain made in England and was the nearest approach to old Sèvres ever made.

MAJOLICA

The name is derived from the island of Majorca, off the coast of Spain, and the chief center of the Hispano-Moresque pottery (q.v.) trade with Italy. At first the term was restricted to tin-enameled wares decorated with metallic lustres. The body, usually buff in color and porous, was dipped in the liquid enamel preparation, and after drying the decoration was painted on the absorbent surface. The ware was then covered with the glaze and fired, which fixed the colors. The earliest example of this ware that is known was executed by Luca della Robbia in 1438. Strictly speaking the term should only be applied to Italian wares, although it is often used to describe other wares decorated in the Italian manner. The best known of the old Italian factories are Gubbio (q.v.), Faenza (q.v.), and Urbino (q.v.), with many others of good reputation.

REFERENCES

Italian Ceramic Art, H. WALLIS; *Majolica and Fayence*, ARTHUR BECKWITH; *A History and Description of Italian Majolica*, M. L. SOLON; *Early Italian Majolica*, ANTIQUARIAN, June 1930.

MARKS

On earthenware the marks, if any, are made either with a metal stamp, impressed in the ware while in a plastic state, or by painted or printed marks. Both methods may be regarded as genuine "marks" on old pieces, provided they are under the glaze. The classification of English porcelain of the 18th century is made difficult by frequent absence of factory marks, and by evidence that the marks of the larger factories were often copied by their minor rivals. According to Litchfield an exaggerated value is placed upon the "mark." This should be used as a confirmation of other points of evidence that the piece is genuine, rather than the evidence itself. No marks whatever were used on early American pottery. It was not until early in the 19th century that wares of some of the potters were marked, and until Barber compiled a partial list in his *Pottery and Porcelain of the United States*, no attempt was made to record them.

REFERENCES

Marks and Monograms on Pottery and Porcelain of the Renaissance and Modern Periods, CHAFFERS—Ed. by LITCHFIELD; *Handbook of Marks on Pottery and Porcelain*, BURTON and HOBSON.

MARL

A term loosely applied to mixtures of clay and limestone. Much used in the early composition of earthenware.

MARSEILLES WARE

As early as 1607-10 Marseilles became an important center, noted for its manufacture of faience. It is distinguished for its graceful shapes and artistic modeling. There are still potteries in the vicinity. A hard-paste porcelain factory was started about 1776 but it was discontinued in 1793. The production of the later years had a white body, a good, clear glaze and was well decorated with flowers in the manner of Mennecy and Sèvres.

MASON WARE

MILES
MASON

Produced at a factory established at Lane Delph, Staffordshire, by Miles

Mason in the 18th century and continued by his son, Charles Mason. The ware is generally in the character of Oriental porcelain although the paste bears no resemblance. The coloring was in reds and blues, and some enriched with gilding. The factory also produced printed ware and excellent enameled ware. See IRONSTONE CHINA.

MAZARINE BLUE

The origin of the name is doubtful. There may be a disputed connection of Cardinal Mazarin with it. It is the "gros-bleu" of Sèvres and the dark blue of Chelsea, and resembles the "powdered" blue of Oriental porcelain, although the ground is solid. Powdered blue is blown, not brushed, upon the body of the piece, before glazing and firing, leaving a mottled appearance.

MEDICI PORCELAIN
    See FLORENCE.

MEHWALDT WARE

An American pottery located at Bergholtz, near Niagara Falls, established about 1851 by Charles Mehwaldt, a German who came to this country because of the political unrest in Germany at that time. Mehwaldt was a master potter and he came of a long line of potters. The ware was of a reddish-brown color mottled with dark spots, lead-glazed, and somewhat resembles the ware of the Bennington potteries, although it lacks the hard metallic glaze of Bennington; it is of same coloring.

The production was chiefly ware for domestic use. The works were destroyed following Mehwaldt's death in 1887.

REFERENCE
    Mehwaldt, ANTIQUES, Sept. 1922.

MEISSEN PORCELAIN
    See DRESDEN.

MENNECY PORCELAIN

A factory producing porcelain of soft paste, established about 1735, famous for its production of small objects such as figurines, animals, toilet boxes and cream pots. The paste is of a creamy color, the glaze and potting both good. The decorations were in landscapes, birds and flowers. Borders were in blue instead of gold. Specimens are among the rarest of the early French porcelains. Factory was closed about 1774.

REFERENCE
    Practical Book of Chinaware, EBERLEIN and RAMSDELL.

MIDDLESBROUGH POTTERY
    See LINTHORPE ART POTTERY.

MINTON WARE

Made at a pottery started in 1798 at Stoke-on-Trent, Staffordshire, by Thomas Minton. At first he made only earthenware and his blue and white

American Blown Glass Decanters—The Keene Olive Amber Decanter in Center
Is One of the Rarest of Three-mold Pieces

Sandwich Whale Oil Lamps and Stiegel Type Mug

IRISH CUT GLASS, LATE 18TH AND EARLY 19TH CENTURIES

ware in imitation of Nankin porcelain was very popular. True porcelain was not made here until 1821, although a semi-translucent ware had been produced about twenty years earlier. The paste of the porcelain was soft and white and the work was always refined, sometimes beautiful. Parian ware (q.v.), a feature of the Copeland (Spode) factories, also of Bennington in this country, is said to have been an invention of the Minton potteries. Thomas Minton died in 1836 and the works were then carried on by his son Herbert. The most marked improvement in Minton porcelain dates from 1851 under the management of Campbell, a nephew of Herbert Minton, and Arnoux, the art director. A new body of special softness and whiteness was introduced and the decoration was in the style of Sèvres. In 1870, M. L. Solon went from Sèvres to the Minton factory where under his direction the pâte-sur-pâte form of decoration was perfected. The factory is still in existence.

REFERENCE
A B C of 19th Century English Ceramic Art, BLACKER.

MOLDS
Molds of plaster of Paris were introduced into the potteries in 1743 by Ralph Daniel of Cobridge. They have since been used in the manufacture of all wares except such as are "thrown."

MUFFLE
A small enclosed kiln for trial purposes for firing enamel colors at a temperature insufficient to disturb the first painting.

MUSKINGUM COUNTY (Ohio) POTTERS
Numerous small potteries were included in this district early in the 19th century, and the following years, producing red, brown and yellow earthenware for domestic use. Experienced potters from Staffordshire reproduced the forms familiar in England. None of these potteries used identifying marks.

REFERENCE
ANTIQUES, July 1924.

N

NANTGARW PORCELAIN

NANT-GARW
C. W.

A soft-paste porcelain, containing a considerable portion of bone ash, produced at Nantgarw, Wales, from 1813 to 1822, of a beautiful white tint and clear glaze. It was painted with tinted grounds in many different colors and with birds and flowers in their natural colors. The factory was started by William Billingsley, the flower painter, who worked successively at Derby, Worcester, Pinxton, Nantgarw, Swansea and Coalport, which helps to explain why the decorations of different factories so closely resemble each other. Nantgarw porcelain is highly translucent, but it was apt to collapse in the kiln, making it costly to produce. A great deal of spurious Nantgarw china is to be found. Any mark not impressed in the paste should be avoided.

REFERENCES

The Ceramics of Swansea and Nantgarw, Turner; Old English Porcelain, W. B. Honey.

Naples Porcelain

A soft-paste porcelain was made here about 1736. See Capo-di-Monte.

Nashua (New Hampshire) Pottery

Established by Martin Krafts in 1838 and continued for six years. Salt-glazed stoneware in the form of jugs and jars with blue decoration was made there.

Newcastle Ware

At Newcastle-on-Tyne from about 1777 to 1825 were made the familiar mugs and jugs with ships in black transfer decoration and with verses appropriate for the sailors for whom they were made. One of the potteries also made blue-printed ware equal to the best Staffordshire. Newcastle ware and Sunderland ware (q.v.) are frequently classed together. Numerous modern potteries carry on the Newcastle tradition.

REFERENCE

A B C of 19th Century English Ceramic Art, Blacker.

New England Pottery

The earlier New England earthenware, though humble and crude, was quaint and not lacking in decorative qualities. Made from local clay, by local potters, for local use, it had that handmade look that appeals to us. No pottery of consequence was made here until after the middle of the 18th century, and the most significant part of the history of American ceramics lies in the early 19th century.

Two kinds of earthenware were produced in New England, red ware first, then stoneware. The former was lead-glazed and decorated, more or less, in colored slip. The stoneware was grey in body and harder than the red ware. Decoration and forms were all English in type. Connecticut, where stoneware only was produced, seems to have led in number and output of potteries. Peabody, Massachusetts, became a center of the industry. Then, of course, Bennington, Vermont (q.v.) takes a leading place.

A terra-cotta works started in Weston, Massachusetts, by A. H. Hews about 1765, produced bean pots, milk pans, jugs and other red earthenware. None of the early earthenware bore a distinguishing mark, so that it is extremely difficult to identify any particular potter. See Pottery.

REFERENCE

Early Pottery in New England, ANTIQUES, Jan. 1922.

New England Pottery Company

Started in 1854 at Cambridge, Massachusetts, making Rockingham and yellow ware. In 1875 L. W. Clark assumed control and began making cream-colored and white granite ware. The pottery also made, later, porcelain of admirable quality and style and decorated in mazarine blue and old ivory.

New Geneva (Pennsylvania) Pottery

Established in 1849 and continued for about fifty years. Grey stoneware with blue decoration for household purposes was made there. A ridged collar was characteristic of this ware. See Greensboro.

REFERENCE
New Geneva Pottery, ANTIQUARIAN, Sept. 1931.

New Hall Porcelain

A hard-paste milk-white porcelain, very translucent, was made at this factory at Shelton in Staffordshire, by a group of Staffordshire potters who bought the patent rights of Richard Champion when he closed the Bristol works in 1781. Only useful ware, generally tea services, was made and the decoration was mostly floral with occasional figure subjects. Their pink lustre tea sets are the triumph of the lustre potters' art. The factory was started about 1780 and closed in 1825.

New York Pottery

The earliest potteries in New York were those of William Crolius and John Remmey, both of these located on Manhattan Island just north of the present City Hall. The product of these potteries was stoneware, consisting chiefly of jugs, jars, pots and other similar household ware. See Crolius Ware and Remmey Ware.

Norton Stoneware Co.
See Bennington.

Norwich (Connecticut) Pottery

Founded about 1836 by Sidney Risley, who continued to operate the pottery until his death in 1875. Stoneware crocks, pitchers, jugs and bottles were the principal products. In later years some glazed and decorated ware was added to the lines. The pottery was discontinued in 1895.

REFERENCE
The Norwich Pottery Works, ANTIQUES, Oct. 1923.

Nottingham Ware

English stoneware late 17th to early 19th century. Earliest dated piece 1700. The color of the body is a warm, reddish-brown and the salt-glaze is decidedly lustrous in appearance. It is smoother in its surface than old Staffordshire, and it is a species of stoneware highly regarded. What are known as "bear" jugs were a feature of Nottingham stoneware, although not peculiar to that pottery.

Nuremberg Ware

Nuremberg is said to have been the

pioneer in the manufacture of majolica in Germany. Large tiles of dark copper-green with subjects in relief, used for the earthenware stoves in vogue early in the 16th century, were produced there. From that time to the present day there have been many potteries at Nuremberg.

Nymphenburg Porcelain

This porcelain was made at a factory in Bavaria established in 1747. The work of Bustelli, a modeler from 1754 to 1763, was exceedingly good. The products of this factory were of great beauty and they are highly prized at the present time.

REFERENCE

Pottery and Porcelain, Hannover.

O

Opaque China

See Semi-China.

Oriental Lowestoft

See Lowestoft.

Orleans (France) Porcelain

In 1753, a factory for the manufacture of soft-paste porcelain was established here. The body was very translucent, white in color and of beautiful quality. In 1770, following the fashion of other French factories, the soft paste was discontinued for the more durable, but less beautiful hard paste. The ground color of this porcelain is nearly always white and the decoration carefully painted. It may readily be taken for late Sèvres. The factory was closed early in the 19th century.

REFERENCE

Pottery and Porcelain, Frederick Litchfield.

Orvieto Ware

A pottery at Orvieto, Italy, in the early decades of the 15th century produced a grey earthenware, lightly painted in purple or green with a transparent lead glaze, which preceded and prepared the way for majolica (q.v.).

Oven

There are three principal ovens: the biscuit oven, which is to harden the piece; the "glost" oven for firing the glaze and the under-glaze decoration; and the enamel oven, called kiln, for fixing the over-glaze decoration. For jasper ware or unglazed stoneware, etc., the biscuit state is the final one. The ware to be fired is placed in "saggers" (q.v.) before going to the oven. See Glost Oven and Kiln.

Over-Glaze

The term applies to painted or printed decoration on pottery, done after the glaze has been applied and fired. The over-glaze is then fired at a lesser heat than is required for the glaze, to fix the colors.

P

Painting

Pottery and porcelain were painted in colors very early. In Europe, at first, it followed the styles of the Oriental artists but by 1740, Herold, an artist at Meissen, had created a distinctive European style in porcelain painting which was copied by other porcelain factories. Distinctive English styles were developed at Bow, Chelsea, Derby and Worcester. The Chelsea factory was pre-eminent in most respects, although during the Dr. Wall period at Worcester there is an especially English quality which endears it to the collector. Pottery painting was common during the same period at Staffordshire and other earthenware factories. All colors applied to pottery or porcelain are mineral, not vegetable.

Parian Ware

This is a hard-paste unglazed porcelain which resembles marble. It differs from "biscuit" only in being fused at a lower temperature. It is said to have been originated by Thomas Minton, but it was a leading product of the Spode (Copeland) factory about 1840, and of Bennington in this country a little later. It is superior to the ordinary "biscuit" formerly used for busts and figures. As a rule, the proportions of these are graceful and the decorations delicate.

Reference

Bennington Cameo Parian, ANTIQUES, Sept. 1929.

Paste

The name given to the body of the ware. There are two kinds; soft paste, made of a mixture of various materials, and hard paste, made of natural clay. Earthenware and artifical porcelain are of soft paste; stoneware, ironstone china and modern porcelain are of hard paste. Since about 1800 the manufacture of porcelain has been altered by the mixture of bone ash and some other materials and true hard-paste porcelain is not now made. See Bone China.

Pâte-sur-Pâte

A method somewhat similar to the slip process, of applying the decoration in plastic form upon the unbaked body of the piece, one thickness being laid on another until the desired strength is obtained, after which the pieces are fired. It was a form of decoration used at Sèvres about 1850 and afterwards perfected by M. L. Solon. It is to be seen in the modern work of the Minton factory in England where Mr. Solon worked for over thirty years, and of the Rookwood factory in Cincinnati. This form of decoration had its origin in China.

Pennsylvania Slip Ware

This slip ware was the first decorated pottery to be made in this country. It was made on a dark-red, brownish clay by the early German settlers in Pennsylvania, who brought their methods and designs from the home country, from the first quarter of the 18th century through a period of more than a hundred years. The slip consisted of a white or light-colored clay and it was either applied to the surface of the ware and then fired, or the design was scratched through the slip (sgraffiato), exposing the brown clay body, before the piece was fired. Sometimes color was added by a brush. This ware was for household use and it was never made in large quantities. The Pennsylvania Museum in Philadelphia has a collection of about 150 pieces of this ware. Slip ware was made in other of the American colonies to some extent, but it obtained most prominence in Pennsylvania.

REFERENCES

Lead Glazed Pottery, ANTIQUARIAN, Nov. 1929; *Pennsylvania Slip Ware*, ANTIQUARIAN, Nov. 1929.

Persian Ceramics

Some of the earliest Persian pottery, with a body of red clay covered with a lead glaze, shows signs of lustre in the decoration. The time of highest excellence was in the 16th and 17th centuries. The decoration of Persian ware is generally floral and the coloring very artistic and striking.

REFERENCE

Persian Ceramics, ANTIQUARIAN, Aug. 1931.

Petuntse

China stone (q.v.). A partially decomposed granite containing some feldspar, used with kaolin for making porcelain.

Phoenixville (Pennsylvania) Pottery

Organized in 1867. Between 1880 and 1890 Griffen, Smith and Hill operated the pottery and made a good grade of Etruscan Majolica. A great deal of care was taken in the molding and the colors used were perfectly blended. An English artist named Bourne was the designer. The quality and beauty of this ware make it desirable for collectors of ceramics. It consisted not only of tableware but vases and various fancy-shaped pieces were also produced. The factory was destroyed by fire in 1890.

Pink Lustre

See Lustre Ware, Gold.

Pinxton Porcelain

Pinxton.

A small factory was started here in Derbyshire in 1796 by John Coke, which produced some fine pieces, similar to Derby porcelain and generally unmarked. Many of the workmen were from Derby. Some of the ware was even whiter and more translucent than Derby, due to William Billingsley, who was with Coke at the time and who had invented a soft-paste porcelain of great translucency. Some has the glassy body afterwards made at Nantgarw, where Billingsley was subsequently employed. The works were closed in 1812. Identified specimens of Pinxton porcelain are comparatively rare, as no mark was in general use.

REFERENCE

Pottery and Porcelain, FREDERICK LITCHFIELD.

PIPKIN

A small earthen pot or jug. See PART 5.

PITCHERS

LUSTRE   STAFFORDSHIRE

See JUGS.

PLAQUE

A medallion or disc of porcelain used as a decorative feature on furniture. In the late 18th century placques of jasper ware, as made by Wedgwood, were inserted on cabinets, commodes, etc.

PLASTER OF PARIS MOLDS

See MOLDS.

PLYMOUTH (England) PORCELAIN

Factory established before 1768 by William Cookworthy, a chemist, produced the first English porcelain to be made from native ingredients; also, this factory was the first to produce cobalt blue from the ore. The product was of hard paste with a milky white color, possessing all the qualities that good, hard-paste porcelain should have, and a fine glaze, although sometimes imperfect, due to imperfect firing. The decoration was in red and blue in the Chinese style and with birds and flowers.

The product consisted of tableware, excellent figures and groups, and some admirable vases. Much of the decoration was in under-glaze blue. The plant was sold to Richard Champion about 1770 and removed to Bristol. It is difficult to distinguish Plymouth China from that of Bristol (q.v.). Plymouth porcelain more nearly approaches true Oriental porcelain than that of any other English factory.

PORCELAIN

All porcelain, broadly speaking, is divided into two classes, namely: hard-paste porcelain and soft-paste porcelain. Hard paste is made from a mixture of kaolin and china stone (petuntse), it can not be scratched, it is cold to the touch and it has a bell-like ring when struck. It resists water and fire and all acids excepting hydrofluoric. The colors used in decoration seem to remain on the surface. In China the body and the glaze are fired at one operation as a rule. All Oriental china and all modern china is of hard paste.

It was first successfully produced in Europe at Meissen in Saxony in 1709 and later in England. Since about 1800, owing to the mixture of bone ash with the other ingredients, "true" hard-paste porcelain has not been made. Porcelain is fired at the highest heat of any pottery. The colors used in decorating are of two kinds, the under-glaze colors applied before glazing and firing, and the enamel colors and gold applied after glazing. These last require a second firing at a low heat to make them permanent.

Soft-paste porcelain is made by mixing white clay with "frit" (q.v.) or some other substance to give it translucency. It was first made in Florence in 1568 but its great development came in England and France in the 18th century. Soft paste can be scratched, it is warmer than hard paste to the hand, and the colors used in decoration sink in so that the effect is softer. The soft paste was the most perfect vehicle ever achieved for decorating, far more so than the hard paste. Soft-paste porcelain is very fragile, liable to crack at the touch of hot liquids, and to lose shape in firing, although these obstacles were overcome to some extent by the use of soapstone.

The productions of the English factories of the 18th century were of soft paste, excepting those of Bristol, New Hall and Plymouth. The most interesting were those made between 1744, when porcelain was first produced in England, and 1800. Early Sèvres porcelain was of soft paste but its later productions are all of hard paste.

REFERENCES
Porcelain, EDWARD DILLON; *Pottery and Porcelain*, FREDERICK LITCH-FIELD; *Porcelain of All Countries*, R. L. HOBSON.

American Porcelain. Not until 1769 was there any serious attempt to manufacture china (porcelain) on this side of the Atlantic. This was in Philadelphia and the projectors of the enterprise were G. Bonnin, who probably learned his trade at Bow, and George A. Morris. The attempt proved to be a financial failure after running a few years, and Bonnin returned to England. No examples of the porcelain made there are known, although some pieces of white cream ware, similar to delft, have been identified as their work. Porcelain was made in New York early in the 19th century, probably by Dr. Mead. How long this factory was in operation is not known, but it is believed that a fine grade of ware was made there of American materials. A vase, fifteen inches in height, of soft paste and exceedingly white glaze but without gilding or coloring, from this factory is in the Pennsylvania Museum.

William Ellis Tucker of Philadelphia has the honor of being the first to supply the home market with a strictly American product. In partnership with a son of Judge Joseph Hemphill, he established the American China Manufactory about 1831. The following year Tucker died and Judge Hemphill took over the business. Artists and artisans were brought from England, France and Germany. Sèvres forms were successfully copied and some of their ware has been sold in recent years for French work. The factory was discontinued in 1838. Since that time several porcelain factories have been established in various parts of the country, notably at Trenton, New Jersey, with the object of producing here more or less successfully ware fully equal in every respect to any that can be made abroad.

REFERENCES

Pottery and Porcelain of the United States, BARBER; Early American Pottery and China, SPARGO; Tucker and Hemphill Porcelain Works, ANTIQUES, June 1928; Philadelphia Porcelain by WOODHOUSE, ANTIQUES, Oct. 1933; Footnote to Tucker History, ANTIQUES, Oct. 1936.

Austrian Porcelain. See VIENNA (Austria) PORCELAIN.

Chinese Porcelain. It is not known when porcelain was first made in China, but it has been identified in some of the productions of the Sung dynasty 960-1229. Plain white porcelain known as blanc-de-Chine and blue and white were produced from the earliest period down to modern times. The blanc-de-Chine ware of the Ming dynasty was held in great esteem and all of the factories in Europe tried to copy it. There was never any soft-paste porcelain made in China. The so-called later wares followed from the fall of the Ming dynasty in 1644. They were made principally at the imperial factory at Ching-tê-Chên and include the K'ang Hsi (1662-1722) blue and white ware, the Yung Chêng (1723-1735) and the Ch'ien Lung (1736-1795) porcelains of a high standard of merit in technical perfection, in grace and variety of forms produced and beauty of decoration.

CHINESE PORCELAIN FORMS

The height of excellence may be said to have been attained in the K'ang Hsi period. To this period belong those beautiful self-colored pieces produced from metallic oxides in a variety of tints, of which sang-de-boeuf is an example. The introduction of flambé, or splashed colors, was also of this period. Decorations on Chinese porcelain are largely symbolic. The colors include Famille Verte (green), Famille Jaune (yellow) Famille Rose, Famille Noire (black) and powdered blue, all in great demand by collectors.

A good deal of white porcelain was imported into Europe and there decorated, in England, France, Italy, Holland and Germany. Some of the so-called Lowestoft is of this kind. The first Chinese porcelain brought to this country was from Canton to New York in 1784, and followed soon after by that brought by Elias Hasket Derby in the ship "Grand Turk" to Salem, Mass.

REFERENCES

> Chinese Porcelain, W. G. GULLAND; Chats on Oriental China, J. F. BLACKER; The Later Ceramic Wares of China, R. L. HOBSON; Chinese Porcelain, MONKHOUSE; Chinese Armorial Porcelain, ANTIQUES, Aug. 1928; Legend and Romance in Chinese Porcelain, ANTIQUES, Dec. 1933.

Danish Porcelain. See COPENHAGEN.

Dutch Porcelain. See AMSTEL, and HAGUE.

English Porcelain. From the collector's point of view, the history of English porcelain begins with the foundation of the Bow factory in 1744 and ends with the Rockingham factory which began to make porcelain in 1820. The obscurity which surrounds their early history may be accounted for by the fact that these factories were all private ventures, started for commercial purposes. In France and Germany much of the production was under royal patronage.

In all seventeen factories were started, viz.:

Bow	(1744-1775)
Chelsea	(1745-1770)
Longton Hall	(1752-1758)
Worcester	(1751-)
Derby	(1756-1849)
Lowestoft	(1756-1803)
Plymouth	(1768-1770)
Chelsea-Derby	(1770-1784)
Bristol	(1770-1781)
Caughley	(1772-1814)
New Hall	(1780-1825)
Coalport	(1790-)
Pinxton	(1796-1812)
Spode	(1800-)
Nantgarw	(1811-1822)
Swansea	(1814-1824)
Rockingham	(1820-1842)

Each of these factories is described under its respective alphabetical heading. Almost all of the production of the English porcelain factories in the 18th century was of soft paste, the only exceptions being the factories at Bristol, New Hall and Plymouth.

REFERENCES

A History and Description of English

Porcelain, BURTON; *English Porcelain*, CHURCH; *Ceramic Art of Great Britain from Prehistoric Times to the Present Day*, JEWITT; *Old English Porcelain*, HONEY; *Powdered Blue in English Porcelain*, ANTIQUES, Jan. 1928; *The First Century of English Porcelain*, BINNS.

French Porcelain. The history of porcelain-making in France begins about 1673 when a factory was started at Rouen (q.v.). A few specimens of this early product still survive. This factory was followed with one at St. Cloud (q.v.), Chantilly (q.v.), Sèvres (q.v.), Vincennes (q.v.) and others, and France has taken a leading part in the production of porcelain of high quality and artistic merit since that time. The production of Haviland at Limoges is one of the best of modern porcelains.

REFERENCES

Practical Book of Chinaware, EBERLEIN and RAMSDELL; *Pottery and Porcelain*, FREDERICK LITCHFIELD.

German Porcelain. To Germany must be given the credit for discovering and introducing into Europe the art of making true hard-paste porcelain of the Chinese type. The invention of Böttger in 1709 paved the way for the establishment of the famous Meissen factory near Dresden (q.v.). Excellent work was done in their best periods by several other German factories; Berlin (q.v.),

Frankenthal (q.v.), Fürstenberg were among the most prominent. The German factories in particular excelled in the development of sculpture in porcelain, inaugurated at Meissen. This was extensively copied in the earliest English china-works. Nearly all German porcelain of the 18th century was made under the ownership and control of the rulers of the various countries and they, of course, had first choice of the products.

REFERENCES

Pottery and Porcelain, FREDERICK LITCHFIELD; *Dresden China*, W. B. HONEY.

Italian Porcelain. Although there is evidence that experiments in making porcelain were made at Venice as early as the first quarter of the 16th century, there are no known examples remaining. Towards the end of the century porcelain was successfully made at Florence (q.v.), specimens of which still survive. Porcelain is not heard of again in Italy until the 18th century, at which time factories were established at Doccia (q.v.), Capo-di-Monte (q.v.), and Venice (q.v.), also at Nove, Vinovo, Este and Treviso.

Japanese Porcelain. The early porcelain of Japan, which dates from early in the 16th century, is of a very hard paste, the ground has a bluish tint and the decoration is very striking and effective in coloring and design. Figure subjects are not common, but one finds representations of the crane, emblem of prosperity, of the tortoise, emblem of longevity, the phoenix, the lion and other animals, as well as birds and fishes of different kinds. Landscapes rarely occur although floral subjects are common. Porcelain in Japan developed under Chinese influence. The decoration of Japanese china brought to Europe by the Dutch in the 17th century influenced the earliest decorations on Meissen, Chelsea, Bow, Derby, Worcester, St. Cloud, Chantilly and other European China. See Imari Ware.

REFERENCE

Keramic Art of Japan, AUDSLEY and BOWES.

Russian Porcelain. The early porcelain of the Imperial factory established at St. Petersburg in 1758 was of a hard paste with a bluish tint and distinctly Russian. During the reign of Catherine II the influence of Meissen and Sèvres is noticed. From about the time of the reign of Czar Alexander I until the Revolution, the entire output of the factory was taken by the court for its own use and for diplomatic gifts. The Imperial factory served as a model for a number of privately owned potteries, of which in 1800 there were about twenty in operation. By 1861, the number had increased to about seventy. The porcelain of the Imperial factory and to a certain extent that of the private potteries reflect the culture of Western Europe rather than the native Russian taste. The figurines of Russian racial types, however, constitute a striking and original contribution to ceramic art. Russian porcelain has been well received by collectors in this country, and it makes an interesting addition to the antique china here obtainable.

REFERENCE

Imperial Russian Porcelain, ANTIQUES, Jan. 1933.

Spanish Porcelain. See BUEN RETIRO.

PORTLAND VASE

For an account of this famous glass vase see PART 3. In 1787 Wedgwood made copies of this vase in pottery, and as an example of modern ceramic art they could not be excelled.

PORTO BELLO WARE

The name given to a white, salt-glazed ware probably made by Astbury in honor of the capture of Porto Bello from Spain by Captain William Vernon in 1739.

POSSET-POT

See TYG.

POTTER'S WHEEL

This wheel, which was used from ancient times until well into the 19th century, consisted of a perpendicular beam about two feet in height, on top of which was a circular disc about a foot in diameter. At the bottom of the beam was a horizontal wooden wheel, four feet across, with four inclined spokes which extended from the beam to the rim of the wheel, which the workman pushed around with his feet, rotating the disc. This contrivance was called a "kick-wheel." A great advance was made later by the introduction of the "throwing-wheel" (q.v.). At the present time a kick-wheel operated by a treadle with the left foot is still used in some of the smaller potteries.

REFERENCE
ANTIQUES, Jan. 1931.

POTTERY

Pottery is the oldest of the arts and in all ages reflects the condition of every branch of art. The term may be applied to all kinds of earthenware but the usual modern distinction is to apply it to ware that is opaque when it comes from the kiln or oven. There are three stages incident to the production of all pottery. The clay state, before the ware has been fired at all; the biscuit state, when the ware has been passed through the oven and fired once; and the glazed state, after the ware has been covered with the glaze and fired a second time. All under-glaze colors or printing are applied to the biscuit before the second firing. If enamel or other decoration is applied over the glaze, the ware is subjected to another firing at a comparatively low heat in the enamel kiln.

REFERENCES
Pottery and Porcelain, FREDERICK LITCHFIELD; The Art of the Old English Potter, M. L. SOLON.

American Pottery. One writer on the subject says that "the history of pottery in this country is pathetic, for while it has had some triumphs, it has worked against an almost inert public opinion. Its votaries have had little but poverty to compensate them." This was probably true, at least, until after the middle of the 19th century, when American enterprise succeeded in overcoming the obstacles to success. The earliest pottery in this country producing white ware, of which there is definite record, was that of Dr. Daniel Coxe, erected at Burlington, New Jersey, previous to the year 1685. Its exact location as a pottery is not known. A stoneware factory was started in New York in 1735 and continued there until 1820, at which time it was removed to South Amboy, New Jersey.

During the latter half of the 18th century many small potteries were started in the German settlements in Eastern Pennsylvania, where slip ware and sgraffiato had been produced before the middle of the century, and several potteries were also started in New England and elsewhere. The ware was crude and largely anonymous, but plain and simple though it was, it brings us closer than almost anything else to the early American pioneer. The bulk of this product was ware for domestic use, adding to the tableware imported from England and France. During the first half of the 19th century many potteries such as Bennington and those in the Ohio River Valley were established, which will be found described under their respective headings. Several of the more important potteries of the last half of the 19th century are also given space. See NEW ENGLAND POTTERY.

REFERENCES

Early American Craftsmen, WALTER A. DYER; Early American Pottery and China, JOHN SPARGO; Pottery and Porcelain of the United States, BARBER; The Methods of Early American Potters, ANTIQUES, April 1924; Early American Pottery—A Resumé, ANTIQUES, Oct. 1931; Marks of American Potters, E. A. BARBER.

Chinese Pottery. The discovery of the secrets of the manufacture of pottery in China is doubtless of great antiquity. Very probably, the Chinese acquired the processes gradually, resulting in a

certain degree of excellence while the world elsewhere was yet young. Chinese pottery differs from any other in the density of the paste, and translucency, with few exceptions, is absent. A kind of decoration peculiar to the Chinese is the crackle (q.v.). Chinese ceramics are bound up with the history, the literature, the mythology of this ancient people, and the whole range is so extensive as to require a lot of study to understand its significance. See CELADON WARE.

REFERENCE

Art of the Chinese Potter, HOBSON and HETHERINGTON.

English Pottery. The products of early English earthenware potteries have an interest for collectors little less in importance than that connected with early English porcelain. The art of the old English potters is of special interest to students of ceramic art, as many processes were invented by them and English earthenware has won for itself a healthy recognition everywhere, from a technical point of view. Examples in existence of the work of the medieval potter, and of the early Staffordshire potters particularly, show a constant striving to improve their wares. The earliest date which appears on any piece of pottery of undoubted English make is 1571.

The factories were so many and the potters who achieved fame and reputation so numerous, that it is a practical impossibility to attempt to enumerate them here. It will suffice to say that the standards set by Wedgwood were never surpassed by potters anywhere, and that no other pottery district in the world became so conspicuous for quality and quantity of production as Staffordshire (q.v.). The practical potters of England succeeded in creating by gradual improvements a ware so superior that all Europe was influenced and benefited by their work. The work of the potters of the 19th century is not less important. Doulton (q.v.) and Minton (q.v.) products are wonderful wares, resembling no others, and many other potteries produced fine wares which won their way by sheer merit into all of the world's markets. See EARTHENWARE.

REFERENCES

Chats on Old Earthenware, HAYDEN; Ceramic Art of Great Britain, JEWITT; Art of the Old English Potter, SOLON; Staffordshire Pots and Potters, RHEAD; Josiah Wedgwood, Master-Potter, CHURCH; The Heritage of the Great English Potters, ANTIQUARIAN, April 1930. A B C of 19th Century English Ceramic Art, BLACKER.

French Pottery. It is known that tin-enameled and slip-decorated pottery was made at Nevers, Rouen, and at various other places in France but very few pieces have been preserved, among which may be found a few of sgraffiato work. The earliest tin-enameled pottery was made by Italian potters in imitation of majolica, but gradually a national style was produced by French potters who succeeded them. Painting by these potters is more carefully executed and includes a wider range of colors. They never used a lead glaze over the enamel. See ROUEN.

German Pottery. Tin-enameled pottery (q.v.) was produced extensively in various parts of Germany toward the end of the 17th century and through the 18th. Its principal features are a soft body and preponderance of purple and blue in the decorations. Tureens, wine jugs, beer mugs, plates and dishes were among the product. Sgraffiato ware (q.v.) was also produced in Germany more than two hundred years ago. Slip-decorated pottery was even earlier. The tulip was the favorite subject of decoration. See PENNSYLVANIA SLIP WARE.

Japanese Pottery. It is uncertain when Pottery was first made in Japan, but it is probable that potters from Korea were at work in Japan early in the Christian era, and while to China is awarded the first place in porcelain, Japan took and held the lead in pottery. The Japanese were and are potters without rivals. Suitable clays for pottery were found in many parts of Japan. The tea ceremony and the burning of incense required a great variety of pieces. Amongst all the pottery Satsuma (q.v.), buff in color with a finely crackled glaze and decorated in gold and colors, takes first place. Genuine pieces of old Satsuma are rare, but imitations are plentiful.

Spanish Pottery. See HISPANO-MORESQUE WARE.

PRATT WARE

Made by Staffordshire potters of that name, of which there have been six generations. Felix Pratt, probably the third of that name, worked from about 1780 to 1820 and his product takes a high place in modeling, color and glaze. He made vases and jugs, and white stoneware with blue figures in relief. See FENTON WARE.

PRINTING

See TRANSFER-PRINTING.

PUG MILL

A bowl-shaped vessel with a shaft having protruding knives used for grinding clay. A horse hitched to a beam walked around and around, revolving the knives. Water was mixed with the clay to give it the right consistency.

PUZZLE JUG

Perforated with holes or fretted patterns which made it impossible to take a draught of liquor without spilling it unless the drinker understood the trick. One or more of the holes would have to be covered with the fingertip.

Q

QUEEN's WARE

About 1760 Wedgwood improved the then recently new cream ware, and he presented to Queen Charlotte of England a decorated breakfast service of his new product. She was much pleased with the ware and ordered complete table services of it and Wedgwood, in her honor, gave it the name of "Queen's Ware."

R

REMMEY WARE

The name given to heavy stoneware made at the Remmey pottery in New York in the 18th century. This ware is heavier than the Crolius ware (q.v.), also a New York product. It has a semi-glazed surface in blended brown colorings with but little attempt at decoration.

RESIST

A term common to several crafts, in general meaning a method of decorating by coating a background with a soluble film, which is later removed, so that the actual decoration will be retained only where desired. Here the term is often used to describe silver lustre ware made by a resist process, with the ground of

AMERICAN PRESSED GLASS COMPOTES, 19TH CENTURY

SANDWICH GLASS COMPOTES, 19TH CENTURY

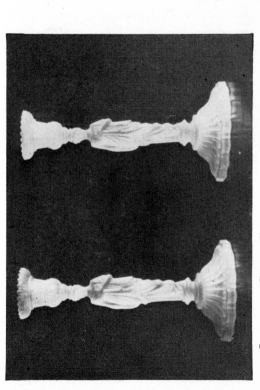

SANDWICH GLASS CANDLESTICKS, 19TH CENTURY

RARE STIEGEL COBALT BLUE GLASS VASE,
18TH CENTURY

BLUE FLINT GLASS SUGAR BOWL AND
COVER. AMERICAN, EARLY 19TH CENTURY

SOUTH JERSEY TYPE BLUE PITCHER, CIRCA 1800

STODDARD AMBER GLASS LILY-PAD PITCHER
MID-19TH CENTURY

platinum (silver) and the ornamentation in white or color. See LUSTRE WARE.

REVERBERATORY FURNACE

This is a kiln so constructed that ceramics fired in it do not come into direct contact with the fuel. The flame goes over a fire bridge of brick and is reflected or reverberated on the material beneath.

RIDGWAY WARE

Job Ridgway, the founder, one of Wedgwood's apprentices, started in business in 1794 at Shelton, Staffordshire, and in 1802 built the works known as Cauldon Place. Later, the businesses of several others of the Staffordshire potters were combined with this factory. Ridgway made a good grade of earthenware similar in many respects to ironstone china, and also made porcelain of excellent quality. The firm flourished, especially during the management of John Ridgway, son of the founder, from 1814 to 1855. During that time they made a set of dark blue design called "Beauties of America" with a border of rose-leaf medallions.

ROCKINGHAM WARE

This ware was first made at a factory located at Swinton, England, established in 1757 by Edward Butler. It took its name from the Marquis of Rock-

ingham, on whose property the factory was located, and the cream ware made

there, covered with a heavy lead glaze richly and warmly colored in brown, became very popular and was copied by other English potters. The so-called "Cadogan" tea-pots without any cover and filled through a hole in the bottom were a celebrated Rockingham product. In 1806, Brameld & Co. took over the works, and continued the various manufactures. In 1820 and until the factory was closed in 1842, porcelain of good quality was also made at Swinton. This porcelain is famed, both for its beautiful ground colors and for the exquisite finish of its painting in enameled colors, and for its gilding. Rockingham ware as made in this country is made from natural buff-colored clays, covered with a dark brown glaze and often mottled by spattering the glaze before it is fired. It was first made here by James Bennett, an English potter at work at East Liverpool, Ohio, in 1839. Later many of the factories were producing it. It was a notable production of the Bennington potteries.

ROOKWOOD POTTERY

It is safe to say that no ceramic establishment in this country has come nearer to fulfilling the requirements of a distinctively American institution than this pottery at Cincinnati, Ohio, and it equals, if it does not surpass, anything produced by European potters. The works were established in 1880 by Mrs. Maria Longworth (Nichols) Storer, who surrounded herself with skilled workmen and able artists. They at first made domestic white and yellow ware of a superior quality for which native clays were used, with blue and brown underglaze printed decoration.

This ware was gradually superseded by the more elegant and decorative forms, which have since attracted so much attention. The ware since produced at Rookwood is a true "faience" and may be classed under three general headings: Cameo or shell-tinted ware, dull-finished ware and, most characteristic of Rookwood, the richly-glazed "faience" in rich tones of black, yellow, red, olive, green, brown and amber. The body partakes of some of the qualities of stoneware and some of the properties of semi-porcelain. The surface is only equaled by the finest Oriental porcelains, and Copenhagen porcelain is the only Occidental porcelain which rivals Rookwood in its management of high-light colors. The harmony of all of the elements, color, decoration and glaze combined, makes Rookwood beau-

tiful. Today, the exquisite ceramic creations of Rookwood may be found in every prominent art museum in this country and in almost every home of culture and refinement.

ROUEN (France) WARE

A manufactory of artistic pottery is believed to have been located here in the 16th century. From about the middle until the close of the 17th century a true French "faience" was produced extensively at several different factories. It was characterized by accuracy of drawing, elegance of modeling and richness of coloring. About 1673, soft-paste porcelain was made here, specimens of which are very rare. The body has a slightly greenish hue. The painting, nearly always in blue, is over the glaze before the firing, and the decoration is French in design. None of it was marked. Factory was closed in 1696.

REFERENCE

Pottery and Porcelain, FREDERICK LITCHFIELD.

ROYAL WORCESTER PORCELAIN

See WORCESTER.

RUSSIAN PORCELAIN

See PORCELAIN, Russian.

S

Sagger

A fire-clay box in which the earthenware is placed when being fired in the oven. This is dusted with material infusible at the oven heat to prevent the pieces' adhering. Also called seggar.

Saint Cloud (France) Porcelain

Faience was made at St. Cloud previous to 1670 and porcelain-making was started about 1696. Although porcelain was made earlier at Rouen (q.v.), St. Cloud was the first enduring factory in France. The porcelain made was of soft paste, the decoration quite simple and the coloring was mostly blue, although sometimes of red. The factory was burned down in 1773 and not rebuilt.

REFERENCE

> Pottery and Porcelain, Frederick Litchfield.

Saint Johnsbury (Vermont) Pottery

Richard Webber Fenton, uncle of Christopher Fenton of Bennington fame, was the founder of this pottery in 1808, and his son, Leander, was associated with him. They made all sorts of domestic ware and the pottery gained a good local reputation. It was closed in 1859.

Saint Porchaire (France) Ware

The ware produced here in the 16th century, also known as Henri II and faience d'Oiron, was an encrusted faience and notable as being the most costly of all ceramic gems. There are sixty-five pieces of the ware known to be in existence at the present time.

Salopian Ware

The porcelain made from 1772 onwards at the Shropshire factory of Caughley (q.v.).

Salt-Glaze

This is an exceedingly hard glaze produced by throwing into the heated kiln common salt, which vaporizes and settles on the ware in minute drops, thin and perfectly transparent. The process was introduced into England in the latter part of the 17th century, superseding the dull lead glaze before used, and early in the 18th century, Staffordshire became the chief center of salt-glazed earthenware. The best pieces of this ware were made from about 1720 to 1760, and during this period decoration in enamel colors over the glaze was introduced. The improvement of the body led to the disappearance of salt-glaze and the enameled ware gave place to transfer-printing. Some of the pottery made in this country in the early 18th century was salt-glazed, and it has been used extensively since. In England, too, some factories are still producing salt-glaze ware.

REFERENCE

> A B C of English Salt-Glaze Stoneware, Blacker.

SAMIAN WARE

The name is derived from the island of Samos in the Aegean Sea, which was noted in ancient times for its glossy, red pottery. The paste was of a fine red, with smooth, close texture and covered with a thin glaze. It was very hard, turned on a lathe and ornamented with applied molded forms. The early Romans copied this ware in a pottery at Aretrum, and it is thought that some of it was also made in England during their occupancy of the island.

SAMSON

The name of Samson is more or less familiar to experienced collectors of old china. The founder of the house, M. Edmé Samson, began business in 1845. He was a decorator of porcelain and his son Émile was a potter. The factory is located in Montreuil with a salesroom in Paris, and from it have come clever copies of Oriental and European porcelains. Some of the work is excellent as far as technique is concerned, and it includes their own private mark in addition to the marks of the factories whose productions they imitate. At one time the factory employed more than two hundred skilled workers, and is still in existence. Copies of antique faience, enamels and bronze work are included in their work.

REFERENCE
The House of Samson, ANTIQUES, May 1923.

SATSUMA WARE

A Japanese product first made by potters brought from Korea at the end of the 16th century by a prince of Satsuma. The old Satsuma ware stands foremost in the pottery products of Japan, and surpasses any other earthenware. In size, pieces of real Satsuma are small, in color they range from cream to old ivory, covered with a minute crackle. Enamel colors, gold and raised ornament are used in the decoration. Old Satsuma is very rare and many potteries in Japan have imitated it.

SCEAUX (France) WARE

This ware is notable for its beautiful shapes in imitation of porcelain, artistically decorated in colors, frequently with gold. The factory, located near Paris, was started about 1750 and was in existence until early in the 19th century. Porcelain was made here from about 1765 onward. Its early products resemble those of Mennecy, as the factory was controlled by the same men operating Mennecy.

SEGGAR

See SAGGER.

SEMI-CHINA

Also called semi-porcelain. These terms were applied to early 19th-century earthenware having a very white semi-opaque body, due to a large admixture of feldspar. It had the outward appearance of china and represented the last word in earthenware. It had but one drawback, it was not translucent. Sometimes the term "opaque china" appears in describing it. The product of the Spode factory was particularly noted for its fine quality, beautiful decoration, often in the Oriental manner, and for its comparative cheapness. See IRONSTONE CHINA.

SÈVRES PORCELAIN

There is no continental porcelain better known by name to everyone or more desirable for the collector than the French porcelain of Sèvres. This remarkable porcelain was first made at Vincennes (q.v.) about 1745, under the auspices of the King of France. The early product was in plain white or with gilding only. In 1756 a factory was built at Sèvres where at first a porcelain of soft paste was made, and this production up to 1769 was the best of the Sèvres porcelains.

The first specimen known of the hard-paste porcelain, which gradually displaced that of soft paste, is dated 1765, and until 1804 both were made, the latter at a continually diminishing rate. Both the soft-paste and hard-paste Sèvres are absolutely white, translucent and flawless. Sèvres product from 1801 to 1852 is regarded with less interest by collectors than any of its earlier ware. Sèvres porcelain is distinguished for its wonderful colorings and its beautiful designs, strictly French in outline. The decoration was by some of the most gifted artists and modelers of the time. The bleu-de-roi of old Sèvres is one of the most famous of ground colors on old porcelain. The rather lavish use of gold was a feature of the decoration of the Empire period. The collector must be on his guard against numerous forgeries and imitations of old Sèvres.

REFERENCES

The Soft Porcelain of Sèvres, E. GARNIER; Royal Sèvres China, EGAN MEW; Pottery and Porcelain, FREDERICK LITCHFIELD; Practical Book of Chinaware, EBERLEIN and RAMSDELL; Bleu de Roi, ANTIQUARIAN, Feb. 1931.

SGRAFFIATO

A method of decorating earthenware of the 15th and 16th centuries, of Italian origin. It consisted of cutting or incising the surface of the ware by means of a sharp pointed instrument before glazing. It gradually found its way into Germany, Holland and other parts of Europe. By that time it was the practice to coat the brown earthenware with a light-colored slip and to cut the incisions through that. It was usually finished at a single firing. In this country the Germans of Eastern Pennsylvania produced considerable quantities of ware in that form in the 18th and early 19th centuries. See PENNSYLVANIA SLIP WARE.

SILVER LUSTRE
See LUSTRE WARE, *Silver.*

SINO-LOWESTOFT
See LOWESTOFT.

SLIP
This is a thick semi-solid fluid composed of clay and water into which the ware was dipped when it was dry enough to be fired. It was also dropped on the ware in the desired design from the spout of a little vessel. The porous body of the piece quickly absorbed the water in the slip and the piece was then ready for the glaze and firing. Various colors were obtained for the slip by use of colored oxides. For example, oxide of iron produces red; copper, green; cobalt, blue; and manganese, a color varying from a purple-brown to almost a black. This method of decoration is of ancient origin, having been used by the Romans and by various countries during medieval times. It was extensively used by English and German potters during the 17th and 18th centuries, especially at Staffordshire, and it is still in use in Switzerland and in Italy. See SLIP WARE.

REFERENCE
Lead Glazed Pottery, E. A. BARBER.

SLIP WARE
This quaint, rough, slip-decorated ware was usually lead-glazed and was generally subjected to but one firing. When the design is dropped upon the ware from the slip cup, it is slightly raised from the surface. The slip wares of the 17th century represent one of the most vital developments of English ceramics. Foremost among slip potters of England were Thomas and Ralph Toft. On account of the distinctive character of the work of the Tofts, all slip-decorated ware in England has come to be generally known as Toft ware (q.v.). Slip decoration was the forerunner of the modern art of applying on the unbaked ware the colored clays which are found on the pâte-sur-pâte process of the Minton factory in England. See PENNSYLVANIA SLIP WARE.

SMEAR GLAZE
This is a glaze applied indirectly to the surface of the ware by painting a coat of glaze on the inside of the closed container in which the ware is baked. During the baking process, this glaze vaporizes and settles like a fine mist on the surface of the ware. It is to be seen on English Parian ware.

SOUTHERN PORCELAIN MANUFACTURING Co.
This factory was established in 1856 at Kaolin, South Carolina, by William

Farrar to make porcelain from clay native to that region. Some of the ware produced was of excellent quality. The plant was a financial failure and was burned in 1863 or 1864. Among the products were porcelain, making of which was discontinued in 1860, Parian and Rockingham ware, and white and cream-colored earthenware. At the close of the Civil War a new company was organized to produce porcelain, but after twelve years of varying success, the factory was closed.

SPANISH PORCELAIN
See BUEN RETIRO.

SPANISH POTTERY
See HISPANO-MORESQUE WARE.

SPATTER WARE

This is a relatively heavy, whitish earthenware, a large part of whose surface is covered with a stipple design in some bright color. In the midst of this stipple work, a clear spot is usually reserved for other decoration. It is also referred to as "sponge ware." Adams of Greenfield, England, was a principal producer of this ware early in the 19th century. It was a Staffordshire product.

REFERENCE
Spatter Ware, ANTIQUARIAN, Oct. 1930.

SPODE WARE

In 1770 Josiah Spode established a factory at Stoke-on-Trent. The factory produced under-glaze blue-printed cream ware of excellent quality, stone china, black and jasper ware. The stone china was of exceptional quality. It was a semi-porcelain and frequently translucent. It became very popular on account of its comparative cheapness and its beautiful decoration.

Transfer-printing in blue and other colors was one of the foundations of their prosperity. About 1800, the factory began to make porcelain, and it is with that ware that their product is best known. The body of the porcelain is soft and white with a fine glaze and much of it is decorated in the Oriental manner. As a rule the decoration is less pleasing than on porcelain of his contemporaries, although an enumeration would include nearly every type of decoration used on china at that time. Josiah Spode, Jr., invented a superior kind of "bone china" (q.v.), which combines the best qualities of both soft-paste and hard-paste porcelain, and his formula later became the English standard and remains unaltered to the present time. The porcelain, stone china and the ordinary earthenware, in their body, glaze and decoration rank with the best of the period.

All of the product of Spode the Elder, who died in 1797, is marked and it is eagerly sought by collectors. An interesting chronology of Spode patterns appears in ANTIQUES magazine, Vol. 15, p. 394. The works are still in operation by W. T. Copeland & Sons, descendants of William Copeland, a partner of Josiah Spode, Jr., and the products worthily sustain the reputation of the earlier periods.

REFERENCES

Spode and His Successors, ARTHUR HAYDEN; Old Spode, T. G. CANNON; A B C of 19th Century English Ceramic Art, BLACKER.

SPONGE WARE

See SPATTER WARE.

SPURS

During the glazing of earthenware, little tripods, called also cockspurs and stilts, are used between the pieces in piling them up in the kiln. On old ware "spur" marks are to be found where it has rested on these supports. Usually three spurs were used.

STAFFORDSHIRE

This is a generic term applying to the products of many potteries in Stoke-on-Trent, Hanley, Cobridge, Etruria, Burslem, Fenton, Tunstall, Longport, Shelton, Lane End and some other lesser-known places, where for centuries potteries and potters have flourished. What is known as the pottery district was then about ten miles long and from three to five miles wide. Some of the better-known names of the Staffordshire potters include Ralph Wood, father and son, Enoch Wood, Aaron Wood, Josiah Wedgwood, Thomas Whieldon, Josiah Spode, John Turner, R. Wilson, William Adams and Job Ridgway.

There were potteries there dating from the 17th century, although the prominence of Staffordshire was identified more particularly with the next century. The isolated position of the Staffordshire potter kept him comparatively free from outside influences and enabled him to develop his stronger, if somewhat ruder, personality. Among the wares produced there owing nothing to foreign sources are slip wares, agate, tortoise-shell, black basalt and jasper ware. No other group of potters in the world at any period has produced such a variety of wares.

From the days of the Elers, 1690-1710, to the days of Wedgwood in 1760, Staffordshire pottery was in a transitional stage. Salt-glaze stoneware was made there until it was superseded by the cream ware of Wedgwood. Under-glaze blue transfer-printing (q.v.), invented by Sadler at Liverpool about 1750, was introduced by John Turner, and Josiah Spode produced the new "willow pattern" in 1784, and from that time onward Staffordshire production was enormous. Much of it was designed for the American market.

Staffordshire pottery can usually be identified from the design on the border, as nearly all of the potters there made use of exclusive border patterns. Of course, exceptions to every rule occur at times, but the theory is generally reliable. Border designs are composed of graceful combinations of sea shells and mosses, roses and scrolls, acorns and oak leaves, grapes and vines or fruit, birds and flowers.

Beginning with the 19th century Staffordshire products were devoted largely to blue transfer-printed wares. At first the willow pattern was used extensively. About 1820, someone conceived the idea of using views of actual places instead of imaginary landscapes with Oriental themes. Views of English cities, scenes in France and Italy, and a series of American subjects became very popular both here and abroad, and resulted in a great prosperity for the potters (q.v., HISTORICAL CHINA). At first of deep blue, later light colors in pink, green, lavender and other colors were included. Some interesting accounts of the American views and of the artists who designed them may be found in the magazine ANTIQUES, July 1923, Nov. 1929, Nov. 1936 and July 1937.

Transfer-printing was succeeded by the lithographic method, a cheaper process, and the collector's interest in Staffordshire usually stops at that point.

Staffordshire potters were noted particularly for figures, Toby jugs and groups. The modeling on such work from 1740 to 1780 is superior to that produced later. During that time, also, the figures were colored by the use of pigments under the glaze. Later enamel colors were used on the surface of the glaze, with lurid effect, and much of the beauty of the old school vanished. Porcelain was also made in the Staffordshire district, but to a much lesser extent than earthenware. The potteries here continue to provide the greater amount of both earthenware and porcelain now produced in England. See MINTON WARE — SPODE WARE — WEDGWOOD WARE.

REFERENCES
Staffordshire Figures, ANTIQUES, Jan. 1927; Staffordshire Pots and Potters, RHEAD; Josiah Wedgwood, Master-Potter, CHURCH; Chats on Old Earthenware, HAYDEN; Staffordshire Pew Groups, ANTIQUES, Sept. 1936.

STANNIFEROUS FAIENCE
See ENAMELED POTTERY.

ST. CLOUD (France) PORCELAIN
See SAINT CLOUD.

ST. JOHNSBURY (Vermont) POTTERY
See SAINT JOHNSBURY.

ST. PORCHAIRE (France) WARE
See SAINT PORCHAIRE.

STILT MARKS
See SPURS.

STONEWARE

Stoneware is a highly-fired, partly-vitrified opaque pottery, covered usually with salt-glaze, originating in Germany. It is composed of plastic clay with a larger percentage of silica than other earthenware, which, when fired, insures closeness and hardness. It more nearly approaches porcelain in its characteristics than other earthenware. John Dwight at Fulham and the Elers brothers at Staffordshire were among the earliest of the English potters to make it. A century later the stone china of Spode (q.v.) and also the ironstone china (q.v.) of Mason met with great success.

REFERENCE
English Earthenware and Stoneware, A. H. CHURCH.

SUNDERLAND WARE

Several potteries were established near Sunderland, the earliest about 1775. The ware is noted for its pink lustre and for the mugs and jugs decorated in black transfer-printing with ships and with verses appropriate for the sailors for whom they were made. Sunderland and Newcastle (q.v.) ware are much alike in this respect. Rose-spotted Sunderland ware is highly regarded by collectors. Much of the Sunderland product was unmarked. Numerous modern potteries are located in the district.

SWANSEA PORCELAIN

SWANSEA

In 1814 a factory here under the ownership of Lewis Dillwyn began making porcelain which has been described by one writer as the most beautiful of all English porcelains in paste or body. It was of soft paste, beautiful in color, glaze and decoration. The most characteristic decoration of Swansea china consisted of flowers painted by Billingsley. Dillwyn remained there four years, and from 1818 to 1824 the factory was run by Bevington & Co., producing lustre and transfer-printed earthenware. Swansea porcelain is scarce and highly prized by collectors. See CAMBRIAN POTTERY.

REFERENCE
Pottery and Porcelain, FREDERICK LITCHFIELD.

SWANSEA WARE

SWANSEA

Pottery established in 1750 at Swansea, Wales, produced earthenware of a high artistic order. Under-glaze blue-printed ware, notably the "willow pattern," salt-glazed ware decorated in enamel colors, and fine black basalt ware were among the wide range of examples. They also made an "opaque china," in reality a whiter and finer kind of cream ware. For a brief period in its later years Etruscan ware of black body with red Grecian designs painted in enamel was made. In 1790 the factory came into the possession of George Haynes, who gave it the name of the Cambrian Potteries (q.v.).

REFERENCE

The Ceramics of Swansea and Nant-garw, WILLIAM TURNER.

SWINTON WARE
See ROCKINGHAM.

T

TEA CADDIES

A bottle-shaped receptacle of rectangular, circular or other form, for holding tea leaves. Also called canister.

THROWING

The art of fashioning shapes on the potter's wheel (q.v.). It is the oldest method of pottery-making employed by civilized man and is still in use in many potteries.

THROWING WHEEL

This is an improvement over the old potter's wheel and is composed of a plate or disk, which is revolved by means of a belt which passes around two spindles and extends to a large vertical fly wheel operated by a crank in the hands of a second person. The revolving plate is often ten or more feet from the crank wheel.

TILES

The earliest attempts at ceramic art included enameled tiles. Tiles of an-cient Roman origin and of the Moors are splendid specimens of this kind of decoration. Many so-called encaustic tiles followed by inlaid tiles with lead glaze were made in medieval times in the monasteries in England. Old delft tiles are other good examples. Encaustic and other tiles were made in the 19th century at Minton's and other potteries in England.

In our country the manufacture of encaustic tiles has grown to be a large industry. Some of the best work has been done by the American Encaustic Tile Co., of Zanesville, Ohio, the Beaver Falls Art Tile Co., of Beaver Falls, Pennsylvania, and the Low Art Tile Co., of Chelsea, Massachusetts. The first tiles produced in this country are said to have been made by Abraham Miller in Philadelphia in 1845.

TIN-ENAMELED POTTERY

Ware covered with a heavy, opaque,

putty-like white enamel, distinguished from glaze which is transparent or translucent. Decorations of tin-enameled pottery must be painted on or in the dense white enamel. Tin enamel is a composition of glass and oxide of lead with a certain portion of oxide of tin which produces the white, opaque effect. Old delft is an example of this stanniferous pottery.

REFERENCE

Tin Enamelled Pottery, E. A. Barber.

Toby Jug

The origin of the Toby jug is uncertain. The early Whieldons were probably produced before 1759. The Toby Philpot jug by Ralph Wood, Sr., was probably the original of a type afterwards imitated by all the potters. Genuine old Tobies always have hollow legs and feet and this is generally apparent. Toby jugs are among the most interesting of early ceramic productions.

Toft Ware

THOMAS·TOFT

Slip-decorated pottery made by Ralph

and Thomas Toft in Staffordshire in the latter half of the 17th century. The material of this ware was usually a coarse reddish clay and the decorating is done in a rather crude manner. The glaze was applied before the ware was fired, but after the slip was placed on it, and this gave to the piece a rich yellow tone. This ware marks a distinct advancement in the history of English potting, and has given the general name of Toft ware to all slip-decorated pottery since. Much of it is in imitation of real "Toft Ware." Thomas Toft was one of the really great English potters.

Torksey Porcelain

The ware made at Torksey in Lincolnshire was from an unsuccessful pottery conducted by William Billingsley from 1803 to 1808. It bore no mark and is almost impossible to identify.

Tortoise-Shell Ware

This ware, made famous by Thomas Whieldon, was made by several Staffordshire potters, but it is doubtful if any of them produced anything quite as fine as Whieldon. The tortoise-shell effect was obtained by covering the body of light color with oxides put on with a sponge.

Tournai Porcelain

A soft-paste porcelain was made here in a factory established about 1750. The salmon scale was a favorite form of decoration.

Transfer-Printing

It is claimed that this method of decoration on ware by means of paper was discovered by Sadler and Green at Liverpool about 1750. The process consists of first engraving the design on copper, inking the plate and transferring the design to specially prepared paper, and while the ink is still wet the paper is carefully laid on the piece to be decorated and the design transfers itself to the ware. It is used on both under-glaze and over-glaze ware, and this invention revolutionized the decoration of all earthenware products, as well as glass, and it helped to make English pottery famous throughout the civilized world. In general, the blue-printer strove to be decorative, representing scenery and designs of an Oriental nature. Blue-printing was essentially a Staffordshire process. Black and white may be said to depict events and chronicle popular sentiment. This was characteristic of Liverpool ware.

REFERENCE

Transfer-Printing on Enamels, Porcelain and Pottery, TURNER.

Trent Tile Co.

At Trenton, New Jersey, made a specialty of alto-relievo tiles, treated by a sand-blast process after glazing. The effect is a soft, satin-like finish, very pleasing to the eye. They also made glazed and enameled varieties in several sizes. In 1886 William Gallimore, an English artist modeler, joined the company, and until his death in 1891 all of the modeling was his work. His style is vigorous and versatile.

Trenton Potteries Co.

At Trenton, New Jersey, is one of the largest concerns in the industry in this country. It is a combination of several older companies.

Tucker and Hemphill Porcelain Works
See CHINA, American.

Tudor Jugs

A class of Elizabethan ware, five or six inches in height, of brown and blue mottled surface with a tin glaze. They are exceedingly rare and valuable and some of them are mounted with silver. A great deal of mystery surrounds their origin, but they are supposed to be of English make.

Turning

Finishing of pottery by lathe work. The Elers Brothers made a very hard, red pottery which, by turning in the lathe, was much thinner than if done on the potter's wheel.

Tyg, Tig

A slip-decorated mug of red ware of the 17th century, made in various sizes with several single or double loop handles. A posset-cup. They were popular for use at Christmas Eve. When made with two handles and with a cover, they were called posset-pots. It is thought that the tyg originated in Staffordshire.

U

UNDER-GLAZE

Decoration, printed or painted, done before the glaze is applied and the piece fired. This is a more difficult process than over-glaze (q.v.), because the high temperature required for the glaze spoils almost all colors excepting cobalt blue, and was first attempted in England about 1750.

UNION PORCELAIN WORKS

Established in 1864 at Greenpoint, Long Island, by Thomas C. Smith. The porcelain made was composed of kaolin, quartz and feldspar mix, and the glaze was applied by the same process used at Sèvres, Meissen and other foreign factories. Mr. Smith was probably the first potter in this country to apply decoration on hard porcelain by the underglaze method. He also used later the over-glaze method, in order to obtain a greater variety of coloring. The work exhibits a high degree of excellence.

UNITED STATES POTTERY CO. (Bennington, Vermont)

See BENNINGTON.

URBINO (Italy) WARE

The majolica produced here was at its best about 1530-1540 and maintained its excellence for about thirty years. The style of decoration is that known as "Raffaelesque" with scrolls and grotesque ornament forming the ground work and medallions of cupids or mythological subjects in the center. Among its products were plaques, vases and drug pots, sometimes with serpentine handles and mask spouts. The large plaques are frequently decorated with Biblical or historical subjects.

REFERENCE

A History and Description of Italian Majolica, M. L. SOLON.

V

VENICE (Italy) PORCELAIN

A manufactory of both hard- and soft-paste porcelain was located here as early as 1719 and continued until 1742. The production was of excellent quality and the decoration was in pure Italian style.

Another factory was established in 1765 where porcelain of great artistic merit was produced until it was closed in 1812.

VIENNA (Austria) PORCELAIN

This ware is renowned for the raised

gold ornamentation, done usually on a body of deep crimson or blue. The body was of hard paste of excellent quality and the glaze was good. The decoration consists chiefly of the copies of famous paintings, although flowers, fruit, figures and landscapes were also used. The factory was established in 1718 and workmen from Meissen were employed. In 1744 it became an imperial institution, remaining under State control until 1864, when it was discontinued.

VINCENNES (France) PORCELAIN

The most important of the early soft-paste factories in France, and apart from the excellence of its product, it is celebrated for being the parent of the great Royal Sèvres factory, through the interest of the King in the enterprise. The products of Vincennes from 1745 to 1756, when the factory was merged with that of Sèvres, are highly prized by collectors. The articles made were varied and included tableware and other household articles of utility and many elaborate pieces upon which special efforts were bestowed. Among these last was the fashioning of porcelain flowers, which were immensely popular with the nobility.

In 1753, the King sanctioned the use of the royal cipher (the L's interlaced) which had already been adopted as a mark. The decoration of the earlier pieces was chiefly copied from Oriental designs. After removal to Sèvres, the factory at Vincennes was used for several years for making hard-paste porcelain, which product must not be confounded with the earlier soft-paste porcelain.

REFERENCES

Pottery and Porcelain, FREDERICK LITCHFIELD; Practical Book of China-ware, EBERLEIN and RAMSDELL.

W

WEDGWOOD WARE

WEDGWOOD

Josiah Wedgwood in 1759 started the business at Burslem, Staffordshire, which was eventually to become one of the most famous potteries in the world. At first he made the usual run of pottery products, but in 1762 he produced a cream ware which not only improved upon the earlier product but was to supplant salt-glaze ware and was to be copied by other potters, as well. Black basalt ware, of which Wedgwood is said to have been the inventor, was first produced in 1766 but the finest work in this ware was not done until much later.

In 1769 he established his works and built a village at Etruria. About 1775 he perfected his well-known jasper ware, and at about the same time he engaged the services of Flaxman, the famous sculptor, and his work has given a distinctive character to the Wedgwood work of the period. The most important piece of this ware was the reproduction in 1790 of the celebrated Portland Vase (q.v.).

Old Wedgwood is considered to be the finest pottery that England has ever produced in workmanship, design, material and color. No earthenware, native or foreign, combined so many technical perfections. The basalt and the jasper ware are the best known and most sought after by collectors. With one unimportant exception, a white biscuit with smooth and wax-like surface, Wedgwood made no porcelain, and only a few pieces of this are now in existence. In 1878, the manufacture of porcelain was revived, and has continued since. Josiah Wedgwood died in 1795, but the works have since been carried on by members of the family, some of the old molds still being in use. The firm continues to produce jasper, basalt, red, cream-colored, and all the other wares for which the factory is famous.

REFERENCES

Wedgwood, and His Works, E. METEYARD; *Josiah Wedgwood, Master-Potter*, CHURCH; *Chats on Wedgwood Ware*, BARNARD; *Josiah Wedgwood and His Pottery*, BURTON; *Two Centuries in Retrospect*, ANTIQUARIAN, May 1930.

WHIELDON WARE

A term derived from the tortoise-shell ware made by Thomas Whieldon, and applied to all classes of ware of a mottled, cloudy or splashed character. Whieldon's tortoise-shell ware was soft, light in weight, with an excellent glaze and it was extremely rich in effect. Whieldon also made a solid agate ware (q.v.) more artistic than had before been attempted and his tortoise-shell wares have always been looked upon as masterpieces of their time. All Whieldon's wares are comparatively rare and command high prices. He was one of England's greatest potters. Wedgwood was a partner 1754-1759, Aaron Wood was a modeler, and Spode and several other potters, who became noted, were apprentices of Whieldon, which doubtless helped to qualify them for their own future success.

WILLETS POTTERY

Started in 1853 by William Young & Sons at Trenton, New Jersey. This pottery became one of the largest in the Eastern states. At first, they made Rockingham and common white ware, but later, decorated pottery, opaque china and porcelain were made. Their Belleek ware is also noteworthy.

WILLOW PATTERN

Thomas Minton in 1780 engraved for Thomas Turner of Caughley this famous pattern, certainly the most popular design ever applied to pottery. Specimens

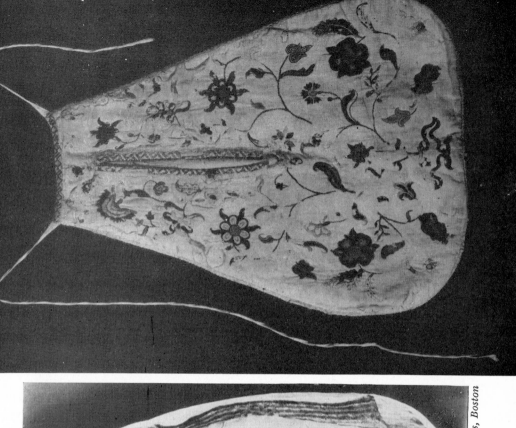

AMERICAN CREWEL EMBROIDERED POCKET, 18TH CENTURY

AMERICAN CREWEL EMBROIDERED CHAIR SEAT, 17TH CENTURY

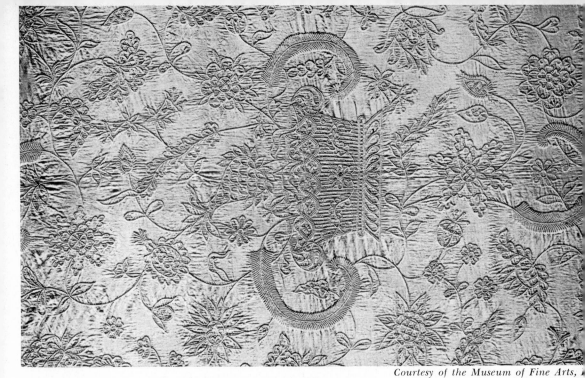

DETAIL OF AMERICAN QUILTED COVERLET, 19TH CENTURY

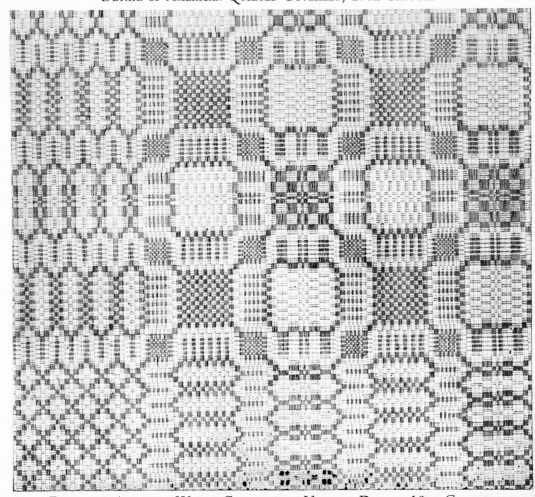

DETAIL OF AMERICAN WOVEN COVERLET OF UNUSUAL DESIGN, 19TH CENTURY

of this earliest ware bear Turner marks. Minton afterwards joined Spode at Stoke-on-Trent and Spode was the first potter in Staffordshire to apply the pattern to earthenware. There were variants of the pattern and the Spode "Willow" can be distinguished from Wedgwood, Davenport from Adams, etc. The design is adapted from designs on Chinese porcelain imported into England, founded on a Chinese legend. By 1800 the pattern was pretty much common property among potters of both earthenware and porcelain, and it was also copied by Continental potters.

WINCANTON WARE

This pottery was established in Somersetshire about 1720 and the peculiarity of this ware is a slight pinkish hue in an excellent delft-like glaze, resembling that of Lambeth faience. The factory was closed about 1748.

WIRKSWORTH PORCELAIN

A factory established in Derbyshire about 1757 and continuing in operation until 1777. Closed for a time, it appears to have re-opened about 1804. The products were chiefly household ware. The paste was of good quality and fairly translucent. Decorations were similar to those of Lowestoft.

WORCESTER PORCELAIN

The Worcester Tonquin manufacture was founded in 1751, and Dr. John Wall was the active head until his death in 1776. Its history has been compara-

tively uneventful, but, alone of all the English porcelain ventures of the 18th

century, Worcester has survived with a record of continuous activity down to the present day. No china has had so much written about it as old Worcester. The earliest china was made of "frit" paste (q.v.), which may be told by its density and by a greenish tint when seen by transmitted light. These earlier productions, consisting largely of tableware, were perhaps the most distinctive of all 18th-century porcelains. Their well-proportioned forms and careful finish are quickly recognized by the collector. Eventually a certain number of ornate pieces were made, but the main emphasis of the factory was always placed on useful ware. Worcester figures of the early period are very uncommon.

Imitations of Chinese porcelain with blue decoration on white ground were followed by the more brilliant colors and designs of the Japanese and Meissen motives. Among the most characteristic of all Worcester inventions were the so-called Japan patterns, which continued to be made from the earlier days until well into the 19th century. The best period of old Worcester china and the china richest in decoration was that made from about 1760 to 1783, the so-called Dr. Wall period, and this porcelain commands very high prices today. The salmon-scale blue ground was one of the characteristics of that period, and the gilding was of superlative quality.

Transfer-printing was introduced at Worcester about 1775, and their early printed china is the best of its class ever made in England. Printing was done in lilac and red, as well as in the usual brown or black or in under-glaze blue. Later, the printing was done by the "bat" process (q.v.).

The Dr. Wall period extended until 1783, at which time the company was taken over by Thomas Flight, the company's London agent, and the Flight name was connected with it until 1840 when the original company and Chamberlain and Company, another Worcester factory started in 1786, were combined. In 1862 the present Royal Worcester Porcelain Company came into existence. The prefix "Royal" was adopted by permission of the King in the Flight period. In Royal Worcester, gilding is the most important feature of the decoration, by means of which great delicacy is produced upon the creamy white lustreless surface for which the Worcester ware is noted. During its long period of existence Worcester porcelain has maintained a front rank for the superb beauty of forms, colors and decorations and for the immense variety of its designs.

REFERENCES

Worcester Porcelain, R. L. Hobson; Old English Porcelain, W. B. Honey; Pottery and Porcelain, Frederick Litchfield; A Century of Potting in the City of Worcester, W. R. Binns; A B C of 19th Century English Ceramic Art, Blacker.

Wrotham Ware

WR⊙THAM

This ware made in Wrotham, Kent County, in England from 1612, the earliest dated example, to about 1710 is noted for its superior slip decoration on tygs, posset-cups and bowls, with a reddish brown body. Medallions and other molded ornaments applied to the body to be decorated were frequently employed at Wrotham, also.

Z

Zaffre

An impure oxide of cobalt of an intensely blue color, used in pottery. A small quantity was sometimes mixed with the glaze.

PART III

GLASS

PART III

GLASS

A

Agata Glass

Made at Cambridge, Massachusetts, resembling peachblow, with a spattered mottling on a glossy finish.

Agate Glass

See GLASS, *Agate*.

Amberina Glass

A lead glass, usually blown, with a lustrous finish of a pale amber color shading to ruby made by the New England Glass Co. of Cambridge. It was very popular and a similar glass is now being made by the Libbey Glass Co. (q.v.), successors to the New England Glass Co. A quite similar glass was also made at Mt. Washington Glass Works at New Bedford.

Amelung Glass Works

At New Bremen, Maryland, variously known also as New Bremen Glass Works, Etna Glass Works and the American Glass Manufactory. This factory was established by John Frederick Amelung, a German who came to America in 1784 and brought with him German glass-workers, and in the following year began to produce glass in a variety of kinds; window glass, flint table glass, bottles, decanters and looking-glass for mirrors, etc. The quality of the product will compare favorably with the glass of other early makers. The works were in operation about six years. There were three or four other glass factories nearby of which little is known. Authenticated pieces of Amelung glass are very rare. At least one marked piece is known to exist.

> REFERENCES
> *Early American Glass*, RHEA M. KNITTLE; *Amelung*, ANTIQUARIAN, Dec. 1930; *Safe Clues in the Amelung Quest*, ANTIQUARIAN, Sept. 1934.

American Flint Glass Works

South Boston, Massachusetts. Prior to the organization of this company about 1850, there had been a factory in Essex Street (q.v.), Boston, which in 1811 was moved to South Boston, continuing until about 1820, when it failed. There were five successive attempts by five different firms to revive the industry, until finally the above company was established under the direction of Patrick Slane. Their product consisted of all kinds of pressed and cut glassware. About 1870, the concern went permanently out of business.

AMERICAN GLASS

Glass-making was one of the first crafts to be started in the American colonies. Glass was made in 1608 at Jamestown, Virginia, but was soon after abandoned. Salem, Massachusetts, had a glass factory in 1639 which continued for three or four years. A dark glass of poor quality was made at Quincy, Massachusetts, between 1750 and 1760. The first successful factory was that at Wistarberg (q.v.), New Jersey, started by Caspar Wistar in 1739. The factory at Glassboro (q.v.), New Jersey, was started in 1775 and that at Kensington (q.v.), Pennsylvania, a few years earlier. These two are still in operation and they are the oldest existing factories in this country.

The first American glass was usually of a greenish color, coarse and full of bubbles. Blue and brown glass made their appearance later. Window glass was the chief product of all of these early factories. Doubtless, the early glassware was influenced in style and design by the workmen drawn from glass-works in England, Ireland, Holland, Germany and France. These workmen drifted in time from one glass-works to another, leaving something of their influence in each. Because of their knowledge and experience they had little difficulty in finding employment. Some of the finest glass ever made in this country was produced by these craftsmen, especially in their off-hand pieces made for their own use or for gifts to others.

In early factories, window-glass and bottle-making seemed to go together. About 1837, factories were built exclusively for making bottles and flasks, and this became an important branch of the industry. The factories where flint glass was made manufactured table and other ware, both blown and pressed. Cut glass began to be advertised about 1830. After the beginning of the 19th century the development of glass-making in this country became more a matter of industry than craft, and much of the product was below the standard of the earlier factories. The introduction of lime glass, cheaper than lead flint, in the last half of the 19th century, increased the production of pressed glass to enormous proportions. Excellent examples of early American glass are to be seen in our museums, notably the Metropolitan Museum in New York, the Pennsylvania Museum in Philadelphia, and the Garvan collections at Yale and Andover. See GLASS.

REFERENCES

American Glassware, Old and New, EDWIN A. BARBER; Early American Glass, RHEA M. KNITTLE; Early American Pressed Glass, RUTH WEBB LEE; Early Glass-Making in Virginia,

Maude P. Hull; ANTIQUES, Aug. 1933.

American Glass Manufactory
See Amelung Glass Works.

Antique Glass

The collecting and classification of antique glass is a difficult undertaking, and, to the uninitiated, not especially satisfactory. All varieties of early glass have many points in common. Generally speaking, it is not easy from the color, form, quality or decorative technique of a piece of glass to determine the particular factory of its origin. Quality and shape are, in later times, easily imitated. Old glass never was buffed; the new glass is buffed. The bottom of a piece of old glass which has been used is almost like ground glass in appearance, and old glass is seldom true to form. The presence of the pontil-mark is reassuring, but it is not a positive means of identification, as some glass is made today with the pontil rod.

In the field of American glass many of the finest specimens, bearing every apparent indication of 18th-century production, were blown in relatively obscure factories in various parts of the country during the early and mid-19th-century period. The only training for the collector who would guard against imposition is the constant handling of old and authentic pieces. Not only the eye but the hand must be trained. In any case of doubt, refer the question to someone who can speak with authority. See Frauds.

REFERENCES
Collecting Old Glass, English and Irish, Yoxall; The Glass Collector, Percival; Old Glass and How to Collect It, J. S. Lewis; Old Glass, European and American, Moore.

B

Baccarat Glass

A crystal glass made at Baccarat, France, with a leaden composition. The factory was founded in 1765 but it was not until about 1820 that the Baccarat products began to count in the history of glass. Although colored glass in various colors is made, the clear crystal produced is much greater than the colored crystal. At first only blown glass was made but later on they adopted the pressed-glass method of Sandwich. Cut glass was also a Baccarat specialty. Baccarat glass was, and is, turned out in a great variety of forms, but table glass constituted the greater part of their product. See French Glass.

REFERENCE
The Crystals of Baccarat, ANTIQUES, Dec. 1927.

Bakewell, Pears & Co.

A glass works at Pittsburgh, Pennsylvania, was founded in 1808 by two

Englishmen, Thomas Bakewell and Benjamin Page, and continued until 1882. The firm name was changed to Bakewell, Pears & Co., in 1836 and this factory is said to have been the first successful flint glass factory in America. The early output included decanters, bottles, pitchers, flasks, vases, drinking glasses and candelabra. In 1810, they made the first crystal chandelier to be made in this country, and the product of their later years was also much diversified. They made glassware for every purpose for which glass was used, and a large part of their product was exported to South America.

REFERENCES
Early American Pressed Glass, RUTH WEBB LEE; *Bakewell, Pears & Co.*, ANTIQUES, March 1927.

BALTIMORE GLASS WORKS
This factory at Baltimore, Maryland, started making glass about 1790 and was continued under various owners and names as the Federal Hill Works, The Patapsco River Glass-House and the Hughes Street Works. Bottles and flasks in various colors were the principal product.

BALUSTER
The term used for stems of glasses having an outline similar to balusters of wood.

BARBERINI VASE
See PORTLAND VASE.

BAY STATE GLASS Co.
Cambridge, Massachusetts, organized in 1849, incorporated in 1857 and in existence until 1874. They made a general assortment of flint glass wares, blown, pressed and cut, of good quality.

BEVELING
Beveling was done in the early days by pressing the glass while molten. The use of the sand wheel for the purpose was not adopted until the 18th century.

BLOBS
Small lumps of molten glass applied as a decoration to the surface of blown glass. Variously known as prunts, seals, mascaroons, etc. See PRUNTS.

BLOWING IRON (or Blow-Pipe)
A hollow tube about four feet long employed in making blown glass. It had its origin before the time of the Christian Era.

BLOWN GLASS
See GLASS, *Blown*.

BOHEMIAN GLASS
Bohemian crystal glass, composed of silicate of potash and lime, is comparatively easy of recognition, but most of it is not so old as we would like to think. Probably very little 18th-century Bohemian glass came to this country. In 1820 and thereafter considerable of this glass came in through Baltimore and it became extremely popular in the Southern states. The roots of Bohemian glass are, perhaps, in the old glass factories of

Venice. It was famous in the 16th century and for a long time Bohemia was the center of the crystal glass-making. The range of colors, also, is considerable; reds, blues, ambers and greens, all in various shades. The gold ruby is the most popular. Much of the effectiveness of Bohemian glass lies in its engraving and in the cutting through of an opaque colored outer surface to disclose a clear or a ground-glass pattern beneath. Further embellishment is often added by painting or gilding, and it was in Bohemia that the art of etching on glass was discovered by Henry Schwanhardt about 1670. See GLASS, *Etched*.

REFERENCE

    Bohemian Glass, ANTIQUES, June, 1923.

BOSTON CROWN GLASS CO.

The Essex Glass Works began to make "Crown" or window glass of excellent quality in 1792 and continued until about 1825. In 1809 the name of the company was changed to the Boston Glass Manufactory and "Boston Crown" glass became synonymous with the best, the country over. This factory was one of the earliest in this country to make flint glass.

BOSTON AND SANDWICH GLASS CO.

    See SANDWICH GLASS.

BOTTLES

During the 17th and 18th centuries the manufacture of bottles in England was an important branch of the glass industry. Enormous quantities were made both for home use and for export.

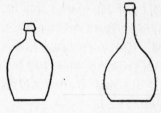

In the history of glass-making in America, glass bottles and flasks played an important part, also. Their production was chiefly from 1808 to 1870. From about 1837 factories were built exclusively for bottle-making, and many of them specialized in flasks, which were in great demand for liquor containers.

There are several hundred varieties of these flasks and bottles. They range in size from half-pint to quart, and they were made in almost every color of glass used at that time. Flasks were blown in two-piece metal molds with patterns cut intaglio on the inner surface of the molds, which produced a corresponding pattern on the surface of the flask. Some of them are to be found with the name of the factory blown in them. All early glass bottles were blown in engraved metal molds and made in several different colors. Bottle glass of the common kinds is composed of a silicate of lime and alumina, with smaller quantities of silicate of potash or soda, iron and manganese. A collection of these old bottles and flasks is novel and attractive.

REFERENCES

Early American Bottles and Flasks, VAN RENSSELAER; *American Bottles Old and New,* WILLIAM S. WALBRIDGE; *Early American Glass,* RHEA M. KNITTLE; *Some Early Bottles,* ANTIQUES, Mar. 1923; *The Lowell Railroad Bottle,* ANTIQUES, Feb. 1923.

Booze Bottles. This name was applied to bottles for whiskey, especially those

produced in 1860 by the Whitney Glass Works for Edmund G. Booz of Philadelphia, often reproduced at present.

REFERENCE

Booz and His Bottle, ANTIQUES, Nov. 1926.

Case Bottles. Four-sided bottles made to fit into the compartment of cases or boxes.

Violin Bottles. Name given to shape of bottles used primarily as containers for

whiskey, produced in the glass-works of the Ohio River district, middle of the

19th century. They were made of various sizes and the color range is widest of any American bottle.

REFERENCE

Epic of American Glass, ANTIQUARIAN, April 1930.

BRISTOL GLASS

It is certain that glass was made in Bristol, England, in the 17th century but all records of this early glass have disappeared. However, in 1760 there were fifteen glass factories in Bristol, and the influence of Bristol glass-makers was far reaching. White and colored glass, also cut glass, were produced at Bristol and the list of objects made comprises nearly all the pieces that could be made of glass. Much of their colored glass resembles our American Stiegel glass, and Venetian glass, especially the ruby. The blue glass is of a very rich hue, on the thicker pieces showing a royal purple tinge when held to the light, and on thinner pieces almost a sea blue. There were other colors used and mixed colors are not uncommon.

The rarest and most interesting of

Bristol glass is the white, opaque milky glass made from 1762 to about 1787. In tint it resembles porcelain or Battersea enamel. The effect was produced by the use of much lead and a small amount of tin in its composition. The color is a solid white and, when held to the light, is translucent to about the same extent as Oriental porcelain. The surface is fine and smooth and soft to the touch. The glass is heavy, owing to the lead used in its manufacture, and it is very brittle. On the white ground the decoration was painted in enamel colors and then fired. Some pieces were decorated in oil gilt. Michael Edkins, noted for his decorations on Bristol pottery,

was one of the artists employed in decorating Bristol glass during the years 1762 to 1787. The art of making this milky glass probably originated in Venice. Bristol glass is certainly the most beautiful of old English glasses, and one of the rarest. See GLASS, *Milk*.

REFERENCES
Bristol Glass, ANTIQUES, March, 1924; *Two Centuries of Ceramic Art in Bristol*, H. OWEN.

BULL'S EYE GLASS
See ROUNDEL.

BUMPER
See FIRING GLASSES.

C

CAMEO GLASS
See GLASS, *Cameo*.

CANDLESTICKS
The earliest glass candlesticks were made in England during the reign of Charles II. At first it was customary to mold these in two sections and fuse the sections together, leaving some irregularity. A straight, clean seam indicates pressing in a machine mold, and is therefore later. Candlesticks were made of pressed glass after the first quarter of the 19th century. The so-called "dolphin" candlestick is a familiar type to the collector.

CAPE COD GLASS CO.
Sandwich, Massachusetts, started by

Deming Jarves in 1858, after his resignation from the Boston and Sandwich Glass Co., with which company he had been associated for more than thirty years. The new company was never very successful and after the death of Jarves in 1869 the factory was closed. Ware similar to that of "Sandwich" was produced.

CASE BOTTLES
See BOTTLES, *Case*.

CAST GLASS
Cast in a mold very much after the manner of molten iron. When taken from the mold it is very apt to be rough and to require subsequent polishing of surfaces and edges. The mixture in cast

glass is heated to a higher temperature and is more liquid.

CHAMPLAIN GLASS WORKS

Established at Burlington, Vermont, in 1827 to make window glass with a side production of bottles. The glass was of excellent quality and heavier than most of the window glass of its time. Bottles were distinguished by a bluish-green cast. The "off-hand" blown examples of the Burlington works form some of the choicest specimens of our native glass-craftsmanship in existence. The high price of fuel put an end to the business in 1848.

CHANDELIERS

The glass chandelier or lustre was in vogue in England and to a lesser extent in this country throughout the 18th century. At the beginning of the 19th century the design became decadent and metal chandeliers gradually replaced the glass. In their best period some were very elaborate and expensive. The first glass chandelier to be made in this country was made at Pittsburgh in 1810. The New England Glass Co. at Cambridge, Sandwich, and other factories also made them throughout their existence, some of them very elaborate. See CHANDELIERS, PART 5.

CHELMSFORD GLASS WORKS

Established in 1802 at Chelmsford, Massachusetts, by Hunnewell and Gore. The enterprise was successful for a time but in 1827 the firm failed, and the business was taken over by others and operated for about twelve years, when it was removed to Suncook, New Hampshire, where operations were continued until about 1850. It is believed that the "Lowell Railroad" bottle was made at Chelmsford in 1829.

CHEVAL-GLASS

A large glass or mirror, introduced late 18th century, swinging between framed-up supports.

CHINESE GLASS

China does not appear to have given the attention to making glass in early times that she gave to the ceramic arts. The Chinese have, however, for some time past, been making glass of extreme beauty and of graceful shapes. The Chinese snuff-bottles (q.v.), of infinite variety, make one of the most charming items for a collector.

CLEVELAND GLASS WORKS

There were three glass factories at Cleveland, New York. Anthony Landgraft and Sons was founded in 1840, the Union Glass Company in 1851 and the Empire Glass Company. A superior quality of sand found nearby gave to the glass produced here exceptional brilliance. The off-hand pieces now in existence resemble the product of Southern New Jersey glass-works.

COLORED GLASS

See GLASS, *Colored*.

COLUMBIA GLASS WORKS

At Columbia, New Jersey, in operation from about 1812 to 1833. Principal product was a good grade of crown glass for windows. Tableware was occasionally blown from the "pot-ends" of the window glass for home use by the workmen.

CONGRESSVILLE GLASS WORKS

See SARATOGA GLASS.

CORK GLASS

Glass-works were established in Cork, Ireland, late in the 18th century and were carried on by various manufacturers for about sixty years. Cork glass resembles that made at Dublin with a slightly amber tinge. Much of the product was exported to America and to various places in Europe. Cork glass is rarer than that of Waterford. It is not so heavy nor is it as deeply cut.

REFERENCES

Old Irish Glass, STANNUS; Irish Glass, WESTROPP.

CORNING GLASS WORKS

Organized in 1875 at Corning, New York, the successor of the South Ferry Glass Works of Brooklyn, which moved to Corning in 1868. It is at the present time one of the leading glass factories in this country. They make exquisite glass of all kinds, particularly in colors.

COVENTRY GLASS WORKS

This company was started in 1813 at Coventry, Connecticut, and continued until 1848, when the works were closed on account of lack of fuel. They made hollow ware, decanters, demi-johns, and some of the earliest historic flasks in shades of green and amber, notably the General Lafayette and DeWitt Clinton flasks. Their flasks are among the finest, in both design and metal, produced by American makers. Thomas Stebbins, the proprietor, first conceived the idea of stamping the busts of our state and national heroes upon American-made bottles.

REFERENCE

Connecticut Glass, ANTIQUES, Sept. 1935.

CRACKLED GLASS

See GLASS, Crackled.

CULLET

Name given to broken or refuse glass, with which the batch in the pots is mixed. From one quarter to one half in bulk is used in addition to the regular ingredients in making flint glass.

CUP PLATES

Small plates, usually from three to four inches in diameter, in which the cup was set, when the tea was poured into the saucer for cooling before drinking, to protect the table or linen from marks or stains. The first glass cup plates in America were probably made at Sandwich. They were of pressed glass, both transparent and opaque, and were very much in demand for more than thirty years. The design upon them was at first conventional, followed by those of a historical nature, of which alone there are more than forty designs.

Some of the more prominent of these are the "Bunker Hill," "Constitution," "Washington," "Henry Clay," "William Henry Harrison," "Chancellor Livingston," "Benjamin Franklin," these last two being what are known as "Steamboat" designs. The octagonal Washington cup plate is one of the most desired by collectors. There are altogether more than 600 different patterns, and the old cup plates have been frequently imitated in modern glass. There is a size somewhat larger than the usual cup plate, known as the "toddy" plate, and a six-inch diameter plate, the tea plate, both of pressed glass. These are both sufficiently rare to make them desirable for collection also.

REFERENCES

Early American Glass, RHEA M. KNITTLE; Historical Glass Cup Plates, ANTIQUES, Feb. 1922, Jan. 1923; Colored Cup Plates, ANTIQUES, Aug. 1933.

CUT GLASS

See GLASS, Cut.

D

DECANTERS

The decanter became very popular in England, late 17th and early 18th centuries. The necks were ringed, the bodies globular, and the stoppers were often very decorative. The rings, sometimes one, two or three, were of different designs. English decanters of white glass are descendants of the wine flasks of the Renaissance period. In the 19th century, although the body shapes varied somewhat as the years went by, they still maintained the ringed necks.

REFERENCE

Old English Decanters, ANTIQUES, June 1929.

DOERFLINGER GLASS

Established by Christopher Doerflinger at Brooklyn, New York, in 1852. At first flint glass was made of excellent quality, and later glass cutting was included, done at a factory built at Greenpoint, Long Island.

DRINKING GLASSES

There are three groups of English drinking glasses, for wine, ale and beer, and cordial or spirit glasses, and five types: baluster stem, plain stem, air-twist stem, white air-twist stem, and cut stem. In the baluster stem the bowls were thick, their stems bulbous and embellished, if at all, with the tear. First half of the 18th century saw more slender stems and engraved bowls with the tear elongated, also bubble twists, termed air twists, which persisted until about 1760. The twist on 18th-century glasses always descends from right to left. In imitation a reverse direction is usually taken. The white twist stem is much like the air twist, excepting that the twist itself is opaque in white or other color. The white twist had its origin in Venice. Cut-stem glasses eventually superseded the earlier types. See FIRING GLASSES and RUMMER.

REFERENCES
Old English Glasses, ALBERT HARTSHORNE; *English Table Glass*, PERCY BATE; *Development of Twist Stem Drinking Glasses*, ANTIQUES, March, 1929; *English Drinking Glasses*, ANTIQUARIAN, May, 1931; *Jacobite Drinking Glasses*, ANTIQUES, July, 1932.

DUBLIN GLASS
Glass-making became an important industry in Dublin early in the 18th century. The production included every kind of glassware, of a slightly yellowish tint, including chandeliers, girandoles and colored glass, which was made for various purposes, plain, gilt and enameled. The first mention of molded Irish glass occurs at Dublin in 1746. Cut glass became a specialty, also, as at Waterford (q.v.). Glass-making in Dublin ended in 1895.

REFERENCES
Old Irish Glass, STANNUS; *Irish Glass*, WESTROPP.

DUTCH GLASS
See LOW COUNTRIES GLASS.

DYOTTVILLE GLASS WORKS
Originally known as the Kensington Glass Works, started in 1771 and passing through several hands, until in 1831 Dr. Thomas W. Dyott bought the works. Since that time the factory has been known as the Dyottville Glass Works. This is one of the two oldest glass-works in the country to have had an existence to the present time, the other being at Glassboro, New Jersey. This company in its earlier years made a specialty of bottles and flasks of every kind, and more of their designs were copied by other glass factories than those of any other factory. Dr. Dyott was a manufacturer of patent medicines, and great quantities of the factory products were made especially for medicine for several years. In 1838 he went into bankruptcy and retired from the glass factory.

REFERENCES
Early American Glass, RHEA M. KNITTLE; *A Dyott Note*, ANTIQUES, Oct., 1936.

E

ENAMEL GLASS
See GLASS, Enamel.

ENGLISH GLASS

The glass-making industry in England dates from the beginning of the 17th century, although some glass was made in England before that time. This old glass, of which very few examples remain, is generally of a light green tinge. The 18th century saw great development in all branches of the glass industry by the use of coal and the covered crucible and the use of lead as a base, and in the beauty and character of the glass for domestic use. The making of flint glass was perfected, the art of glass cutting reached its greatest beauty, and the fame of English glass was spread throughout the world on the ground of the excellence of the material. Besides glass in great variety, both white and colored, for domestic purposes, and drinking glasses (q.v.) of all descriptions, large quantities were made to be sent to America. The period between 1780 and 1810 is said to have been the most important in English glass-making. See BRISTOL GLASS, NAILSEA GLASS, NEWCASTLE GLASS.

REFERENCES

History of English and Irish Glass, W. A. THORPE; History of Old English Glass, FRANCIS BUCKLEY; Glass Making in England, HARRY J. POWELL; Old English Glasses, ALBERT HARTSHORNE.

ENGRAVED GLASS
See GLASS, Engraved.

ESSEX GLASS WORKS

Organized about 1787 by Robert Hewes and Charles F. Kupfer, a German, and a factory was erected on Essex Street in Boston. The enterprise was successful and large quantities of window glass were produced. In 1809 the name of the company was changed to Boston Glass Manufactory, and in 1811 the company moved to South Boston where a larger factory had been erected. Here, they met with various difficulties and were finally compelled to suspend. The works were later used by the American Flint Glass Works (q.v.).

ETCHED GLASS
See GLASS, Etched.

ETNA GLASS WORKS
See AMELUNG GLASS WORKS.

F

FAVRILE GLASS
See TIFFANY GLASS.

FEDERAL HILL GLASS WORKS
See BALTIMORE GLASS WORKS.

FIRING GLASSES

These drinking glasses were always short and stumpy, not exceeding four and one-half inches in height, and were

DETAIL OF BEDSPREAD, AMERICAN CREWEL EMBROIDERY, 18TH CENTURY

AMERICAN CREWEL EMBROIDERY, EARLY 18TH CENTURY

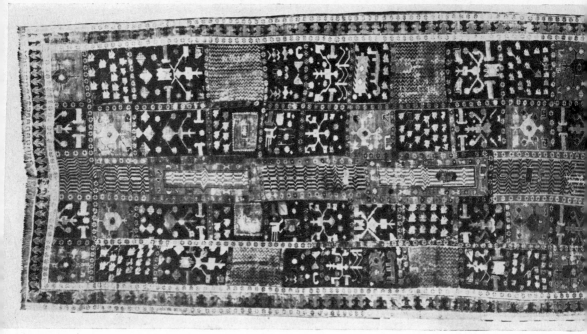

Persian Flower Garden Rug, about 1700; Length, 12 feet, 4 inches; Width, 6 feet, 4 in

Rare Antique Hamadan Rug—Length, 8 feet, 8 inches; Width, 4 feet, 4 inches

called "firing glasses" from their very thick and solid feet (bases) with which the table was rapped in response to a toast, which was supposed to resemble a volley. They were made chiefly from 1740 to 1770, and they are among the most interesting of the old English drinking glasses. See DRINKING GLASSES and RUMMER.

FLASKS
See BOTTLES.

FLEMISH GLASS
See LOW COUNTRIES GLASS.

FLINT GLASS
See GLASS, *Flint.*

FOOT
The foot or base of a glass is a most important point to consider in judging the period of the glass. The earlier glasses have high feet, sloping up well towards the stem. Flat feet are always a sign of late glass. The "folded" foot is to thicken and strengthen the rim. A number of folded-foot glasses are early, but it is not an infallible sign of age, as it continued to be made until nearly the middle of the 19th century. The English foot was folded over from the top, differing from the Venetian style, which was to fold the foot under. Domed feet, made principally about the middle of the 18th century, are those which rise markedly in the middle. These were difficult to make and the number made was small.

FRAUDS
There is probably no department of antiques in which there is so much room for fraud as in old glass, none in which imitation has been carried to a finer point. The reason for this is that the demand, of course, is much greater than the supply. Glass-works in New Jersey for some time have been making glass in imitation of the shape, color and design of the glass produced in earlier days by the South Jersey glass-makers. Examine at leisure any piece that you contemplate purchasing and by daylight, if possible, so as to make the color test, which is often, but not always, the most reliable. If you can compare the piece with other pieces of whose authenticity there is no doubt, it will be helpful, and do not hesitate to ask the advice of a glass expert if you know of one whose opinion you can seek. Do not be hurried in making your decision, and insist upon a "money back" guarantee in writing if you make the purchase.

FRENCH GLASS
Glass-making in France appears to have been carried on from Roman times to the present day. During the 15th and 16th centuries, the glass made showed a strong Venetian influence, although the shapes are simpler and rather heavier. A French glass-maker rediscovered in 1688 the process of making cast glass plates of almost unlimited size, and the great glass mirrors at Versailles were

made by that process. Although there were quantities of glass made all over France through the centuries, there is at the present time no representative gathering of the old glass that can properly be called a collection. A few scattered examples are in the Louvre and in the Musée de Cluny. Modern French glass ranks high among the glass of the world. See BACCARAT GLASS.

REFERENCE
Glass, EDWARD DILLON.

G

GERMAN GLASS

Early German glass was much influenced by Venetian methods and shapes. During the 16th century, however, the characteristic enameled glass was made in distinctively national shapes and continued to be made during the 17th and 18th centuries. The best known and most popular are the large cylindrical beakers of white or green glass, enameled with the coat-of-arms of the owner or the arms of the different states. These beakers have been copied by the glassmakers of later periods.

REFERENCE
Glass, EDWARD DILLON.

GIMMAL FLASK

A flask or bottle, containing two separate compartments, each with a spout. Used as a container for oil or vinegar, usually.

GLASS

The invention of glass dates from the earliest antiquity and may probably be attributed to the Egyptians. Glass, at first, was doubtless opaque, then translucent and finally transparent. These various steps meant long centuries of experiments. In Rome, the art of glassmaking was developed to a high pitch of excellence, and it is said that glass was employed there for a greater number of purposes than it is today. Colored and ornamental glass held much the same place then that china does among us today. It was also used in slab form for wall decoration, colored in imitation of veneers of marble or porphyry. In Europe, for nearly a thousand years little glass of artistic interest was produced, excepting the stained glass (q.v.) used in the windows of the Gothic churches. Glass-making flourished in Constantinople throughout the Dark Ages, and Venice, where glass-making became a monopoly in the 13th century, received its impulse from Constantinople. From Venice glass-making made its way gradually to France and to England, until in the 16th and 17th centuries it was established in those countries and in other parts of Europe, notably Bohemia.

The history of modern glass begins with the Venetian crystal glass of the

16th century, the first since the time of the Romans. The base of all glass is sand or silica, and the alkalies used are principally soda, lime, and potash. Lead is sometimes used to replace the alkalies, in whole or in part. Glass is formed by the fusion of the mixture to form silicates in various proportions, according to the qualities required. Glass has certain peculiar properties: in ductility, when heated, it ranks next to gold; it is flexible and elastic when heated but extremely brittle when cold; it can be drawn into a thread sufficiently fine to be woven into a fabric, and to such a degree of thinness that it may remain suspended momentarily in the air; it resists the action of all acids excepting hydrofluoric acid.

The composition of the principal kinds of glass is:

Window and plate glass; silica, soda and lime.

The so-called crown glass is the best of the window glass.

Flint and crystal glass; silica, potash and lead.

The greater ease with which flint glass could be fashioned led to its adoption for tableware, decanters and the better grades of bottles.

Bottle glass; silica, lime and alumina.

Bottle glass is the cheapest of all glass.

Any of the above kinds of glass may be colored by the use of metallic oxides. See *Colored Glass.*

REFERENCES

Glass, G. A. EISEN and F. KOUCHAKJI; *Glass,* EDWARD DILLON.

Agate Glass. Also called slag glass. It is the glass made from iron slag, which is very fusible, cryolite and manganese, producing a variety of curious color combinations. Glass of this description was made, especially at one period, from 1900 to 1903, in chocolate and golden agate color. See AGATA GLASS.

Blown Glass. The methods of glass blowing and the tools with which it is done are now very little different from those which have served workers in glass from the remotest times. The blowing-tube was in use by the Romans at the beginning of the Christian Era, and specimens of blown glass of that period are numerous. Blown glass was also made in Spain, in Gaul and in Southern England during the Roman occupation. Until glass blowing by machine was perfected, blown glass was just what its name implies; blown by the air from the lungs of the glass-worker. All glass was blown glass up to the time of the invention of a method of pressing glass in molds by an American mechanic about 1827, which process, by reducing cost of glass manufacture, revolutionized glass-making in this country and abroad. Blown glass, however, is more lustrous and more desirable from the collector's viewpoint than pressed glass. See *Three-Mold Glass.*

Cameo Glass. Glass, usually colored, with a partial or complete coating of opaque white glass, upon which the relief ornament was carved. It was known to the skilled glass-makers about the time of the Christian Era, and the Portland Vase (q.v.) is a survival of that period. Glass of that description was not again made successfully until the last half of the 19th century, by Thomas Webb & Sons at Stourbridge, England.

REFERENCE

Cameo Glass, ANTIQUES, Sept. 1936.

Colored Glass. Colored glass was a feature of both early Venetian and Bohemian glass. It was also made by the Romans, both opaque and transparent, in a variety of colors with the exception of ruby red, which appears to have been unknown to them. The earliest made in England was at Stourbridge about 1750. Excellent colored glass was also made later at Bristol, London, and other places in England and in this country. Stiegel colored glass was at once one of the earliest and one of the most beautiful. The industry was well established before the end of the century both here and abroad, and a great variety of table ware and toilet articles were made of colored glass. The formulas for making this glass include the following oxides in addition to that for flint glass:

Blue transparent glass:—oxide of cobalt

Red ruby:—oxide of gold

Amethyst or purple:—oxide of manganese

Emerald green:—copper scales and iron ore

Orange:—iron and manganese

Gold topaz:—oxide of uranium

Hard white opaque:—putty prepared from tin and lead

Soft white opaque: arsenic and antimony

See *Stained Glass.*

REFERENCE

English Colored Glass, ANTIQUES, April and May, 1931.

Crackled Glass. This kind of glass is said to have been first made in the 16th century by the Venetians, and the effect probably was obtained by suddenly cooling the surface when the object was half blown.

Crown Glass. A superior quality of window glass made without lead.

Cut Glass. All cut glass is, of course, easily distinguishable. It is usually of thick-walled vessels of flint glass, sharp to the touch and heavy. The cutting is produced by pressing the glass against grinding wheels, and the ground parts are finally polished on a wooden wheel supplied with a fine polishing material. Cutting on glass originated probably in Bohemia in the 17th century. It does not seem to have spread into other European countries until about the second decade of the 18th century. In England, it was first mentioned about 1720, and it was not made in Ireland until after about 1740. In this country it was not generally made until during the second quarter of the 19th century. The fine early English, Irish and American cut glass was always from blown glass, not pressed. See LIBBEY GLASS COMPANY.

Enameled Glass. The enameled glass of the Saracens during the 13th, 14th and 15th centuries was the most decorative and magnificent of all glass ever made. It was, furthermore, the first application of solid enamels to the surface of glass, porcelain or faience. It probably had its origin in the enamels used on metals of the Byzantine Era. On the opaque white glass made at Bristol, England, in the second half of the 18th century, enameled colors were applied in a most artistic fashion and then fired.

Engraved Glass. Engraved patterns are produced by applying emery powder, mixed with oil, to the edges of small revolving copper discs. Engraving by the use of a diamond preceded the use of the wheel. Some of the best engraved glass produced here was made by the New England Glass Co. at Cambridge.

Etched Glass. By the use of hydrofluoric acid an exquisite form of decoration is obtained, seeming hardly more than a shadow of a design blown upon the glass. The glass is first coated with wax and the design is then scratched upon it.

Oddly, according to chemical history hydrofluoric acid was not discovered until 1771, by Scheele, although Henry Schwanhardt of Bohemia first etched glass about 1670, by what he called *"aqua fortis."* It is probable that there was a considerable amount of fluorspar in the glass and that, through the reactions in his process, Schwanhardt may unwittingly have been the real discoverer of hydrofluoric acid.

Flint Glass (or *Crystal Glass*). This glass, essentially a silicate of lead and potassium or sodium, was developed, it is claimed, in England in the last half of the 17th century. A certain amount of the earlier glass was actually made with flints, from which it derives its name, but by the end of the 17th century, lead glass displaced the flint. The materials used are carefully selected as the glass must be of great purity. It is heavy and, in the best quality, of great brilliance and lustre. It cuts and polishes as finely as rock crystal. England claims to have been the first country to have perfected the glass as we now know it.

Lime Glass. A substitute for lead flint glass discovered in 1864 by William Leighton, a chemist employed in a glass factory at Wheeling, West Virginia, which enabled glass manufacturers to produce a glass for tableware and other purposes at a greatly reduced cost. This discovery had a very injurious effect upon some of the leading glass-works, notably those of New England, before they could adapt themselves to this new competition. Lime glass cools and is finished more quickly than lead glass.

Milk Glass. An opaque, white and translucent glass resembling porcelain. This glass, for which Bristol glass (q.v.) is famous, was known to the Egyptians and it was in use by the Romans. Its revival is credited to the Venetians, and it was made at various glass factories in the Low Countries, Germany, Bohemia, France, and Spain, besides England. All decorated it after the manner of porcelain with gilding and enamel colors. None of it, however, is quite equal to that of Bristol, and genuine old Bristol glass of that kind is exceedingly rare. Much of the glass that collectors and dealers call Bristol is German or Dutch.

REFERENCES
    A *Note on Milk Glass*, ANTIQUES, Oct., 1928; *Milky and Milk White Glass*, ANTIQUES, July 1935.

Mirror Glass. This glass was at first made only at Venice, but mirrors backed by lead or tin were produced in the 13th century, and in the last half of the 17th century mirror glass was made in France and in England. A Frenchman rediscovered a way about 1688 to make large mirrors from flat, cast plates of glass, and his product is to be seen in the Palace at Versailles. This result was obtained by casting and by subsequent rolling and polishing the plates, after which they were coated with a tin-mercury amalgam. The same method was introduced into England about a hundred years later. Specimens of the early English mirrors are to be found in many places in England, notably at Hampton Court Palace. Most of this early English glass was made at Vauxhall (q.v.), from blown glass in cylinder form, split open, flattened and polished; the backs being silvered by mercury floated over tin foil.

Molded Glass. Glass was blown in molds before the time of the Christian Era and the process has been continued to modern times. In the blowing in the full-size mold, the air forced the plastic glass into the form of the design cut in intaglio on the inside surface so that the finished piece, when taken from the mold, showed a depression on the inside to correspond to each protuberance on the outside. This glass, known to collectors as "three-mold glass" (q.v.), is much sought for. The patterns used in this country are roughly in three forms: geometric, arched and Baroque, and constitute one means of differentiating this type from other types of glass. The patterns of old English and Irish glass are simpler. Similar molds are used for pressed glass (q.v.) but the patterns, as a rule, are more intricate than those designed for blown glass. The mold marks are more prominent, the inside of the glass is smooth, and the glass lacks the lustre of the blown glass.

REFERENCE

Molded Glass, ANTIQUES, Dec., 1928.

Off-Hand Glass. This name was given to that work of the early American glass-makers done in their spare moments, designed for their own use or for gifts to friends. Both useful and ornamental articles were made from the left-over ends of batches, and examples of this glass are eagerly sought by collectors.

Opal Glass. See *White Glass.*

Opalescent Glass. See *White Glass.*

Overlay Glass. See GLASS OVERLAY.

Pattern Glass. Name given to the pressed glass produced by all American factories in large quantities from about 1840 onwards. Until about the time of the Civil War this was all lead flint glass, after which lime glass, being cheaper, was substituted. This last does not have the bell-like ring of the flint glass. The number of the patterns used

and their variations are almost without end. One writer asserts that there are nearly three hundred patterns that are collectible in sets. The low price of this

glass, compared with blown glass, and the demand for it gave the manufacturers opportunity for quantity production and they took advantage of it. See PATTERNS IN GLASS.

REFERENCES

Early American Pressed Glass, RUTH WEBB LEE; Rarities in Pattern Glass, ANTIQUES, Mar., 1935.

Pressed Glass. Pressed glass is so-called because the glass is pressed into the mold by means of a plunger with a long handle or lever, instead of being blown into it. By this method, the piece is smooth on the inside, regardless of how deep the design or pattern may be on the outside surface. The molds are similar in construction to those for blown glass, although the patterns differ in style and variety of design. It is a less expensive and quicker process of making glass.

Experiments in pressing glass began about the same time (1827) at both Cambridge and Sandwich, Massachusetts, and the method, once firmly established, revolutionized glass-making everywhere. In 1836, it was being made at Birmingham, England, and in France, Germany and Austria at about the same time. This caused a bad break in the prices of glass abroad, but in this country it seemed to put the glass industry on its feet. By the middle of the 19th century it had invaded every market here and abroad and three-fourths of the product of American glass-works was pressed glass. Pressed glass is considered less desirable from the collector's standpoint, as it lacks the lustre of blown glass, for as a rule the glass is not of as good metal. See *Pattern Glass*.

REFERENCES

Early American Pressed Glass, RUTH WEBB LEE; *Pressed Glass of Old Sandwich*, ANTIQUES, Feb. 1922; *Early Glass Pressing at Cambridge and Sandwich*, ANTIQUES, Oct. and Dec. 1935.

Silvered Glass. This type of glass was made by blowing a thin glass object and coating this with a silvery substance, after which another thin layer of glass was "cupped" over the silver surface. Another method was to pour the silvery substance into the space between the glass layers through a hole where the pontil was located, and the hole afterwards was plugged. This plug or seal must be kept closed, for if the air is allowed to enter, the silver coating gradually disappears. This kind of glass was made by the New England Glass Company at Cambridge as early as 1850.

Stained Glass. The stained glass, which in the later Middle Ages was restricted to use in the windows of the churches, is actually colored and painted glass. It had a high potash content, which served to promote the brilliancy of the colors. The most ancient stained glass window in existence today is in the Abbey of St. Denis near Paris, dedicated in 1142. The most beautiful, perhaps, are those of the Church of St. Chapelle in Paris, and in the Cathedral of Chartres, where there are 146 windows of stained glass, depicting about five thousand human figures. Stained glass for windows was also made in England in the 15th century and probably even earlier. See *Colored Glass*.

REFERENCES

Ancient Stained and Painted Glass, F. SYDNEY EDEN; *Stained Glass*, ALFRED WERCK; *Stained Glass of the Middle Ages in England and France*, ARNOLD and SAINT.

Three-Mold Glass. The abbreviation of the term, blown contact, three-section mold. (See also *Insufflated*). Only the earlier glass which was blown, not pressed, into a mold is properly called "three-mold" glass. It is blown in full-size three-piece contact molds or in a small open-top mold. In the open-top mold, the glass is reheated and expanded by blowing and shaping in the open, leaving a suggestion on the surface of the pattern of the mold. This type of glass is a product peculiar to America of the early 19th century. The patterns used for this glass are a distinctive feature, and are quite different from those for pressed glass. They are, however, more elaborate than those used in making English and Irish blown glass. Nearly all of the so-called three-mold glass was made before 1850. A large proportion of this glass was made at Sandwich and at the New England Glass Co. in Cambridge. The pressed "pattern" glass is chiefly of a date later than 1850. See *Molded Glass*.

REFERENCES

Three-Mold Glass, ANTIQUES, August 1924; *Early American Glass*, RHEA M. KNITTLE.

White Glass. Opaque white glass (called opal) owes its opacity to oxide of tin added to the regular glass formula. See *Milk Glass*.

GLASS COLLECTING
See ANTIQUE GLASS.

GLASS OVERLAY
This effect was obtained by blowing the desired object and one or two corresponding "cups" to fit over the first piece. After cooling the design was obtained by cutting through the outer layer or layers to the under surface.

GLASSBORO (New Jersey) GLASS WORKS
This factory was started about 1780 by Stanger Bros. About 1840, Whit-

ney Bros. purchased the plant, since known as the Whitney Glass Works. Bottles and flasks were their principal product. In 1850, they produced the "Jenny Lind" flask, with globular bottle and long slender neck, with a relief portrait on the side, which was very popular. This is one of the two oldest glassworks in the country to have had a continuous existence, the other being the Dyottville Glass Works (q.v.) at Kensington, Pennsylvania. The Glassboro plant is now a part of the property of the Owens Bottle Company.

GREENSBORO (Pennsylvania) GLASS WORKS
This was a glass factory, established by Christian Kramer and other Germans about 1807, who had earlier come to this country with Amelung (q.v.) and after the failure of that enterprise had drifted west. Here were produced some of the choicest pieces of our early glassware in amber, green, cobalt and other colors and in various attractive designs. This glass is also referred to as "Kramer family" glass. The factory continued in operation until 1849.

REFERENCE
Greensboro Glass, ANTIQUARIAN, Aug. 1931.

H

HAMMONTON (New Jersey) GLASS WORKS
This factory was started about 1820 and continued operations until about

1858, making bottles and flasks, also window glass. In the years 1836-8 they made some of the best designed flasks in the American catalogue. The color is usually of a light aquamarine.

HANDLES

See KNOBS.

HOBBS, BROCKUNIER & Co.

Manufacturers of glass at Wheeling, West Virginia, at which plant William Leighton, formerly superintendent for the New England Glass Co. at Cambridge, discovered a process of making glass at a greatly reduced cost by the use of lime in the formula instead of lead. See WHEELING GLASS WORKS.

INSUFFLATED

A term used to indicate early glass hitherto known as "contact three-section blown mold." The molds used in making this glass were always full-sized. The patterns are usually distinctive of this type of glass, and the mold marks are, as a rule, visible upon its surface. It was also more iridescent than other American glass, owing to its being thinner and to the method of manipulation. See GLASS, *Blown* and GLASS, *Molded*.

IRISH GLASS

Glass-works flourished at Belfast, Cork, Dublin and Waterford, in Ireland, during the 18th and 19th centuries.

HUGHES STREET GLASS WORKS

See BALTIMORE GLASS WORKS.

HURRICANE GLASSES

This name was given to the glass, resembling an oversized lamp chimney, used with candlesticks to prevent the wind or draft from blowing on the light.

I

Irish glass is very tough; it sings with a clear note when struck; it is interesting and, in most cases, beautiful, although Waterford glass appears to have the preference of the collectors. But it is probable that the workmen traveled from one place to another, using the same materials for the metal, the same patterns for the objects made and the same designs for decoration. Great quantities of Irish glass were exported to this country until the glass industry in Ireland came to an end, largely through the effects of English competition. See CORK GLASS, DUBLIN GLASS, WATERFORD (Ireland) GLASS.

REFERENCES

Irish Glass, M. S. DUDLEY WESTROPP; *Irish Cut Glass*, ANTIQUES, June 1928; *Old Irish Glass*, Mrs. GRAYDON STANNUS.

K

KEENE (New Hampshire) GLASS WORKS

A factory for making glass bottles, flasks and decanters was started here in 1816 on Marlboro Street, but it was not until some years later, under the management of Justus Perry, that success crowned their efforts. The factory remained in operation until 1850. In the earlier years of its operation clear flint glass was produced to some extent, also blown three-mold glass in amber and olive-green. Another factory called the New Hampshire Glass Factory was started on Prison Street at about the same time as the other, producing window glass, bottles and "off-hand" pieces blown by the workmen for home use. This plant was destroyed by fire in 1855. Most of the Keene bottles and flasks are in varying shades of green and amber, although some are of a bluish color. Those best known are the "Sunburst" and Masonic-Eagle designs, of which the "Sunburst" is, perhaps, the best. The glass is heavy, rather coarse in texture, and in a wide range of colors. The off-hand pieces, which the blowers were allowed to make for themselves for home use, are very rare.

REFERENCES

The Keene Glass Works, ANTIQUES, May 1926 and June 1927; The Keene Masonic Bottle, ANTIQUES, Feb. 1924.

KENSINGTON GLASS WORKS

See DYOTTVILLE GLASS WORKS.

KENTUCKY GLASS WORKS

This factory started at Louisville, Kentucky, in 1850 and made bottles, demijohns, jars and flasks. After a few years the name was changed to the Louisville Glass Works (q.v.).

KNOBS

Glass handles or knobs for furniture were usually made of pressed glass in a wide range of patterns and sizes. Some were also of blown glass and some of cut glass. There was a considerable variety of colors: clear white, opaque white, opal and light blue, the most common. The larger ones were also used to support pictures and mirrors and to hold back curtains. Quantities of these glass knobs were made at Sandwich, Pittsburgh and other glass factories.

REFERENCE

Glass Knobs, ANTIQUES, May 1928 and April 1929.

KRAMER FAMILY GLASS

See GREENSBORO GLASS WORKS.

L

Lacy Glass

See Sandwich Glass.

Lamps

Although glass lamps may have been produced in some of the 18th century glass-works, there is no existing example of their product. Until the end of the first quarter of the 19th century, lighting in the home was chiefly by means of metal lamps. Soon after starting operations, the New England Glass Works, Cambridge, and the Boston and Sandwich Glass Company began making glass lamps which became at once very popular, gradually displacing the metal lamps and soon becoming an important branch of the glass industry.

Lamp bases were among the earliest of pressed objects, and the tops were more often blown and ornamented by cutting and engraving. They were made in a variety of shapes and sizes, of clear and colored glass, at first with burners for whale oil, then the flat wick burners for kerosene, and glass lamps maintained leadership for home lighting from that time until the introduction of electric lighting. See Part 5, Lamps.

REFERENCES

Colonial Lighting, Arthur Hayward; Cambridge Glass, 1818 to 1888, Lura W. Watkins.

Lancaster (New York) Glass Works

In 1849, a group of Pittsburgh workmen started a factory here. A variety of bottles and flasks for liquor, medicines and perfumes in amber, aquamarine, green and clear glass was the chief product. One of their flasks, "Success to the Railroad," is considered to be the chief Lancaster prize. They also made a Masonic flask. The plant was operated under various names until in 1881 it became known as the Lancaster Cooperative Glass Works, Limited.

REFERENCES

The Lancaster Glass Works, ANTIQUES, Oct. 1927; ANTIQUES, Aug. 1933.

Libbey Glass Company (Toledo, Ohio)

This company, the successor to the New England Glass Company (q.v.), has brought the art of cutting glass to the highest state of perfection. Libbey cut glass surpasses in mechanical and artistic qualities the best wares of a similar nature produced elsewhere, and its fabrications are world-famous for the depth and richness of their designs, their purity of color and their prismatic brilliancy.

Lighting

See Lamps above, also Lamps and Lights in Part 5.

Looking-Glasses

See Glass, Mirror, also Mirrors, Part 1.

LOUISVILLE (Kentucky) GLASS WORKS

Succeeded the Kentucky Glass Works in 1856, and for a few years was successful. After undergoing several changes in name, the business was finally abandoned, owing to the competition of Pittsburgh Glass Works and of the newly opened glass factories in the natural-gas belt in Ohio. Their scroll flask and their fluted flask are both attractive, but the fluted flask is the more rare. Some of these are marked and they are made in a wide range of colors: amber, brown, sapphire blue, olive and clear glass among them.

REFERENCE
The Kentucky Glass Works, ANTIQUES, Feb. 1926.

Low COUNTRIES GLASS

In and around Antwerp, Brussels and Liége the making of glass during the 15th and 16th centuries seems to have been attended with greater success than in many other parts of Europe. Glass after the style of the Venetian product, although rather heavier, was made. England imported from Antwerp a considerable amount of glass in the 17th century and the export trade to other countries from this center was large. For a time there was an active rivalry between the glass-makers of Antwerp and Amsterdam. During the 17th and 18th centuries, engraving on glass with a diamond was carried to a high state of perfection, especially on the roemer (q.v.) in Holland, and much glass was sent from England to be so engraved. Immense quantities of glass were made at Liége in the 18th century in great variety and of excellent quality.

REFERENCE
Glass, EDWARD DILLON.

LYON (JAMES B.) & COMPANY

In 1852, this company purchased the old O'Hara Glass Works at Pittsburgh and greatly enlarged them and soon became one of the foremost producers in this country. It was the first to adopt pressed glass as its main line of production. Deming Jarves of Sandwich considered Lyon glass as the exemplification of all that was best in the industry. The Lyon Company received many medals and other honors for superiority in pressed glassware. The house held a foremost rank until 1886.

M

MANTUA (Ohio) GLASS Co.

A glass-works was established there in 1821 and for a few years produced window glass and tableware of a light green color, aquamarine and amber, some of which was of excellent quality. The factory was closed in 1829.

REFERENCE
ANTIQUES, Vol. 26, 27 and 28.

MARLBORO STREET GLASS WORKS
See KEENE GLASS WORKS.

MARVER
See TOOLS.

McKEE (S.) & Co.

Pittsburgh glass factory started in 1834 to manufacture window glass and bottles, chiefly. In 1850 five sons of Thomas McKee, one of the partners, organized the firm of McKee and Brothers, specializing in pressed-glass tableware in great variety.

MEXICAN GLASS

The making of glass began in Mexico soon after the Conquest, became an important industry, and continued so for two hundred years. Some of it is not only beautifully incised but further enriched with painting, chiefly in gold. In the opinion of Dr. Edwin Atlee Barber this particular style of glass was made at Pueblo, where glass factories are still in existence making flasks, bottles and drinking glasses, clear in color and of pleasing shapes. None in the cut or gilded style is made now, but many small glass-works are making at the present time tableware resembling the early American blown glass.

METAL

The term used for the molten glass without regard to its fashioning. By the addition of broken glass (cullet) (q.v.) to the regular mixture a better quality of metal is obtained.

MILK GLASS
See GLASS, Milk.

MILLEFIORI GLASS

An Italian word, meaning the glass of a thousand flowers. Rods of glass of different colors were arranged in bundles, exposed to heat, and then the air squeezed out until they formed a solid mass. When cut across, the design showed exactly the same at each cross section. These were often set in a ball of plain glass for a paper weight. This type of glass was first made by the Romans. The art of making it was rediscovered by the Venetians, and in France in the 19th century paper weights of this glass became very popular. In this country they were made by the New England Glass Co., Sandwich, and other glass-works.

MIRROR GLASS
See GLASS, Mirror.

MOLDED GLASS
See GLASS, Molded.

MOLDS

Molds were made in sections of wood or metal, hinged together, some opening vertically, others horizontally, and the design was cut in intaglio on the inside surface. The glass, whether blown or pressed, was very apt to have a seam where the sections joined unless the mold was new or it fitted tightly. Sometimes the patterns were so arranged that the seams would fall upon part of the ornamentation. Three-section molds were probably used first in the late 18th century and continued in favor until about the middle of the 19th century. The so-called part mold, used with blown glass, was small, with an open top, which gave to the glass its preliminary form, after which it was taken from the mold, reheated and expanded to the required size and shape by blowing in the open. Molds in one piece were used in making glass objects like tumblers, where the top was the largest part. When a piece was small at the top or it had a curved outline, such as a bottle, it was necessary to use a two-piece or a three-piece mold and some pieces were made in four-section molds. The molds for pressed glass are similar to those used for blown glass but the results obtained are quite different. See GLASS, *Molded*.

MT. VERNON GLASS WORKS

A New York State glass company organized in 1810 and located in the same town. The factory was operated by the Granger brothers for several years. The product appears to have been chiefly bottles, flasks and decanters.

REFERENCE
ANTIQUES, Vol. 16, pp. 193 and 394.

MT. WASHINGTON GLASS CO.

At New Bedford, Massachusetts, was organized in 1837 by Deming Jarves for his son George. Prior to the closing of the factory, 1870, W. L. Libbey was connected there, leaving New Bedford to go to Cambridge as manager for the New England Glass Co. Interest of collectors is chiefly in the late colored ware produced at these works, among which so-called peachblow glass was prominent.

MURANO

The island near Venice where the glass-making was done. See VENETIAN GLASS.

MUSKINGUM COUNTY (Ohio) GLASS WORKS

There were several glass-works in this territory, the earliest of which was established in 1815. Among them were the Whitney Glass Works (q.v.), the Putnam Glass House, the Flint Glass House and the Window Glass House. Their product was mainly bottles, flasks and carboys.

REFERENCES
Early American Glass, RHEA M. KNITTLE; Muskingum County Glass Works, ANTIQUES, Oct. 1924.

N

NAILSEA (England) GLASS WORKS

The glass-works at Nailsea, England, about nine miles from Bristol, were

started by John R. Lucas in 1788 and glass-making was carried on there until 1873. The ware was, in general, cruder and cheaper than that of Bristol. It is inferior in style, color, texture and

workmanship. Ornamental flasks were Nailsea's chief product. These flasks vary in height from three to ten inches, and they were made in various colors as well as in the ribbon effects. Bottles, jugs and bowls were also made. A characteristic of Nailsea bottle glass is a scattering of spots and blotches in thin milk and clear glass. Another is decoration by threads, loops and stripes of white enamel on clear glass. These also were made in colors (polychrome). Old Nailsea glass is now quite rare and commands a high price. See ENGLISH GLASS.

REFERENCE

Classification of Nailsea Glass, ANTIQUES, Jan. 1932.

NEW BREMEN (Maryland) GLASS WORKS
See AMELUNG.

NEWCASTLE (England) GLASS

Drinking glasses were made here late in the 16th century, but specimens of this early glass are not known to exist today. A century later when lead (flint) glass was introduced here, two factories

were in operation and continued to produce glass for about two hundred years. Some of this was the best flint glass ever produced in England, of which its clarity (whiteness) is an evidence. Toward the end of the 18th century new glasshouses were erected which emphasized quantity rather than quality, and the reputation of Newcastle glass declined. Imitations of Bristol opaque, white and colored glass were made, and later Bohemian glass was imitated. For a cen-

tury Newcastle has also produced pressed glass. See ENGLISH GLASS.

REFERENCE

Some Types of Newcastle Glass, ANTIQUES, June 1933.

NEW ENGLAND CROWN GLASS CO.

Cambridge, Massachusetts. Organized in 1824, and although separate from the New England Glass Co., intimately connected with it. They made crown glass in various grades and for a time were very successful. The business became insolvent in 1838 and the works were finally taken over by the New England Glass Co.

CHINESE ANIMAL CARPET, CH'IEN-LUNG PERIOD (1736-1795)
LENGTH, 11 FEET, 7 INCHES; WIDTH, 11 FEET, 5 INCHES

FRENCH (AUBUSSON) TAPESTRY CARPET, 18TH CENTURY—LENGTH, 21 FEET, 6 INCHES; WIDTH,
15 FEET, 9 INCHES

EXAMPLES OF VENETIAN LACE—THE TWO UPPER, 17TH CENTURY; NEXT BELOW, 16TH CENTURY; LOWEST, 18TH CENTURY

REFERENCE

Cambridge Glass, 1818 to 1888, LURA W. WATKINS.

NEW ENGLAND GLASS BOTTLE CO.

Cambridge, Massachusetts. Another factory closely connected with the New England Glass Co., established in 1826 and in existence for nineteen years. Their object was to produce black and green glass wares, and presumably this factory was the source of some of the early bottles and flasks now sought for.

REFERENCE

Cambridge Glass, 1818 to 1888, LURA W. WATKINS.

NEW ENGLAND GLASS COMPANY

This company, founded at Cambridge, Massachusetts, in 1818 by Edmund H. Monroe and others, purchased a property known as the Boston Porcelain and Glass Company for the site of their works. It continued in operation for about seventy years and a great variety of objects in plain blown, molded, pressed, colored and cut glass were produced. Beautifully engraved ware was also a product of this company. Success attended the efforts of the company from the start, and by the middle of the century it was said to be the largest glass manufactory in the world. Deming Jarves, who in 1825 founded the Boston and Sandwich Glass Company, was previously general manager at Cambridge. The method of making pressed glass (q.v.) was introduced here and at Sandwich at about the same time, and credit for perfecting this method is given by some to one company and by others to the other company. Practically all of the glass of this factory was lead flint, whether plain or cut. The pontil-mark appears on only the earliest pieces. After a successful career for about fifty years, the competition from lime-glass makers and the excessive cost of fuel, compared with oil and natural gas of the western manufacturers, brought disaster to the New England Company. In 1878 the works were leased to W. L. Libbey, who had been agent for the company since 1872, and ten years later they were moved to Toledo, Ohio. See LIBBEY GLASS COMPANY.

REFERENCE

Cambridge Glass, 1818 to 1888, LURA W. WATKINS.

NEW GENEVA (Pennsylvania) GLASS WORKS

This factory was established in 1797 by Christian Kramer and others of the German workmen who were brought to America by John Frederick Amelung in 1784. See AMELUNG GLASS WORKS. It continued at New Geneva until 1807 when it was removed to Greensboro (q.v.). During the first six years Albert Gallatin, afterwards Secretary of the Treasury of the United States, was a partner. The product was mainly window glass, although bottles, pitchers, etc., were made of a pale green shade.

Later, a factory was started here again and continued to make glass until 1857.

REFERENCE

New Geneva Glass, ANTIQUARI-AN, Aug. 1931.

NEW HAMPSHIRE GLASS FACTORY

See KEENE GLASS WORKS.

NEW JERSEY GLASS WORKS

There were many glass-works in New Jersey during the early 19th century. Among these see SOUTH JERSEY GLASS, COLUMBIA GLASS WORKS, GLASSBORO GLASS WORKS, HAMMONTON GLASS WORKS, WATERFORD GLASS WORKS, also WISTARBERG GLASS. Consult Early American Glass, RHEA M. KNITTLE.

NEW LONDON (Connecticut) GLASS WORKS

A factory here operating under various names from 1856 to 1874, produced colored glass and aquamarine flasks, jars and demijohns.

NEW YORK STATE GLASS HOUSES

New York State was among the first of the states where glass was made. There were at least thirty to forty little glass factories scattered about the state making window glass and bottles, but most of them were short-lived and their production was small. The glass was usually amber or aquamarine. Practically none of them produced blown tableware or decorative glass as a commercial product. Many of the workmen were employed formerly at South Jersey works, and carried into their new employment, traditions of style and methods earlier used. See ONEIDA GLASS FACTORY.

REFERENCE

ANTIQUES, July, Sept. and Nov. 1929 and July and Sept. 1930.

NORTHUMBERLAND GLASS COMPANY

Located at Leamington, England, near Newcastle, the factory here, founded in 1787, carried on glass-making successfully throughout the 19th century.

O

OFF-HAND GLASS

See GLASS, Off-hand.

O'HARA GLASS WORKS

See PITTSBURGH GLASS HOUSES.

OHIO GLASS FACTORIES

For an account of some of the early glass-works in Ohio see MUSKINGUM COUNTY GLASS WORKS, MANTUA AND WHITE GLASS WORKS, also consult Early American Glass, RHEA M. KNITTLE.

ONEIDA (New York) GLASS FACTORY

This factory was organized in 1809 and continued operations successfully until 1836 at Vernon, New York. Their product was chiefly window glass, bottles and flasks.

REFERENCE

ANTIQUES, July, 1929.

OVERLAY

See GLASS OVERLAY.

P

PAIRPONT GLASS COMPANY

New Bedford, Massachusetts. This is the last remaining 19th century glass-works in this country that has used hand-blowing methods continuously.

PAPER WEIGHTS

Glass paper weights were very much the fashion in the Victorian period. They were made at glass-works both here and abroad, but the finest specimens are probably those of Baccarat in France. The Millefiori (q.v.) weights were the most beautiful but others were made with fruit and flower centers. The convex top of the glass served to magnify the design. Pressed-glass, cheaper paper weights were also made.

PATAPSCO RIVER GLASS WORKS

See BALTIMORE GLASS WORKS.

PATTERN GLASS

See GLASS, *Pattern*.

PATTERNS IN GLASS

BELL-FLOWER

The great number of patterns of pressed glass produced in almost endless variety last half of 19th century present one of the hardest problems in glass classification. Much of the glass falls, however, into a few principal types;

the geometrical, the waffle, and thumb-print and others, for example (these are not to be confused with the geometrical designs on three-mold blown glass); the floral, such as bell-flower, rose and other flower subjects; the animal—the lion and Westward Ho are examples; the fruit group, including among others the currant, grape and pineapple; and the historical group with likenesses of Washington and Grant and the Lincoln Drape. Besides these are numerous minor classifications. The most complete illustrated reference book on this subject is *Early American Pressed Glass* by RUTH WEBB LEE. See GLASS, *Pattern*.

PEACHBLOW GLASS

A name derived from the Chinese peachblow porcelain and applied to a glass made by the New England Glass Co. of Cambridge, the Mt. Washington Glass Works at New Bedford, and other factories. Although it was a beautiful glass, it was not a success commercially and very little of this ware was made. Specimens are accordingly rare. Cambridge peachblow shades from a cream white to a violet red; the Mt. Washington peachblow from a bluish white to a blush pink.

REFERENCE

ANTIQUES, Aug. 1933.

PEG LAMPS

The name given to glass lamps with

a peg-like base intended for use in the top of a candlestick.

PHILADELPHIA GLASS WORKS
See DYOTTVILLE GLASS WORKS.

PHOENIX GLASS WORKS
See PITTSBURGH GLASS HOUSES.

PITKIN GLASS WORKS

Glass was made at Manchester, Connecticut, by Captain Richard Pitkin and his two sons William and Elisha from 1783 to 1830. The product was bottles, flasks and demijohns made from olive-green and amber glass. Few authentic specimens exist and these are closely held. The "Pitkin type" ribbed flask is known to every American collector. They were later made at Keene, New Hampshire, and by some of the Ohio glass factories.

REFERENCE
Connecticut Glass, ANTIQUES, Sept. 1935.

PITTSBURGH   (Pennsylvania)   GLASS HOUSES

The O'Hara Glass Works started in 1797 by James O'Hara and Isaac Craig was the first of the pioneer glass-houses in the Allegheny region that endured more than eighty years in the same location. In 1813 there were five glass factories in Pittsburgh, in 1826 eight, and in 1857 there were thirty-three, nine of which were flint glass-houses. Window glass, bottles and hollow ware were the products of the early factories. The O'Hara plant was the first in this country to use coal for fuel. In 1819 O'Hara died; Frederick Lorenz leased his plant, and in 1838 William McCully, who was to become one of the most prominent of Pittsburgh glass-makers, joined Lorenz. The Phoenix Glass Works was established in 1833 for making bottles and in 1840 was merged with the O'Hara works, then known as the Pittsburgh Glass Works. In 1851, McCully withdrew from the company, purchased the Sligo plant, one of the O'Hara factories, and operated for many years as William McCully and Company. Bakewell, Pears & Co. (q.v.) and James B. Lyon and Company (q.v.) were two others of the prominent Pittsburgh concerns, which produced molded (blown) and pressed glass in great variety and in enormous quantities. Some of the pressed glass was of such a superior quality that it was difficult to tell it from cut glass.

REFERENCES
Early American Glass, RHEA M. KNITTLE; Early Pittsburgh Glass Houses, ANTIQUES, Nov. 1926; Pittsburgh Versus Sandwich, ANTIQUES, Aug. 1933.

POMONA GLASS
A variety of clear glass blown in a part-sized mold, then expanded and ornamented by etching and staining, made by the New England Glass Co.

at Cambridge. There are but few remaining specimens of this glass.

PONTIL

See TOOLS.

PONTIL-MARK

This is a rough circular scar found on the bottom of old blown glass caused by the breaking of the glass from the pontil or punty rod which held it while the workman finished the piece. As methods improved the mark was ground down smooth and after 1850 the pontil mark disappeared completely. Modern reproductions of old glass, as a rule, have a rough pontil-mark but the fracture is generally cleaner and sharper than on the genuine old glass.

PORCELAIN AND GLASS MANUFACTURING Co.

See NEW ENGLAND GLASS Co.

PORTLAND (Maine) GLASS WORKS

Pressed glass tableware in sets, both clear and colored, was made at a factory here from 1864 to 1873. Some pieces are marked P. G. Co. especially in the "Tree of Life" pattern.

REFERENCE

ANTIQUES, Aug. 1933.

PORTLAND VASE

A celebrated ancient Roman glass vase supposed to have been made in the time of Augustus, found in the 17th century in a marble sarcophagus near Rome. The ground of the vase is dark blue glass and the figure subjects which adorn it are cut in cameo style in an outer layer of white opaque glass. It was at first called the Barberini vase from the name of the palace where it was placed, but later coming into the possession of the Duchess of Portland, it became known thereafter as the Portland Vase. It was finally placed in the British Museum, and in 1845 a visitor dashed it to pieces, but all of the pieces were saved and the vase was restored to the semblance of its original beauty.

REFERENCE

The Portland Vase, ANTIQUES, Aug. 1929.

POTICHOMANIE

A word derived from the French, indicating a type of decoration on glass vases in imitation of porcelain or pottery, in vogue in the middle of the 19th century.

REFERENCE

ANTIQUES, Aug., 1927.

PRESSED GLASS

See GLASS, Pressed.

PRUNTS

The name given to the projections or bosses of varied forms scattered on the sides of some early glass. They are characteristic of early German and Dutch glass and they are also seen on old English glass. The name should be restricted to those cases where the "blob" is sufficiently large to melt away the surrounding glass. Where it is small and merely dropped on the glass, the word "tear" better expresses the form.

R

REDFORD (New York) GLASS WORKS

On the Saranac River near Plattsburg a glass factory started operation in 1832 and continued for about twenty years. Its chief product was window glass but the workmen produced for their own use many fine examples of blown glass of a beautiful green color. John S. Foster, the superintendent, was one of the most able of glass-makers.

REDWOOD (New York) GLASS WORKS

This factory, founded in 1833, was located at Alexandria, and John S. Foster was for a time connected with it. During the thirty years of its existence the workmen made some notable pieces of glass for home use.

ROEMER

A drinking glass much used in Germany and the Netherlands in the 17th century and later, with a cup-like bowl and ribbed feet, built up out of threads of glass. The stem consists of a hollow bulb almost as large as the bowl, often ornamented with blobs (prunts) of glass. See RUMMER.

ROSETTES

Glass in this form in opaque and clear colors, attached to metal screws, was used for the support of mirrors and pictures and for holding back curtains. They were popular first half of 19th century. See KNOBS.

ROUNDEL

The so-called Bull's-eye glass was known also as roundel. This glass was used for windows, door lights, for mortar and pestle and other household purposes, also for lenses on lighting devices.

RUMMER

A drinking glass made in England last half of the 18th century with a curved bowl and a short, thick stem, sometimes collared and supported by a square or round flat foot. Some of them were engraved. They were for use in taverns. See FIRING GLASSES.

S

SANDWICH GLASS

The glass made by the Boston and Sandwich Glass Company at Sandwich, Massachusetts, is everywhere known as Sandwich glass. The factory was established in 1825 by Deming Jarves, who continued with the company until 1858, when he was succeeded by Lafayette

Fessenden, as manager. The factory was located at Sandwich because of abundance of local fuel (wood) and easy transportation. The sand used was from New Jersey and from the Berkshires in Massachusetts. The glass made here was for every purpose for which glass was suitable. The grade was flint glass of the best quality, the designs were equal to those of any other factory in the country, and the output grew steadily to enormous proportions. Pressed glass was introduced here about 1828 and became one of the principal products. Many of the conventional patterns of this flint glass had a stippled background producing an effect of old lace—the so-called "lacy" glass, so much desired by collectors. The making of colored glass and opal glass began about 1830 and the ruby glass of Sandwich was especially noteworthy. Later, cut and etched glassware in great variety was made.

From 1843 to 1867 the factory was in operation twenty hours of the day, four days to the week. Four shifts of men were used. A large proportion of this product at that time was in glass lamps. At one time the factory employed more than five hundred workmen and their weekly melts were more than one hundred thousand pounds. Their export business was also very large. Genuine Sandwich glass of the earlier days is much sought for by collectors. The historical cup plates (q.v.) of that period are especially prized, but nearly all Sandwich glass now in existence, that can be identified as such, is desirable. The works closed down in 1888.

REFERENCES

Early American Glass, RHEA M. KNITTLE; *The Romance of Old Sandwich Glass*, F. W. CHIPMAN; *Pressed Glassware of Old Sandwich*, ANTIQUES, Feb. 1922; *The Boston & Sandwich Glass Co.*, ANTIQUES, April 1925; *Positively Sandwich*, ANTIQUES, April 1935; *Directions for Making Sandwich Glass*, ANTIQUES, Dec. 1925; *Secrets of Sandwich Glass*, ANTIQUES, April 1926; *Sandwich Models*, ANTIQUES, March 1927; *Sandwich Lacy Glass*, ANTIQUES, Aug. 1933.

SARATOGA (New York) GLASS

A factory was erected here in 1844 by Oscar Granger who had earlier been making glass at Mt. Vernon, New York. In 1854 Granger sold the factory and it became known then as the Congressville Works. The product of this factory was chiefly bottles, but the "offhand" glass of the workmen, consisting of tableware and decorative objects, is eagerly sought by collectors. This glass, with many of the characteristics of early South Jersey glass, was made in light and dark green, amber and aquamarine colors and their shapes are marked by a fine feeling for form.

REFERENCE
Saratoga Glass and Its Personality,
ANTIQUARIAN, Mar. 1930.

SCONCES

Glass sconces as a support for candles with mirror backs were in use in the late 17th and early 18th centuries.

SILVERED GLASS

See GLASS, *Silvered.*

SLAG GLASS

See GLASS, *Agate.*

SNUFF-BOTTLES

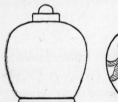

Glass or crystal Chinese snuff-bottles are about two and one-half inches high, decorated on the outside or inside with inscriptions or with painting, and with a stopper to which is attached the tiny spoon for removing the snuff (or medicine, as they are also used by the Chinese for medicines). Snuff-bottles were also made from jade, porcelain and rock crystal with carved and incised surfaces. Those of the Ch'ien Lung reign (1736-1795) are considered the best. They make a desirable addition to any collection.

REFERENCE
Chinese Snuff Bottles, ANTIQUES, Oct. 1928.

SOUTH FERRY GLASS WORKS (Brooklyn)

Established about 1823 by John Gillerland who had formerly been connected with the New England Glass Co. at Cambridge, Massachusetts. Much of our fine cut glass of the "Forties" and "Fifties" came from these works. See CORNING GLASS WORKS.

SOUTH JERSEY GLASS

Under this general heading may be grouped the products of a number of glass factories which were located in various places in Southern New Jersey, late 18th and early 19th centuries. Several of them were operated by former Wistar workmen and those who followed the methods and designs of the product of that factory. On this account, the attempt to differentiate between true Wistarberg and these other South Jersey products is futile.

The commercial output of these factories consisted of window glass, bottles, and other similar hollow ware. Bowls, pitchers, mugs and other similar articles were not a commercial product, but were individually blown pieces, generally cherished and handed down in the families of the workmen who made them or for the friends and relatives for whom they were made, and this practice continued for more than one hundred years. Probably most of the existing South Jersey glass was produced after 1800. Despite the bulbous body, South Jersey type of glass is never top-heavy;

plain, crimped or uneven of foot, its base remains sturdy; ample of mouth, its pitchers pour without dripping; the handles are made for hands, not for two fingers. A variety of color combinations and various methods of decoration add to the charm of this glass.

REFERENCES

Early American Glass, RHEA M. KNITTLE; Wistarberg and South Jersey Glass, ANTIQUES, Oct. 1926; Various South Jersey Operations, ANTIQUES, July 1928.

SPANISH GLASS

During the 15th, 16th and 17th centuries choice glass was made at Barcelona and glass factories were located in various other places in Spain. Early records show that common glass and a pure white glass, more like rock crystal, were made. The Catalans early became the rivals of the workers at Murano (Venice), in form, design and excellence of workmanship. All sorts of glass for everyday use were made, but Spanish glass is not often met with, the manufacture having been mainly for home use. The glass of Southern Spain was blue, green and dark olive in color and the shapes are of Oriental or native form.

REFERENCES

Glass, EDWARD DILLON; Spanish Glass, ANTIQUES, July 1928.

STAINED GLASS

See GLASS, Stained.

STEMS

The stem of a drinking glass may be either a plain rod or cylinder or of baluster shape. This last is a modification of the double knops of some 17th-century glass. The plain stem is varied by opaque white or colored twists or clear air-twist. In a general way a loose, widely twisted spiral is indicative of the earlier glass, while the tightly twisted specimens are of a later make. This type of stem, if not an English invention, was more commonly used there than elsewhere. See DRINKING GLASSES.

STIEGEL GLASS

This, perhaps the most famous of all early American glass, was made at Manheim, Pennsylvania, between 1765 and 1774 by Henry William Stiegel. It was a flint glass, the first in America made for tableware, possessing the clear resonant ring of the finest Bohemian glass, with clear and even colors. This was due to the skill and methods of the English, German, Irish, and possibly Italian workmen brought from Europe by Stiegel for employment at Manheim. Although Stiegel made window glass and bottles, it is to the articles for domestic use that Stiegel glass owes its fame. This is the most beautiful glass ever blown in the American colonies, and in quality it frequently excelled the finest of European glass. Besides clear white, the colors include a rich blue, Stiegel's favorite color, green, amber,

amethyst and opaque white. The surface of many of his pieces was engraved
or enameled in colors.

Stiegel competed with English factories for the trade of the colonies and
his product was sold in Philadelphia,
New York and even so far away as in
Boston. At the present time few collectors will attribute any glass to Stiegel
unless it is well authenticated, although
genuine examples of this glass are the
gems of any collection. Examples are to
be seen in the Metropolitan Museum in
New York, the Pennsylvania Museum at
Philadelphia, the Garvan collection at
Yale and at Andover, and in some other
of our larger museums.

REFERENCES
Stiegel Glass, FREDERICK WM. HUNT-
ER; Early American Glass, RHEA M.
KNITTLE.

STODDARD (New Hampshire) GLASS
WORKS
There were three or four glass factories here between 1842 and 1873
making bottles and flasks, chiefly coarse
in quality and of a dark amber-green in
color. A considerable variety of "off-
hand" specimens, including pitchers,
bowls, jars, salts and a number of other
shapes, were made by the glass-blowers
for home use and for presentation to
others. The introduction of clear glass
for bottles at a lower price than the
colored glass compelled the owners of
the works to discontinue operations.

REFERENCE
Stoddard Glass, ANTIQUES, Aug.
1933.

SUNCOOK, (New Hampshire)
See CHELMSFORD GLASS WORKS.

T

TEMPLE (New Hampshire) GLASS
WORKS
The first glass factory to be started
in the Colonies after the Revolution was
started here. The life of the project was
short and the output limited. Bottles
and some decanters and probably some
other shapes were made of glass of a
greenish color, but little, if any, genuine
Temple glass is now known to be in
existence. Robert Hewes of Boston
started the works in 1780 and the history of the works is a story of an inter-

esting personality rather than that of a
successful industry. He was a man of
versatile talents, not only familiar with
glass-making but a good surgeon. In
1787 he became identified with the
Essex Glass Works in Boston (q.v.).

REFERENCE
The Temple Glass Works, AN-
TIQUES, Oct. 1923.

THREE-MOLD GLASS
See GLASS, Three-Mold.

Tiffany Glass

Known as Favrile Glass, an invention of Louis C. Tiffany in 1893 as a medium for use in making stained-glass windows. Later it was used for blown-glass forms but it was always hand-made. The tinting of the glass is wonderfully rich, and the iridescent and gem-like effects are astonishingly brilliant. The name Favrile is a derivation from an old Saxon word meaning hand-wrought. Each article is marked with the Tiffany name or initials and all unusual pieces bear a number with the letters of the alphabet being used, at first as a prefix, later as a suffix to the number.

Tools

No great variety of tools are used in glass-making, and they have undergone but little change since the time of the Romans. The principal ones are the pucellas, a pair of blunt shears working like a pair of sugar tongs, used in shaping blown glass; the spring tool, a kind of simple tongs; the blowing-iron, a hollow tube about four feet long; the pontil or "punty" rod, made solid in various sizes and attached directly opposite the blowing iron; and the marver (French *marbre*, meaning marble), a slab of iron on which the lump of glass is rolled to smooth the outside before blowing.

U

Union Glass Company

A company organized in 1854 by members of the Houghton family, at Somerville, Massachusetts. This company made only flint glass and their pressed tableware patterns corresponded closely with those of other factories. They also produced silvered glass for reflectors, knobs and other purposes. Later, cut-glass and ornamental vases

and an iridescent glass after the style of Tiffany glass (q.v.) were also made. Competition with Western factories producing glassware under more favorable conditions compelled the factory to close in 1924.

REFERENCE

Union Glass Company, ANTIQUES, Nov. 1936.

V

Vauxhall Glass

This glass was made at the factory of Dawson, Bowles & Co., located near the famous Vauxhall gardens in London, late in the 17th century. Glass-makers

from Venice were brought to supervise the work. The production was a glass with a bluish tinge used chiefly for mirrors. The reflecting quality was obtained by attaching thin sheets of tin foil coated with mercury to one side of the glass. Many of these mirrors were used as wall panels, and they are still to be seen in some of the old palaces. Beveling of the edge was about one inch wide and hand ground.

VENETIAN GLASS

Glass-making at Venice received its impulse from Constantinople where glass-making flourished throughout the Dark Ages. The earliest known date for glass-making at Venice is 1083. The glass-makers were incorporated in 1268 and at the close of the century they were segregated on the island of Murano, near the city. The history of modern glass begins with the Venetian crystal glass of the 16th century, the first since the time of the Romans. They also produced at about the same time milk-white glass in imitation of the porcelain of the Orient and crackled glass. Rigid laws were passed to prevent workmen from going to other countries but the rewards for breaking them were very tempting, and apparently flight was not uncommon.

Venetian glass enjoyed for a long time the monopoly of commerce and it became the marvel of the civilized world. The making of mirrors started in the 13th century and during the 16th century the metal of their glass was improved, it was made thinner, and different colors were employed. In the 18th century they engraved and cut glass with the wheel. Although during the 17th century the trade was still very large, by the end of the century the fortunes of Venice began to wane. By that time every country in Europe was making its own glass to a great extent and the competition of Bohemian glass (q.v.) was particularly strong. Old Venetian glass represents the most wonderful achievement of the glass-blowers' art. Its characteristics are its extremely light weight, its fragility, a slight cloudiness in hue, and in the design a sense of perfect poise and balance. During the 19th century the industry has been revived and it is now again one of the foremost artistic crafts in the world.

REFERENCE

Glass, EDWARD DILLON.

VERNON GLASS WORKS
See MT. VERNON GLASS WORKS.

VIOLIN BOTTLES
See BOTTLES.

W

WATERFORD (Ireland) GLASS

The making of glass at Waterford, Ireland, was begun in 1729 and continued for eleven years. From 1740 to 1783 no glass was made there, but from that time until 1851, when the works were closed, the output was very large. The early glass was common green glass with only a very small quantity of flint glass. The later Waterford glass is de-

scribed by some writers as having a bluish tinge in its body, although Mr. Westropp, an authority on Irish glass, disputes this claim, and its style is similar to English glass of the Georgian period. Cut glass became the chief part of the Waterford product, although glass was made for every use to which glass was adapted. As early as 1786 Waterford was sending large quantities of glass to American ports, which business continued increasing until about 1822, after which the trade dwindled. Besides Waterford, there were flourishing glassworks at Belfast, Cork and Dublin. See IRISH GLASS.

REFERENCES
Irish Glass, M. S. DUDLEY WESTROPP; Old Irish Glass, MRS. STANNUS; How About Waterford Glass? ANTIQUES, Sept. 1923.

WATERFORD (New Jersey) GLASS WORKS
The manufacture of window glass was carried on here as early as 1825-30. At a later period glass bottles and flasks were made. Their quart flasks are among the rarest of American flasks. Different proprietors carried on the works until about 1880. One of the early owners, Joseph Porter, introduced many innovations into the glass industry; among them certain alterations permitted Sunday shut-down, where previously all glass plants operated on Sundays. This change spread rapidly to other plants until Sunday shut-down became general. Porter also increased the wages of his employes, enabling them to enjoy a better mode of living. This, too, spread and before long other employers were obliged to adopt the new scale of wages.

REFERENCE
Early American Glass, RHEA M. KNITTLE.

WELLSBURG (West Virginia) GLASS HOUSES
Isaac Duval & Co. operated a glassworks here from 1813 to 1828, when Duval died. An excellent grade of flint glass was blown. Cobalt blue and amber were the usual colors. Others became interested in glass-making at this place and the industry was active for a number of years.

WESTFORD (Connecticut) GLASS WORKS
From 1857 to 1873 glass-works here produced flasks in three sizes in various shades of amber.

WESTMORELAND GLASS CO.
At Grapeville, Pennsylvania—a factory still producing glass, some of which is from the original molds of the Sandwich Glass Co.

WHEELING (West Virginia) GLASS WORKS

Various glass-works were established in this region from 1810 onward, which resulted in its becoming the world's greatest bottle-producing section up to 1860. In 1864 a Wheeling concern brought about a great change in the manufacture of glass by making a clear, brilliant glass with the aid of bicarbonate of soda and lime, at about one-third the cost of lead or flint glass. This discovery was made by a chemist formerly employed at the New England Glass Co. at Cambridge, but then at work for Hobbs, Brockunier & Co.

REFERENCES

Early American Glass, RHEA M. KNITTLE; Glassmaking in Wheeling, ANTIQUES, Aug. 1933.

WHITE GLASS

See GLASS, White.

WHITE GLASS WORKS

This factory was started in 1815 at Zanesville, Ohio, by Isaac Van Horn, and continued under various managers until 1851. They made bottles, flasks and domestic hollow ware, turning out much of the fine early glass which is to be found in Ohio. Of their production, the best known are the Masonic and reverse Eagle flasks, and their bulbous bottles in various colors.

REFERENCE

Zanesville Glass, ANTIQUES, Dec. 1932.

WHITNEY GLASS WORKS

See GLASSBORO GLASS WORKS.

WILLINGTON (Connecticut) GLASS WORKS

In operation at West Willington from 1815 until 1872. Hollow ware such as bottles and jars was produced of amber and green. The product is of little interest.

WISTARBERG GLASS

Caspar Wistar started making glass in Salem County, New Jersey, in 1739. He brought from Holland four skilled glass-makers and the earliest production was undoubtedly Dutch in design. Bottles, bowls, pitchers and drinking glasses were made, although window glass and bottles were the chief products. The other articles were more in the nature of by-products made by individual workmen for their own use or for gifts to others. The factory was in successful operation until about 1780, being carried on after the death of Caspar Wistar in 1752 by his son Richard. Wistar is credited with having made the first flint glass in this country. Although plain colors were preferred, he made two and three-color pieces by fusing. The usual colors were turquoise, amber, greens, browns and blue. Characteristic marks of Wistar glass are the thin threads of glass wound spirally near the top and the wave design of decoration.

One of the best authorities on early

American glass (McKearin) doubts that there are in existence half a dozen pieces of glass which can be authenticated as the product of the factory of Caspar Wistar and his son Richard. With the possible exception of Stiegel, not any word in the realm of American glass has been so loosely used as Wistarberg. Examples of Wistarberg glass are to be seen in the Metropolitan Museum in New York and in the Pennsylvania Museum in Philadelphia, and some other Museums.

REFERENCE

Wistarberg and South Jersey Glass, ANTIQUES, Oct. 1926.

Z

ZANESVILLE GLASS

In 1815 the White Glass Works (q.v.) started a factory here, and in 1816 the New Granite Glass Works began producing bottles, flasks and hollow ware, continuing operations until 1848.

American "Star of Bethlehem" Quilt, Early 19th Century

Star Pattern Hooked Rug, dated July 1879

FLORAL TYPE OF NEW ENGLAND HOOKED RUG, EARLY 19TH CENTURY

NEW ENGLAND PATRIOTIC HOOKED RUG CIRCA 1800; LENGTH, 4 FEET, 4 INCHES;
WIDTH, 2 FEET, 7 INCHES

PART IV

TEXTILES

PART IV

TEXTILES

A

ALPACA

A warm fine woolen cloth, made from the hair of the alpaca goat. The fiber is small but strong, elastic, lustrous and silky. The alpaca goat is common to Chile and Peru.

AMERICAN TAPESTRIES

See TAPESTRIES, *American*.

AMERICAN TEXTILES

Early American textiles did not approach the skill and sophistication of foreign weaves. Spinning and weaving were employed by the early settlers, particularly those of New England, though they lacked the skill to produce fabrics other than the simplest weaves. In Virginia in the 17th century, linen and silk, as well as linsey-woolsey (woolen cloth) were produced to some extent. These materials were spun and woven by Colonial women for purely utilitarian purposes. The first woolen factory in America was started in Rowley, Massachusetts, in 1643 and by the beginning of the 18th century textile manufacturing was carried on in the North, not only as a household industry, but as a trade. In domestic circles, spin-

ning and weaving flourished briskly through that century, and the women wrought in their leisure hours stitches and designs with which they had been familiar at home in England.

In 1816, a mill was in operation in Waltham, Massachusetts, where for the first time all stages of manufacturing, from the preparation of the raw material to the production of the finished product, were carried on under one roof, by power. Early in the 19th century American factories began to equip with the improved English machinery, and by 1809 there were in operation in New Hampshire, Massachusetts, Rhode Island, Connecticut and New York eighty-seven mills, more or less, supplied with power machinery. The factory had now become a part of American life and was to make this a nation of manufacturers.

REFERENCE

Early American Textiles, FRANCES LITTLE.

ANGORA

A light, silky dress goods made from the hair of the angora goat of Turkey.

229

APPLIED WORK, OR APPLIQUÉ

The superposition of one material upon another of contrasting ground, velvet on damask for example, the design being cut out from the one and sewn down upon the other. See EMBROIDERY.

ARABESQUE

Curving scrolls that cross and interlace ornamented with the forms of leaves and flowers.

ARRAS

The term usually denoting the tapestry hangings used in medieval halls. It is derived from the name of the Flemish town Arras, where in the 14th century some of the finest of early tapestries were woven. See TAPESTRIES.

ARTIFICIAL SILK

See RAYON.

AUBUSSON RUGS

See RUGS, *Aubusson*.

AUBUSSON TAPESTRIES

See TAPESTRIES, *Aubusson*.

AXMINSTER CARPETS

See CARPETS, *Axminster*.

B

BARCELAND, BARCELONA

A kind of silk handkerchief or neckcloth said to have been made originally at Barcelona, Spain.

BARGELLO-WORK (Flame-stitch, Hungarian-stitch)

Originated in Italy, where it was worked in silks. English work was carried out in crewels. The figure is usually a series of pointed or flame-like forms.

BAUDEKIN

A rich cloth sometimes mentioned in connection with bed-hangings in the Middle Ages. Now called brocade (q.v.).

BAYEUX TAPESTRY

This is not strictly a tapestry, but a specimen of early medieval embroidery with a border, top and bottom, resembling sampler work, using woolen thread of various colors on a heavy brown linen cloth. It is 214 feet long and 20 inches wide, and is a panorama representing the invasion and conquest of England by William the Conqueror in 1066. It contains the figures of over 600 men, 200 horses, 40 ships and boats, besides numerous birds, animals and other objects in 72 scenes, with Latin inscriptions giving the subjects and names. Tradition asserts it to be the work of Matilda, wife of William, and the women of her household. It is now preserved in the library at Bayeux, episcopal city of Normandy.

REFERENCE

The Bayeux Tapestry, FRANK R. FOWKE.

BAYS, BAYES, BAIZE

A coarse woolen stuff having a long nap used chiefly for linings, curtains, etc., introduced into England from France in the 16th century. In finer texture used for clothing.

BEAUVAIS TAPESTRIES

See TAPESTRIES, *Beauvais.*

BED-HANGINGS

These consisted of tester, celour, curtain and bed-coverings in the Middle Ages. In the 16th century, when the bed took the form of wainscot head and tester, supported by two posts, the hangings were limited to curtains and valances. Later, the beds were entirely covered and draped in textiles, until in the Georgian period they became again less pronounced.

BERLIN WOOL WORK

A type of needlework invented in Berlin, Germany, early in the 19th century, the design being blocked and colored on canvas, and done by the cross-stitch. The best Berlin-work was for furniture coverings in flower and conventionalized designs. The so-called zephyr wool, a fine dyed worsted, gave the best results, but silk, chenille and beads were also used. This work was very popular here, also in England, following the decline of the sampler in the Victorian period.

REFERENCE

Berlin Wool Work, ANTIQUES, July 1927.

BLEACHING

This is the process of whitening textile fibers and fabrics by exposure to the sun and weather, as it was practised before the Christian era, or by treatment with chemicals. In the 18th century a bleaching solution of potash and lye was used and in 1785 the powerful bleaching quality of chlorine was discovered, since which time various other bleaching processes have been discovered.

REFERENCE

Bleaching, Dyeing and Chemical Technology, TROTMAN.

BOBBIN LACE

The name is derived from the bone bobbin used, in distinction from the needlepoint lace. This form of lace-making was introduced into England in the last half of the 16th century and in the time of Queen Anne had become a prominent industry. It was first made in this country at Ipswich, Massachusetts, in the 18th century by workmen from England. See LACE.

BOMBASINE (also spelled BOMBAZEEN)

A twilled or corded dress material composed of silk and worsted. In black, much used for mourning.

BRAIDED RUGS

See RUGS, *Braided.*

BROADCLOTH

A fine woolen double-width cloth with a smooth-finished surface.

BROCADE

The term, derived from the Spanish *broche*, meaning the pointed bobbin of the high-warp loom, originally meant the combination of bobbin and shuttle effects. The pattern is woven over a shuttle fabric during the process of weaving, thus bringing the design into relief. Brocades were used for bed-hangings and for the upholstery of chairs in England in the 17th and 18th centuries.

BROCATEL

A coarse brocade of linen, chiefly used for tapestry effects in wall hangings.

BRUSSELS CARPETS

See CARPETS, *Brussels*.

BUCKRAM

At first a fine linen or cotton fabric; later, stiffened with gum or paste.

C

CALAMANCO

See CALIMANCO.

CALICO

A somewhat coarse cotton fabric. It took its name from Calicut, a city on the coast of Malabar, where it was first manufactured. In Colonial times it was imported from England and the prints of Robert Peel of Lancashire were widely worn by the women of this country. See COTTON PRINTING.

CALIMANCO

A glazed woolen stuff of Flanders woven with satin twill and checkered in the warp, so that the checks are seen on one side only. Much used in the 18th century.

CAMAK

Also called Camorca, a fabric of silk and fine camel's hair in use in the 14th and 15th centuries.

CAMBLET (or CAMLET)

A stuff originally of silk and camel's hair, popular in the 18th century for bed-hangings and upholstery. Later, made of silk and wool.

CAMBRIC

A very fine, thin linen.

CANVAS

Stout, heavy cloth woven in the same way as linen, usually of unbleached cotton or of flax, sometimes of jute.

CARDING

The process of cleaning cotton of any foreign substances after "ginning," and to reduce it to a ribbon of thin fleece to be run through the drawing and roving machines into a thread-like form before it is wound on the bobbin.

CARPETS

Carpets probably originated in Persia where they were for centuries hand-woven, both as carpets and rugs. (See RUGS, *Oriental*). The art spread eastward through India and China and westward through Turkey in Asia. Early importations into Europe were from Asia Minor, which gave the name Turkey-work (q.v.) to the product, and those made in England and in France in the 17th century of hand-knotted pile went by the name of Turkey-work. By the middle of the 18th century the making of pile carpets had become an important English industry. It received a great stimulus by the influx of French Hugue-not carpet-weavers. In England, during early times, the word "carpet" was applied to the coverings of beds, tables, cupboards, etc., and the same practice was followed in this country. It was not until the middle of the 18th century that the word was applied to floor coverings. The first factory in this country for the manufacture of yarn carpets was started at Philadelphia, late in the 18th century.

Axminister Carpets. Originally made at Axminster, England. The texture was chenille, soft and very agreeable, resembling Smyrna rugs, and the patterns were usually of pronounced Baroque or Rococo design. Carpet-making at Axminster began about the middle of the 18th century and continued actively for nearly one hundred years.

Brussels Carpets. In the 18th century Brussels was the leading carpet-producing center in Europe, but in England carpet factories at Axminster and Wilton captured the English market. Brussels carpets are made with the velvet weave uncut, applied to floor coverings.

The patterns follow French designs. They are woven usually the width of the Flemish ell (27 inches).

Embroidered Carpets. A name given to a type of carpet of domestic make in this country early in the 19th century. A description of one made by Lucetta Smart of Rumney, New Hampshire, in size 86 by 58 inches, states that it is made of two strips of heavy woolen blanketing sewn together and on this ground the design is worked in a curious kind of chain stitch. The border shows a flowering vine, the field a woven basket from which arises a tree, amidst which disport birds. The colors are grey-green, three shades of blue, browns and reds varying in hue. It is quite probable that the so-called embroidered carpet was a forerunner of the hooked rug, a type of floor covering more quickly made, yet durable.

REFERENCE

A *Note on Embroidered Carpets,* ANTIQUES, June 1926.

Kidderminster Carpets. Carpet-making was first established at Kidderminster, England, during first half of the 18th century. The product was a two-ply ingrain carpet showing warp and pile on each side, and reversible.

Wilton Carpets. These were first made at Wilton, England, in the 18th century in imitation of the velvet weave of Brussels carpets, but with the loops cut. The English patterns were largely Oriental and average much better than those of Brussels. Of the Wilton products of the 19th century the finest were of lamb's wool only, noted for its luster and long and beautiful fiber. The weaving was done by hand and only vegetable dyes were used.

REFERENCE
European and American Carpets and Rugs, FARADAY.

CARTOON
A study or design executed on strong paper and of the size to be reproduced in tapestry or other weaving.

CASHMERE (Kashmir) SHAWLS
See SHAWLS.

CASTOR
Usually describes a hat, either of beaver fur or resembling it.

CHAIN-STITCH
A loop-stitch. See STITCHES.

CHENILLE
A silk or worsted cord used in weaving, having short threads set at right angles, forming a velvety thread.

CHEYNEY, CHENEY
See CHINA.

CHINA
An English weave of worsted or woolen stuff allied to serge. In Colonial times it was variously spelled "chaney," "cheney" and "cheyney." There was also a reference in old inventories to "cheney satten" and "cheney taffetas," which may have been of silk.

CHINTZ
A cotton cloth, usually glazed, and printed in various colors. The name was originally applied to the printed cotton cloth from India imported into England in the 17th century. It afterwards was applied to the glazed hand-printed calicoes of European and American manufacture. See TOILE-DE-JOUY.

REFERENCES
The Chintz Book, PERCIVAL; Two Centuries of English Chintz, ANTIQUES, April 1929.

COACH LACE
Not a lace at all, but an ornamental braid used to adorn the interior of coaches. When used in Europe for coach or livery it bore the arms of noble families, or seal of a city if designed for official use, but in this country it was designed on purely ornamental lines and in various colors.

COMFORTER
A bed-covering, usually of cotton and filled between the outer surfaces with loose cotton or wool and knotted at regular intervals to prevent the interlining from slipping out of place.

CORDUROY
A ribbed cotton material.

COTTON
A vegetable fiber, distinguished from all other fibers by the peculiar twist it possesses, which makes it exceedingly valuable for spinning. It is grown under a wider range of climatic conditions,

over a greater area, and by a greater number and variety of people, and is useful for a larger number of purposes than any other fiber. Its by-products are also of great importance. The Sea Island and Egyptian long-staple cottons are among the most valuable species. The invention of the cotton gin (q.v.) by Eli Whitney in 1794 gave great impetus to the growing of cotton in this country, by the facility with which the seeds were removed from the boll by the use of that machine. In 1789 the first cotton mill in New England was started at Beverly, Massachusetts. See SPINNING.

REFERENCES

> Cotton from the Raw Material to the Finished Product, PEAKE; Story of the Cotton Plant, WILKINSON; King Cotton, WATKINS.

COTTON CLOTH

Was first produced in England about 1760, and in this country by the beginning of the 19th century it had become an established industry. In Colonial times, cotton was used to some extent for home weaving.

REFERENCE

> Cotton Weaving and Designing, TAYLOR.

COTTON GIN

A machine for separating cotton fiber from seed, invented by Eli Whitney in 1794. Previously the work had been done by hand, a slow and tedious proc-

ess. Two types of the gin are now in use—the saw gin of the Whitney type, which does very rapid work and is generally used, and the roller gin, which is much slower but is less likely to injure the fiber. It is preferred for the long-staple cottons.

COTTON PRINTING

In Europe there were crude but ambitious attempts to imitate the cottons of the Orient imported in the 17th century by the East India trading companies. In France the Toile-de-Jouy (q.v.) factory, near Versailles, was started in 1760 and work of good quality had been done in other parts of Europe at about the same time. In this country, a few isolated instances of cotton printing are recorded prior to the Revolution but as an industry it dates from the last quarter of the 18th century. At the turn of the century numerous establishments sprang up, particularly in New England and Pennsylvania, and the activities of these manufacturers foreshadowed the development of the enterprise which now occupies so important a part in the economic life of America. In 1803 cottons were first printed by the cylinder process, and rollers were first engraved with the design for calico printing in 1825.

REFERENCES

> Early American Textiles, FRANCES LITTLE; The Cotton Industry, HAM-

MONG; *Early Cotton Printing in America*, ANTIQUES, Jan. 1928.

COUNTERPANE (or Counterpoint)

A bed-covering first mentioned in the Elizabethan period, so-called from being worked in square or diamond-shaped figures, or panes, derived from the Latin *pannus*, a piece of cloth. Before the time of Elizabeth it was known as counterpoint. See COVERLETS.

COVERLETS (French *Couvre-Lit*)

Embroidered. Made with heavy wool yarn drawn through rather coarse homespun blanketing. They are of late 18th- and early 19th-century make. Of these early American embroideries, very few are to be found at the present time. The method used was similar to that later employed in making hooked rugs.

REFERENCES

Note on Certain Early Coverlets, ANTIQUES, Nov. 1927; *Embroidered Coverlets*, ANTIQUES, Dec. 1932.

Quilted. These were made on a quilting frame. The earlier ones were usually of linen, but those of the 19th century are of cotton, as a rule. Over the lining was spread a thin layer of cotton or wool and covered with the pieced top. The pattern consisted of single, double or triple lines, diagonal or in squares, diamonds or other design, in fine running-stitch, not an extraneous thing but a part of the making. They were frequently adorned with an appliquéd design pieced together from bright colored fabrics. Some were quite elaborate in composition. Another method was to lay cords of soft cotton or candle wicking between the top and the lining and quilt them in by a row of stitches on each side. Either method made a most durable and comfortable bed covering. See QUILTING.

Woven. Coverlet weaving was practiced in all of the colonies from New Hampshire to Georgia from early 18th century to the middle of the 19th. They were woven on a hand loom in two strips, usually about thirty inches wide and of the desired length, and then sewed together to make a spread. The warp was usually of white cotton or linen and the woof of colored wool, grown, spun, dyed and woven into the coverlets by the housewife. Blue and red were the favored colors, but yellow, green and brown were also used. These colors were obtained from home-made vegetable dyes and have retained their brilliancy unfaded.

REFERENCES

Book of Hand-Woven Coverlets, ELIZA C. HALL; *Some Hand-Woven Coverlets*, ANTIQUES, Feb. 1925.

CRETONNE

A French substitute for chintz, heavier, and not in common use until about 1860. It is an unglazed cotton fabric, printed on one side.

CREWEL-WORK

Embroidery in wool on linen. The

word is derived from the German *Knaul*, meaning a ball of wool. This was a type of embroidery that met with great favor in England and the American colonies in the 18th century. Such work was used for curtains, cushions, bedhangings, and for table covers. It continued in popularity until well into the 19th century. See EMBROIDERY.

REFERENCE

Crewel Embroidery, ANTIQUARI-AN, Nov. 1931.

CROCHET

A form of needlework, employing silk, wool or cotton and a hook or needle, and for some years in the 19th century it was the most popular of all of the various forms of fancy needlework.

CROSS-STITCH

Probably the oldest stitch known for use on a woven material, formed by two stitches, crossing at right angles.

CUPBOARD CLOTHS

Used in England and here in Colonial times to cover the tops of cupboards, on which it was customary to display china, pewter or glass. Frequently mentioned in inventories of the 17th century.

CUSHIONS

Cases of woven stuff, leather or needlework, filled with hair, feathers or down.

CUT-WORK

The forerunner of certain lace stitches and used for the decoration of household linens and clothes. It appeared in France as early as the 16th century and it is found on early English embroideries, also. See EMBROIDERY.

D

DAMASK

A rich flat fabric first made in Damascus, which in the 12th century achieved a great reputation for the weaving of splendid patterned stuffs. From there the manufacture spread to Italy and it was introduced into England late in the 16th century. It is a weave with a warp satin ground with a weft satin twill or taffeta pattern, the lines of the figures contrasting sharply with the lines of the ground, causing the shifting sheen as viewed from different angles. Damask was a favorite material for upholstery throughout the 18th century.

DARNICK, DORNECK, DORNICK

A coarse kind of linen fabric used generally for hangings, originally made (17th century) at Dorneck, Dutch name for Tournay. The name was also applied to a coarse variety of checkered table linen.

DENIM

A cotton fabric with a twilled weave on the face side.

DIMITY

A stout cotton or linen cloth used in England in the 17th century, with the name from Latin *dimitum*, double thread.

DORNECK, DORNOCK

See DARNICK.

DRAPERY

Textile cloths or fabrics used for hangings.

DRESDEN WORK

A combination of lace medallions and embroidery in linen thread or colored silks, made during the 18th century.

DRILL—DRILLING

A fine, heavy, twilled linen or cotton fabric of a satiny finish.

DRUGGET

A coarse cloth of wool or wool mixed with silk used for wearing apparel.

DUCAPE

A stout silk fabric of soft texture, sometimes woven with a stripe. Introduced into England by French refugees in 1685.

DUCK

An untwilled fabric of cotton or linen, not so heavy as canvas, but used for similar purposes.

DUFFEL

A coarse woolen cloth having a thick nap or frieze, originally made at Duffel, near Antwerp in Flanders.

DYEING

The art of dyeing was practiced in some sort by all primitive peoples, the dyes being derived from vegetable sources. The so-called Tyrian purple was known in the early days of the Roman Empire. It was so expensive that only the very rich could afford it and by the Middle Ages the dye had been lost to commerce. Towards the close of the Middle Ages the art of dyeing was greatly developed in northern Italy, especially at Florence. Subsequently, discoveries of new dyestuffs and the application of improved processes brought dyeing with vegetable colors into general use. It was not until 1856 that the first artificial dyestuff derived from aniline was discovered, since which time first aniline, then other colors from coal-tar have superseded the vegetable dyestuffs. Dyeing may be done in various stages of fabric manufacture, depending upon the material and the purpose for which it is to be used.

REFERENCE
Dyes and Dyeing, PELLEW.

DYES

From remote times to the middle of the 19th century, dyes made of vegetable coloring matter were the only dyes available. Indigo made any shade of blue; madder, all reds from pink to rose; the barks of walnut, chestnut and hickory trees gave a brown dye; and black oak and hickory made green; sumac, wild cherry, and goldenrod gave various yellows; scrub oak, black. Logwood and cochineal were also used. Alum was used for "fixing" the colors. The women of colonial times were very skillful in making and using these dyes, and the colors of the fabrics of those early days that are still in existence remain unfaded today.

REFERENCE

Dyes and Dyeing, PELLEW.

E

EMBROIDERED CARPETS

See CARPETS, *Embroidered.*

EMBROIDERY

The art of producing ornamental patterns by needlework on any fabric which can be sewed over. It dates from the earliest times, and arrived in Europe from the nations of the East. The greatest perfection in European embroidery came in medieval times, and the most highly appreciated examples are of English origin. The fabrics principally used in embroidery work are linen, silks, satins, velvets and flannels. The materials employed are colored worsted yarns (crewels), and silk. Some of the principal stitches are the chain or tambour-stitch, the button-hole stitch, the feather-stitch and the Berlin-work stitch. A distinct class of embroidery consists of appliqué or cut-work, in which designs of different materials and colors are cut out and sewed down on the surface of the fabric to be ornamented. A pattern entirely covering the underlying material, or nearly so, would be described as needlework (q.v.).

REFERENCES

Embroidery Book, ARTHUR; *Embroidery and Needlework*, FRY; *The Lace and Embroidery Collector*, HEAD; *An Embroidery Pattern Book*, ANTIQUES, Mar. 1925.

ENGLISH TAPESTRIES

See TAPESTRIES, *English.*

ENGLISH TEXTILES

By the end of the 18th century English mechanics by their inventions had revolutionized textile manufacturing and had turned it from a hand industry to one run by power. This gave England great advantages over other manufacturing countries, and the secret of the designs of these new machines was carefully guarded. The earlier inventions of Hargreaves, Crompton and Arkwright needed but the power loom to make them effective in a large way, and Cartwright provided that in 1785. From that day to the present time Manchester, England, has been a leader in textile production. See SPINNING.

F

Farandine

A cloth of silk and wool or hair, invented about 1630 by one Ferrand.

Feather Edge

Ribbons and braids, ornamented on one edge with loops or tufts.

Flame-Stitch

See Bargello-Work.

Flax

The vegetable growth from which linen is made. It was the most used fiber until superseded by cotton at the close of the 18th century.

Flemish Tapestries

See Tapestries.

Flushing

A heavy coarse cloth made from shoddy, taking its name from Flushing, Holland.

French Tapestries

See Tapestries.

Frieze

A coarse woolen cloth with a rough, shaggy nap, usually on one side only.

Fringe

An ornamental border of hanging cords. See Upholstery.

Fulling

A textile term for a process of scouring and pressing whereby woolen goods are cleaned of grease and thickened into a compact finished material.

Fustian

A coarse, twilled cotton or linen material such as corduroy, frequently used for bed-hangings in early times.

G

Galloon

A cotton, silk or worsted fabric, used for dress trimmings, also a thin tape of silk woven with metal, used for uniforms.

Gimp (French *Guimpure, Guipure*)

A lace trimming for dress made from silk, wool or cotton in which fine wire is twisted into the cord. Gold and silver wire are used in the manufacture of military cord.

Gingham

A cotton fabric of a light or medium weight, woven from colored yarns in stripes or checks. The woven design differentiates the fabric from printed calico, some of the designs on which resemble those of ginghams.

Gobelin Tapestries

See Tapestries, *Gobelin*.

Gros-Point

Needlework, on a coarse, canvas ground, of wool or silk, which crosses two meshes of the canvas as distinct from petit-point (q.v.), which crosses only one mesh. See Needlework.

H

Hair-Cloth

A covering for chair seats and for other purposes, made from horse hair, woven on a warp of cotton, linen or worsted, and in use in this country even before the Revolution and continuing for more than one hundred years. It was economical because of its long-wearing qualities.

Hangings

In their application to the history of furniture, hangings include not only bed and window curtains but wall coverings of the various materials used. Tapestries (Arras) were the favored coverings on the walls of the houses of the wealthy. Leather was less used as a wall covering in England than on the Continent. The lighter textiles were naturally preferred for the curtains of beds and windows. Then, from the beginning of the 17th century through the 18th century can be traced the development of the use of paper as a wall covering. See Bed-Hangings.

Harrateen

A kind of linen fabric mixed with wool in use in Colonial times. It was also used in England for wall-hangings and the drapery of beds in the 18th century.

Hatchel, Hackle

A wooden comb with iron teeth used in the preparation of flax for spinning.

Holland

A linen fabric originally made in Holland.

Honiton Lace

A form of lace made in Honiton, England, introduced there by Flemish refugees in the middle of the 16th century. The lace made there never attained the celebrity of that from the great centers in Flanders and the north of France. See Lace.

Hooked Rugs

See Rugs, *Hooked*.

Horsehair

See Hair-Cloth.

Hungarian-Stitch

See Bargello-Work.

I

Irish Lace

Similar to point-lace and known also as Irish guipure. It is distinctly a home industry in Ireland and very little commercialized.

Italian Lace

See Lace.

Italian Tapestries

See Tapestries.

J

JACQUARD LOOM

This loom, which has played so important a part in textile weaving since its invention, was perfected by Joseph Marie Jacquard of Lyons, France, about 1806. The Jacquard attachment may be applied to almost any style of loom and it is used in weaving large and complex patterns. One of the earliest used in this country was at the Northrup Woolen Mill at Roanoke, New York, in 1820.

JEAN

A twilled cotton cloth resembling fustian.

K

KERSEY

A coarse, smooth-faced narrow wool fabric something like broadcloth but lighter in weight, distinguished by the diagonal ribbed appearance of its upper surface, where the nap, not being raised, allows its structure to be seen.

KIDDERMINSTER CARPETS

See CARPETS, *Kidderminster*.

L

LACE

Lace presumably originated in Italy, supported by the fact that the earliest manuals were printed in Italy and by the markedly Italian character of the designs of early lace. Apparently lace evolved during the late 15th century. It departed from the earlier embroidery principles, first by what is known as "drawn-work," then by "cut-work," and with this, lace really started its long evolution. The industry centered in Venice, and in the first half of the 17th century, Venetian point-lace took Europe by storm. From Venice the art of making point-lace traveled to other Italian towns and westward to France and Flanders, and the Alençon lace of France attained great beauty in the 18th century.

There were two varieties of early hand-made lace, needle or point-lace, made throughout with button-hole stitches, and bobbin or pillow-lace, woven, plaited and twisted. While point-lace-making has always been the distinguishing characteristic of Italy and the south, pillow-lace remains distinctively associated with the Flemish towns and with England. The needle and bobbin governed the making of antique lace as they do today. The early lace was made with linen thread, occasionally with metallic or silken thread,

FLEMISH HUNTING TAPESTRY, EARLY 16TH CENTURY; HEIGHT, 9 FEET, 2 INCHES; WIDTH, 8 FEET, 4 INCHES

BRUSSELS TAPESTRY, 16TH CENTURY—HEIGHT, 11 FEET, 3 INCHES; WIDTH, 8 FEET, 6 INCHES

French Tapestry, 17th Century—Height, 12 feet, 6 inches; Length, 16 feet, 5 inches

never with cotton thread, and white linen thread is still used for hand-made lace.

Technically, lace consists of two elements, the pattern, forming the more solid portion of the fabric, and the ground, which serves to hold the pattern together. The pattern is sometimes stitched down after being separately made, such lace being known as appliqué or applied. In guipure lace the pattern is cut out of cambric and applied to stitchwork. Machine-made lace of the present time, in which cotton thread is largely employed, cannot rival handwork in delicacy and strength of ornamental structure.

REFERENCES

How to Know Laces, ROBERTS; *American Lace and Lace-Makers*, VANDERPOEL; *A History of Lace*, PALLISER; *Lace and Its Development*, ANTIQUES, May 1922; *Spanish Blonde Lace*, ANTIQUES, Aug. 1922.

LAMBREQUIN

A festooned drapery at the top of a window or around the top of a bed.

LAWN

A kind of very fine linen, resembling cambric.

LINEN

Linen is made from flax and flax, like wool, has been used as a material for woven fabrics from a remote period. The use of linen for wrapping mummies in ancient Egypt is well known, and the Bible tells of the rich man clothed in purple and fine linen. Linen is manufactured in most European countries and in this country, too, although its manufacture has never been extensive here since cotton took the lead at the end of the 18th century. Irish and Scotch linens are famous. In Colonial times flax was raised in nearly every community here, and was cured, spun and woven into cloth for sheets, pillow cases, towels, table-cloths, clothing and other useful purposes. Most of the linen was plain and the quality varied. Sometimes, for table-cloths, it was woven to pattern. The work of spinning and weaving took up more of the housewife's time than any other one of the household crafts.

REFERENCES

Homespun Handicrafts, ELLA SHANNON BOWLES; *Handicraft Art of Weaving*, THOMAS WOODHOUSE.

LINSEY-WOOLSEY

At first coarse woolen stuff with linen used as a warp. Later it became a dress material of an inferior grade of wool woven on a cotton warp.

LOOM

The loom is a machine for weaving yarn or thread into a fabric. In many primitive looms the bobbin, on which the weft was wound, was passed by hand, and the loom on which the flax and wool of Colonial times was woven was the same in principle as that used by the nations of antiquity. The shuttle carrying the bobbin was devised to throw the bobbin the full width of the loom. Bobbin looms are divided into treadle looms and those without a treadle, called high-warp looms. In 1733, John Kay of England invented the flying shuttle, and the first successful power loom was invented by Edmund Cartwright, also an Englishman, in 1785. Then came the Jacquard loom (q.v.) in 1806, which provided for weaving large and complex patterns. The modern power loom combines a number of appliances which make it possible for one weaver to operate several looms.

Lustring or Lutestring

A glossy, silk fabric with a ribbed pattern used for clothing and for furniture upholstery in the 17th and 18th centuries. Although it was made in England, large quantities were imported there from France and Italy.

M

Mantilla

The national head-dress of lace for women in Spain. The name is derived from *manto*, the veil with which Spanish ladies were accustomed to cover the face, after a custom of Moorish women.

Mantua

A silk fabric made in Italy.

Mockado

Inferior cloth made in several parts of Europe, and much used for clothing in the 16th and 17th centuries.

Mohair

A fabric composed of the hair of the angora goat, mixed with silk or wool, used occasionally in the 17th and 18th centuries for upholstery and hangings. Later, the name was applied to a material of silk.

Moravian-Work

See Needlework Pictures.

Moreen

A woolen fabric, sometimes mixed with cotton, in imitation of watered silk (moiré), used for hangings in the 18th century.

Mortlake Tapestries

See Tapestries, *English*.

Mule Spinner

A machine for spinning fine threads. The invention of this machine by Samuel Crompton (q.v. Part 6) in 1779 revolutionized the cotton-spinning industry. The spindles were set in a traveling frame to reduce the strain of the process of spinning, by rollers, producing finer strands, which enabled English textile makers to manufacture muslins equal to those formerly imported from India, and brought great prosperity to Manchester. See SPINNING JENNY.

MUSLIN

A fine cotton fabric of Oriental origin deriving its name from Moslem. It somewhat resembles gauze in appearance, but it is woven plain without any looping of the warp threads on the weft. The term "muslin" is now also applied to a coarser and heavier cotton cloth suitable for sheets and pillow cases.

N

NANKEEN, NANKIN

A buff-colored cloth originally made in the district of Nanking in China from a naturally buff-colored type of cotton fiber. The original Nankeen has been superseded by ordinary cotton cloth, colored to imitate the genuine fabric.

NEEDLEWORK

Needlework is a broad, general term applying to embroidery, lace, and tapestry work. In the Tudor period chairs, upholstered with satin or velvet, were frequently enriched with applied needlework. During the William and Mary and Queen Anne periods in England needlework was particularly devoted to tapestries, in which a coarse canvas ground is entirely covered by close-set stitches of wool or silk. This work was accounted the duty of the women folk in country houses in England. Many examples are today in good state of preservation. The stitch generally used is a diagonal called the tent-stitch. Grospoint and petit-point are terms used also for this work, gros-point crossing two meshes of the canvas, and petit-point, the smaller, crossing but one mesh. In general, the designs follow those for tapestries and other textiles of the periods. Crewel-work was popular, also designs in imitation of the Chinese silks, embroideries, and other textiles imported at that time from the East. Some of the most important needlework panels were those designed for wall-hangings in imitation of woven tapestry. About 1770, needlework covers for seat furniture were superseded by silks, satins and tapestry.

Needlework in the American colonies was largely utilitarian, although as time passed and the conditions became somewhat easier for women, they indulged their taste for decoration and ornamentation by means of their needle. Firescreens, chair seats, bed-coverings and articles of clothing gave evidence of their skill and taste. Samplers, too, afforded work for the younger generation. See EMBROIDERY and LACE.

REFERENCES

Art in Needlework, DAY; *Embroidery and Needlework*, FRY; *English Needle-*

work, KENDRICK; *Dictionary of Needle-work*, CAULFIELD and SAWARD; *Tent Stitch Work*, ANTIQUES, Dec. 1922.

NEEDLEWORK PICTURES

In England needlework pictures in imitation of tapestry were made as early as the Tudor period and they were continued until the days of the Stuarts, corresponding roughly with the years during which tapestries were produced. The subjects consisted of Biblical scenes, chiefly, although there were others of current interest. Some of the later pictures were a combination of needlework and paint. The effect of these, in many instances, approaches the grotesque. One of the finest needlework pictures in existence today is to be seen in the Cluny Museum in Paris. It is a panel in high and low relief of the 16th century, representing the story of Eden.

It is truly a work of art. In this country these pictures were introduced by the Moravians, who came to Pennsylvania soon after 1700. In their schools, they taught fine white embroidery, tambour, crewel-work, and the making of pictures with a needle on silk and satin. In the late 18th and early 19th centuries, this work became very popular in their district, and went under the name of Moravian-work.

REFERENCE
Needlework Pictures, ANTIQUES, April 1926.

NILLA

A cotton fabric imported into England from India in the 17th century. It was either plain or striped.

NOYALS

A canvas fabric made at Noyal, France, in the 17th century.

O

ORIENTAL CARPETS
See CARPETS and TURKEY-WORK.

ORIENTAL RUGS
See RUGS, *Oriental*.

P

PADUASOY

A strong corded or grosgrain silk fabric, originating at Padua, an Italian city long known for the excellence of its fabrics. Much worn by both sexes in the 18th century. A serge fabric, also from Padua, was called paduasay.

PAISLEY SHAWLS
See SHAWLS.

PARAGON

A woolen material used for garments, hangings, and upholstery in the 17th and 18th centuries.

PATCHWORK

See QUILTS.

PERSIANA

A light silk printed with floral designs.

PETIT-POINT

Sometimes called tent-stitch. It is a slanting stitch, worked usually in silk or wool over a single thread or mesh of coarsely woven canvas. It was much used in the walnut period of furniture. Anything above eighteen stitches to the inch is petit-point. The smaller the stitch, the more enduring the work. Petit-point of over twenty-four stitches to the inch will outwear fine velvet. Coarser work, using the same stitch, is known as gros-point (q.v.). See NEEDLEWORK.

PINTADO

A variety of East Indian chintz printed or painted in colors, and used for wall-hangings in England in the 17th century.

PLUSH

A textile fabric with a pile or nap longer than that of velvet. It is made of cotton, wool or silk.

POINT-LACE

It is believed to have originated in Venice in the desire to produce light and graceful effects in embroidery. See LACE.

POPLIN

A fabric with a silk warp and worsted weft, having a corded surface.

PORTIÈRE

A door hanging or curtain.

PRINTING ON TEXTILES

See TEXTILES.

PURL

Fine wire closely bound with silk, then coiled around a fine rod and pushed off in the form of a coiled tube. Short lengths of purl were freely used in needlework of the late 16th and early 17th centuries.

Q

QUILTING

A favorite decoration for coverlets (q.v.), also for table covers, tester valances, petticoats, etc. It consisted of many intricate stitches needed to make the desired patterns, some of which were very elaborate. The feather designs, both single and double, were used more frequently than any others for quilting valued coverlets. Then there were the tulip, the basket of flowers, the running vine, the twisted rope and many others.

REFERENCES

The Ancient Art of Quilting, ANTIQUES, Mar. 1923; Corded and Padded Quilting, ANTIQUES, Nov. 1924.

QUILTS

They were at first plain piece-work of cotton or linen made of small blocks of various shapes and sizes, sewed together, usually of some geometric design, with a lining often fixed in position by stitching. A "patchwork" quilt is one upon which the design is laid on like a patch and sewed into place. In other words the design is cut separately and applied to the quilt. It is also known as a pieced quilt. See COVERLETS.

REFERENCES

Old Patchwork Quilts and the Women Who Made Them, FINLEY; *Romance of the Patchwork Quilt in America,* HALL and KRETSINGER; *Handicraft of the Early American Woman,* ANTIQUARIAN, July 1930.

R

RATTEEN

A thick twilled woolen stuff from France, Holland and Italy, chiefly, and used mostly in linings. It was usually with a nap but sometimes dressed.

RAYON

Formerly known as artificial silk, it is not silk at all, although it is made of practically the same elements that the worm consumes in producing silk, namely cellulose. But the silkworm produces an animal fiber, whereas the cellulose fiber is purely a vegetable product. Spruce wood-pulp and cotton supply the major part of the raw material for manufacturing rayon.

RETICULE

A lady's hand-bag or work-bag, made of net work, originally.

RHENISH TAPESTRIES

See TAPESTRIES, *Rhenish.*

RUGS

A covering for the floor, usually ob- long or square and made in one piece. The use of rugs dates back many centuries, and doubtless they originated among the nations of the East. In medieval times in England and in Europe the floors of the home of the lowly or the castles of the rich were either of dirt or of stone, covered with rushes, and it was not until the time of Queen Elizabeth that oaken floors were introduced and an occasional rug used to cover them. Early in the 18th century, painted canvas came into vogue as a floor covering, followed by Oriental rugs and those made in France. In this country, the early settlers covered the wooden floors with sand or with the skins of animals. It is very doubtful if rugs were used here to any extent until toward the end of the 18th century, except in the homes of the wealthy, where rugs imported from England and France were to be found. The hooked rug was in wide use in the 19th century.

Aubusson Rugs. A tapestry-like rug made at Aubusson, France, on low-warp looms, which attained great prominence in the 18th century. These rugs were exported to England, and in this country they were to be seen in the homes of the wealthy.

Braided Rugs. It is very probable that braided rugs were made almost, if not quite, as soon as any form of New England mats. Braiding was a simple craft and rugs made in that manner were very durable. Cast-off wearing apparel usually formed the basis of these rugs.

REFERENCE
As to Braided Rugs, ANTIQUES, Feb. 1926.

Hooked Rugs. The best of the old hooked rugs exhibit a fine and patient workmanship, and they are of a time when the making of objects for use was also a means of amusement. The patterns of these older rugs express the designer's own personal interest, whether it was in flowers or animals or other simple subjects. The typical foundation of hooked rugs is burlap or gunny cloth, but they are occasionally found made on a linen cloth foundation. The time of the earliest use of the hooked rug has not been definitely established, but it is believed to have been before the end of the 18th century. Before the middle of the 19th century it had become very popular. The work was attached to a wooden frame which held it tight and smooth while the surface was being covered with the design. Woolen or cotton rags cut in strips and woolen yarn were the materials used. In some rugs the loop top was sheared off, making the surface resemble an Oriental rug.

REFERENCES
Collecting Hooked Rugs, WAUGH and FOLEY; The Hooked Rug, KENT; The Craft of Hand-Made Rugs, HICKS; Distinguishing Good Hooked Rugs, ANTIQUES, Jan. 1927.

Needlework Rugs. These were made with woolen yarn by use of stitches with a needle, producing an embroidery effect resembling the so-called Turkey-work (q.v.). See CARPETS, *Embroidered.*

Oriental Rugs. The making of these rugs is everywhere the same, the warp being stretched between two rollers, the pile being formed by the ends of rows of woolen (or silken) knots tied to the warp between weft threads that hold them in place. Sheep's wool, camel's hair, mohair from the angora goat, and silk are all used as materials from which these rugs are woven. The fineness of a rug depends largely upon the quality of the wool and the number of knots to the square inch. History and religion are woven into the fabrics of all Oriental rugs, if one can but read the signs aright.

Persian rugs excel those of other countries in artistic designs as well as in harmonious coloring, and they are unsurpassed in technique. The warp and weft of these rugs are usually of cotton, and both the Sehna and Ghiordes knot are employed in weaving. There are numerous rug-making centers. Some of the well-known names are: Ferghana, Saruk, Serebend, Mosul, Kashan and Bijar. Among the good antique Persian rugs there are, in all, about thirty original designs, all with different borders, but there are many variations of these designs. Turkish rugs are not so finely woven as the Persian rugs, and the Ghiordes knot is always used. Warp and woof are usually of wool or of goat's hair, and the rugs are made with a longer pile and looser texture. The Anatolian are probably the best known of the Turkish rugs. The Chinese rugs of antiquity are remarkable and very rare, in fact, almost unprocurable.

Blue is the typical Persian color, as red is typical of Turkestan and yellow of China. Kazaks are North Caucasian fabrics that rank high today. The Khilims (Kilims) are woven with a form of weaving which dates back to Egyptian times, before the pile fabrics had been evolved. They are particularly appropriate for hangings and for couch covers. Any Eastern rug over fifty years old may be classed as old. Genuine antiques are almost priceless.

REFERENCES

How to Identify Oriental Rugs, WOLFE; The Practical Book of Oriental Rugs, GEORGE LEWIS; Oriental Rugs and Carpets, DILLEY.

RUSSEL

A woolen fabric formerly used for clothing, especially in the 16th century. It was made in various colors.

RUSSIAN TAPESTRIES

See TAPESTRIES, Russian.

S

SAMPLERS

The earliest mention of samplers in England is 1502, and in the first stages they are purely a record of stitching patterns. The earliest samplers were long and narrow because the loom on which the foundation material was woven was narrow. Numberless examples of English samplers are in existence dating from the middle of the 17th century to the middle of the 19th century. Linen, bleached or unbleached, always hand-woven, is the foundation material of all early samplers. The stitches were usually in linen thread. Another variety is the lace sampler, belonging chiefly to the 17th century. Only three authentic examples of the 17th century samplers of this country are known. One is by Anne Gower of Salem, one by Loretta Standish at Pilgrim Hall in Plymouth, and one, dated

1654, bearing the names of Miles and Abigail Fleetwood.

In Colonial days every well-brought-up girl made a sampler on homespun linen. As a rule the earliest were without name or date but many of those made in the 18th century bearing both name and date are still in existence, particularly in New England, New York, New Jersey and Pennsylvania. Borders appeared about 1726. The alphabet and figures are commonly seen on them and subjects chosen vary from Biblical scenes to pictures taken from nature and geometric designs. The later English sampler was often the product of a mature young lady who was filling her wedding chest, while the American sampler was wrought laboriously by the child as a part of her education. The great numbers of samplers in existence warrant a lengthy study of the subject.

REFERENCES

American Samplers, BOLTON and COE; *Samplers and Tapestry Embroideries*, M. B. HUISH; *Samplers in Our Alley*, ANTIQUES, June 1923.

SARCENET, SARSENET

Name for a very fine and soft silken fabric said to have been first made by the Saracens. It was a material for luxurious hangings and coverings in England in the 17th century.

SATEEN

A cotton or woolen fabric made to resemble satin.

SATIN

A silk fabric in which so much of the weft is brought uppermost in the weaving as to give a more lustrous and unbroken surface to the cloth than is seen when the warp and weft cross each other more frequently.

SATINETTE

An imitation of satin woven in silk or silk and cotton.

SAVONNERIE

A woven fabric hand-knotted like a heavy wool velvet, called Turkey-work, made at a factory in Paris, where it was established early in the 17th century. It was finally absorbed by the Gobelin factory. The stitch used had its origin in the East, and although the product was given the name of tapestry it more nearly resembles a carpet surface.

SAY

A cloth of fine texture, resembling serge, made of wool and in use in England in the 17th century.

SERGE

A woolen twilled stuff made on a loom and frequently used in England for the linings of curtains and for the covers of furniture in the late 17th and early 18th centuries.

SHAGREEN

A textile used in England in the 18th century for hangings and linings.

SHALLOON

A closely woven woolen cloth first

made in Châlons, France, and utilized for linings.

SHAWLS

The cashmere shawls are made at Kashmir, a native state of India, where they form the principal industry, from the hair of the Kashmir goat, which is long, fine and silky. Paisley shawls were made at Paisley, Scotland, in the first half of the 19th century, at which time they were very popular. Their double shawl was made to imitate the pattern and appearance of the cashmere shawls. Others, called "broche," had woven stripes of various colors, the alternate stripes being patterned. Another kind was the half shawl, so worn that one half of each side showed the face of the pattern, the other half, the reverse of it. This was folded across the middle when worn, so that the exposed part displayed the face of the pattern.

SHODDY

The wool of old woolen fabrics, torn to pieces and remade with an admixture of fresh wool into new cloth.

SILESIA

A linen cloth that took its name from Silesia, where it was first made. Sometimes it is referred to as "sleazy."

SILK

Silk is made from the fiber derived from the cocoon of the silkworm. It was known to the ancient nations of the East, presumably having its origin in China, where the mulberry tree was cultivated for feeding the silkworms, long before the Christian era. Silk culture in Europe is now practiced in Italy, Spain, Portugal and France, and in this country the first attempt was made in Virginia in the 17th century. In 1759, silk from Georgia sold in London at three shillings a pound higher than that from any other part of the world. Silk was also being produced in South Carolina, Connecticut and several other states during the last half of the 18th century. In England the first silk mill was at Derby, where it was started in 1719 by Thomas Lombe, and in this country the first mill was started in 1810. During the 19th century silk mills were started in various parts of the country and some of them were very successful. The center of this industry in this country is Paterson, New Jersey. At the present time all the silks used for manufacturing in the United States are imported, and Japan is the leading silk-producing country.

REFERENCE

Early American Textiles, FRANCES LITTLE.

SPANISH TAPESTRIES

See TAPESTRIES, Spanish.

SPINNING

Spinning is the art of drawing, twisting and combining animal and/or vegetable fibers, so that they are formed into continuous threads for the further operations of weaving, knitting or sewing. The principal textile fibers are silk, wool, flax, cotton, jute and rayon. The earliest spinning apparatus was the spindle with the distaff. During the last half of the 18th century, three inventions were made which completely revolutionized the art of spinning: Hargreaves' spinning-jenny (1764), which spun several threads at one time, Arkwright's roll-drawing spinning machine (1769), by means of which cotton produced a thread so strong that it could be used for the warp instead of linen, which was before required, and Crompton's mule spinner (1779). This machine spun threads so fine that muslins could then be made in England. All of these machines were made much more effective by the invention of the power loom by Cartwright in 1785. During the 19th century many important improvements were made but the general principles of earlier machines remain.

REFERENCE

Early American Textiles, FRANCES LITTLE.

SPINNING-JENNY

A mechanism invented by James Hargreaves (q.v. PART 6) in 1764, by means of which several threads were spun at one time. The name "Jenny" was that of the inventor's daughter. See MULE SPINNER.

SPINNING-MULE

See MULE SPINNER.

SQUAB CUSHION

Movable cushions for chairs and settees, frequently mentioned in 18th-century inventories. They were one of the features of every room in the Jacobean period in England.

STENCILING

In stenciling on textiles the colors are applied with a brush through the pattern, and the process is nearer painting than printing. The Japanese are especially skillful in the use of stencils.

STITCHES

Almost hopeless confusion exists as to the proper nomenclature of stitches. It is hardly too much to say that nearly every stitch has something like half-a-dozen different names. The stitches are described under the names by which they are most commonly known or which seem to describe them most clearly. The tent-stitch is the first half of the familiar cross-stitch. All the rows of stitches slope the same way as a rule. It is taken over a single thread only. The tapestry or Gobelin-stitch resembles a tent-stitch, save that it is two threads in height, but only one in breadth. The Florentine and Hungary-stitches are upright, which, arranged in a score of different ways, have been called at times by as many different names. The satin-stitch is long and flat and is seen on Japanese embroideries of all periods. The laid-stitch is of long thread laid on the foundation and held down by short couching-stitches, placed at intervals. These are to be seen on Italian and Spanish embroideries. Knot-stitches, also called looped-stitches, were used to represent the hair of the human figure or the coats of animals, etc., seen in stump-work pictures. Plush-stitch, known as velvet- and rug- and raised-stitch, is a series of loops, secured to the foundation by tent- or cross-stitch, after which the loops are cut as in raised Berlin-work. The needlepoint lace-stitches are as a rule of a close and rather heavy type. Cross-stitch taken over two threads was much used on samplers. Bird's-eye stitches are short, even stitches surrounding the eyelet. Names of stitches also include cable, stem, reticella, briar, the chain-stitch, buttonhole, feather, herringbone, cat-stitch and French-knots, and the list is far from complete.

Stump Work

An embroidery in which some parts of the pattern appear in high relief, raised by a foundation of wool or cotton wool, with knot-stitch, a method almost exclusively of the Restoration period. It is likely that stump-work was purely an amateur or home art.

REFERENCE
The Stitches of Stump Work, ANTIQUES, June 1933.

Swanskin

A fine, thick flannel, so-called on account of its extraordinary whiteness, 17th century.

Swedish Textiles

In Sweden, the textile art is not only one of the oldest of Sweden's industries, it is also most highly developed. Early in the 16th century Flemish weavers were brought to Sweden, bringing with them the skill in design and color of their native land. Weaving of rugs and tapestries became firmly established as a home industry. The earlier textiles resembled the Oriental in design and the coloring materials were from native sources.

REFERENCE
The Background of Swedish Textiles, ANTIQUARIAN, June 1930.

Swift

A frame supported on a standard with two cylinders, one above the other, to which two skeins of yarn were attached and wound into one ball. The revolutions of the cylinders twisted the yarn into one firm strand.

T

Tabby, Tabinet

A thick silk taffeta with a watered or variegated surface introduced into England late in 17th century. Tabinet is sometimes distinguished from tabby, in its use chiefly as upholstering.

TAFFETA

A fine silken stuff, smooth, plain and closely woven, with a lustre or gloss, used for hangings.

TAMBOUR-STITCH

A loop-stitch, similar to the chain stitch in embroidery.

TAMBOUR-WORK

A type of embroidery that was popular in both the 18th and 19th centuries. It takes its name from the drum-like hoop that held in place the material that served for the foundation. It was much used for the embroidery of muslin.

TAMMY

A fine, worsted cloth of good quality, often with a glazed finish.

TAPESTRIES

Tapestry-making is weaving, and its principle is simple. Colored threads, usually of wool or silk, constitute the web, and are woven across other threads, generally of linen, which constitute the warp. A tapestry is a pictured cloth with a ribbed or rep surface woven either on a vertical, high-warp (haute lisse) or on a horizontal, low-warp (basse lisse) loom. In the former the warp is vertical and the woof horizontal; in the latter, the woof is vertical and the warp is horizontal. The high-warp tapestry was known to antiquity and in the celebrated periods of weaving in Europe the high-warp loom has been the one in use. The low-warp loom came into use in France about 1600. It is almost impossible to distinguish the difference in the product of the two methods. The weavers of the 18th century put a single red thread along the top and bottom of a tapestry woven on the low loom to distinguish it. All old tapestry, is of course, hand-woven.

From very early times the inhabitants of Western Europe were renowned for their woven fabrics. The weavers at Arras are said to have begun weaving in the 9th century. Weaving was done in monasteries in France for several centuries. In the 13th century the craftsmen organized guilds and from that time tapestry weaving became an established industry. In tapestry there are four important groups; Gothic, 14th and 15th centuries; Renaissance, 16th century; Baroque, 17th century; Rococo and Classic Revival, 18th century. Before the 14th century there were primitive tapestries only.

The art of tapestry-making came to Europe from the East, and in the 14th century at Paris and at Arras in Flanders designers and weavers were able, with a few colors, to manipulate threads into the strongest and liveliest contrasts of form, color and tone that can be achieved on a flat surface. France is the mother of Gothic tapestries, and Arras gained such distinction that its name became the synonym for tapestry of the finest quality. In the last quarter of the 14th century the craft of the tapestry weaver was in the most prosperous condition it knew in France in the Middle Ages. In the next century Brussels and Bruges and Tournai in Flanders took the lead under the influence of designs by Flemish and Italian artists, and by the middle of the 16th century Flemish tapestry attained a degree of perfection which has never since been surpassed. Much of the wool for the finest French and Flemish tapestries was imported from England. In return, the tapestries of Arras and Flanders were sold in England. In Italy, Ferrara, Florence, Milan and Rome were also noted for fine tapestries in that century.

In the 17th century Brussels lost its leadership through haste and excessive production, and the tapestries woven at the Gobelins' (q.v.) factory in Paris, fostered by King Louis XIV, took first place before the end of the century, and in England tapestries were produced at the Mortlake factory, founded in 1619 by Sir Francis Crane, which were of the highest order of merit. The best tapestries of the 18th century were those of Beauvais (q.v.) but the high standards of the early tapestries had degenerated. The difference is mainly of texture, though also caused by the different character of the designs and by the attempt to use too many shades of coloring. Since the 18th century no really great tapestries have been made.

Gothic and 18th-century tapestries have narrow borders or none; Renaissance and Baroque tapestries have wide borders, some of them of great beauty. Gothic tapestries excel in reds; Renaissance in whites and golden yellow; Baroque in blues; Rococo in rose; while Classic Revival colors are weak and pale. The most important distinguishing feature of old tapestries is the open slits which separate the different parts of the design, different in this respect from damasks, brocades and other weaves. In the prominent museums in this country and in Europe, and in some private collections too, there are to be seen many of those early masterpieces of woven art. A great many have been destroyed by the ravages of time and by the wilful purpose of man, especially in France during the time of the French Revolution. Those tapestries that survive well deserve the care and admiration now bestowed upon them.

REFERENCES

The Tapestry Book, HELEN C. CANDEE; Tapestries: Their Origin, History and Renaissance, GEORGE HUNTER; The Practical Book of Tapestries, HUNTER; A History of Tapestry, THOMSON.

American Tapestries. The first tapestry produced in America was woven on a small loom in New York in 1893 by a Frenchman. Since that time other looms of the low-warp pattern have been set up, workmen obtained from abroad, and some creditable copies of old tapestries have been made.

Arras Tapestries. See above, directly after TAPESTRIES.

Aubusson Tapestries. Weaving of tapestry was established here before the 17th century, and as early as 1637 had more than two thousand workers on low-warp looms. The industry was greatly injured by the Revocation of the Edict of Nantes in 1685 and by the hard times that prevailed in France in the last decade of the 17th century. In 1731, the French Government assisted by sending a dyer and a designer from the Gobelin factory; prosperity began anew, and the best period of tapestry weaving in Aubusson is from 1740 to 1790. Distinguishing features of the early product are the dazzling whites and the loose texture.

Bayeux Tapestry. See BAYEUX.

Beauvais Tapestries. This famous factory was founded in 1664. It was a step in the campaign that transferred the tapestry supremacy from Flanders to France. The factory here produced tapestries for the general public, while the Gobelin factory was devoted to work for state purposes. Compared with those made at Gobelins' the Beauvais tapestries were inexpensive. In the 18th century, largely because of the designs of the artist Boucher, the work of Beauvais is comparable with the best tapestries of the earlier centuries.

English Tapestries. The first English factory of any continuity appears to have been the Sheldon Looms, established at Barchester in Warwickshire by William Sheldon about the middle of the 16th century. The tapestries produced there compare favorably with the finest contemporary Flemish weavings. Some of these consisted of large tapestry maps of English counties. The great name in the history of tapestry-making in England is Mortlake in Surrey County in the 17th century. From 1620 to 1636 these tapestries, made under Sir Francis Crane by expert weavers from Flanders, rival those of the later Gobelins and surpass those of Brussels of the period. Sir Francis Crane died in 1636 and the establishment became known as "The King's Works." The factory lost royal support in the troubled times of the reign of Charles I and, after struggling through the times of the Commonwealth and the Restoration, finally passed out of existence in the reign of Queen Anne. There were also some other minor factories in England during this period, and one in Ireland. Several are of record during the 18th century, Lambeth, Fulham and Soho.

REFERENCES
Tapestry Weaving in England, THOMSON; *Elizabethan Sheldon Tapestries,* HUMPHREYS.

Flemish Tapestries. See above, directly after TAPESTRIES.

French Tapestries. See above and Gobelin Tapestries.

Gobelin Tapestries. The history of Gobelins begins with the establishment on the banks of the Bièvre river in Paris of a dye factory, by Jean and Philibert Gobelin, brothers, at the end of the 15th century. In the following century they added to their dyework a tapestry manufactory. In 1662, the factory attracted the attention of Colbert, French finance minister, who purchased the works, and in 1664 the King, Louis XIV, established it as a royal manufactory under the direction of Charles Le Brun, the great master of decorative art of that period, who with a great number of artists and artisans brought the production of tapestry to a high state of perfection in design and weave. From that time the Gobelins have been the most artistic tapestries anywhere produced. The finest set was the History of the King (Louis XIV), a grand historical document. The set numbered fourteen hangings. The History of Alexander in eleven hangings is another famous set. During the 18th century the Gobelin tapestries failed to reach the high standards of the earlier work. The Savonnerie (q.v.), an establishment founded by Henry IV for velvet pile carpets and hangings, was combined with Gobelins' in 1826.

Mortlake Tapestries. See *English Tapestries,* above.

Rhenish Tapestries. Along the banks of the Rhine from Basle to Mayence, there existed through the entire 15th century a flourishing industry of tapestry weaving. The production was small, the work was quite individual, and in type different from the Flemish tapestries of the same period.

REFERENCE

    15th Century Rhenish Tapestries, ANTIQUARIAN, Jan. 1930.

Russian Tapestries. Peter the Great established the Imperial Tapestry Factory at St. Petersburg in 1716 with French weavers from Beauvais. Some notable tapestries were made there but the factory was discontinued in 1859.

Spanish Tapestries. The Royal Tapestry Factory was established in Madrid in 1720 and is still in operation. The best were those woven in the last quarter of the 18th century from designs by Goya.

TAPESTRY EMBROIDERIES

    See NEEDLEWORK PICTURES.

TAPESTRY FURNITURE COVERING

    As furniture became much more diversified in the 18th century, tapestry coverings became common. France set the example and most of these coverings were made at Beauvais on low-warp looms and at the Gobelin works. Aubusson also produced many attractive sets. Tapestry coverings all in silk are much inferior to those that have the proper proportion of wool.

TENT-STITCH

    See NEEDLEWORK.

English Brass Chandelier and Andirons, Georgian Period, 18th Century

English Pewter, 17th Century, Tankards, a Charger, a Paten, Snuff Boxes

English Pewter, 17th Century, Alms Dish, Salts and Candlesticks

TEXTILE PRINTING

In printing fabrics the color is stamped on from an engraved block or roller. The process, in one form or another, can be traced back to remote times. In the 17th century the industry was revived, and in 1676 textile printing was introduced into England by a French refugee who opened an establishment on the Thames River near Richmond. In the last half of the 18th century the art was brought to a high state of perfection in France, especially at the Toile-de-Jouy factory (q.v.) of Oberkampf. The first factory for printing fabrics in America was started in 1774 at Kensington, near Philadelphia, by John Hewson, an Englishman who had gained his knowledge of the business in England. Although the industry grew rapidly in this country American prints have never quite reached parity with those from abroad. At the end of the 18th century metal rollers took the place of wooden blocks and the modern machine period had begun. The printing of woolen and silk cloths is similar to that of cotton or linen except that the woolen cloth requires more preparation and the silk cloth less.

REFERENCE
Painted and Printed Fabrics, CLOUZOT and MORRIS.

TIFFANY

The term for transparent silk, gauze muslin or cobweb lawn, 17th century.

TOILE-DE-JOUY

French chintz manufactured at Jouy-en-Josas in the Bièvre valley near Paris, in a factory established in 1760 by Christophe-Philippe Oberkampf (1738-1815). The chintzes were printed with designs by master artists of the period, of whom Jean Baptiste Huet from 1773 to 1811 was the most prominent, and they became very popular in France, and later in England. Colors used were sepia, mauve, blue, grey, green, black and madder red. After the death of Oberkampf the factory gradually dwindled in importance and in 1843 it was torn down.

REFERENCES
Le Manufacture de Jouy, ANTIQUES, May 1927; Toiles de Jouy, ANTIQUARIAN, May 1931.

TOILINETTE

A cloth for waistcoats with weft of woolen yarn and warp of cotton and silk. Name from the French toilinet, in turn from toile, a canvas.

TOW

The short fibers of flax made into a heavy thread, used for burlaps and coarse clothing stuff, and, when woven, called tow cloth.

TURKEY-WORK

A home product of Colonial times in this country, also imported from England, made in imitation of Oriental pile rugs by threading woolen yarns through a coarse cloth of open texture (canvas or burlap) then knotting and cutting the ends. It became very popular for chair coverings and table and cupboard cloths.

U

UPHOLDER

Called also Upholsterer. The individual who prepared the upholstery fittings. In the 18th century upholstery formed an important part of the trade of the leading cabinet-makers.

UPHOLSTERY

The earliest forms of upholstering in England were state canopies and beds. A diversity of material was employed, plain and embroidered velvet, satin, tapestry, needlework, and even leather was used. Later, chintz and Indian calicoes came into favor. In the 17th century, fringes became an important feature of upholstery and continued in use until the end of the 18th century. Metal fringes and tasseled silk floss fringes were introduced from France and Italy during the Restoration and afterwards copied in England. Allusions to upholstery are numerous in the 18th century in all of the cabinet-makers' books of the period, and the upholsters' trade reached its zenith at that time. In this country, chair seats were covered early and by the end of the 17th century upholstered furniture was comparatively common. During the 18th century the use of upholstery in general paralleled its use in England.

V

VALANCE

A hanging drapery for beds, windows, etc.

VELVET (French, *Velours*)

A silk fabric with a short, close, soft nap. It is believed that the first velvet was made in China, but the early centers of velvet-making in Europe were the cities of Lucca, Genoa and Florence in Italy. Later Venetian velvets became noted, and the art was taken up in the Low Countries. After the Revocation of the Edict of Nantes, French silk weavers migrated to England, and plain and figured velvets were made at Spitalfields, though not equal to Italian velvets. Velvets were then much used for hangings, but in the 18th century velvet lost favor, being replaced by lighter fabrics. A cheaper product known as Utrecht-velvet, consisting of worsted mohair, or of mohair and cotton, was also used for upholstery and hangings. The pile of modern velvets is produced by extra warps that loop over wires, which are withdrawn after the passage of the binding weft. So-called velvet carpets such as Wilton (q.v.) are made by the use of the velvet weave applied to floor coverings of wool.

VIRGINIA CLOTH

A mixture of cotton and tow used for servants' clothing in Colonial days.

W

WEAVING

Weaving is the art of making cloth on a loom (q.v.). There are three fundamental weaves—plain, twill and satin. Others, such as taffeta, damasks, brocades and velvets are merely variations or complications of these three. For many centuries weaving was carried on as a household industry with little or no change in the style of the loom or in the methods employed, and though the loom was remarkably simple, even crude, the operators produced fabrics that have never been excelled in fineness of texture, even at this later day. The materials in early use in this country for weaving were wool, flax and hemp. Cotton came later. The periods just before and following the Revolutionary War are considered the high spots in American home-weaving. It was not until the latter half of the 19th century that all of the processes connected with weaving were grouped together in one establishment, the mill.

REFERENCES

Shuttle-Craft Book of American Hand-Weaving, ATWATER; Early American Textiles, FRANCES LITTLE; Homespun Handicrafts, ELLA SHANNON BOWLES.

WILTON CARPETS

See CARPETS, Wilton.

WOOL

Next to cotton, wool is the most extensively used of all fibers. A pound of the finest wool will yield nearly 100 miles of thread. Although the typical wool is produced by sheep, goat's hair furnishes a long, fine silky material, much used in making beautiful textile fabrics. The angora goat yields mohair, the alpaca goat a fiber known as alpaca, and the wool made from the cashmere (kashmir) goat of India is said to be the most costly of all wools. The fine soft hair of the camel approximates sheep's wool in its structure. The wool grown in this country was much improved in quality early in the 19th century by importation of large numbers of merino sheep from Spain, where cross-breeding had been carried on scientifically for generations.

WOOL-CARD

A leather pad backed with wood and set with bent wire teeth.

WOVEN COVERLETS

See COVERLETS, Woven.

PART V

METALS

PART V

METALS

A

ALLOY

A compound produced by the mixture of two or more metals, effected by fusion.

AMERICAN PEWTER

See PEWTER, *American*.

AMERICAN SILVER

See SILVER, *American*.

ANDIRONS

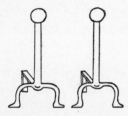

Also called FIRE DOGS (q.v.). Until late in the 17th century all fireplace fittings, including andirons, were made of iron. Prior to the beginning of the 15th century when cast iron was first introduced, fire dogs were made of wrought iron. Andirons, usually, are made with jog or curve in the shank, which makes one right-hand, the other left-hand, and usually, too, with a knob on the upper surface of the shank to hold the log in place. Old andirons may be identified by the iron bolt welded to the log support directly under the uprights. The modern ones are fastened with a regular nut and bolt. Andirons are made in various sizes and in various patterns.

ANGEL

The Angel mark on pewter is of Continental origin, broadly speaking. It is seldom seen on English pewter. This touch-mark is used in conjunction with the maker's mark. The Angel may be flying, or standing with a palm branch in hand or with sword and scales. The use of this mark was strictly reserved for metal of the finest quality. It was adopted throughout most European countries, except France, as a sign of the very best, from the middle of the 17th century.

ANTIMONY

A metal much used for alloys, particularly in fine old pewter. It is a brittle metal of a bluish white color and does not tarnish or rust. It is obtained principally from Borneo and China and is also to be found in various parts of this country and Europe.

APOSTLE SPOONS

See SPOONS.

Appliqué

A piece of metal cut out and fastened to another piece—applied. See Cut-Card Work.

Argand Burners

See Burners, Lamp.

Ashbury Metal

A hard pewter used for forks, spoons, etc., with 25% antimony in the alloy, which gave the required hardness.

Astral Lamp

The name given to a lamp with the Argand burner—improved by Count Rumford, late 18th century. See Burners, Lamp.

B

Bail Handle

A metal handle curved upward at the ends, depending from the sockets of the mount. See Handles.

Basins

The basin was used in the 15th and 16th centuries with the ewer for cleansing the hands after meals, and has continued in use for domestic purposes since. In this country early in the 18th century, it was also used for baptismal rites. Basins were made of pewter or silver, sometimes even of glass.

Beaker

A pewter or silver cup, varying in height, with a flat bottom and sides tapering outward from the base, usually engraved. They were without handles, as a rule, although some of the early American beakers were made with handles. During the Middle Ages they were used as domestic vessels but later were made for both church and domestic use. Beakers were among the earliest objects in silver in New England, and the Puritans adopted them almost exclusively as communion cups.

Bell-Metal

A bronze made of copper and tin in proportion of three or four parts of copper to one of tin, together with a small amount of zinc. Besides its use for bells, it was also used for mortars and for standard weights and measures.

Betty Lamp

See Lamps.

Bezel

The metal ring, usually hinged, surrounding a clock-face glass.

Black Metal

See Lay Metal.

Bleeding Dishes

Sometimes called in England blood-porringers. Bowls to contain blood, sometimes made in nests, of silver or pewter. They were usually graduated, so as to show in ounces the quantity taken, and were made with but one handle. They first appeared in England in the first quarter of the 17th century.

Boss

A protuberant part in ornament.

BRASS

An alloy of copper and zinc, and sometimes containing tin, ductile, and capable of being hammered or rolled into thin leaves. Also much used for castings. The proportion of copper varies from 60% to 75%. From the days of Queen Elizabeth onward it has been much favored for domestic utensils. Furniture mounts (See BRASSES, FURNITURE), candlesticks and andirons are other fields for its use. See BRASS UTENSILS, and ORMOLU.

BRASSES, FURNITURE

The pendant drop brasses came into use the last half of the 17th century, followed by the chased brass plates, with loop handle. Chippendale made popular the so-called "willow" brasses, and after these came the oval plates of Hepplewhite and Sheraton. Many of the earlier brasses used were cast, some with flat surfaces, others with raised design. The handles of these earliest brasses were held in place by narrow strips of brass or iron thrust through a hole drilled in the drawer and clinched inside. These were called "cotter-pin" brasses. Prior to the Revolution most of the brasses used on furniture made in this country came from England. Brasses on old furniture should be of the same period as the antique. It is better to make use of good reproductions than to use a later style, although old.

REFERENCES

Furniture Hardware, ANTIQUES, Vol. 11, p. 477; Vol. 12, pp. 54 and 140; *Development of Old Brass Handles*, ANTIQUES, Nov. 1935.

BRASSES, MONUMENTAL

Large plates of brass or of latten (q.v.) inlaid on slabs of stone forming a part of the pavement, or placed on altar tombs of old churches in Europe. They flourished in England in the 13th and 14th centuries.

BRASS UTENSILS

Included among them were the kettles, warming-pans, basins, pots of various sizes, candlesticks, fire sets, braziers, lamps, fenders and cooking utensils. Some of these were made of copper also. Those of the 17th century used in this country were brought from England or Holland. Early in the 18th century braziers began producing brass and copper utensils here, although castings of brass were not made here until late in the century. Old brass has a soft sparkle and brilliancy not found later.

REFERENCE

Chats on Old Copper and Brass, BURGESS.

BRAZIER

A portable metal pan or hearth in which charcoal or coke is burned. Its earliest use was for live coals for heating. It later became a domestic utensil, the forerunner of the modern chafing dish, first made in the 15th and 16th centuries, in England and the Low Countries, of copper or brass. During the 18th century it was also made of silver by both English and American silversmiths. Among the earliest were those of John Coney of Boston about 1720. BRAZIER also is used to designate the brass-worker.

REFERENCE

Two Chafing Dishes by Peter Van Dyck, ANTIQUES, Oct. 1936.

BRIGHT-CUTTING

A form of engraving on metal in which the designs are lightly cut into the metal in such a way as to offer a reflective surface.

BRITANNIA METAL

An alloy which contained no lead, superseding ordinary pewter because of its supposed injurious effect on health. As first made in the middle of the 18th century, Britannia metal was strictly first-grade pewter. Although there were many variations of the proportions, tin 85%, antimony 10%, zinc 3% and copper 1% was a standard composition. Bismuth was also used at times. It afterwards changed its pewter-like character and adapted itself to the new factory methods of manufacture. Britannia metal can be "spun" more readily than pewter and can also be electroplated.

BRONZE

An alloy of copper and tin, sometimes with traces of zinc, phosphorus, etc., used for domestic utensils from a prehistoric period. Bronze was almost universally used by the Romans for metal objects other than those of gold and silver, and during the so-called Bronze Age bronze was used as the material for cutting implements and weapons. Bronze has been extensively and beautifully wrought by the Chinese and Japanese through many centuries.

BUCKLES

Comparatively little has been written about the Colonial shoe- and knee-buckles. About the time of Charles the Second, the ornamental shoe-buckle came into fashion in England, small at first, but destined to increase in size and in richness of design. Shoe- and knee-buckles were immensely popular throughout the 18th century and later, and thousands of pairs were exported to America. They were made of pewter, pinchbeck, silver, and sometimes of gold, set with jewels, real or paste.

Bull's-eye Lamp

A lens lamp, first half of the 19th century, used for reading. It was usually of pewter and mounted on a low stand.

Burners, Lamp

The earliest burners were of 18th-century invention, when the flat wick was introduced and connected between the oil and the flame by a metal casing, with the wick adjusted by a spur-wheel. In 1783 A. Argand, of Geneva, invented a round burner with holes in the side, through which more air was drawn against the flame, making it a steadier and brighter light. The upright-wick burner was an epoch-making contribution to the development of lighting. During the first half of the 19th century many patents for burners to improve the lighting qualities were issued. Few of them were practical, and their further development was discouraged when gas and electricity became popular.

REFERENCE

Colonial Lighting, Arthur Hayward.

C

Caddy

See Tea Caddy.

Camphene Lamps

A lamp made in early 19th century to burn a fluid known as camphene and very inflammable. The wick tubes are smaller and longer than those of the whale oil burner, and they point away from each other.

Can

A drinking cup important in Colonial America, of silver or other metals, with a rounded bottom and molded base. See Mugs, and Tumblers.

Candelabrum

This may be described as an ornamented, branched candlestick, as the name was applied to the candle-holder (girandole) with two or more branches attached to a mirror, as well as to the more elaborate branched candlestick, also sometimes called girandole, mounted on glass, pottery or marble bases, with two or more branches. These last were usually made in sets of three (two of them for a single candle) for the mantle, and were, as a rule, fitted with hanging glass prisms. They were introduced in the late 18th century and became very popular.

Candle Box or Holder

This was made of sheet metal, usually of tin plate, and hung on the wall, horizontally. In common use in England and in the Colonial period here.

CANDLE MOLDS

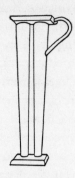

Made of tin, tin plate, or of pewter, in tube form, into which the melted grease was poured after the wick had been hung in place. The number of tubes ranged from two upward. This process was much quicker than dipping.

REFERENCE
ANTIQUES, June 1937.

CANDLE SNUFFERS

These first came into use in England in the first quarter of the 17th century and were used to trim or snuff the candle-wick when the flame became yellow and smoky, or to extinguish the candle. They were at first made of iron, later of brass and silver. Those of silver are very rare. Usually a tray was provided for the snuffers to rest upon, and in the Georgian period short legs were attached to the snuffers to raise them from the surface of the tray. In the 18th century the snuffer formed part of the equipment of every household. With the snuffer the extinguisher (q.v.) was usually to be seen.

REFERENCE
Iron Snuffers, ANTIQUES, Nov. 1929.

CANDLE STANDS

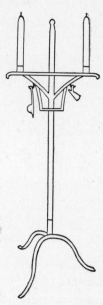

The wooden or wrought-iron floor stand of the Colonial period for holding candles. It was usually adjustable by moving up or down on the pole or standard. Often branched for two or more candles.

CANDLESTICKS

A support with a socket for holding candles. The earliest candlesticks, however, were surmounted by a pricket (q.v.), which, although common in Europe, was not used in this country. Throughout the 16th and 17th centuries the candlestick was of a somewhat dwarf pattern. In this country in the 17th century, tall candle-holders or stands were made of wrought iron with tripod support. From the middle of the 17th century the candlestick constantly gained in use, until it was being made of pewter, brass and silver, rather taller and more ornate. Candlesticks of American silver of the late 17th or early 18th century are extremely rare, as are the English candlesticks dating earlier than the reign of Charles I. Many candlesticks were made with a slide for ejecting the stump of the candle. Some of the old brass candlesticks were cast in two parts and show a seam where they were welded together. The bedroom candlestick had a saucer at the bottom, with a ring for carrying and a cone-shaped extinguisher attached. Later candlesticks were also made of glass and of pottery.

CANISTER
See TEA CADDY.

CASTERS (or Castors)
The roller casters for furniture were used on English furniture early in the 18th century, and they were imported here along with other brass furniture hard-

ware. They were at first generally of wood, but soon after made of brass.

Casters for holding condiments at table were small vessels of silver, cylindrical in shape, tapering toward the top with a high domed lid or cover, perforated and with a finial in the center. They were first made in England during the reign of Charles II, and they are among the early 18th-century products of the American silversmiths. They were later made of cheaper metals and became very common.

CAUDLE-CUP (Also called Porringer or Posset-Cup)

A gourd-shaped silver or pewter drinking cup with two handles. Its origin is traced to the time of Henry VIII, but during the reign of Charles II it became very popular, and next to the tankard in common use. Frequently it was made with a cover. It was a fore-runner of the so-called loving cup of a later day. Although the caudle-cup was copied and made by Boston silversmiths as early as 1665, it does not appear to have been made by any other Colonial silversmiths. See POSSET-CUP.

CAULDRON

From earliest historic times the cauldron (called also kettle and pot) has been among the most important of household utensils. Usually made of iron, but often of brass or copper, it was constantly in use for cooking all boiled foods. In Colonial times meat was more often cooked by boiling than it was by roasting or baking.

CHAFING DISH
See BRAZIER.

CHALICE

A sacramental cup with a stem and foot, with straight or flared sides, often with a cover. The earliest piece of silver, whether ecclesiastical or secular, with an English hall-mark is a chalice with the London date letter 1479. The chalice was usually of silver, but pewter was sometimes used in Colonial times, and it was the only vessel in the Colonial churches that was never used for domestic purposes.

CHANDELIERS

The term applied to lights suspended from the ceiling. Chandeliers of rock crystal were made in England shortly after the Restoration. Wood, carved and gilded, or silver was employed. In the second half of the 18th century, chandeliers of cut glass and crystals, modeled after those of Versailles, became very elaborate. See LIGHTS.

CHARGERS

The largest of the pewter flatware. They were made in three or more sizes, the largest being nearly two feet in diameter.

CHASING

Chasing is much employed in the decoration of silver. It is usually done with tools without a cutting edge, that displace the metal by pressure, contrasted with engraving the metal by means of a sharp tool, which removes a portion of the metal surface. The term is also applied to refining the rough edges of castings.

CHIMNEY CRANE
See CRANE.

CHINESE PEWTER

This product dates back at least two thousand years, and it has ever since then been a leading industry.

CHOCOLATE-POTS
See TEA-POTS.

CLOCK JACK (Also called Roasting Jack)

A contrivance for turning roasting

meat, hung on a hook in front of the fire-place. Those made in England were heavy and cumbersome. Simon Willard, of clock fame, made one lighter and more compact, enclosed in a brass case.

COFFEE-POTS
See TEA-POTS.

CONTINENTAL PEWTER
See PEWTER, *Continental*.

CONTINENTAL SILVER
See SILVER, *Continental*.

COPPER UTENSILS
See under BRASS UTENSILS.

COPPERSMITH
The coppersmith has taken a prominent place among the craftsmen of all nations, and at all periods, and in many instances he has been acknowledged as an artist of no mean order. The product and the activities of the coppersmith in England were for centuries regulated by the Worshipful Company of Founders. During the first half of the 18th century coppersmiths from England came to this country and by the middle of the century were making here a large part of the brass and copper utensils used. The tools with which the ancient copper-smiths wrought and fashioned the most beautiful works are still used by the modern coppersmith.

CRANE, CHIMNEY
A wrought-iron bracket hung against the wall of the fireplace in the 17th and 18th centuries and made to swing to and fro over the hearth. In large fireplaces there were sometimes two of these cranes in place. Pot hooks were attached to them for suspending the cooking utensils.

CREAM PITCHERS
See PITCHERS.

CURTAIN-HOLDERS
Metal curtain-holders for holding back window draperies made their appearance in the second half of the 18th century. See ROSETTES.

CUT-CARD WORK
This is a surface ornament on silver in relief, cut from a separate sheet of metal and applied. Usually it is employed as a border or as a decorative plate to receive the rise of a knob or handle. The style was derived from France and it was in use in England and in this country from late 17th century until well into the 18th. Early examples were usually solid. Later they were frequently pierced.

REFERENCE
Cut-Card Ornament, ANTIQUES, Nov. 1933.

D

DISH CROSSES
An X-shaped table stand, used for holding dishes.

DISH RINGS
Rings used as stands for dishes holding hot foods, to protect the surface of

the table. They were made of silver in Ireland, last half of the 18th and early 19th centuries, and were called "potato rings."

REFERENCE

Irish Dish Rings and Their Tradition, ANTIQUARIAN, Jan. 1930.

DOOR KNOCKER

See KNOCKER.

DOOR LATCHES

See LATCHES.

DRINKING CUPS

The earliest cups were made of horn, later of maplewood (see MAZER BOWL), and even of leather and other materials in medieval times. In Tudor days there were cocoanut and ostrich shell cups, mounted with silver and with feet of the same metal. From the time of Elizabeth these cups were of pewter or silver, and took the form of tankards, flagons, caudle-cups, beakers, cans and mugs.

DROP HANDLE

A pendant brass or iron drop used on furniture, last part of 17th century. See HANDLES.

E

ÉCUELLE

The French name for a vessel resembling an English porringer, very popular in France in the 18th century. It was usually of silver, although sometimes made of pewter or faience, with two handles, and as a rule a domed cover was added.

EMBOSSING

Producing raised or projecting figures or designs in relief on the surface of metalwork.

ENGLISH PEWTER

See PEWTER, English.

ENGLISH SILVER

See SILVER, English.

ENGRAVING

Marking with a sharp tool which removes a portion of the surface. This was the decorative process most commonly used on early silver.

EPERGNE

An ornamental silver table stand for sweetmeats, etc.

ESCUTCHEON

A key-hole plate of metal, first of iron or bronze, later usually of brass. The design followed the style of the handles

American Pewter by J. Danforth From the Kerfoot Collection, Early 19th Century

English Pewter, 17th Century, Plates, Candlesticks, Snuffboxes and Mug

AMERICAN PEWTER TANKARDS AND CUPS, EARLY 18TH CENTURY

on furniture. It was an important detail during the 18th century.

REFERENCE
Furniture Escutcheons, ANTIQUA-RIAN, Nov. 1931.

ESTAMIER
The old French name for pewterer.

EWER
A jug-like shape, the earliest of which dates from the 15th century. Accom-

panying it was a basin or a salver, and water from the ewer was poured into the basin for cleansing the hands after meals. They were rarely made after the middle of the 18th century.

EXTINGUISHER
A cone-shaped cap for putting out the flame of a candle or whale-oil lamp, instead of blowing this out. It usually had a hook attached. See CANDLE SNUFFERS.

F

FEEDING CUP
See SPOUT CUP.

FENDER

A guard of pierced metal or wire, to place before an open fire. They were often made of sheet brass with a design cut from the metal in the desired pattern. First used about the middle of the 18th century.

FIRE BACKS
Plates of cast iron set into the backs of open fireplaces to prevent the destruction of the back wall of the hearth. The outward surface of these was usually covered with a relief design for ornament. Fire backs have pedimented tops which distinguish them from stoveplates (q.v.).

REFERENCE
American Firebacks, ANTIQUES, Feb. 1934.

FIRE DOGS
Fire dogs was the early name given to andirons, due to their shape, more or less resembling dogs. See ANDIRONS.

FIREPLACE TOOLS
The tools and accessories of the fireplace in Colonial times were usually made of iron and were of many kinds, for a great variety of purposes. They included the crane (q.v.), pot hooks, shovel, tongs, slice bar, fire fork for manipulating the logs, pots and kettles (cauldron, q.v.), spit for roasting, clock jack (q.v.), gridiron (q.v.), skillet (q.v.), trivet (q.v.), frying pan, toaster (q.v.), toasting fork, skimmers, ladles, and, of course, the fire dogs (andirons, q.v.). Kitchen paraphernalia was shaped mainly on English lines, although

in some of the Colonies examples show
the influence of other European countries.

FLAGONS

The flagon was an elongated tankard
(q.v.) of silver or of pewter, which generally served as a sacramental vessel,
although not confined to such purpose.
At first the lid was flat, but later it was
shaped as a dome with a finial. Sometimes the flagon was made with a spout.
It was not until early in the 18th century
that the flagon was made in this country.

FLUTING
See GADROON.

FOOT WARMER

A sheet iron or tin-plated box, usually
about eight or nine inches square and six

inches high, with holes punched in the
sides and top and set into a wooden
frame with a wire handle to carry it by.
They were used for keeping the feet
warm when traveling or were taken to
church, where in the winter time there
was no heat. They were filled with live
coals from the fireplace.

FORKS, TABLE

Forks first appeared in Italy in the
15th century, but they did not come
into general use there until the next century. Their use gradually spread to other
European countries and appeared in
England early in the 18th century.
With two, three or four prongs, the
stems or handles followed designs of
contemporary spoons. Forks were not
made to any extent by Colonial silversmiths, although iron or steel forks with
bone handles, sometimes with silver
handles, were in common use in this
country in the 18th century.

REFERENCE
The Evolution of the Knife and Fork,
ANTIQUARIAN, Dec. 1929.

FRANKLIN STOVE
See STOVE.

FRENCH SILVER
See SILVER, *French.*

G

GADROON
An ornament on silver or pewter similar to fluting or more correctly, reed-

ing, as the repoussé (q.v.) work between the lines is usually convex. The
term gadroon is generally applied to the

narrow borders or edges, while the deeper work on the bodies is called fluting.

GARNISH

The pewterer's trade term for a complete set of a dozen platters, a dozen flat bowls and a dozen small flat plates.

GILDING

The processes of applying gilding to metal and to wood are very unlike. With metals, the early method was to apply to the metal surface a nitrate of mercury solution, then to rub this over with a thick amalgam consisting of gold and mercury. The article was then subjected to heat, which caused the gold to adhere and the mercury to evaporate. This process was known as mercurial or fire-gilding, and was very expensive. It was, however, effective, and under favorable conditions permanent. The modern method of gilding is by electroplating the article.

GIMBAL LAMP

A lighting device for ships, suspended so as always to remain level.

GIRANDOLE

See CANDELABRUM.

GOBLET

The name of goblet was given to the standing cup (q.v.) in Colonial times in this country.

GODDARD

A drinking cup.

GRIDIRON

A wrought-iron kitchen utensil much in use in Colonial days for cooking over the fire. The form has changed but little during the long period of its usefulness.

H

HALL-MARKS

The term hall-mark derives literally from the guild hall of the Goldsmiths' Company of London, and the marks were established to prevent fraud and to secure a certain standard of purity. The bulk of English plate from the 14th century on was marked. The marks signify: first, the leopard's head, adopted about 1300, denoting that the work was done under the surveillance of the Goldsmiths' Company; second, the maker's own mark, adopted 1363; third, the year mark with the secret date letter, adopted about 1438; fourth, assayed and found to be standard, the stamp of the lion passant, adopted about 1540; finally, the King's head, adopted in 1784 as proof that the duty had been paid. It has been estimated that more than ninety per cent of old English silver bears the London hall-mark. The study of hall-marks is of a complex nature and adds no inconsiderable task to the collecting of English silver. The standard work on the subject is *English Goldsmiths and Their Marks* by SIR CHARLES J. JACKSON. Much of the plate of Holland, France, and Germany also was marked, due to the influence of the powerful trade guilds existing in all European countries to protect the interests of the trade. In this country, as there were no trade guilds here, the only official stamp was the maker's mark, usually in the form of his initials, often combined with a device or emblem. The present "sterling" (q.v.) mark now required was not adopted until 1865.

REFERENCES

> *Hall Marks on Gold and Silver Plate*, CHAFFERS; *Old Silver and Old Sheffield Plate*, OKIE; *Chats on Old Silver*, ARTHUR HAYDEN; *English Goldsmiths and Their Marks*, JACKSON; *Hall-Marks. The Heraldry of English Silver*, ANTIQUES, Aug. 1932.

HANAP

The name of a standing cup (q.v.) with cover for use at the table in medieval times. It came next to the salt in importance as a table accessory, and in the halls of the wealthy was made of costly metal, or sometimes, of an ostrich egg or a cocoanut shell, mounted in silver and having feet of the same metal.

HANDLES

The pendant drop handle, at first made of wrought iron, later of brass,

was the style in use on furniture in the 17th century. This was followed by the bail handle of brass, attached with cotter pins or wire, and later the more elaborate so-called "willow" brasses, attached with screw and nut. This style of handle remained in vogue until the time of Hepplewhite and Sheraton, when their handle with the oval or hexagonal plate displaced them. The handles on bowls, cups, vases, porringers and other forms in metal and ceramics are definite clues to style and origin.

HINGES

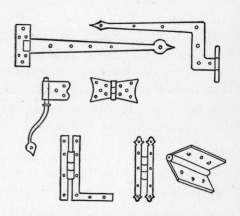

Strap hinges were in early use on the lids of chests and on doors, both in England and in this country. The so-called "butterfly" hinge was also one of the earliest hinges made here. It was made in a variety of sizes, and the iron of the spread ends was usually thinner than towards the center. These were chiefly for use on tables with drop-leaf. H and HL hinges were used extensively on doors and cupboards throughout the 18th and early part of the 19th centuries, especially in New England. In New York and Pennsylvania the so-called "rat-tail" found favor. It was seldom seen in New England. All of these hinges were hand-wrought. In 1772, an English invention of cast-iron butt hinges served eventually to displace the wrought-iron hinges.

HOB GRATE

A basket-like grate of English design that sits inside the fireplace.

HOLLOW WARE

Name given to bowls, pots, measures, tankards, flagons and other hollow pieces, in both metal and ceramic ware.

HORSE TRAPPINGS

Fanciful frets of perforated brass, similar to ornaments which had been used on horse harness from time immemorial. These ornamental brasses were regarded as charms against danger and perils unknown today.

REFERENCE

Horses Brasses and Their Symbolism, ANTIQUES, Oct. 1929.

I

INKSTANDS

Pewter and silver inkstands of the 18th century included receptacles for sand and wafers as well as for ink, and also a pen stand.

IRISH PEWTER

See *Irish Pewterers* by COTTERELL and WESTROPP, 1917.

IRISH SILVER

See SILVER, *Irish*.

IRON

Iron seems to have been the first native metal to be used in the American colonies. In 1630, a deposit of iron ore (bog iron, it was called) was found at Saugus, a few miles north of Boston, which could easily be obtained and smelted. A company was organized by John Winthrop, Jr., a crude smelter was set up, also a foundry, producing both wrought- and cast-iron. It was one of the first native industries of New England, and it supplied the colonists with iron for pots, kettles, hinges and latches, fireplace and farm tools. Later, when candles came into common use, iron candlesticks and the tripod candle stands were made. In 1648, the same company built a forge in Braintree and, in 1652, another at Raynham near Taunton, Massachusetts.

REFERENCES

Early American Wrought Iron, SONN; *Iron in Early American Lighting,* ANTIQUES, May 1923; *Early American House Hardware,* ANTIQUES, Aug. 1923; *Iron Hardware for Buildings,* ANTIQUES, Oct., Nov., Dec. 1927.

J

JAPANESE PEWTER

This ware has been made in a variety of forms for more than one thousand years. Examples of the antique pewter are on exhibition at the Museum of Fine Arts, Boston.

JAPANNED WARE

Although fine japanned work, which is lacquering or varnishing on metal, was done in Holland, France, and Spain following the early importations of Chinese lacquer, the best of the early work was done on tin-plated iron at Pontypool, England, near Wales, late 17th century, where a fine varnish, heat-resisting, hard-drying and with a surface peculiarly well adapted for decoration, had been discovered. The first mill for rolling iron was erected at Pontypool in 1664, and the invention of tin-plating speedily followed. The manufacture of japanned ware began next, lasting a hundred years. Examples of that work are things of beauty, worthy of a place of honor today. The chief difference to be noted between modern japanned ware and that of older date is the delightfully mellowed coloring of the old and the shiny brightness of the new. Japanning was done on pewter and on tin, also, in the 18th century. In this country, japanned tin ware was made and sold in great quantities and variety during the first half of the 19th century. See TÔLE.

REFERENCES

The Art of Japanning, ANTIQUES, Aug. 1922; *Pontypool and Usk*, ANTIQUARIAN, Feb. 1930.

K

KITCHEN PARAPHERNALIA
See FIREPLACE TOOLS.

KNIVES, TABLE

These began to appear in England in the Restoration period, although they did not become common until the 18th century. Early knives were of steel with bone or ivory handles. Later handles of porcelain or silver were used.

KNOCKER, DOOR

The earliest knocker was of the S type and its knock was deep, sharp and resounding. These were at first made of wrought iron, then of brass. Early

brass knockers came from England, as casting in brass here was not begun until late in the 18th century. In the Georgian period, the "urn" knocker came into favor, and continued in use until well into the 19th century. These knockers were often hand-chased and they were attached to the door by wrought-iron bolts. After the Revolution knockers were made in this country, cast in sand molds from wood-carvers' models of the English pattern, in a variety of shapes and designs.

REFERENCE

Latch and Door Knocker, ANTIQUES, Feb. 1923.

KNOP

An architectural term often applied in other fields, and used in early times to designate the terminal of a spoon.

L

LAMPS

No great improvement over the flat, shallow lamps of antiquity—made of stone, clay or metal, containing oil in a covered reservoir from which it was drawn by the capillary action of the wick, passing through a small hole to the tip of the ignited wick—took place until the end of the 18th century. The earliest lamp in use in this country was

the "Betty" lamp, usually made of iron, oval or triangular in form, the basin of which was filled with grease in which a rush or a twisted rag was placed for a wick. At first, the Betty lamp was made with open top. Later, a cover to the oil bowl was added and lamps of that type continued to be in use well into the 18th century. As a rule, the Betty lamp had a hook or chain attached for suspending from a beam in the ceiling or for hanging on the wall. Some of the Betty lamps were made double. The "Phoebe" lamp was similar to the Betty, but with a shallow cup beneath for catching the drippings.

In the latter part of the 17th century pewter lamps for use with sperm (whale) oil were made in a great variety of shapes and sizes, and continued to be used throughout the next century.

Beginning with the 19th century the tin and pewter whale-oil and camphene (q.v.) lamps with two spouts were to be seen in every household until, about the middle of the century, the growing use of glass lamps, which had first appeared about 1820, and were made in many patterns in the following years, gradually displaced them. Many of these glass lamps had patented devices of various kinds to improve the lighting qualities.

A marked advance over the saucer-shaped lamps toward the modern lamp came with the introduction of the flat wick late in the 18th century, adjusted with a spur wheel, followed by the invention in 1783 of the Argand round burner, which procured a steadier and brighter light. The lamp with a flat wick for kerosene oil came into use about 1865. But the discovery that transformed the whole method of oil lighting was accidental. One of Argand's workmen, in heating a bottle over the open flame, cracked off the bottom and held the remainder in such a way over the flame that it acted as a chimney, and in that manner the lamp chimney came into existence, an improvement in artificial lighting only paralleled by the invention of the electric lamp of modern times. See LIGHTS.

REFERENCES

Colonial Lighting, ARTHUR HAYWARD; Light and Lamps of Early New England, CONNECTICUT MAGAZINE, 1903-04; On the Trail of the Betty Lamp, ANTIQUES, Feb. 1924; Further Light on the Betty Lamp, ANTIQUES, April 1929; Some Old Lamps, ANTIQUES, Dec. 1926; Early American Lamps, ANTIQUES, Dec. 1927, Jan. 1928; The Light of Other Days, ANTIQUES, March 1932; American Glass Lamps, ANTIQUES, April 1936.

LAMP BURNERS
See BURNERS.

LANTERNS

A receptacle for a light enclosed by some substance which protects it from a draught and permits of reflection. The origin of the lantern is lost in obscurity. It was in use long before the Christian Era and has continued in use ever since. Early lanterns in this country (spelled lanthorn in Colonial days) were of three kinds: hand lanterns, hanging, and wall lanterns. Of these the hand lantern is most frequently seen. The circular type, usually of tin, sometimes of brass, with domed top, punched with holes for the light of the candle to show through, was in use in the 17th and 18th centuries. Some of these early lanterns used candles, others had small oil lamps. The later ones were made square in form with sides of glass. The hanging lantern was for use in lighting halls, staircases and corridors, and they were usually made of iron or brass. The wall lanterns were similar in type to the hanging lantern and used for the same purposes. Cheaper examples of both of these were made in a great variety of shapes and sizes, of tin and japanned. Towards the end of the 18th century lanterns were gradually superseded by lamps, for indoor lighting. See LIGHTS.

LATCHES, DOOR

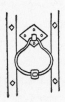 

Those on early buildings of the English colonists of the 17th century were made by the local blacksmith and, naturally enough, he followed training he had received in England, so that the early English styles persisted for many years. The pear-shaped ring, set slightly off-center, acted as a door handle, latch, and knocker. In the first quarter of the 18th century a separate door handle with latch was used. It was finely wrought and tapered to fit the hand, and with some variation continued to be used until the modern door-knob was devised. Locks were not used in connection with latches in early times.

REFERENCE
Latches and Door Knockers, ANTIQUES, Feb. 1923.

LATTEN (French *Laiton*)
A hard medieval metal made of copper and zinc, much resembling brass. It was formerly used chiefly for making church utensils, but was also used for domestic purposes.

LEAD
This metal was used as an alloy in making pewter, while oxide of lead was employed as a base in fusion with silica or sand in making glass.

LEY (or Lay) METAL
This was the lowest grade of pewter, consisting of 80 parts of tin and 20 parts of lead. The cheapest was known as black metal, 60 parts of tin and 40 of lead, an inferior product.

LIGHTS
Early lighting was primitive in its character. It is impossible to determine whether candles, which are of great antiquity, or a wick floating in oil was the earlier method of lighting. Candles can be traced back to the beginning of English history. A socket for holding the candle did not become common until the 16th century. Rush lights, the holders for which were crude iron affairs, were in use in England, throughout the 17th and 18th centuries, while in this country the pine-knot, aptly called "candlewood," and the "Betty" lamp were among the earliest lighting devices. The

introduction of candles was an improvement, especially when they were set in holders with two or more branches or in sconces (q.v.) with reflectors. Candles were a luxury for some time. They were at first made from tallow obtained from wild animals or from beeswax or the wax from the bayberry, and were either dipped or molded. Gradually the use of the hanging or wall lantern (q.v.) developed into the chandelier of the 18th century. This was a frame of metal or wood generally suspended from the ceiling to hold numerous candles. These in England in time became very elaborate with cut glass or crystal decorations, modeled after those of Versailles. The most famous chandeliers were made in France. The first glass chandelier in this country was made at Pittsburgh in 1810. Later the New England Glass Co. at Cambridge specialized in this form of lighting equipment. Few chandeliers dating previous to 1775 have survived. Lamps of metal or glass in a great variety of forms and sizes gradually gained ascendancy over other forms of home lighting. See CHANDELIERS and LAMPS.

REFERENCES
Colonial Lighting, HAYWARD; *Light and Lamps of Early New England*, CONNECTICUT MAGAZINE, 1903-04; *From Flint to Matches*, ANTIQUES, March 1929.

LIGHT FIXTURES
Candle fittings of the 17th and 18th centuries may be placed in three classes, viz.: the candlestick and the candelabrum; the candle fitting that hung on the wall, the lantern and the sconce; those that were suspended from the ceiling, or the lantern and the chandelier.

LOCKS
Locks are of ancient origin. In Rome they were made of bronze or iron. During the 15th, 16th and 17th centuries, ingenious and complicated locks, ornamented with hammered ironwork, were made and the locks in use up to the beginning of the 19th century were all on the same spring-lock principle of the earlier locks. Mortise locks were introduced about the middle of the 18th century. In the 19th century invention of the tumbler lock and the cylinder lock brings us to the modern locks.

LOVING-CUP
Another name for the caudle-cup (q.v.), a generic name for presentation cups.

M

MARKS
See HALL-MARKS and TOUCH-MARKS.

MARROW SPOONS
See SPOONS.

Mazer Bowls

A drinking bowl of medieval times made of mazer (maple) wood, bound and mounted on silver or pewter. Sometimes the bowls were lined 'with the metal also. This was the earliest type of domestic plate, and came into use in England in the 15th century. They were not made after the 16th century, and almost without exception, those preserved are of maple wood. The "Scrope" mazer at York is 12 inches across and 3½ inches deep, dating from the beginning of the 15th century.

Metal Mounts

A means of opening and shutting lids and doors in the form of hinges (q.v.), locks (q.v.), and handles. See also Brasses.

Monteith

This name was given to a silver punch bowl or basin with a notched or indented rim, to which the glasses were attached, made in England late in the 17th century. The rim was moveable. The name that is of the fashionable gentleman of the day, Monteith, for whom the bowl was first made.

Mortars

These were in domestic use from the 16th to the 18th centuries, with the accompanying pestle, in the preparation of home remedies. The form may be described as resembling an inverted bell.

Mounts

The handles, escutcheons and any ornamental metal work used on desks, bureaus and other furniture. Until the end of the 16th century, mounts appear to have been the work of the blacksmith. In the 17th century increasing use of mounts made their manufacture a separate industry. See Brasses.

Mugs

These were made of pewter or silver, usually similar to the bodies of the tankards of the same period, with a handle but without a cover. Some were of the shape of the beaker, the caudle-cup, or the stoneware jug. They always had a flat bottom. The so-called "can" or "cup" used in America was made with a rounded bottom and molded base. Mugs were a popular form of drinking vessel throughout the 18th century.

N

NAILS

Hand-forged nails, made from a soft, fine iron in England, were brought to this country by the early colonists. Soon after, the local blacksmith was making nails from iron smelted here, which was tough and strong. They bent easily but did not break, and these hand-forged nails continued to be used until the end

of the 18th century. Ezekiel Reed of Massachusetts at that time invented a machine for cutting nails from the plate.

NIELLO

A kind of ornamental engraving in black, inlaid enamel on metal, derived from Italy.

NOGGIN

A pewter drinking cup holding a gill.

O

ORMOLU

A metal composed of brass made to resemble gold by the use of more copper and less zinc than usual. Much used by the French for decorative purposes on furniture in the 18th century, frequently gilded in addition.

OXIDIZING

A finish imparted to metal work by chemical treatment, or by continued exposure to the air. Many examples of Colonial silver especially show designs in which oxidized areas are used to provide a striking contrast to parts in relief.

P

PAINTED TIN WARE

A method of decoration common in late 18th century and early 19th. See TÔLE.

PAKTONG

Also called tutenag, crude or alloyed zinc. A silver-white Chinese alloy, imported into England between 1750 and 1800. It was then believed to be a rare metal, Chinese white copper, mined only in the East, but was later discovered to be in reality an alloy of copper, nickel and zinc. It was tarnish-resisting and was used for candlesticks and other metal objects.

PATEN

A small circular salver or plate employed for the wafers or bread in the eucharistic service. It is always of the same material as the chalice, often richly chased or engraved, and at first was the cover of the chalice. They were first made separately in England early in the 17th century. See TAZZA.

PATINA

Originally, the greenish surface film on copper-containing metals, formed in the course of time by oxidation. Today, the term has been enlarged to include the films formed similarly on other metals, and also the characteristic surface appearance of antique furniture.

PEG LAMP

A glass lamp with a projection at the bottom of the oil reservoir for insertion in a socket. First half of 19th century.

PEPPER BOXES

These were made in silver, first half of 18th century, and were used sometimes as a sugar sifter, also. They were about four inches high and were round or octagonal in form with a perforated cover.

PETTICOAT LAMPS

So-called from their flaring shape. Made in metal and in glass.

PEWTER

Pewter, an alloy of tin with other metals, was in use by the ancients and by European countries for several centuries before it became a great industry, that had its golden age in the 16th and 17th centuries. Until silver came into common use on the tables of the rich, pewter held first place for church services and for household use. The ware was too expensive for common use, even far into the 16th century.

Old fine pewter consisted of 112 parts of tin and 26 parts of copper, or, in place of copper, brass. Another fine grade was 100 parts of tin, 4 parts of copper and 8 parts of antimony. Common pewter was 82 parts of tin and 18 parts antimony. "Ley" or "lay" metal was a cheap grade of pewter consisting of 80 per cent of tin and 20 per cent of lead. The cheapest, often known as black metal, was 60 per cent tin and 50 per cent lead. Copper, bismuth and antimony were used to harden pewter. Lead, when used, was to cheapen it.

Pewter, though it darkens and dulls easily, oxidizes but little. For trenchers, platters and the larger flat ware (sad ware), the metal was cast in flat pieces and rolled into sheets of the desired thickness and then hammered into shape. Hollow ware and practically all other pewter was cast in molds, in sections, soldered together, and finished with hand tools, or later, by the lathe. In the pewter days, all mugs, pitchers, basins and porringers were made to scale, and even pewter bottles of exact quarts and pints were made. Pewter, more strictly than other forms of metal, has been kept within the confines of household use. Pewter maintained its popularity until the work of the potters in the 18th century, with their more sanitary and more easily cleaned ware, caught the public taste and ultimately gave the coup-de-grace to an industry which had flourished so long.

In collecting pewter one may safely follow these general directions. Straight or slightly waved lines preceded swelling curves, flat unadorned lids came before domed tops with knobs and crests, few and simple moldings were the forerunners of many and elaborated ones.

In pewter containers the thumbpiece offers the most readily recognized mark of nationality.

REFERENCES

Pewter Down the Ages, H. H. Cot-terell; *National Types of Old Pew-ter*, H. H. Cotterell; *Smaller Objects of Pewter*, ANTIQUARIAN, Dec. 1929.

American Pewter. Although Thomas Bumstead is known to have been making pewter in Boston in 1654, pewter-making in America really had its beginning about 1700, and continued through the first half of the 19th century. (The earliest known American piece is a plate by Simon Edgell (died 1742) of Philadelphia.) During this time, something over two hundred pewterers are known to have come and gone. Their names are preserved and their marks stamped upon much of their product. After 1820, crockery and Britannia ware began to displace pewter, and its manufacture gradually dwindled. Tankards, flagons and porringers, plates, basins and bowls were among their product, now much sought after by collectors. The eight-inch plate is usual and is the foundation of American pewter collecting. Plates were seldom larger than 13 inches. Examples by some of the makers are exceedingly rare; and the covered tankard is among the greater rarities. The "Betty" lamp in pewter is said to be the rarest of all pewter objects to be

found today. Practically no embossing or chasing is found on early pieces.

The native quality of American pewter is said to be inferior to that of England. It becomes less mellowed by time and neglect, and is improved by cleaning. On the other hand, early American pewter has a solidity, a simplicity of form, a sincerity that is very fine, resembling in design English pewter of the Stuart times. The later pewter is lighter and in general follows the designs of the silversmiths.

Because of English laws with regard to marking pewter, there has been a tendency to regard all unmarked pewter in this country as American. Except for the whale-oil lamp, which was a distinctively American creation of the 19th century and unmarked, this rule does not apply. Unmarked pewter, in spite of the rules of the Pewterers' Society, has always been made in England and a good deal of it found its way to America, especially in the Colonial days, and one authority claims that the greater part of the pewter used in this country during the 18th century was imported from England. Pewter made here before 1750 was often unmarked, but since that time pewter plates were generally marked, but basins were not. Next to the plate, the basin was the most important article for household use. These ranged in size from 6½ to 12 inches in diameter. Pewter plates and chargers can usually be dated by the style of their rims.

The methods of marking pewter have always been the same and during the last years of the 18th century, American pewterers generally began to use a "touch-mark" (q.v.). The "eagle" touch-mark dates from the last decade of the 18th century. The state seals of Massachusetts and Rhode Island were also used by some makers. Other makers invented "hall-marks" similar to those on English pewter of that time. To the collector, familiarity with the marks of the various makers will be needful, as he is generally a student of makers' touches to a degree that is in no sense true of the collector of the European metal. These can be found in detail in Kerfoot's *American Pewter*, which is an extensive book on the subject. After 1825 the making of pewter in America rapidly ceased to be a handicraft and became an industry.

REFERENCES

American Pewter, J. B. Kerfoot; *Some Notes on American Pewterers*, Louis G. Myers; *Rhode Island Pewterers and Their Work*, Calder; *American Pewter and Pewterers*, ANTIQUES, Jan. 1923; *Marked American Pewter*, ANTIQUES, May 1926; *Three Maine Pewterers*, ANTIQUES, July 1932.

Continental Pewter. According to one authority (Cotterell) some of the most beautiful types of pewter known to collectors are to be found nowhere except in European ware. Many difficulties are to be encountered in making a collection of these because of the number of different countries where they were made, each with different rules and regulations and each with its own organization of pewterers with their various marks. From the beginning of the 17th century what is known as the "three-touch" system of marks has obtained. This consisted of (a) the town or city arms or other local device indicating place of origin; (b) maker's name, initials, touch or device; (c) quality marks—of these quality marks the most frequent is the "Angel," (q.v.) the use of which was strictly reserved for metal of the finest quality, and was adopted throughout most of the European countries. The "Rose and Crown" (q.v.) was also used as a quality mark, sometimes as first, sometimes as slightly inferior.

Pewter forms and decoration varied in Continental pewter, but not in that of Great Britain, according to the influence of the successive periods from the Gothic to that of the Empire type.

THUMBPIECES

There are various characteristics such as the thumbpieces, the handles, the handle finials, the lids, the bases,—all of

FINIALS

which are distinguishing features of the different countries of Europe and must be studied as a part of the subject. One thing, remembered, will help in identifying Continental pewter; it is not hand-hammered. As a rule, English pewter generally is.

REFERENCES

National Types of Old Pewter, COTTERELL; Pewter Down the Ages, COTTERELL; Old Pewter, Brass, Copper, and Sheffield Plate, MOORE; European Continental Pewter, ANTIQUES, Vols. 11 to 16 inc.; French Pewter, ANTIQUES, Nov. 1927.

English Pewter. Interest in collecting pewter in England began in 1904, following the issue of Pewter Plate by MASSÉ and an exhibition of pewter arranged by him in London in the same year. The art of the pewterer was practised in England as early as the 12th century, but it was not until after the Restoration that it, even among the rich, came into daily household use. In the 18th century, for the better part of a hundred years, all of England, more or less, ate off pewter, drank from it, and used it for half the adjuncts and utensils of ordinary living. The London guild, chartered in 1473 under Government authority, supervised the handicraft all over England. English pewter is hammer-finished generally, while most American pewter is not, nor is Continental pewter; and English pewter may be allowed to accumulate a film of oxidation without losing its charm.

England stood alone in the high quality of her metal. Pewter "blended" in the English manner stood for excellence on the Continent. Again, England, with the Netherlands, stood alone against the decoration of pewter. Plates and chargers were made by the so-called "sadware" men, and the pots and vessels for liquids, by the "hollow ware" men.

English pewter marks are given in Old Pewter, Its Makers and Marks, by COTTERELL, and MRS. MOORE in her book Old Pewter gives many interesting details of the growth of that handicraft in England from early times, and of the many difficulties encountered

AMERICAN SILVER BRAZIERS, CHAFING DISHES, AND STRAINER, 18TH CENTURY

ENGLISH SILVER CUP, EARLY 18TH CENTURY

SILVER CAUDLE CUP, WILLIAM AND MARY PERIOD,

Courtesy of the Fogg Art Museum

SILVER CUP BY JOHN CONEY (1655-1722)

by the "Company of Pewterers" in enforcing the many regulations surrounding the craft. The rules of the Scotch guild were much like those of England, and it is often difficult to find a difference between pieces of English and of Scotch make.

REFERENCES
Old Pewter, Its Makers and Marks in England, Scotland and Ireland, H. H. COTTERELL.

PEWTERERS
For a fairly reliable list of names of American pewterers, consult *American Pewter* by KERFOOT and *Practical Book of American Antiques* by EBERLEIN and McCLURE. English pewterers are listed in great detail and marks illustrated in the standard reference work, *Old Pewter, Its Makers and Marks in England, Scotland and Ireland*, H. H. COTTERELL.

PHOEBE LAMP
See LAMPS.

PINCHBECK
An alloy of about five parts of copper and one of zinc, invented by Christopher Pinchbeck (1670-1732). It had the appearance of gold and was much used in England for buckles, sword hilts, chains, etc.

PINS
The lowly pin of today has its ancestry in ancient Greece and Rome, where they were made of bronze. Even the safety pin is by no means new.

PIPKIN
The name given the brass coal scuttle made for use after the introduction of coal in England, middle of the 18th century. See PIPKIN, PART 2.

PITCHERS

These were usually known as jugs in England. Cream pitchers with pear-shaped bodies, usually supported on three scroll feet, were made about the middle of the 18th century. Later ones were made with a base.

PLANISH
To condense, smooth and toughen a plate of metal by blows of a hammer.

PLATE
In England all silver articles have been since early times, and still are, designated as "plate." The term should not be confused with "plated" ware. In America, early silver is usually referred to as "silver," but since 1865 *it* is marked and known as "sterling."

PLATES
Silver dinner plates made their appearance in England late in the 17th century and during the 18th century they were quite common there and came into use in this country. Pewter plates were common both in England and here

throughout the 17th and 18th centuries, until pottery and porcelain ware gradually displaced both silver and pewter.

PONTYPOOL WARE
See JAPANNED WARE.

PORRINGERS

One of the most useful pieces of household ware in Colonial times. These were made of pewter or of silver by our earliest craftsmen of the 17th century, and continued in use until gradually displaced by pottery ware about the middle of the 18th century. They ranged in size from three to six inches in diameter of bowl, and a flat handle set nearly flush with the rim was placed on one or both sides of the bowl. The American porringer is usually larger and quite different (see BLEEDING DISHES) from those of England, where they were variously known as ear-dishes, bowls, bleeding dishes, posset-cups and tasters.

REFERENCES
The American Pewter Porringer, ANTIQUES, May 1930; Early American Silver, AVERY.

POSSET-CUP
Another name for caudle-cup (q.v.)

used for drinking posset, curdled milk with spices and hot sack (wine). It was usually made with a cover to keep the contents warm. In England it was also called a porringer (q.v.).

POT
See CAULDRON.

POT HOOK (also called POT HANGER)
Attached to chimney cranes for suspending the cooking utensils. They rank among the earliest of domestic metal implements.

POTATO RINGS
See DISH RINGS.

PRICKET
The pointed spike of a candlestick upon which the candle was forced when required for use. Its origin is earlier in date than the candlestick with socket, and it was commonly used in Europe in medieval times. It was not used in this country.

PRINCESS METAL
A composition of copper, brass and arsenic.

PUNCH BOWLS
In England in the 15th and 16th centuries the Mazer bowl (q.v.) was commonly used for a drinking vessel. Silver bowls for mixing punch first appeared after the Restoration, the Monteith bowl (q.v.) somewhat later, followed by bowls of porcelain and pottery.

Q

QUAICH, QUAIGH

A shallow, circular Scotch drinking vessel, somewhat like a deep saucer and made in several sizes. The larger ones were used for porridge. The quaich was made of pewter, brass, silver, and of wood, usually quite plain and furnished with two solid ears by which to hold it. It is often confused with the porringer, which it resembles somewhat.

R

REPOUSSÉ

Relief decoration, usually done on comparatively thin metal, accomplished by hammering instead of by slow pressure as in chasing. Similar to embossing (q.v.).

ROASTING JACK (or SPIT)

See CLOCK JACK.

ROSE AND CROWN

One of the marks used by pewterers. In England it was required to be placed upon pewter ware made for sale outside of London. Users of the mark were forbidden by the Company of Pewterers to place either their initials or date or other private mark on such pewter. On the Continent where the Rose and Crown was a favorite mark, there were no such restrictions, so that Continental pewter (q.v.) with this mark will be found to have the private mark or marks of the pewterer upon it. Where initials appear either in the Crown or on the heart of the Rose, such pieces are of European origin. American craftsmen were also apt to use the Crowned Rose in addition to their private marks.

ROSETTES

Brass rosettes, sometimes with enamel ornamental face, for the support of mirrors and pictures and to hold back curtains, were common throughout the 18th century. Rosettes with glass fronts superseded those of metal in the 19th century.

S

SAD WARE

Flat articles in pewter, such as plates, dishes, chargers and trenchers, were known as sad ware.

SALTS (SALT CELLARS)

Among the rarest pieces of old silver and pewter is the ceremonial "salt," the principal article of domestic plate in early English houses of whatever degree, and the salt cellar was an honored guest at every feast. Many of the customs surrounding its usage emanate from the medieval manners of the European continent. The salt cellars known as standing salts were large, monumental in design, marking, by their presence, the

upper and lower table. By the middle of the 17th century the position of the standing salt lost its significance. Supplementary to these salts were the trencher salts, used at the lower end of the table and by the side of the trencher, probably the style first used here in the Colonial period. These were small in size and made in various forms of pewter

and of silver. The circular salts with three feet and the salts with the glass lining belong to the Georgian period.

REFERENCE
The Silver Salt of Tradition, ANTI-QUARIAN, June 1930.

SALVER

A tray on which anything is presented. Salvers were seldom used in churches, where the paten or tazza served the purpose of passing the ceremonial bread.

SCONCES

In early use here for a support and reflector for candles, and hung on the wall; usually, at first, made of tin, sometimes of brass, and in various shapes. It is quite difficult to find two alike and it is quite impossible to allocate the period or locality of manufacture. They superseded the "Betty" lamp of earlier days. Silver sconces were popular in England last half of the 17th century, and during the 18th century they were made here for the homes of the wealthy. These last may be identified by makers' marks.

SCOTTISH PEWTER

See *Old Pewter, Its Makers and Marks in England, Scotland and Ireland*, COTTERELL.

SCOTTISH SILVER

See SILVER, *Scottish*.

SCREWS

The earliest use of screws here was about 1725. In England, their use dates from late in the 17th century. They were hand-made with coarse threads and the slots in the top were of uneven depth and frequently off-center. They were cut off squarely at the lower end so that it was necessary to drill a hole for them before using. It was not until the middle of the 19th century, long after machine-made screws were made, that the gimlet-pointed screw appeared.

SHEFFIELD PLATE

Sheffield plate is artistically the most satisfactory substitute for silver yet discovered, according to Frederick Bradbury, considered to be the best authority on old Sheffield. It differs from all other plated ware in that the plating is done on the sheet metal, usually copper, before the article to be made is formed. The process was discovered by accident by Thomas Boulsover, a Sheffield cutter, in 1742, and soon after Joseph Hancock set up a factory at Sheffield for the manufacture of domestic ware, and smaller articles. The ware became popular, others began to make it, and the manufacture of Sheffield plate grew to large dimensions, until electroplating, developing about 1840, displaced it. Factories opened in Birmingham and London and in France, and the term Sheffield was applied to the production of these factories as well.

For about sixty years the plating was on one side of the copper only until a process was discovered that plated the metal on both sides at the same time. The most artistic as well as the most prolific period was from 1774 to 1784. In 1785 a method of finishing cut edges by a silver wire was invented. Gadroon and bead edges, stamped in rolled plate, were a favorite form of decoration on early pieces. The interiors of bowls, pitchers and cups were sometimes gilded. Before 1784, Sheffield plate is unmarked, after which marking was made legally permissible. There was no system like the hall-mark on English silver to distinguish the makers. Between 1784 and 1836, fifty-one manufacturers at Sheffield and seventy-four at Birmingham registered their marks, and occasional specimens are found bearing the stamped marks of the manufacturer. The majority of fine Sheffield pieces are unmarked. The Sheffield Assay Office published in 1908 a list of the marks recorded with them.

REFERENCES

Old Sheffield Plate, JULIA W. TORREY; Chats on Old Sheffield Plate, ARTHUR HAYDEN; History of Old Sheffield Plate, FREDERICK BRADBURY; Sheffield Plate, HENRY N. VEITCH; Old Silver and Old Sheffield Plate, HOWARD P. OKIE; Treasure in Old Sheffield, ANTIQUES, March 1922; Old Sheffield Plate, ANTIQUES, Dec. 1927.

SILVER

Working in silver is one of the oldest arts and crafts of man, and the manners and customs of its users are reflected in the purposes for which it was made. The work of the craftsman in silver of medieval times has never since been excelled, perhaps not equaled. There were two principal reasons for this condition: first, the rivalry between royalty and nobility in splendor of display called for many elaborate decorative pieces. Also, the Church of the Middle Ages required much silver and gold work. The second reason is that all of these wonderful pieces could only be made by hand and the cost of labor in those days was inconsequential. Today, it would be prohibitive. Nearly all of this silver has been lost or destroyed by wars, invasion, and the fierce contests in the name of religion.

Articles of silverware may be broadly classified as domestic and ecclesiastical. The first includes silver for drinking purposes, table accessories, containing or pouring, and silver for miscellaneous household and personal uses. Ecclesiastical silver includes chalices, patens, beakers, flagons, cups, bowls, basins and plates. The collector of antique silver should rely upon a responsible dealer in making his selections unless he is exceptionally well informed. English silver of the 18th and early 19th centuries is copied by modern makers and the hallmarks of the period are forged. Genuine old silver is altered in shape, "transformed" into pieces much more desirable.

American Silver. More silverware was produced in New England in the 17th century than in any other colony, and it not only was of a very high quality, but it followed the changes in English design quite closely. Boston silversmiths took the lead, and the energy and skill which they displayed as craftsmen brought them not only commercial success, but official posts. John Hull, with his partner Robert Sanderson, heads the list and these men, together with Jeremiah Dummer, John Coney and Edward Winslow, kept Boston in the lead not only in the production of silver through the first half of the 18th century, but they also excelled in quality. At the same time, the work of the silversmiths in Newport, New York and Philadelphia gained prestige in their respective communities. Samuel Vernon of Newport, Peter Van Dyck and Jacob Boelen of New York, and Philip Syng, father and son, of Philadelphia, were among the most prominent of these. The New England silversmith patterned after English silver, the New York silver of the 17th and 18th centuries never loses the mark of its Dutch ancestry, and Philadelphia silver of the 18th century developed certain distinctive features of its own.

Most of the early silver was made from coin, which was melted and refined to the desired standard. An addition of copper was used to toughen it. Drinking vessels, tankards, mugs, beakers, caudle-cups and flagons, formed the chief group of silver utensils of the early New England and New York silversmiths.

Candlesticks of the 17th and early 18th century are extremely rare. In making hollow ware, the metal was rolled or hammered into thin sheets and beaten with a mallet into desired shapes on an anvil. After this, surface decoration, engraving, chasing, piercing or repoussé work was added. The beauty of these early American pieces depends partly upon the form, partly upon the decoration, and partly upon the beautiful color and surface modeling. Early silver possesses a soft lustrous color or texture, unapproachable in modern ware. It may be likened to patina on old furniture. Incidentally, buffing, the process by which old silver is sometimes polished nowadays, is harmful to the surface and should never be employed.

Early American silver is thoroughly characteristic of the taste and life of the period in America. There was no attempt to imitate the magnificent baronial silver formerly made in England. It is dependent for its undoubted charm on the simplicity of its lines and graceful forms, without the prodigality of ornament which mars the beauty of much contemporary European work. During the period from 1650 (the earliest known dated piece is by Hull and Sanderson, 1659) to the end of the 18th century, the names of several hundred American silversmiths have been recorded and the list is probably by no means yet complete. Until recent years it was taken for granted that most of the old silver to be seen in this country was English, but careful study of the subject reveals the fact that comparatively little is English. Of about 2000 pieces of church silver, 1640 are found to be by American makers, and to a great extent donated to the churches by their original owners, by means of which they have been preserved to the present time. In an article printed in *Harper's Monthly Magazine* in 1896, written by Dr. THEODORE W. WOOLSEY, the field of old American silver was first called to the attention of collectors. Splendid specimens are to be seen in the Museum of Fine Arts in Boston and in the Metropolitan Museum in New York, and the Garvan collections at Yale and Andover.

REFERENCES

Historic Silver of the Colonies and Its Makers, FRANCIS HILL BIGELOW; *A List of Early American Silversmiths and Their Marks*, HOLLIS FRENCH; *Old Silver of American Churches*, E. ALFRED JONES; *Early American Silver*, C. LOUISE AVERY; *Early New York Silver*, ANTIQUES, Nov. 1924; *Early New England Silver*, ANTIQUES, Sept. 1925; *Silver of the New England Churches*, ANTIQUARIAN, July 1930; *Silversmiths of Early Boston*, ANTIQUARIAN, July 1931.

Continental Silver. The use of silver, as of gold, for luxurious purposes, was common in all of the Continental countries during the Middle Ages and later, and many magnificent things were produced. Of these, some were enameled and enriched with pearls and precious stones. All of those countries have suffered losses of immeasurable value, particularly in those things made for secular use. One of the pieces that escaped destruction, known as the "Cup of the Kings of France and England," is one of the great treasures of the British Museum in London. It was probably made in Paris about 1380, by a goldsmith and enameler unsurpassed in technical skill by any modern craftsman.

The early royal plate of France, as well as all other plate, was converted into coin by Louis XIV in 1687 for the prosecution of his wars, and he prohibited the further making of it. In Holland serious losses of old plate are recorded and in Italy nothing now remains of the splendid plate made for the Medici by the great goldsmiths of Florence. No other country suffered more severe losses in secular plate; precious objects in gold and silver were consigned to the crucible without a pang. In Poland, precious objects in gold and silver were lost in the division of the country in 1794. All of the great treasures of Spain of the time of its great wealth in the 16th century have been converted into coin, and the Royal collection of today contains no Spanish plate of that century, nor is a representative collection to be seen in any Spanish museum. An interesting

account, together with many illustrations of surviving Continental silver, giving also the names of a large number of silversmiths of European countries, including England, is to be found in *Old Silver of Europe and America* by E. ALFRED JONES, M.A. See *French Silver*.

English Silver. One reason for the high regard in which English silver is held is because of the precautions which have been taken to keep its standard high and to prevent counterfeiting. The "Sterling" (q.v.) standard, consisting of 925 parts of silver alloyed with 75 parts copper, has been maintained with a few brief exceptions, since 1300, in the reign of Edward I. In the three or four centuries preceding the Reformation, the wealth of gold and silver in the shrines and treasuries of the cathedrals and abbeys was immense, so immense as to be almost incredible. Comparatively few examples of this work now remain, those of any importance very few indeed. Little or no communion plate of any kind is now to be found in the cathedrals older than the Restoration Period, and the Wars of the Roses were to secular plate what the iconoclastic zeal of the Reformation was to the treasuries of the church. Finally the Civil War of the first half of the 17th century, and the Royal need for money in the last half, nearly completed the destruction of all old plate, gold or silver. The capture of Spanish silver-laden vessels from the New World by English sea captains in the 16th and 17th centuries, which served to replenish the silver stock in England, was the source from which much of the destroyed plate of that period was made. The earliest silver consisted mainly of flagons, cups, spoons and chalices. Mazer bowls (q.v.) of the 15th and 16th centuries are among the comparatively few things that escaped destruction. The first example of tankards recorded is about 1650, and from that time onward silver has been used for an ever increasing number of purposes.

The bulk of English plate from the 14th century on was hall-marked, that is, stamped with certain Guild Hall marks, which was a guarantee of its quality and lawful manufacture. Besides these hall-marks (q.v.), there was the date (year) and the mark of the maker, registered with the Goldsmiths' Company of London. It has been estimated that over ninety per cent of old English silver bears the London hall-mark. This method of marking English silver has been the means of identifying and dating old examples with far greater accuracy than is the case with any other work of the early craftsmen that has come down to our time. The standard work on the subject is *English Goldsmiths and Their Marks* by SIR CHARLES J. JACKSON. Another excellent authority is *Old Silver and Old Sheffield Plate*, HOWARD P. OKIE. *Old English Plate Marks* by W. J. CRIPPS contains a reliable history of the begin-ning and the gradual development of this important branch of art craftsmanship.

Since the Restoration the work of the English silversmith compared favorably with the best of those on the Continent, and influenced to some extent the work of our own Colonial silversmiths. Following the Revocation of the Edict of Nantes in France in 1685, many of the best French workmen fled to England, and some of the best of English silver from the time of William and Mary and Queen Anne bears the names of those workmen. During the period from 1720 to 1765 the silver produced in England has never since been surpassed for beauty of outline and ornamentation, doubtless influenced to some extent by French designs.

REFERENCES

Old English Silver, WILLIAM W. WATTS; Old Silver of Europe and America, E. ALFRED JONES; Chats on Old Silver, ARTHUR HAYDEN; and authorities mentioned in the text; English Provincial Silver, FINE ARTS, May 1933.

French Silver. Old French silver is imperfectly known, and much history of French silver remains to be written. The comparatively few pieces that have survived bear witness to the technical and artistic excellence of the work of the French silversmith. Many of the finest pieces of their work are to be found in collections in foreign countries.

Domestic silver of the 18th century and before is exceedingly rare. The marks on French silver are of three kinds: the silversmith's mark, the date mark, and the duty mark. A brief but quite comprehensive account of the work of the French silversmith is contained in *Old Silver of Europe and America* by E. ALFRED JONES. For marks consult *Old Silver and Old Sheffield Plate*, OKIE, and *A Guide to Old French Plate* by LOUIS CARRÉ.

Irish Silver. Old records show that goldsmiths were working in Dublin in the 13th century, but the earliest Irish marks are those of a maker in Dublin in 1605. Dublin was the center of the silversmiths and in 1637 the Goldsmiths of Dublin were chartered by Charles I. The standard mark is the harp, used with the crown added to it. Other marks were used, varying with the date, showing that the duty had been paid, the maker's device, and the date letter. Marks of all known Irish silversmiths are listed in *Old Silver and Old Sheffield Plate* by OKIE.

Scottish Silver. The manufacture of silver in Scotland extends back to the 15th century, and, in comparison with England, seems to have covered a wider area. Edinburgh was the chief center for assaying silver, although many towns and burghs also did so. The art of the silversmith in Scotland has always been on a high level, and the statutes governing the marks are many in number. The

identification of Scottish silver requires close study of an intricate field. There were no marks struck on Scotch silver before 1457. For a complete list of marks consult *Old Silver and Old Sheffield Plate* by OKIE.

SILVERSMITHS

An extensive list of names of American silversmiths may be found in *American Silversmiths and Their Marks* by ENSKO. For English silver, *English Goldsmiths and Their Marks* by SIR CHARLES J. JACKSON is regarded as the best authority.

SKILLET

An iron utensil of the early fireplace. It was the equivalent of the modern saucepan but the term is, however, applied without much distinction apparently to various pots as well as pans.

SNUFFERS

See CANDLE SNUFFERS.

SNUFF-BOXES

Made in many materials, common and precious, in many countries, especially during the 18th century.

REFERENCE

The Story of Snuff and Snuff Boxes, CURTIS.

SOLDER

A metal or metallic alloy of low melting-point, used when melted to join metallic surfaces.

SPANDRELS

Term for the irregular triangular spaces formed by the outlines of the circular face of the clock and square corners. At first the decorations were of cast brass, carefully chased and finished with hand tools; later, the tool work was omitted. When the painted clock-dial came into use these decorations were painted also. The form and design of the ornaments in these spaces are, to a certain extent, an indication of the age of the clock.

SPIDER

The term applied to cast-iron frying pans with handles, originally made with short legs. When the kitchen range became common, the legs were omitted.

SPINNING

A lathe process by which a thin plate of metal, rotating rapidly, is forced to take the shape of a wooden core.

SPLICE

The splice was a fireplace tool in Colonial days, with a broad, flattened end and a rather long handle, used to remove bread or pies from the brick oven.

SPOONS

The spoon is an utensil of very great antiquity. During the Roman period spoons were often elaborately carved and turned. Throughout the Middle Ages spoons were quite plain, those for use by common folk being made of wood or horn. In England, during the 14th and 15th centuries, they became more elaborate, and handle terminals were

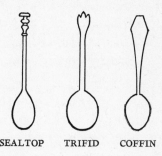

SEALTOP   TRIFID   COFFIN

ornamented with busts and figures. Sets of thirteen spoons were made of silver or of pewter from the end of the 15th century through the 16th century, with the handle terminal ornamented with figures of the Apostles, with appropriate symbol for the purpose of identifying each. At the present time but five complete sets are known to be in existence, although many partial sets and single spoons are to be seen in the Museums. Spoons were made of bronze, pewter and latten (q.v.) during this period for ordinary use, because of their low cost compared with silver. Early spoons of silver are among the rarest pieces of English hall-marked plate in existence. In the evolution of the spoon to its modern form, it passed through many interesting stages, in the shape of both the handle and the bowl, so that these are usually a reliable index of the period of origin. Most metal spoons before 1650 had slender hexagonal handles and broad, fig-shaped bowls. Some of the handles had a seal-top in which the stems terminate by means of a disc on the end; others, the maiden-head, so called, from the bust of the Virgin used at the end of the stem. There were other variations also. The stem became gradually thinner and flatter and broadened at its tip, until in the 18th century it became down-curving. Some had a round, slender and tapering support on the under side of the bowl, called a "rat-tail," first seen about 1660 and lasting for 70 to 80 years. At length, its place was taken by a simple scroll, the bowl became pointed as in the modern spoon, and the handle took on the well-known "coffin" shape, which was popular through the last half of the 18th century. A curious custom prevailed in connection with these spoons, thought to be an English Puritan tradition. Two of these spoons were given to the friends helping at the time of a burial, which is given as the reason that they are usually found in pairs. In England they were called funeral spoons. What are known as tea spoons and dessert spoons were not made until the last half of the 17th century. Marrow spoons had unusually long and very narrow bowls, used to scoop marrow from bones.

The study of spoons of American make is more difficult than that of old Eng-lish spoons because there is no date-letter to establish the exact age. Those of the Colonial period were usually made of metal coin, they were crude in design with flat stems, oval bowl, most of them rat-tailed. Gradually, the form changed until, at the end of the 18th century, spoons were dainty in shape. The word "Sterling" appears on all American spoons after about 1865.

REFERENCES
The Craft of the Spoonmaker, AN-TIQUES, Sept. 1929; *Earliest English Spoons of Base Metal*, FINE ARTS, June 1932; *Apostle Spoons*, ANTIQUES, July 1929.

Spout Cup

A silver cup with cover usually, and handle, and with spout at right angle for infants' and invalids' drinking purposes, more popular in New England than in England, where the form originated about the middle of the 17th century, but was seldom made there. It was rarely, if ever, made in New York or Philadelphia. It was sometimes called feeding cup.

Standing Cup

In use from early English times for wine. In wealthy families they were of silver or of gold and very costly. With the lower classes, cups of "treen" (wood) were common. Standing cups, when well proportioned, are among the most delightful shapes wrought by the silversmith. When made with covers, they were called hanaps (q.v.).

STERLING

The term "sterling" is probably derived from the name of the German tribe of Easterling, famous for the purity of its silver coin in the Middle Ages. Sterling is 925 parts fine; that is, it contains 11 ounces, 2 pwts. of pure silver and 18 pwts. alloy in every 12 ounces, or troy pound. This was essentially the standard of all early English silver. During the Colonial period in America, no general laws were passed to establish a standard for silversmiths, but their silver conforms generally to the English standard. As a group these early silversmiths were recognized as men of honor and integrity, and they justified their reputation. It was not until about 1865 that the law compelling silversmiths to adhere to the sterling standard and to stamp the product with the word sterling was adopted in this country. See HALL-MARKS.

STIPPLED

Marked all over the surface with little dots.

STOVE

One of the earliest improvements over the fireplace for heating purposes was the so-called Franklin stove, designed by Benjamin Franklin in 1742. It was a cast-iron structure with an open front and either a grate for burning coal or with andirons for burning wood, that could either be fitted into the fireplace and the surrounding space bricked up, or projected into the room and connected with a flue by means of a stove-pipe. This last was the usual arrangement. As time passed, several improvements were made in the original design and legs were added. The cast-iron box stove was invented a few years after and came into common use. Early in the 19th century cylindrical sheet-iron stoves were first made.

REFERENCE

The Franklin Stove, ANTIQUES, July 1922.

STOVE PLATES

These were used in a section of the chimney adjoining the fireplace to give heat to a room on the opposite side. This form of heating was called a "jamb" stove and it was the forerunner of the box stove. The stove plate is a slab of cast-iron, often confused with the fire back, about two feet square and, if decorated by relief design, was one of the plates exposed in the room. There were five plates as a rule, sometimes six, and this method of heating came into use in some parts of this country about the middle of the 18th century. The majority of them must be ascribed to Pennsylvania.

SUGAR BOWLS

These came into use as a distinctive piece of silver in the last half of the 18th century, when they were made to conform in design with that of the tea-pot. Previous to that time sugar or comfiture boxes, some of them very elaborate, were made by several of the Colonial silversmiths.

SUN DIAL

An ancient instrument for telling time, but limited to those days that the sun shone. They were made both in stationary and in portable form, some of the latter in size for the pocket.

REFERENCES

The Book of Sun-Dials by GATTY; Portable Sun Dials, ANTIQUES, Sept. 1926.

T

TACKS

The lowly tacks, hand-forged until about 1800, had every appearance of tiny, hand-forged nails. They were made in a variety of sizes with sharp points. The early machines for making tacks were operated by hand or foot power.

TANKARD

Silver or pewter drinking vessel with hinged lid, broad, flat base, and with heavy handle. They were of generous proportions and usually cylindrical in shape or tapering to the top. The earliest tankards were made with flat lid, and came into use in England in the time of Elizabeth and so continued until the time of Queen Anne, when the domed tankard made its appearance. In American silver, the early tankards are usually straight-sided in the form of a truncated cone, with flat lids and high thumb-pieces. Some have had, later, spouts added. Barrel-shaped tankards were common in late 18th and early 19th century. Smaller vessels without covers are called mugs (q.v.) and elongated tankards are commonly known as flagons (q.v.).

REFERENCES

Some New England Tankards, ANTIQUES, Aug. 1927; English Silver Drinking Cups, ANTIQUARIAN, Feb. 1930.

TAPPET HEN, TAPPIT HEN

A peculiarly, shaped measure of pewter made and used in Scotland. There are two varieties, the earlier style, un-crested, and the later, crested type having a knob on top. The name may be applied to either the Scot's pint size or two-pint size, equivalent to three English pints, or three English quarts, respectively, although several others were made. The smallest had no lid.

TASTER

A small and distinctive vessel, with handles, usually of silver, sometimes of pewter. They varied in size from less than a quarter to a half pint, and were used for tasting and sampling ale, wine, and spirituous liquors. They were sometimes called dram cups. At one time an official known as the "taster" was employed in every royal household.

TAZZA

A large shallow bowl, usually of silver, with baluster stem with a foot, and sometimes handles, of Italian origin. Like the paten (q.v.) the tazza was for use in church service. The Colonial silversmiths made them in considerable numbers, late 17th and early 18th centuries.

TEA CADDY (or CANISTER)

The early forms of the English silver tea caddy were round or square. Later they became oval in form, and by the end of the 18th century they resembled the designs of the cabinet-maker. As a rule they were fitted with one or two containers for the tea. Apparently Colonial silversmiths seldom, if ever, made tea caddies.

TEA-POTS

The first pewter or silver tea-pots were made in England about the middle of the 17th century, following the introduction of tea into Europe. Incidentally, the price of tea in England in 1660 was 60 shillings per pound. The earliest tea-pots were round and tall, then were bulbous in form with a high-domed lid. Later, in the 18th century, they became pear-shaped, then oval and urn-shaped. Before the introduction of the 18th-century tea-cups, tea was drunk from silver (or pewter) porringers. Coffee-pots and chocolate-pots came into use about the same time as tea-pots, and followed the same general variations in form.

TEA URNS

Used for hot water with tea services. They took the place of tea kettles, late 18th century. They stood on a square base and had a lid with a finial, two handles, and a spigot in the lower front. Some of them were also provided with a spirit lamp.

Thumbpiece

The name given to the lever on tankard or flagon, by pressing on which, with the thumb, the lid is raised. A study of various types of thumbpieces assists in identifying old pewter.

Time Lamps

These were made with a glass reservoir marked in such a manner as to show the passage of time as the fuel burned down.

Tin

The metal entering most largely into the composition of pewter was obtained by the English pewterers chiefly from the mines of Cornwall. It was also used in making many articles for household use and for plating iron. See Japanned Ware and Tôle.

REFERENCE
The Village Tinsmith, ANTIQUES, March 1928.

Tinder Lighting Equipment

This consisted of the tinder, usually made by scorching linen or cotton fabric, the flint, and steel, and was commonly in use during Colonial times as a means for providing fire. The operation might be performed in a few seconds or it might take several minutes, according to the skill of the operator in making and directing the spark and also to the age

of the tinder, which became almost useless after three or four days.

Toaster

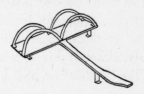

The toaster used before the open fireplace for toasting bread was made of wrought iron and stood on short legs. They were useful on the hearth and later before the grate.

Tôle

French name for a kind of painted tin similar to Pontypool ware. It served for a host of household needs and customs from the days of Louis XV to those of the early Victorian period.

Touch-Mark

The touch-mark on pewter was used for the same purpose as the hall-mark on silver—it is the trade-mark of the maker. It was a custom of early origin which later was enforced by law in England, although it did not apply in America. Much English and some American pewter bears, in addition to the touch of the maker, a series of smaller marks, generally four, struck in a row and called "hall-marks." These are entirely unofficial, even in England. There is also to be seen on English pewter some device like a flower or animal, and on American pewter, generally from the beginning of

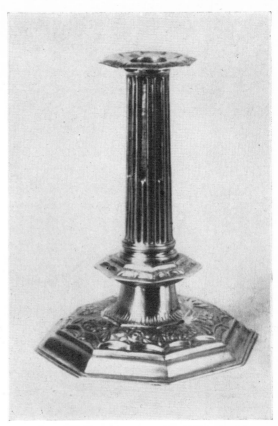

SILVER CANDLESTICK, LONDON, 1684

VER CANDLESTICK, JOHN CONEY (1655-1722)

Courtesy of the Museum of Fine Arts, Boston

SILVER SALVER BY JOHN CONEY (1655-1722)

SILVER PORRINGER BY JOHN CONEY (1655-1722)

SILVER PORRINGER BY JOHN BURT (1691-174

Courtesy of the Fogg Art Museum

SILVER CUP BY JOHN BURT (1691-1745)

Courtesy of the Gallery of Fine Arts, Yale U

SILVER CUP BY JOHN CONEY (1655-172

the 19th century, some sort of decorative device. In England, the "Rose and Crown" (q.v.) was a mark required by the Company of Pewterers on all pewter made for sale outside of London. All other marks were forbidden.

REFERENCES

Chats on Old Pewter, MASSÉ; American Pewter, J. B. KERFOOT.

TOUCH-PLATES

Plates of pewter kept at Pewterers' Hall in London on which the touch-mark of the pewterers was stamped and recorded. It was compulsory for the pewterers so to register their marks. All of the earlier plates were destroyed by the great London fire in 1666. Plates since that date, bearing 1200 separate touches, have been preserved.

TRAYS

The metal tray was first developed and decorated by japanning at Pontypool, England, but the process soon became a trade and as early as 1709 was taken up in Bilston, and later, in Birmingham and Wolverhampton. During the greater part of the 18th and early 19th centuries, these places were the chief centers of the manufacture of what was known to the trade as Pontypool ware. In France a similar ware was known as Tôle (q.v.). The early trays were decorated with simple geometric designs in two or three colors on a plain

black ground. The silver tray came into use about the third quarter of the 18th century. Raised rims and short legs were sometimes attached to these. See CHARGERS, JAPANNED WARE, and WAITER.

TRENCHER

The name applied to early pewter plates, adapted from the early wooden trenchers, use of which antedated metal.

TRENCHER SALT

See SALTS.

TRIVET

An iron fireplace utensil with short legs to set before the fire for the purpose of keeping the contents of a kettle hot. They are sometimes called spiders (q.v.).

TUMBLER

A small silver or pewter cup with a rounded bottom which came into use in England towards the end of the 17th century. They were without handles and the bottoms were extra heavy, which caused them to maintain an upright position. In America these were called "can" or "cup." See CAN, and MUGS.

TUTENAG

See PAKTONG.

V

VANES
See WEATHERVANES.

VICKERS METAL
See WHITE METAL.

W

WAITER
A tray for dishes; also a salver.

WARMING-PAN
An article of common domestic use in this country in the 17th and 18th centuries, usually placed between the sheets for warming the beds. The pan was of brass or of copper, the lid perforated to allow the heat from the hot cinders inside the pan to escape more readily, and with a turned, rather long, wooden handle. In England, the warming-pan dates from the time of Elizabeth.

WATCHES
Watches cannot claim the antiquity of clocks, although they can be traced as far back as the 14th century. The early watches were shaped like an egg. They were introduced into England in the 16th century and by the middle of the 17th century they were quite common. Thomas Tompion, Daniel Quare and George Graham were distinguished early English watch-makers.

REFERENCE
Old Clocks and Watches and Their Makers, BRITTEN.

WEATHERVANES
The vane denotes any flat surface attached to an axis and moved by a fluid, as air or water. Vane was originally fane, a flag, from the Anglo-Saxon "fana." The most common designs in old American weathervanes are the Indian, the ship, and various animals and birds. The foreign vanes often have grotesque designs. Some early vanes were connected with a dial or map in the building below so that every turn of the vane was shown on the dial.

WHALE OIL LAMPS
See LAMPS.

WHITE METAL
Any of several white alloys, especially one of tin, antimony, copper and zinc in imitation of silver. In the late 18th century James Vickers of Sheffield, England, used a similar metal, so like silver that the casual observer would never question its identity as such. The articles which Vickers produced were all made in the best period of design, and closely followed the silver of the time in both form and ornamentation. Most of his pieces are plainly marked Vickers. Competition of Sheffield plate shortened the life of the Vickers enterprise and, as a consequence, examples are rare.

REFERENCE
Vickers White Metal, ANTIQUES, July 1926.

WINE TASTER
See TASTER.

PART VI

BIOGRAPHY

PART VI

BIOGRAPHY

A

ABBEY, RICHARD (1720-1801)

Liverpool potter, who, while working for Sadler and Green, designed the various "Arms" jugs which became famous. In 1790 he went into business for himself and established the pottery which afterwards became known as the Herculaneum Pottery (q.v. PART 2), the largest and most successful pottery in Liverpool.

ADAM, ROBERT (1728-1792)

One ot four brothers from Edinburgh, Scotland, John, Robert, James and William, all archıtects and interior decorators. Robert, who was the leading spirit, spent several years after leaving college in the study of architecture in Italy. Returning to England he applied classical design to his work there and in 1762 he was appointed architect to the King. A famous speculation of the four brothers, The Adelphi Terrace, caused them to be called "The Adelphi," the Greek word for brothers. The influence exerted by them upon furniture came through their use of classic form from Greek and Roman styles and of exquisite painted furniture by An-gelica Kauffmann, Cipriani, Pergolesi and other noted artists of the period. The changes in form and structure due to the inspiration of the brothers Adam were more radical, more sudden, and of wider prevalence than any that had hitherto taken place. Robert Adam designed furniture but was not himself a cabinet-maker. Besides furniture he included designs for carpets, lamps, wall lights, clocks, fire grates, etc. He covered the whole ground of house equipment.

REFERENCE

Robert Adam and His Brothers, JOHN SWARBRICK.

ADAMS, NEHEMIAH (1769-1840)

Cabinet-maker at Salem, Massachusetts. Tables and other pieces of furniture now in existence, attributed to him, are examples of excellent workmanship. Some of his furniture was shipped to southern states for sale there.

ADAMS, PYGAN (1712-1776)

A merchant and one of the best of Connecticut silversmiths. He was, also, a captain in the militia and served as a

311

representative to the General Assembly for several years.

ADAMS, WILLIAM (1745-1805)

The Adams family was one of the earliest and one of the most prominent among the Staffordshire potters. John Adams, great-grandfather of the above William, built in 1657 the "Brick-House" works at Burslem, afterwards occupied by Josiah Wedgwood. William Adams built the Greengates factory in 1787 and continued there until his death. He was a favorite pupil of Wedgwood, and according to some authorities his blue jasper ware is rather finer than that of Wedgwood. His blue-printed ware and his cream stoneware were also of the best quality. He made blue jasper cameos and plaques for the Adam brothers to be used on furniture designed by them. He was not only a great potter but a successful one, too. He left a name that will always testify to his industry, talent and individuality. There were three other William Adams potters, contemporary with above and related to him; viz.: William Adams (1748-1831) of Brick-House and Cobridge Hall, a cousin; William Adams (1772-1829) of Stoke-on-Trent, also a cousin, and William Adams (1798-1865) of Greenfield (Tunstall), a son of the preceding William.

REFERENCE

William Adams, an Old English Potter, WILLIAM TURNER.

AFFLECK, THOMAS (? -1795)

A cabinet-maker who came to Philadelphia in 1763 with Governor John Penn and during the years until his death is said to have labored almost continuously for the Penn family and their associates.

REFERENCES

Blue Book, Philadelphia Furniture, HORNOR; ANTIQUES, May and Nov. 1935.

ALLIS, JOHN

Hatfield, Massachusetts. A maker of Hadley Chests.

ALLISON, MICHAEL

A New York cabinet-maker active from 1800 to 1845. Was a neighbor and contemporary of Duncan Phyfe.

AMELUNG, JOHN FREDERICK (1739-1798)

Born in Bremen, Germany, and came to America in 1784. He was a glass-maker and he brought with him several workmen and together they established the New Bremen (Maryland) Glass Works, later known as Amelung's Glass Works. The glass produced there was second to none in this country. Amelung remained at New Bremen for six years, after which he was identified with several other glass factories. For an account of his wanderings after leaving New Bremen consult Rex Absolutus in ANTIQUES, April, 1928.

APPLETON, WILLIAM (1765-1822)

Cabinet-maker of Salem, Massachusetts.

ARKWRIGHT, SIR RICHARD (1732-1792)

English cotton manufacturer and inventor, born at Preston, Lancashire. He devised the spinning frame, by means of which cotton was spun into thread, and it was put to practical use in Preston in 1768. For several years he struggled against opposition from hand labor to his machines, and his final success was due as much to his admirable system of management as to the improved machinery. He was also one of the first to use the steam engine, which made him independent of water power. He was knighted by George III in 1786.

ASH, GILBERT

New York chair-maker active from 1756 to 1770.

ASTBURY, JOHN (1678-1743)

One of the great early English potters. Astbury is credited with the introduction of ground flint into the earthenware body about 1720, and he was constantly experimenting with methods by which to improve his product. The character of the Astbury ware (q.v.

PART 2) is so individual that it is well nigh impossible for the collector to be mistaken in it.

AUSTIN, JOSIAH

Cabinet-maker of Salem, Massachusetts, and a partner of Elijah and Jacob Sanderson (q.v.).

AUSTIN, NATHANIEL (1741-1816)

Pewterer of Boston and one of the most distinguished of American craftsmen whose name is found on pewter. He was also a silversmith.

AUSTIN, RICHARD (1773?-1817)

Pewterer of Boston, listed in the directory as working at his trade from 1796 to 1813. He made use of the Massachusetts coat-of-arms mark on his ware, which is of excellent quality and rare.

AUSTIN, RICHARD (1774-1826)

Chair-maker, Salem, Massachusetts.

AVERY, JOHN JR. (1732-1794)

Clock-maker and silversmith of Preston, Connecticut, of inventive genius. He was self-taught.

B

BADGER, THOMAS (1764-1826)

Pewterer at Boston, late 18th century. Apparently flat ware was his chief product.

BADLAM, STEPHEN (1751-1815)

Cabinet-maker of Dorchester, Massachusetts, who is given credit for making much of the furniture for the Derby family at Salem, by some attributed to Samuel McIntire (q.v.). He was a Brigadier General in the Revolutionary War.

REFERENCES

A Revised Estimate of McIntire, ANTIQUES, Dec. 1931.

BAGNALL, BENJAMIN (1689-1740)

One of the earliest clock-makers in America, who was born in England and arrived in Boston about 1712. He made eight-day clocks in pine and walnut cases as early as 1722, and found a ready sale for them. His sons, Benjamin, Jr. and Samuel, were clock-makers also. The latter carried on business in Boston from 1740 to 1760.

BALCH, DANIEL (1735-1790?)

Clock-maker of Newbury, Massachusetts, from about 1760 to 1790. His clocks are distinguished by engraved brass faces with chased spandrel decorations and carefully designed hands. After his death his sons, Daniel, Jr. (1761-1835) and Thomas (1771- ?) carried on the business.

BALL, WILLIAM (? -1810)

Philadelphia silversmith.

BARNS, B. (1759-1842)

Pewterer of Philadelphia, known to have worked there from 1812 to 1817 and in that time to have been one of the most prolific producers of pewter in America. His ware is of good quality of metal and workmanship.

BASSETT, FRANCIS (1729-1800)

One of the earliest New York pewterers. J. B. Kerfoot considered his product the most desirable from the collector's point of view, of all of the American makers. He is the only pewterer listed in the first issue of the New York City directory.

REFERENCE

Concerning the Pewtering Bassetts, ANTIQUES, March 1930.

BASSETT, FREDERICK (1740-1801)

New York pewterer of about the same time as Francis, mentioned above. His work is very rare and highly regarded. It is thought that Francis and Frederick were brothers and that they were sons of John Bassett (1696-1761), also a pewterer.

BECK, WASHINGTON (1839- ?)

Born in Pittsburgh and one of the best known glass mold-makers of his time. He not only made molds for American glass-makers but exported his product to foreign countries. His slogan was "a constant succession of new designs," and to him must be attributed many of the designs of the pressed so-called pattern glass of the period.

BELDEN, ——

A partner of John Allis of Hatfield, Massachusetts.

BELTER, JOHN HENRY

A New York cabinet-maker of great popularity in fashionable circles first half 19th century.

BENNETT, EDWIN (1818- ?)

A brother of James Bennett (below) who came in 1841 from England to work in the East Liverpool, Ohio, pottery. In 1846, he left there and started a factory at Baltimore, Maryland, the first to be established south of the Mason and Dixon Line. He made a specialty of the finer grades of ware and was very successful. In 1890 the Edwin Bennett Pottery Company was formed.

BENNETT, JAMES

An English potter who came to this country in 1834, and after working in Jersey City and in Troy, Indiana, he went to East Liverpool, Ohio, where he established the first pottery in that district in 1839. Since that time East Liverpool has become one of the chief pottery centers in this country.

BENTLEY, THOMAS (? -1780)

Partner of Josiah Wedgwood from 1768 to 1780. He resided in London and gave his attention to introducing Wedgwood wares to the trade in London, in which he was very successful.

BILLINGSLEY, WILLIAM (1758-1828)

A decorator of porcelain employed by many of the English factories, Derby, Worcester, Pinxton, Nantgarw, Swansea and Coalport, where he died. The rose was his favorite flower decoration. He was the most famous of all china painters of his time, and for a few years conducted a porcelain factory at Torksey, which was unsuccessful.

BOARDMAN, THOMAS DANFORTH (1784-1873)

Pewterer of Hartford, Connecticut. His mother was Sarah Danforth, a granddaughter of Thomas Danforth (q.v.), the famous pewterer of Norwich, Connecticut. Thomas was the first of the Boardman group of pewterers, rivaled in number only by those of the Danforth group. *American Pewter* by KERFOOT gives a detailed account of the activities of these groups. The best work of Thomas was done before 1825.

BOELEN, JACOB (1654-1729)

Born in Amsterdam, he came to New York in 1659. He was one of the earliest of the New York silversmiths and his work is characterized by the Dutch influence to be seen on all early New York silver. Boelen became very active in civic affairs and occupied several important offices. His son Hendrick was also a silversmith associated with him.

BÖTTGER, JOHANN FRIEDRICH (1682-1719)

A chemist who discovered the secret of true porcelain in 1709 while in search of a process that would convert base metal into gold, and, under the patronage of the Elector of Saxony, established the Dresden (Meissen) China factory in 1713, which produced the first hard porcelain to be made in Europe. After the death of Böttger, Kändler, modeler, and Herold, painter, together produced designs never excelled, which made Dresden porcelain (q.v. PART 2) famous.

BOUCHER, FRANÇOIS (1703-1770)

Noted French painter who was also the most brilliant and successful tapestry designer of the 18th century, first at Beauvais and then for Gobelin.

BOULLE, ANDRÉ CHARLES (1642-1732)

French cabinet-maker noted for his work in ebony, inlays and clever coverings with ornaments of brass, ormolu, and other metals. He was also an architect, carver in mosaic, artist in cabinet work and designer of figures; altogether a man of many abilities. His great success, however, was in his use of tortoiseshell inlay in connection with brass (usually), and his name has since been given to that process although it is disputed that he was the inventor of that form of decoration. Boulle was one of the staff of Charles Le Brun (q.v.), the great master of decorative art under Louis XIV, and resided in the Louvre from 1672 until the time of his death, where the celebrated ébéniste composed his choicest work. His furniture is luxurious and harmonizes only in a rich setting. After the King's death his fortunes dwindled and he died in poverty.

BOULSOVER, THOMAS

A cutlery-maker in Sheffield, England, who in 1742 accidentally discovered that silver and copper could be welded together, which discovery led later to the establishment of the Sheffield plate industry.

BOYD, PARKES

Pewterer of Philadelphia whose name appears in the directory from 1798 to 1819. He was a maker of fine pewter in both quality and finish. Examples of his work are rare.

BRACE, RODNEY

Clock-maker who came from Torrington, Connecticut, and worked at North Bridgewater (now Brockton), Massachusetts, early in the 19th century. He made many small shelf clocks, and these were sold in all parts of the country by means of wagon travel.

BRADFORD, CORNELIUS (1729-1786)

Pewterer of New York, son of William Bradford (below), removed to Philadelphia and there pursued his trade until the death of his wife, after which he returned to New York. His pewter work ranks as high as other pewterers' of his time. In the years just before the Revolution he was a trusted dispatch bearer between the Colonies.

REFERENCE
ANTIQUES, Aug. 1930.

BRADFORD, WILLIAM (1688-1759)

Pewterer. In 1719 he became a freeman of New York, his occupation on the records given as that of a pewterer.

BRECKENRIDGE, J. M. (1809-1896)

The last one of the old Connecticut clock-makers. During his long career he made many improvements in tools for making clocks. He remained at his bench in the shop of the New Haven Clock Company until a few months before his death.

BREWSTER, ELISHA C. (1791-1880)

Clock-maker of Bristol, Connecticut, from 1833 to 1862, when he retired.

He invented a new spring for clocks and manufactured the first spring clocks made in this country. He had a branch house in London for the sale of his goods.

BRIGDEN, ZACHARIAH (1734-1787)

Silversmith whose shop was located in Cornhill, Boston. Marked pieces of his work are to be seen in some collections. He married Sarah, daughter of Thomas Edwards, also a silversmith.

BROWN, GAWEN (1719-1801)

Clock-maker from England who settled in Boston. He made the clock for the Old South Church in that city and was also the maker of tall clocks and watches.

BULLARD, CHARLES (1794-1871)

Noted for the painted glass fronts and dials which he furnished for Simon Willard (q.v.).

BURLING, THOMAS

A cabinet- and chair-maker of New York. Active from 1790 to 1800.

BURNAP, DANIEL (1760-1838)

Clock-maker of East Windsor, Connecticut, and an apprentice of Thomas Harland (q.v.). His clocks always had brass works and tall cases and are among the best made in New England. A characteristic of his clocks is the silver face, beautifully engraved and without spandrel decoration. They often had also the phases of the moon, calendar attachments and chimes. About 1800 he removed to Andover, Connecticut, where he was located at the time of his death.

BURT, JOHN (1691-1745)

A prominent Boston silversmith of the first half of the 18th century. The bulk of his work was simple, useful hollow ware. He was very successful and his business was continued by his three sons, Samuel (1724-1754), William (1726-1752), and Benjamin (1729-1805). The latter made some of the finest ware of his time.

C

CALDER, WILLIAM (1792-1850)

Pewterer of Providence, Rhode Island. He began work in 1817 and made a variety of utensils for household and church use. He used two touches; one, an eagle, the other simply his last name in small capital letters.

REFERENCE

William Calder, ANTIQUES, Nov. 1936.

CAMP, HIRAM (1811-1893)

A Connecticut clock-maker, nephew of Chauncey Jerome (q.v.), who organized the New Haven Clock Company in 1853 and was its president until his death.

CARLILE, JOHN (1762-1832)

Cabinet-maker, born in Boston, who went to Providence while a young man and started cabinet-making there. His cabinet work is closely related to Hepplewhite and Sheraton models, and gives evidence of good workmanship in construction and good taste in simple inlay. He was a public-spirited citizen and in 1824 presided in the town council which received Lafayette. Carlile was also a Mason.

REFERENCE
John Carlile, ANTIQUES, Dec. 1924.

CARTWRIGHT, EDMUND (1743-1823)
The inventor of the power loom in 1785, he was born in Nottinghamshire, England. He was a clergyman by profession but he became interested in cotton-spinning, and besides his power loom, he took out a patent in 1789 on a wool-carding machine, and also obtained patents for various other improvements in textile machinery. His patents yielded him little return, however, and in 1809 Parliament granted him £10,000 in consideration of his inventions. It was not until the beginning of the 19th century that the power loom came into practical use.

CHAFFERS, RICHARD (1731-1765)
A Liverpool potter who made at first blue and white earthenware for exportation to America. In 1756 he was the owner of a soapstone mine in Cornwall, from which he utilized soapstone to make porcelain of excellent quality decorated with subjects of a Chinese character.

CHAMBERS, SIR WILLIAM (1726-1796)
A Scotch architect and designer of furniture in the Chinese style. In his early life he visited China and made notes and sketches of furniture, buildings and gardens, of which he made good use on his return to England. His influence is plainly traceable in many of Chippendale's best productions. He was among the first to treat the art of interior decoration and designing as one congruous whole and give it a worthy place alongside other decorative and applied arts. His accomplishments were recognized by King George III, who appointed him Royal Architect. The Somerset House in London was designed by him.

CHAPIN, AARON (1751-1838)
Born in Chicopee, Massachusetts. In 1783 he removed to Hartford, Connecticut, where he became one of the best workmen of the cabinet-makers of that state. Chapin worked mostly in cherry. One of his highboys, now in the Fine Arts Gallery at Yale University, is particularly notable in design. It is a combination of Queen Anne and Chippendale styles with a bonnet top of his own design.

REFERENCE
Aaron Chapin, ANTIQUES, Sept. 1933.

CHAPIN, ELIPHALET (1741-1807)
A cabinet-maker of East Windsor, Connecticut, thought to be a relative of

Aaron Chapin (above). It is supposed that Eliphalet was the maker of some of the best pieces of cherry cabinet work for which Connecticut cabinet-makers are noted, although there is but little documentary evidence in support of such a theory. A special feature is the spiraled rosettes terminating the broken arch.

REFERENCE

ANTIQUARIAN, April 1931.

CHIPPENDALE, THOMAS (1709?-1779)

It has been generally believed that this most famous of English cabinet-makers was born in Worcestershire in 1709, the son of Thomas Chippendale (died 1753), a wood carver and cabinet-maker, although Oliver Brackett says that he was probably the son of John Chippendale, a joiner, and was born at Otley in Yorkshire in 1718. Thomas married in 1748 and in 1749 was living in London. He was a good business man and attracted a large and fashionable clientele to his shop in St. Martin's Lane, where he was located in 1753. In 1754 he published the *Gentleman and Cabinet-Maker's Director*, which passed through several editions. In 1760, he was elected a member of the Society of Arts. He worked in mahogany almost altogether, was very careful in the selection of woods, and relied upon carving for his decorative effects. As a carver he was without a peer. Chippendale did not find it necessary

to invent. He superimposed, on the sturdy English carcase, designs drawn from French, Gothic, Dutch and Chinese sources, adding, to every style from which he drew, grace, strength and solidity without heaviness, wonderful craftsmanship, and homelike character. When old age was approaching, he took up commissions from Robert Adam and carried out his classic designs, even including inlaying, which he had never done before. After his death, the business was continued until 1796 by his son (Thomas, Jr. 1749-1822) under the name of Chippendale, Haig & Co., and the high level of work which always distinguished the shop in St. Martin's Lane was maintained.

REFERENCE

Thomas Chippendale, OLIVER BRACKETT.

CIPRIANI, GIOVANNI (1727-1785)

A Florentine artist who came to England in 1755 and soon achieved a reputation for painted decoration in public buildings and houses. He probably inspired much of the painted furniture of the period, although there are no known existing examples of his work.

CLAGGETT, WILLIAM (1696-1749)

An early maker of good clocks in Newport, Rhode Island. He is said to have been born in Wales and lived first in this country at Boston. The dials of his clocks were masterpieces of the engraver's art. His brother Thomas was also a clock-maker.

CLARK, DANIEL (1768-1830)

Cabinet-maker of Salem, Massachusetts. He received his training in Boston and started business in Salem in 1796. He made and carved tables, chairs, chests of drawers and other furniture.

CLARK, PETER (1743-1826)

Born in Braintree, Massachusetts, and moved to Lyndeboro, New Hampshire, in 1775 where he erected a kiln for making pottery. After service in the army, he carried on his business for a number of years making jugs, jars and pots for various purposes. The business was continued after his death by his sons.

REFERENCE

The Lyndeboro Pottery, ANTIQUES, Feb. 1928.

CLEWS, JAMES (1786-1856)

Staffordshire potter who bought, with his brother Ralph, the works of Andrew Stevenson at Cobridge in 1819. Clews made a series of American Historical plates and his "Landing of Lafayette" plates, made in 1824, are much sought after by collectors, as are his "Doctor Syntax," his "David Wilkie," and "Don Quixote" designs. The characteristic Clews mark is a circle impressed with a crown inside and the words "Clews Warranted Staffordshire." In 1836, Clews came to this country and started a pottery at Troy, Indiana, which failed, and Clews returned to England. Perhaps no English potter was better known on this side of the Atlantic than James Clews.

REFERENCES

English Tours of Doctor Syntax, ANTIQUARIAN, Oct. and Nov. 1931; English Tours of Doctor Syntax, FINE ARTS, Jan. 1932.

COBURN, JOHN (1725-1803)

Silversmith of Boston, whose shop was located on King (now State) Street opposite the American Coffee House. That he was an excellent craftsman, examples of his work in various collections testify. After the Revolution he was town warden and a census recorder.

CONEY, JOHN (1655-1722)

Silversmith of Boston who learned his trade either under John Hull (q.v.) or Jeremiah Dummer. He was one of the most prolific of Boston silversmiths and his work ranks among the best of Colonial silversmiths. At least 147 examples of his work are in existence today, consisting of beakers, caudle cups, chafing dishes, porringers, tankards and other pieces. The father of Paul Revere was one of his apprentices, and he was a brother-in-law of Jeremiah Dummer (q.v.), another Boston silversmith. Coney was an engraver of unusual skill, and he engraved the plates for Massachusetts in 1690 for the first paper money used in the Colonies. He was successful in his business but took small part in public affairs.

REFERENCE
John Coney, Silversmith, CLARKE.

CONNELLY, HENRY (1770-1826)

Philadelphia cabinet-maker and a real master craftsman after the style of Sheraton. His work places him among those of first rank as a furniture-maker and designer.

COOKWORTHY, WILLIAM (1705-1780)

A Quaker chemist of Plymouth (later of Bristol), England, who established a porcelain factory there, patenting in 1768 virtually the first English porcelain of native ingredients. It is said that he was the discoverer of the clay (kaolin) in Cornwall from which the great potting trade in England has received more benefit than from almost any other source.

COPELAND, WILLIAM (? -1826)

English potter who became a partner of Josiah Spode, Jr., at Stoke-on-Trent in 1797. Descendants of William Copeland are carrying on the business today under the name of W. T. Copeland and Sons.

COWELL, WILLIAM (1682-1736)

A Boston silversmith of some prominence.

CREHORE, CHARLES C. (1793-1879)

Made clock cases for Simon and Benjamin Willard and other clock-makers

of the period. He also made piano cases and violins.

CROLIUS, WILLIAM

One of the early potters of New York, coming to this country from Germany where he learned his trade. His pottery was located about 1735 just north of the present City Hall near that of John Remmey (q.v.), a brother-in-law, and the business was carried on for many years by descendants of William Crolius. See CROLIUS WARE, PART 2.

REFERENCE
ANTIQUARIAN, Jan. 1930.

CROMPTON, SAMUEL (1753-1827)

An English inventor whose spinning mule, perfected in 1779, revolutionized the cotton-weaving industry. He was unable to bear the expense of taking out a patent, and manufacturers made use of the invention without compensation to the inventor. In 1812 Parliament granted him £5000, the only official recognition bestowed upon him.

REFERENCE
Life and Times of Crompton, FRENCH.

CUMMING, ALEXANDER (1732-1814)

Scotch clock-maker who removed to London. He made the astronomical clock now in Buckingham Palace for George III, for which he was paid £2000.

CUMMINS, WILLIAM

Clock-maker at Roxbury, Massachusetts, an apprentice of Simon Willard.

Curtis, Lemuel (1790-1857)

Clock-maker, born in Boston, who started in business at Concord, Massachusetts, from which place he removed to Burlington, Vermont, in 1818. He had been an apprentice of Simon Willard in Boston, and made an improvement in the movement of the Willard banjo clock for which he took out a patent in 1816. He made only wall and shelf clocks, all of which were splendid examples of the clocks of the period. His banjo clocks usually had a rounded bottom for the swing of the pendulum, with a convex glass and classical painting on it, called a "girandole" clock.

Custer, Jacob D. (1805-1872)

Clock-maker of Norristown, Pennsylvania. In 1842 he began the manufacture of clocks to propel the lights in lighthouses. He also made long-case clocks.

D

Danforth, Thomas (1703-1786)

One of the earliest Colonial pewterers, at first at Taunton, Massachusetts, later of Norwich, Connecticut. His pieces show skillful craftsmanship and are treasured by collectors. He retired from active work in 1773. Twelve of his descendants followed the pewterer's trade, of whom Thomas Danforth Boardman (q.v.) was one. The family was active over a hundred years.

REFERENCE
The Danforths, ANTIQUARIAN, March 1930.

Darly, Matthias

An engraver in London and designer of furniture, 18th century. Many of Chippendale's *Director* plates and those of Ince and Mayhew's *System* were engraved by him. He published *Chinese Designs* in 1754, which doubtless influenced Chippendale's Chinese style.

Davenport, John (? -1834)

Staffordshire potter who began work at Longport in 1793. He claims more attention as a maker of porcelain than of earthenware, but his earthenware is highly regarded by collectors. See DAVENPORT WARE, PART 2.

De L'Orme, Philibert (? -1572)

French designer and carver of stone chimney-pieces, gargoyles and capitals.

Disbrowe, Nicholas (1612-1683)

Born in Walden, Essex, England. Came early to America and settled at Hartford, Connecticut, as a joiner. He is given credit for the design for the Connecticut "sunflower" chest. The chest marked "Mary Allens chist cutte and joyned by Nick Disbrowe" is the earliest piece of American furniture for which the maker's name is given.

SILVER PUNCH BOWL AND LADLE, GEORGIAN PERIOD, 18TH CENTURY

ENGLISH SILVER MONTEITH BOWL, 17TH CENTURY

Silver Oval Sugar Basket by Paul Revere (1738-1818)

DIXWELL, JOHN (1680-1715)

Silversmith born in New Haven, the son of Col. John Dixwell, the regicide. He removed to Boston in 1698 and learned the trade of silversmith. He also became active in the affairs of his time and a deacon of the North Church in Boston.

DOGGETT, JOHN

Cabinet-maker of Roxbury, Massachusetts. He was also a carver and gilder. He made clock cases for Simon Willard and carved and gilded the ornaments for them and supplied the glass. Aaron Willard and his son also employed him for similar work, and he did work for the Derbys at Salem.

DORFLEIN, PHILIP (1816-1896)

A maker of metal molds for glass works, who began work in Philadelphia in 1842. He originated a large number of bottle designs with portraits of prominent men. He was one of the best known mold cutters in the trade.

DOWNS, EPHRAIM

Clock-maker at Bristol, Connecticut, active from 1811 to 1843.

DUESBURY, WILLIAM (? -1786)

Son of a Longton Hall potter, for some years prior to 1755 he had been a china painter in London. With the financial aid of John Heath he organized the Derby Porcelain Works in1756. In 1770 he purchased the Chelsea factory and in 1776 the Bow China Works.

He was one of the most influential figures in early English porcelain history.

DUFFIELD, EDWARD (1720-1801)

Pennsylvania clock-maker of Lower Dublin and a friend of Benjamin Franklin, who made him the sole executor of his estate. Duffield's clocks were distinguished for good workmanship and good timekeeping.

DUMMER, JEREMIAH (1645-1718)

A Colonial silversmith, in his youth apprentice to John Hull at Boston. He started in business in 1666, in which he was successful, and he was also a merchant and interested in civic affairs. Also, there are several disputed portraits attributed to him. The fluted band on a plain surface characterized his work. He was a prolific and powerful craftsman, and one hundred and nine pieces listed as made by him have been preserved. He made tankards, beakers, porringers, caudle cups, and various other objects for sacred and secular use. A pair of candlesticks made by him are the earliest known candlesticks made by Colonial silversmiths.

REFERENCES

Jeremiah Dummer, CLARKE and FOOTE; *Jeremiah Dummer, Silversmith*, ANTIQUES, Oct. 1935.

DUNHAM, RUFUS

Made pewter and Britannia ware in Westbrook, Maine.

DWIGHT, JOHN (1638?-1703)

One of the greatest of English potters, and to him must, perhaps, be attributed the foundation of an important industry. Between 1671 and 1676 he settled at Fulham and established his pottery works there, with the product known as Fulham ware (q.v., PART 2). Aside from the usual earthenware, noted for its fine modeling, he made a fine white stoneware resembling porcelain, and stoneware jugs of the Cologne type. Another specialty was making busts and figures. According to Professor Church he stands at the head of all English potters in that field. His portrait bust of Prince Rupert, life size, is regarded as the finest piece of pottery modeling in the world.

DWIGHT, TIMOTHY (1654-1691)

Silversmith of Boston. It is thought that he was one of the apprentices of John Hull. His work is very well regarded.

DYOTT, THOMAS W. (1771-1861)

Born in England, and came to this country in 1795. He was an early promoter, if not the originator, of the "patent medicine" business in this country. A self-styled doctor, he was also one of the most interesting characters in the glass-making industry. After making a fortune in selling drugs and medicines, in which activity he used great quantities of bottles, he bought in 1831 the Kensington Glass Works, changed its name to the Dyottville Glass Works (q.v. PART 3), and continued its operation for several years. In 1838 he was forced into bankruptcy and retired from active business, but the factory continued in operation and is still in existence.

REFERENCE

Early American Glass, RHEA M. KNITTLE.

E

EDGELL, SIMON (? -1742)

A pewter-maker at Philadelphia, whose large hammered plate is considered to be the earliest dated piece of American pewter.

EDWARDS, ABRAHAM (1761-1840)

Clock-maker, Ashby, Massachusetts, active from about 1792 until about 1820. He produced many tall clocks, at first with his brother Calvin (1763-1796), and after his death worked alone. While the brothers worked together

each clock was numbered, totaling about 600. Abraham discontinued numbering them afterwards. The earlier clocks had wooden works but these were soon succeeded by clocks with brass works. Abraham's son John also made a few clocks, inscribed with his name.

EDWARDS, JOHN (1670-1746)

Silversmith. Born in England and served his apprenticeship in London, after which he came to Boston, where he became a partner of John Allen (1671-1760) and one of the most flourishing of the Boston silversmiths. He was also prominent in civic affairs, holding many public offices. His son Thomas (1701-1755) was also a silversmith.

EGERTON, MATTHEW (1739-1802)

Cabinet-maker of New Brunswick, New Jersey, made clock cases, secretaries, bureaus, tables, bedsteads and chests. He is not known to have made chairs. His style, favoring Hepplewhite, and workmanship were excellent, as were, too, the work of his son Matthew, Jr., who followed his father's trade. The work of both is very similar in character and quality.

REFERENCES

Matthew Egerton, ANTIQUES, Sept. and Nov. 1928; Matthew Egerton, Jr., ANTIQUARIAN, Dec. 1930.

ELERS, JOHN PHILIP and DAVID

Two Dutch potter brothers who went to England at the time of William III and established a pottery at Bradwell in Staffordshire, and through their improved methods advanced the standards of Staffordshire wares. The black and red teapots made by Elers, unglazed, with ornaments in Chinese style added in relief were particularly noteworthy. Although the Elers brothers left Staffordshire in 1710 and were afterwards connected with the manufacture of glassware and porcelain in Chelsea, Elers ware (q.v. PART 2) continued to be copied and imitated long afterwards. It was superior to anything before produced in Staffordshire.

ELFE, THOMAS (1718-1775)

Cabinet-maker of Charleston, South Carolina. He made furniture of every description for the best families of Charleston. The greater part of his production was in mahogany, which was in common use at the time not only for furniture, but for doors, newel posts and banisters, and for paneling rooms and other interior work.

REFERENCE

Thomas Elfe, ANTIQUES, April 1934.

ELLICOTT, JOSEPH (1732-1780)

Clock-maker, Philadelphia. In 1769 he made his famous musical clock which includes a planetarium where the planets move in their respective orbits. There is no other clock like it in this country or abroad. The case is of mahogany, and there are glazed doors on each of the four sides of the hood, one for the regular clock dial, one for the planetarium dial, one for the list of twenty-four music-box tunes, and one at the rear exposing the working mechanism of the clock. It is today in good running order. Mr. Ellicott was a member of the American Philosophical Society.

REFERENCE

The Masterpiece of Joseph Ellicott, ANTIQUES, Aug. 1934.

ELLIOT, CHARLES

English cabinet-maker in London of the time of Chippendale.

ELLIOT, JOHN (1713-1791)

A Quaker cabinet-maker of Philadelphia, born in Bolton, England, who came to America in 1753. At the outbreak of the Revolutionary War he retired from business.

ELLIOT, JOHN JR. (? -1810)

Son of the foregoing and who carried on the cabinet-making trade until his death. Both made and repaired mirrors, and several of these have been found with their label attached.

EVANS, DAVID (? -1814)

Philadelphia cabinet-maker. His three books of accounts running from 1774 to 1811, preserved by the Historical Society of Pennsylvania, indicate that he made a great variety of furniture. They also give the prices charged and the names of patrons for whom he worked.

REFERENCE

David Evans, ANTIQUES, Feb. 1932.

F

FENTON, CHRISTOPHER WEBBER (1806-1865)

American potter born in East Dorset, Vermont, and one of a family of pioneer American potters. To Fenton was due much of the success of the Bennington pottery (q.v. PART 2) while he was identified with the factory from 1846 to 1858. Fenton's ability and energy as a business promoter, rather than as a practical potter, give him the important place he holds today in the history of American pottery. While he was at Bennington the factory became famous for its Parian white, granite and Rockingham wares.

REFERENCE

The Fentons, ANTIQUES, Oct. 1923.

FESSENDEN, LAFAYETTE

Succeeded Deming Jarves in 1858 as manager of the Sandwich Glass Works.

FISK, WILLIAM (1770-1844)

A cabinet-maker who made clock cases for Aaron and Simon Willard and other clock-makers.

FLAXMAN, JOHN (1755-1826)

Sculptor and designer employed by Wedgwood. He designed some of the most exquisite of the relief decorations used on Wedgwood's jasper ware, and his modeling work made him famous, and did much to make the fame of Wedgwood. In 1787 he went to Rome and remained there seven years, sculpturing. In later years, he designed many famous monuments and became a leader in the British school of sculpture, although he was more skillful as a modeler than as a sculptor, and more successful in his bas-reliefs than in his treatment of the round.

FORSTER, JACOB (? -1838)

A cabinet-maker in Charlestown, Massachusetts, from 1781 until the time of his death. He was born in Berwick, Maine. A chest of drawers with his label dated 179? shows workmanship of excellent character.

FROMANTEEL, AHASUERUS

From a family of Dutch clock-makers, mentioned as early as 1630, who came to London. He was a member of the Clockmakers Company in 1632 and he is said to have introduced the use of the pendulum in England.

FROTHINGHAM, BENJAMIN (1734-1809)

Cabinet-maker, born in Boston, established in Charlestown in 1756, and with the exception of seven years given to the service of the American cause in the Revolution, he pursued his trade until his death. He was a Major of Artillery in the war and a friend of Washington. His father, also named Benjamin (died 1765), and his son, another Benjamin (died 1832), were also cabinet-makers.

REFERENCE
Benjamin Frothingham, ANTIQUES, Dec. 1928.

G

GAUTIER, ANDREW (1720-1784)

One of the first American furniture-makers to use illustrated newspaper advertising. He was born and lived in New York and specialized in the making of Windsor chairs.

GIBBONS, GRINLING (1648-1721)

England's most famous wood carver was born in Rotterdam, Holland. He carved the choir stalls at St. Paul's Cathedral and in the chapel at Windsor Castle, besides doing much work in the royal palaces at Whitehall, Hampton Court, and Kensington. He also carved wall-panels, mirror frames and chimney-pieces, and was appointed Master-Carver-in-Wood in 1714. He did most of his work under the direction of Sir Christopher Wren (q.v.). Gibbons was not so successful with his work in marble and bronze.

REFERENCE
Grinling Gibbons and the Woodwork of His Age, TIPPING.

GILLERLAND, JOHN

A glass-maker who was considered to be the best metal-mixer of his time in America. Many of his decanters and wine glasses cannot readily be distinguished from the imported ware. He was at first connected with the New

England Glass Company at Cambridge, and in 1823 he went to Brooklyn where he established the South Ferry Glass Works, which was in successful operation until late in the Fifties. Much of our fine cut glass of the Forties and Fifties came from the Gillerland furnaces.

REFERENCE
Early American Glass, RHEA M. KNITTLE.

GILLINGHAM, JAMES (1736-1781)
Philadelphia cabinet-maker with a shop on Second Street. His furniture was simple but of a fine character and he compares favorably with other leading Philadelphia cabinet-makers.

REFERENCES
Blue Book, Philadelphia Furniture, HORNOR; ANTIQUES, May 1936.

GILLINGHAM, JOHN (1710-1793)
Philadelphia cabinet-maker, uncle of James, above. In 1740 he made a desk for Benjamin Franklin.

REFERENCE
ANTIQUES, June and Oct. 1931.

GILLOW, ROBERT (? -1772)
A member of one of the oldest furniture-making families in England, starting in Lancaster in 1724 and opening in London in 1765. He rivaled Chippendale in the excellent quality of his work. Richard (1776-1866), grandson of Robert, was the inventor of the telescopic dining-table, and is reported to

have been a maker of English billiard-tables. The firm is still in existence.

GLEASON, ROSWELL (1798-1886)
Pewterer at Dorchester, Massachusetts, who is said to have begun work about 1830. His ware was in great variety and some of it was very good in quality and workmanship.

REFERENCE
ANTIQUES, Aug. 1931.

GOBELIN
The name of a family of dyers from Belgium which came late in the 15th century to Paris. Jean and Philibert, brothers, established a tannery on the banks of the Bièvre River there and in the following century added a tapestry manufactory, which eventually, through the support of King Louis XIV in the 17th century, became famous. See TAPESTRIES, Gobelin, PART 4.

GODDARD, JOHN (1724-1785)
A cabinet-maker of Newport, Rhode Island, reputed to have been the first to make block-front furniture, although some authorities believe that Job Townsend (q.v.) should have the credit. Goddard was one of the most noteworthy and successful of our early cabinet-makers and rivals in reputation William Savery and Duncan Phyfe. After his death his son Thomas (1765-1858) carried on the business, although it is not known that he made block-front furniture.

REFERENCES

> *Furniture Treasury*, Vol. 3, WALLACE NUTTING; *John Goddard and His Block Front*, ANTIQUES, May 1922; *A Sidelight on John Goddard*, ANTIQUES, Sept. 1936.

GOELET, PHILIP (1701?-1748)

New York Silversmith.

GOSTELOWE, JONATHAN (1744-1806)

Philadelphia cabinet- and chairmaker. He followed English models of the Georgian period very closely and authentic pieces of his work establish him as among the foremost of Philadelphia cabinet-makers. A labeled bureau of his make is in the Pennsylvania Museum and other labeled pieces are known. In 1788 he was chairman of "Gentlemen Cabinet and Chair Makers," a trade organization, and in 1793 he retired from active business.

REFERENCES

> *Blue Book, Philadelphia Furniture*, HORNOR; *Jonathan Gostelowe*, ANTIQUES, June and Aug. 1926.

GOULD, JOHN JR. (1793-1840)

Cabinet-maker of New Ipswich, New Hampshire, whose work has been identified on two chests of drawers of good workmanship by his printed label on each. One of his apprentices was Jonas Chickering, who afterwards achieved fame by making the Chickering piano.

REFERENCE

ANTIQUARIAN, March 1930.

GRAHAM, GEORGE (1673-1751)

A Quaker clock- and watch-maker born in Kirklinton, who went to London in 1688 and began his apprenticeship. Subsequently employed by Thomas Tompion (q.v.), he married the daughter of James Tompion, brother of Thomas. Graham is credited with inventing the dead-beat escapement in clocks, still unsurpassed, and he was acknowledged to be the foremost horologist of his time. He was buried in Westminster Abbey.

GRANGER, OSCAR

Glass-maker early in Vernon, New York, where he learned to make glass at the (Mt.) Vernon Glass Works. In 1844 he went to Mt. Pleasant (Saratoga), New York, and built a glass factory which was successful for a number of years.

REFERENCE

ANTIQUARIAN, March 1930.

GREATBACH, DANIEL

An English potter who came to this country in 1839 from Hanley, Staffordshire, and found employment at the Jersey City potteries until 1848. In 1852 he joined the United States Pottery at Bennington, Vermont, and he was the originator of many of the Bennington models that met with favor from that time until the pottery was closed. Notable among these was the hound-handled pitcher or jug. Greatbach was an artist, but not a good business man, and he died in poverty in Trenton.

H

HAMLIN, SAMUEL

Pewterer at Newport, Rhode Island, active last quarter of the 18th century.

HANCOCK, JOHN (? -1842)

Reputed to have been the first potter to make bronze (copper) lustre ware at Staffordshire. He came to America in 1828 and operated potteries successfully at South Amboy, New Jersey, Louisville, Kentucky, and East Liverpool, Ohio, where he died.

HANCOCK, JOSEPH

About 1750 while experimenting at Sheffield, England, with the process of combining silver and copper discovered by Thomas Boulsover (q.v.), he began the manufacture of small articles of silver plate on copper, which eventually grew to a great industry. See SHEFFIELD PLATE, PART 5.

HANCOCK, ROBERT (1730-1817)

An engraver of designs for transfer-printing on porcelain. He was at the Worcester factory in 1757, and is said to have done work for Bow and for Lowdin's Bristol factory. He was afterwards associated (1775) with the Caughley factory.

HARGREAVES, JAMES (? -1788)

The inventor of the spinning-jenny (q.v. PART 4) was an illiterate weaver, who helped Robert Peel in 1760 in the construction of a carding machine. In 1764 he invented the spinning-jenny, named for his daughter, and later erected a spinning mill, and continued to carry on business as a yarn manufacturer until his death.

HARLAND, THOMAS (1735-1807)

Clock-maker from London who settled in Norwich, Connecticut, in 1773 and made clocks there with brass works, equal to those previously imported from England. He became the foremost clock-maker of his day in this country, and Daniel Burnap (q.v.) and Eli Terry (q.v.) were among his apprentices.

HARRISON, JOHN (1693-1776)

English clock-maker of Yorkshire, who invented a chronometer that would permit longitude to be taken at sea and for which he was paid by Act of Parliament £2,000. He was one of the greatest horologists of England. There is a long-case clock with wooden wheels and pinions by him in the Guildhall Museum in London.

HEMPHILL, JOSEPH (1770-1842)

A partner of William Ellis Tucker (q.v.) at Philadelphia in the first successful production of American porcelain, and proprietor of the factory after the death of Mr. Tucker in 1832 until it was closed in 1836.

HENCHMAN, DANIEL (1730-1775)

Boston silversmith. His Governor Wentworth punch bowl is now owned by Dartmouth College.

HENDRICKS, AHASUERUS

The first recorded silversmith in New York (1675).

HEPPLEWHITE, GEORGE (? -1786)

English cabinet-maker located at St. Giles, Cripplegate, London. Of his early life but little is known. He was the second of the great English cabinet-makers to make a distinct impression upon the styles of the period. His work was lighter and more graceful than that of Chippendale, and he undoubtedly derived most of his classic feeling from the designs of the brothers Adam. Hepplewhite is credited, with Thomas Shearer, a contemporary, with originating the design of the sideboard, which displaced the table and separate pedestals then in use. After his death in 1786, his widow Alice and her partners carried on the business under the name of A. Hepplewhite & Company, and in 1788 published in book form the designs of George Hepplewhite, under the title of *The Cabinet Maker and Upholsterer's Guide*, which became popular and went into several editions. It was a valuable addition to the literature of cabinet-making.

HEWES, ROBERT (1751-1830)

Born in Boston and identified with the glass factory at Temple, New Hampshire, which he started in 1780. This enterprise was not successful and Hewes returned to Boston, where in 1787 he became one of the organizers of the Essex Glass Works (q.v. PART 3). Hewes was a man of versatile accomplishments, an expert fencer, familiar with surgery and with a peculiar talent for bone-setting.

HEWSON, JOHN

An Englishman who came to Philadelphia in 1774 under the auspices of Benjamin Franklin. He was the first calico printer of record there and he maintained his industry until his death, after which it was carried on until 1823 by his son John, Jr.

HITCHCOCK, LAMBERT (1795-1852)

Chair-maker, whose name has been given to chairs of a type said to have been first manufactured by him and afterwards widely copied by other makers. He came from Cheshire, Connecticut, in 1818 to a town afterwards called Hitchcocksville in his honor, and still later changed to Riverton, the name it now bears. In 1826 he erected a factory there and began making "fancy" chairs with stenciled instead of painted decorations on a ground usually painted black, which business was successful for several years. Other makers of chairs made a similar product and undersold him, and owing to this competition he made an assignment, and in 1843 started the Unionville Chair Company, which was unsuccessful. Owing to the superior quality of the Hitchcock chair, his name is applied to all chairs of the same type and period.

REFERENCE

Hitchcock of Hitchcocksville, AN-
TIQUES, Aug. 1923.

HOADLEY, LUTHER and SAMUEL

Makers of wooden clocks at Winsted,
Connecticut, active from 1807 to 1813.

HOADLEY, SILAS (1786-1870)

One of the leading figures in the Connecticut clock-making industry. He began work in 1809 with Eli Terry (q.v.)
at Plymouth and continued until 1849,
at which time he retired from business,
having made a fortune during the forty
years of activity. His product was
highly regarded and today his clocks
are rare.

HOLLINS, SAMUEL (1774-1816)

English potter of Shelton, Staffordshire. Noted for his red and chocolate-
colored unglazed ware decorated with
ornament in the Elers manner. He also
produced some fine examples of jasper
ware.

HOMES, WILLIAM (1717-1783)

Boston. Known as the "honest"
silversmith.

HOOK, WILLIAM (1777-1867)

One of the leading cabinet-makers of
Salem, Massachusetts. He started in
business in 1800, and in the ensuing
years he made furniture of excellent
quality and workmanship for many of
the leading families in Salem and the
vicinity.

HOPKINS, GERRARD (? -1796)

Cabinet-maker at Baltimore, Maryland, for about thirty years. He learned
his trade in Philadelphia and all of his
later work shows the influence of his
training there. His furniture was plainly
but substantially built, with but little
carving.

HOWARD, EDWARD (1813- ?)

Founder in 1861 of the E. Howard
Clock Co. at Roxbury, Massachusetts,
and maker of clocks and watches of excellent quality. The company is still in
existence. Howard was an apprentice
of Aaron Willard, Jr. He retired in
1882.

HULL, JOHN (1624-1683)

Born in Leicestershire, England, he
came to Boston in 1635. One of the
first Colonial silversmiths he was also
appointed mint-master in 1652, in
which year Robert Sanderson (q.v.)
became his partner. For thirty years
these two coined silver for local circu-
lation. The "Pine Tree" shilling and a
sixpence were the first coins made in
America. The dies for these coins were
made by Joseph Jenks of Lynn, the first
Colonial iron-founder. Hull became a
great and prosperous merchant, and
some authorities are of the opinion that
to Sanderson should be given a large
share of the credit for the silverware
produced, although while Hull lived
most of the silver made bore the marks
of both men.

REFERENCES

Historic Silver of the Colonies and Its Makers, BIGELOW; *American Silver of the 17th and 18th Centuries*, AVERY; *Early New England Silver*, ANTIQUES, Sept. 1925.

HUNNEMAN, WILLIAM C. (1769-1856)

Brass-worker of Boston who had been an apprentice of Paul Revere. He made andirons, bells, kettles, candlesticks, warming-pans and other household utensils. He also furnished brass works for clocks for Simon Willard, and also supplied some of the brass fittings for the Frigate Constitution, while she was building.

HURD, JACOB (1702-1758)

A Boston silversmith and one of the largest producers of his time, all of whose work was excellent in quality and design. After his death, his son Nathaniel (1729-1777) carried on the business, but he was more noted as an engraver and designer of bookplates.

HUTCHINS, ABEL and LEVI

Clock-makers at Concord, New Hampshire, who had been apprentices of Simon Willard. They were active from about 1788 to 1819.

HUTTON, ISAAC (1767-1855)

Silversmith at Albany, New York.

I

INCE, (W.) and MAYHEW, (J.)

English cabinet-makers operating as Mayhew and Ince. In 1748, they published *The Universal System of Household Furniture*, which included directions for the workmen in executing the designs for tables, chairs, book-cases, mirror frames, etc. Lockwood says that the work of Ince made him a close rival of Chippendale, and Macquoid ranks him among the best cabinet-makers of the period. He was the most active partner, and the firm continued in existence for many years.

INGRAHAM, ELIAS (1805-1885)

He was born in Marlboro, Massachu- setts, but went early to Bristol, Connecticut, where he began the manufacture of clocks and was the founder of a business still running. He originated the so-called "Sharp Gothic" pattern of case for shelf clocks, which soon became familiar everywhere. He did not patent the design and it was copied extensively by other clock-makers, owing to its popularity.

IVES, CHAUNCY

Chauncy, Joseph and Lawson Ives were clock-makers at Bristol, Connecticut, from about 1810 to 1836.

J

JACQUARD, JOSEPH MARIE (1752-1834)

Born in Lyons, France. He was the son of a weaver and, being familiar with his father's trade, he endeavored to make improvements in the looms then in use, which finally resulted in the loom known the world over as the Jacquard loom, which provided for weaving large and complex patterns.

JARVES, DEMING (1791-1869)

Founder of Boston and Sandwich Glass Company in 1825. He was born in Boston and from 1818 to 1825 had been connected with the New England Glass Company at Cambridge. Jarves was a man of exceptional ability, he understood all of the mechanics of glass-making, was far-sighted and inventive. Under his leadership "Sandwich" glass became known everywhere for its excellent quality and artistic variety. Jarves remained at Sandwich until 1858 when he resigned and started the Cape Cod Glass Company, also at Sandwich. It was not a successful venture and after the death of Jarves it was disposed of.

REFERENCE

Deming Jarves, ANTIQUES, Oct. 1931.

JEROME, CHAUNCEY (1793-1860)

A Connecticut clock-maker born in Canaan. In 1821 he moved to Bristol and started in business for himself. He inaugurated the one-day clock with brass works instead of wooden, for shelf clocks, and it was a great success. It revolutionized American clock-making and brought Jerome a fortune. Wooden works were from that time discontinued by clock-makers generally. A large part of Jerome's product was exported to Europe. His last years were clouded with misfortune but his name will always rank among those of the leaders in the clock-making industry. He was the author of *History of the American Clock Business for the Past 60 Years*, published 1860.

JOHNSON, THOMAS

Cabinet-maker in London of the time of Chippendale. He was notable as a designer of frames for pier glasses, ovals and girandoles in the Rococo style.

JONES, GERSHON

Pewterer of Providence, Rhode Island, at work there before the Revolution and after. Specimens of his pewter are decidedly rare.

JONES, INIGO (1573-1652)

Architect and designer, the "Father of English Classic Revival." Born in London, he was the dictator of style during the reign of Charles I. He left many examples of his work in celebrated palaces and homes of the wealthy. His masterpiece is considered to be the Banqueting House at Whitehall. His classic chimney-pieces were carved in wood, stone and marble by imported Italian workmen.

REFERENCE
Designs of Inigo Jones, JONES.

K

KAUFFMANN, ANGELICA (1741-1807)

A painter of portraits and historical subjects, also celebrated as a decorative artist. She was employed by the brothers Adam in decorating the painted furniture of the period.

KENT, WILLIAM (1684-1748)

English furniture designer and architect of considerable influence. He was also a painter and sculptor. His furniture was designed to conform to his architectural style, in which work he was the forerunner of Robert Adam (q.v.). He designed most of the furniture for "Houghton," the seat of Sir Robert Walpole. An account of the furniture designs of Kent is in the ANTIQUARIAN, Vol. 14, p. 43. He occupied an extremely important place in the arts and crafts of his day.

REFERENCE
William Kent, ANTIQUES, Nov. 1933.

KIERSTEDE, CORNELIUS (1675- ?)

New York silversmith who removed to New Haven, Connecticut, in 1722. His early work is in characteristic Dutch style, but after his removal from New York he appears to have blended the Dutch with the styles of the English silversmiths, to which he added unusual touches which seem to distinguish his work from that of any other craftsman. He was still living in 1753.

KILBOURN, SAMUEL

Pewterer of Baltimore who is listed in the directory as working there from 1814 to 1824. His work is of excellent quality and specimens are rare.

KRAMER, CHRISTIAN (1773-1858)

Glass-maker born in Germany who came to America in his early years. In 1797, he began making glass at New Geneva, Pennsylvania, and later, with others, started a glass factory at Greensboro, Pennsylvania (q.v. PART 3), where flint and bottle glass in various colors and designs was produced of excellent quality. According to one authority he will rank as one of the greatest of our early glass-makers.

L

LAMERIE, PAUL (? -1751)

French silversmith who went to England following the Revocation of the Edict of Nantes. His work in the Rococo style was so good that he stands first in the effect of foreign influence upon the silverware of the 18th century in England. His work was copied long after his death and pieces bearing his mark bring very high prices.

LANNUIER, CHARLES HONORÉ (1779-1819)

Born in Chantilly, France, he came to New York in 1790, where from 1805 until his death he conducted a cabinet-maker's business. He is said to have been the peer of Duncan Phyfe, and that master's chief competitor. Much work attributed to Phyfe was probably by him. After the death of Lannuier, his foreman, J. Gruez, carried on the business until about 1824.

REFERENCE

A Franco-American Cabinet Maker, ANTIQUES, May and June 1933.

LE BRUN, CHARLES (1619-1690)

Famous French artist and designer, considered to have been the founder of modern French art. Appointed in 1662 painter to the King, Louis XIV, he decorated the Gallery of Apollo in the Louvre, following which he became the director of the Gobelin tapestry works, where he made cartoons for those famous tapestries. He was an indefatigable worker, never yielding to flattery, and at his death left a remarkable record of accomplishment in many branches of art. He was, perhaps, the greatest genius in decorative art of modern times.

LEE, RICHARD (1747-1823)

American pewterer born in Scituate, Rhode Island. He removed first to Lanesboro, Massachusetts, and later to Vermont. He is said to have made pewter buttons for the American army during the Revolution. Specimens of his work are very rare. His son, also Richard, made pewter and brass utensils.

REFERENCE

Richard Lee, Pewterer, ANTIQUES, June 1928.

LEIGHTON, THOMAS (1786-1849)

Glass-worker, born in Birmingham, England, who came to this country in 1826 to work for the New England Glass Company at Cambridge as "gaffer" (superintendent or foreman), where he remained until his death. His son John succeeded him as "gaffer," which position he retained until 1874.

LE PAUTRE, JEAN (? -1682)

French cabinet-maker born in Paris. His works, published in 1731, are full of French Renaissance details which were doubtless of considerable influence upon English cabinet-makers, especially those who, like Chippendale, produced florid carving effects. A master carver himself, he supplied the models for most of the wood carvers of his day. All of his designs are heavy in form.

LE ROUX, BARTHOLOMEW (? -1713)

Best known of the Huguenot silversmiths who came from France and located in New York. He was father-in-law of Peter Van Dyck (q.v.).

LE ROUX, CHARLES (1689-1745)

Son of Bartholomew Le Roux and a good craftsman. He was for several years official silversmith of New York.

LISTER, THOMAS (1718-1779)

English clock-maker, native of Luddenden, Yorkshire. His son, also Thomas (1745-1814), was a clock-maker of Halifax, England, for 42 years, where he made long-case clocks of excellent quality both as to case and movement. On the inside of the door he (the son) was accustomed to place a label reading:

> Lo! here I stand by thee
> To give thee warning day and night;
> For every tick that I do give
> Cuts short the time thou hast to live.
> Therefore, a warning take by me,
> To serve thy God as I serve thee:
> Each day and night be on thy guard,
> And thou shalt have a just reward.

LLOYD, WILLIAM (1779-1845)

Cabinet-maker of Springfield, Massachusetts, whose work in the first quarter of the 19th century ranks him among the good cabinet-makers of his time. His label appears on several pieces of his earlier work. His later work is less satisfactory.

LOCK, MATTHIAS

An English designer of furniture, who had at one time a furniture workshop in London. He was a man of artistic attainments with pen and pencil, and also an etcher who engraved his own plates. Associated with a man named Copeland, he published *Original Designs for Furniture*, which appeared at intervals between 1740 and 1765. Another was the *Book of Ornaments*, in which his designs for mirror frames were particularly good.

LORING, JOSEPH (1743-1815)

Boston silversmith.

L'ORME, PHILIBERT DE

See DE L'ORME, PHILIBERT. Also spelled as one word, DELORME.

LUKENS, ISAIAH (1779-1846)

A clock-maker at Philadelphia who was not only a highly skilled craftsman, but a man of considerable scientific ability. He made the clock now on Independence Hall, and others of his clocks are in use today.

M

MANSFIELD, JOHN (1601-1674)

The earliest silversmith on record in this country, although no example of his work is known. He arrived in Boston in 1634 and it is probable that John Hull may have learned his trade from him.

MANWARING, ROBERT

A London cabinet-maker of the 18th century, who made a specialty of chairs.

His best work showed artistic treatment and there was much attention to the detail of ornament. He was one of the leading spirits of the Society of Upholsterers and Cabinet Makers, and in 1765 published *The Cabinet and Chair Maker's Real Friend and Companion*. In nearly all of his drawings there is a marked similarity to those of Chippendale. He was superior to many of the less celebrated chair-makers.

MAROT, DANIEL (1661-1720)

A French Huguenot cabinet-maker, born in Paris and a pupil of Jean Le Pautre (q.v.), whose style he closely followed. He went to Holland in 1686, thence to England when the Prince of Orange became England's King William III. His designs were founded on the school of Charles Le Brun (q.v.) and his style in England shows a blending of Dutch and French design. Although it is disputed that he ever visited England, he became the most prominent figure of his time in the development of English furniture, and he exerted the greatest influence in forming the styles of the Queen Anne period. The work at Hampton Court Palace was designed and supervised by Marot and Sir Christopher Wren, and Marot also designed most of the furniture. The majority of the rooms and grounds are still practically in the same condition as when they were inhabited by William and Mary. Marot made a great use of upholstery, which was an exceedingly important part of decoration at that period.

MARTIN

Three brothers of this name, Julian, Robert, and Simon-Étienne, began the manufacture near Paris in 1723 of a transparent varnish resembling Chinese lacquer, the secret for which one of them had discovered while working for a Dutch inventor. This varnish, which was called Vernis-Martin, was taken under national protection and became famous for its lacquer-like qualities, and was extensively used on the best furniture of the Louis XV period. After the death of Robert in 1765, the business dwindled.

MAYER, ELIJAH (? -1818)

English potter at Hanley, Staffordshire, who produced black basalt tea ware, both glazed and unglazed, cream ware equal to that of Wedgwood in body, shape and decoration. He takes a high rank among English potters.

MAYHEW AND INCE.

See INCE and MAYHEW.

McINTIRE, SAMUEL (1757-1811)

Born in Salem, Massachusetts, and lived there all his life. He was noted for his carved work, done in the style of Sir Christopher Wren and the Adam brothers. Probably the carving done by him on furniture has never been surpassed by anyone in America. He was also noted for his work on mantels, doors, cornices and other interior work.

SILVER SUGAR BOWL BY PAUL REVERE
(1738-1818)

SILVER CREAM PITCHER BY PAUL REVERE

SILVER GOBLET BY PAUL REVERE
(1738-1818)

SILVER MUG BY PAUL REVERE (1735-1818)

Courtesy of the Museum of Fine Arts, Boston

ENGLISH SILVER BARONIAL SALT, 16TH CENTURY

Courtesy of the Museum of Fine Arts,

COCOANUT EWER WITH SILVER MOUNTING,
LONDON, 1574

Courtesy of the Museum of Fine Arts, Boston

SILVER TRENCHER SALT BY JOHN CONEY (1655-1722)

ENGLISH SILVER STANDING CUP
LONDON, 1571

REFERENCES

Samuel McIntire, Carver, and the Sandersons, Early Salem Cabinet Makers, MABEL M. SWAN; *The Wood-Carver of Salem. Samuel McIntire, His Life and Work,* COUSINS and RILEY; *Early American Craftsmen,* WALTER A. DYER; *Furniture Carving by Samuel McIntire,* ANTIQUES, Vols. 18 and 19; *Furniture of Samuel McIntire,* ANTIQUARIAN, Nov. 1930.

McINTIRE, SAMUEL FIELD
Son of above, also a Salem carver.

MEAD, ABRAHAM (1742-1827)
A potter of Greenwich, Connecticut. He made salt-glazed, grey stoneware jugs, crocks, bean-pots, jars and other household utensils. During the Revolution he was a Captain, and assisted in the defense of New York. Later, he became a Deacon in the Greenwich Second Congregational Church.

MEISSONNIER, JUSTE A. (1675-1750)
French designer of furniture in the Louis XV period, whose style evidently influenced Chippendale. He was a master of "rocaille" ornament and of the use of curved lines. Meissonnier, native of Turin, pupil of the Italian Boromini, was also an architect and goldsmith.

MELVILLE, DAVID (1755-1793)
Pewterer of Newport, Rhode Island, and of good reputation as a craftsman. After his death, his son Thomas continued making pewter.

METCALF, JOSEPH (1765-1849)
A brother of Luther Metcalf and himself a good cabinet-maker of Medway, Massachusetts.

METCALF, LUTHER (1756-1838)
Cabinet-maker who began work in Medway, Massachusetts, about 1780, after service in the Revolutionary War. He pursued his trade with success and produced some excellent pieces of cabinet work which are still in use by descendants of the original owners.

MILLER, ABRAHAM (? -1858)
One of the most progressive American potters of his day. His factory was in Philadelphia, and he was probably the first potter in this country to make lustre ware, which had become so prominent in England. He was also one of the first to make porcelain, although for some reason he never produced it for the market. His factory was established about 1791 and continued in operation for many years. His staple productions were red, yellow, Rockingham, and a limited quantity of white ware, all for domestic use.

MILLS AND DEMING
New York cabinet-makers, last decade 18th century.

MINOTT, SAMUEL (1732-1803)
Boston silversmith.

MINTON, THOMAS (1765-1836)
Master English potter, employed first at Caughley, then at Stoke-on-Trent by

Spode. He started in business in 1796 and at first made only earthenware, but later made porcelain, also. After his death the works were carried on by his son and the firm is still in existence.

MONROE, NATHANIEL

See MUNROE.

MOULTON, WILLIAM (1664-1732)

Silversmith of Newbury, Massachusetts. His son Joseph (1694-1756) and five succeeding generations carried on the same line of business. They monopolized the trade in their vicinity for 120 years.

MULLIKEN, SAMUEL (1720-1756)

One of the early New England clockmakers, located at Newbury, Massachusetts, and of good reputation. He was succeeded by his son Jonathan (? -1782) and his grandson, who made clocks in Newbury until about 1807.

MUNROE, NATHANIEL

Clock-maker of Concord, Massachusetts, who worked in company with his brother Daniel from 1800 to 1808 and with Samuel Whiting from 1808 to 1817. Munroe also had an extensive brass foundry where he made bells, clock movements, etc.

MYERS, MYER (1723-1795)

New York. Most prominent early Jewish silversmith. He made the plate for the synagogue at Newport, Rhode Island, and he was president of the New York Silversmiths' Society in 1776.

N

NORTON, JOHN

A native of Goshen, Connecticut, and a captain in the Revolutionary War. He removed to Bennington, Vermont, in 1785, where in 1793 he started the manufacture of red earthenware, the first pottery in Vermont. Captain Norton retired from the pottery in 1823 and the business was continued by his sons, Luman and John, and it eventually became the United States Pottery Company, which under the management of Christopher Webber Fenton (q.v.) made the Bennington ware famous in American pottery products.

NOYES, JOHN (1674-1749)

Boston silversmith, quite prominent in the community and brother-in-law of John Edwards (q.v.).

NOYES, SAMUEL S.

Circa 1810. Cabinet-maker at East Sudbury, Massachusetts, has left several labeled pieces.

O

ONCLEBAGH, GARRETT (1663-1733)
New York silversmith.

OTIS, JONATHAN (1723-1791)
Born in Sandwich, Massachusetts.

He was a skillful silversmith and an ardent patriot. His business was located in Newport, Rhode Island, until after the Revolutionary War. He died in Middletown, Connecticut.

P

PALISSY, BERNARD (1510-1589)
Noted French potter born in Périgord. He was not only a famous potter, but he holds high position among French writers on natural philosophy, agriculture and religion. He spent sixteen long years in perfecting the enamel surface of pottery, enduring in the meantime, for himself and his family, extreme poverty and other hardships. He was in 1557 rewarded with success, and his ware, bearing in high relief plants and animals colored to represent nature, soon made him famous. It is said that he carved his faience plates as Cellini did his gold and silver work. At the same time he was an ingenious inventor of wonderful processes. He removed to Paris in 1564, and although a Huguenot, he was permitted to establish his workshop in the Tuileries and was specially exempted by Catherine de Medici from the Massacre of St. Bartholomew in 1572. In 1585, he was arrested as a Huguenot, and confined in the Bastille, where he died. Fine specimens of his work are to be seen in the Louvre and in the Musée de Cluny in Paris.

REFERENCES
Bernard Palissy, PHILIPPE BURTY;
Palissy the Potter, HENRY MORLEY.

PALLADIO, ANDREA (1518-1580)
The great Italian architect of the Renaissance. The word Palladian has been used throughout Europe as the equivalent of the beautiful and excellent in architecture.

PALMER, HUMPHREY
Staffordshire potter located at Hanley. He was the first to apply bas-relief to his black basalt vases (1769). About 1776 he took J. Neale into partnership and called the firm Neale & Company. They copied Wedgwood, Adams and Turner wares.

PARMELEE, EBENEZER
He has the distinction of having made the first town clock erected in New England at Guilford, Connecticut, in 1726. It had but one hand, struck curfew at nine o'clock, and was placed in the church tower where it remained until 1893. It is now in a museum and still going.

PEEL, SIR ROBERT (1750-1830)

Born in Lancaster, England. In 1773 he began to manufacture cotton goods, and by his enterprise and remarkable aptitude for business he amassed an enormous fortune. His eldest son, Robert, was a famous English statesman.

PENNINGTON, SETH

Perhaps the best known name among the Liverpool potters of the 18th century, mainly for his production of fine bowls, but he is also especially noted for his porcelain.

PHYFE, DUNCAN (1768-1854)

New York cabinet-maker who may, very appropriately, be called the American Sheraton. He was a Scotchman by birth and came to this country in 1784. At that time the name was spelled Fife. He began business about 1795 and was very active for about fifty years. In the years 1795 to 1825 he produced his best work. He is the only American cabinet-maker to whom may definitely be attributed any considerable number of pieces. Phyfe excelled in carved ornamentation. See PHYFE STYLE, PART 1.

REFERENCES

Early American Craftsmen, WALTER A. DYER; Furniture Masterpieces of Duncan Phyfe, CHARLES O. CORNELIUS; Phyfe Né Fife, ANTIQUES, Dec. 1929.

PIERCE, SAMUEL (1768-1840)

Pewterer at Greenfield, Massachusetts. His product is characterized primarily by fineness of metal which still retains its pristine perfection. The eagle touch-mark identifies his pewter but that with the initialed touch is rare. Tools used by him were on exhibition in 1935 at the Pewter Club in Boston.

REFERENCE

Samuel Pierce, Pewterer, ANTIQUES, Feb. 1927.

PLYMPTON, CALVIN (1775-1816)

Cabinet-maker of Medway, Massachusetts, said to have been an apprentice of Luther Metcalf (q.v.) and himself a good craftsman, whose work was well regarded.

POTWINE, JOHN (1698-1792)

Silversmith born in London, but from 1721 to 1737 at work in Boston, whence he removed to Hartford, Connecticut, where he lived for several years, conducting also a general store. In 1754 and until his death he lived in Coventry, Connecticut. His work shows beauty of proportion, careful workmanship and versatility.

REFERENCE

John Potwine, ANTIQUES, Sept. 1935.

PRATT, FELIX

Staffordshire potter, whose work resembled that of the great Italian majolicists. His work is identified by the peculiar blue tinge of the glaze, the style of modeling and the extremely fine quality of the coloring. It was largely imitated by other potters. He was active from about 1780 to 1820.

PULCIFER, FRANCIS (1771-1823)

Cabinet-maker of Salem, Massachusetts.

Q

QUARE, DANIEL (1648-1724)

London clock- and watch-maker. He was admitted to the Clockmakers' Company in 1671, a warden 1705-07, and Master 1708. In 1687 he placed the minute hand concentric with the hour hand on clocks. In 1695, he obtained a patent for a barometer. His clocks are among the finest timekeepers in the world. A clock by him at Hampton

Court goes twelve months with one winding. His reputation is second only to Thomas Tompion (q.v.).

QUINTARD, PETER (1700-1762)

Born in New York, where he learned the trade of silversmith. Removed in 1737 to South Norwalk, Connecticut, where he continued his trade until his death. A number of pieces of his well-wrought work are still in existence.

R

RANDOLPH, BENJAMIN (? -1792)

Philadelphia cabinet-maker with a shop in Chestnut Street larger than that of Savery. He was a man of great artistic ability and in design and workmanship his chairs rival those of Chippendale.

REFERENCES

Blue Book, Philadelphia Furniture, HORNOR; Benjamin Randolph, ANTIQUES, May 1927.

REMMEY, JOHN (1706-1762)

German potter who came to New York in 1735 and started a pottery, at first in partnership with William Crolius (q.v.) but afterwards alone. The product was a rather heavy stoneware sometimes decorated with cobalt-blue or with incised ornament. The pottery

was continued until about 1820 by the son and grandson of John Remmey. This last was a man active in civic affairs, and he also possessed a fine library.

REFERENCE

ANTIQUES, June 1937.

REVERE, PAUL, SENIOR (1702-1754)

A French Huguenot born in France and named Apollos Rivoire. He came to Boston in 1718 and was apprenticed to John Coney (q.v.), the silversmith. Following Coney's death he started in business for himself, anglicized his name, and married in 1729 Deborah Hichborn. Paul, Junior, was the third of twelve children.

REVERE, PAUL (1735-1818)

He was born in Boston and lived there

all of his life. Upon the death of his father in 1754 he continued in the business which was to make him the most celebrated silversmith in America. He belonged to several patriotic societies and was an active member of the Boston Tea Party in 1773. He also made a copper plate engraving of the Boston Massacre (1770). In 1775 he made the famous ride which Longfellow has immortalized, and he was otherwise active in support of the American Revolution. In 1780, Revere began again his work in silver which the war had interrupted. He later started a brass and iron foundry, made the copper bolts, spikes and pumps for the Frigate Constitution, and also engaged in making bells, but he is best remembered for the beauty and quality of his silver work, competing in both, as it did, with that of the best English silversmiths. The Museum of Fine Arts in Boston and Metropolitan Museum in New York have fine collections of Revere silver.

REFERENCES

The Life of Colonel Paul Revere, E. H. Goss; *Paul Revere and His Engraving*, WM. L. ANDREWS; *Early American Craftsmen*, WALTER A. DYER.

RICHARDSON, ELISHA (1743-1798)

Cabinet-maker of Franklin, Massachusetts, some of whose work is still preserved in that vicinity. It was all, apparently, of a distinctly utilitarian use.

RICHARDSON, FRANCIS (1681-1729)

Philadelphia silversmith born in New York. He was the first American-born silversmith to make silver in Philadelphia, and the business was carried on after his death by his son Joseph (1711-1784) and his two grandsons, Joseph, Jr. (1752-1831) and Nathaniel (1754-1827).

REFERENCE

ANTIQUARIAN, May 1930.

RICHARDSON, GEORGE (1747-1830)

Pewterer, located in Boston from 1818 to 1830, where he died. There is evidence that earlier he was at work in Cranston, Rhode Island.

RIDGWAY, JOB (1759-1814)

Staffordshire potter located at Hanley in 1794. Later he took his two sons into partnership and after the father's death the firm name was changed to J. & W. Ridgway. This firm produced the "Beauties of America" series, and their "old blue" is much sought after. Descendants of Job Ridgway continued in business in Staffordshire through the 19th century.

RITTENHOUSE, DAVID (1732-1796)

Born at Norristown, near Philadelphia, and lived to become the most distinguished of Pennsylvania clock-makers. He started in business when he was but seventeen years old, and made altogether probably not more than 75 clocks. The beauty and quality of these clocks is unsurpassed, and nearly all authentic examples are now in museums. He also made mathematical instruments, and in 1768, he made an orrery (q.v. PART 1) for the University of Pennsylvania, and another was made for Princeton College. A man of many talents, he was professor of astronomy at the Pennsylvania University, 1779-1782, president of the American Philosophical Society, 1790-1796, and in 1795 he was elected an honorary fellow of the Royal Society of London. From 1777 to 1789 he had been state treasurer of Pennsylvania. He was notable politically, socially and mechanically.

REFERENCE
David Rittenhouse, ANTIQUES, May and June 1932.

ROBBIA, LUCA DELLA (? -1482)
This talented artist, born about 1400,

is a name synonymous with Italian plastic art. Most of his subjects are in high relief, the enamel is fine in quality, beautifully white, opaque and lustrous, and the modelings of his cherubs, especially the faces, which have been left quite unglazed, are really masterpieces. Luca died in 1482 and was succeeded by two generations of artists who followed his style of work for about fifty years. Some of these later productions were so good as to be confounded with the product of the master.

ROUSE, WILLIAM (1639-1704)
Boston silversmith. Few examples of his work are known to be in existence today, but those give evidence of excellent workmanship. At his death, his estate was appraised by John Coney.

S

SADLER, JOHN (? -1789)
Noted for his discovery in 1752 at Liverpool of the transfer-printing process of decorating earthenware, although, as is usual, some authorities refuse to give him credit for the invention. However, Sadler and his partner, Guy Green, continued that form of decoration for the potters of Liverpool and elsewhere for several years. Wedgwood was one of the Staffordshire potters to send quantities of his product in the biscuit state for decorating in that manner before being fired in the home kilns.

SANDERSON, ELIJAH (1751-1825)
Cabinet-maker of Salem, Massachusetts. A good and active workman for many years. In partnership with his brother Jacob and Josiah Austin they made furniture in great variety. Some of it was sent on speculation for sale in southern states and in foreign ports. Occasionally other cabinet-makers of Salem and vicinity combined their products with those of the Sandersons. The ship captain was the salesman, and good profit sometimes resulted from these ventures.

SANDERSON, JACOB (1757-1810)

Brother of Elijah Sanderson above. Also a good craftsman. He was a selectman of Salem in 1795.

SANDERSON, ROBERT (1608-1693)

Silversmith born in England and settled in Boston about 1640. In 1652 he became a partner of John Hull (q.v.), and although Hull is given much of the credit for the silver made by the firm, Sanderson, who learned his trade in England, is entitled to his full share. The work of the firm consisted chiefly of beakers, standing cups, caudle cups and spoons. A tankard bearing only the mark of Sanderson is at the Museum of Fine Arts, Boston.

SARGEANT, JACOB (1761-1843)

Silversmith and clock-maker born in Mansfield, Connecticut. In 1788 he was doing business in Springfield, Massachusetts, and in 1796 at Hartford. At first, he made clocks with brass works, the cases for which were made for him. His later work was largely as a silversmith.

REFERENCE

Jacob Sargeant, ANTIQUES, April 1931.

SAVERY, WILLIAM (1722-1787)

Philadelphia cabinet-maker, ranked among the best of American craftsmen of the 18th century. His earlier furniture was of the simpler type, neither carved nor otherwise embellished, but his later work was fashioned in the style of Chippendale and of a surprising degree of excellence. Some of it may well be rated with that of Chippendale himself.

REFERENCES

Blue Book, Philadelphia Furniture, HORNOR; ANTIQUARIAN, July 1930.

SEYMOUR, JOHN

Cabinet-maker of Boston active 1790 to 1810. Examples existing of his Sheraton-type work place him high in rank among the craftsmen of the period. Often used light-blue paint for interior of secretaries.

SHAW, GEORGE (1750-1792)

Philadelphia cabinet-maker, whose business was continued by his son Alexander (? -1828). Two bureaus with labels of his son are on record.

SHEARER, THOMAS

English cabinet-maker whose work had many points of strong similarity to that of Hepplewhite and Sheraton. Neither surpassed him in the combination of daintiness and simplicity. Shearer in one respect, however, stands clearly forth as the leader whom both followed. He was the one who began the development that resulted in the graceful sideboard with which the names of his two contemporaries became so prominently identified, and his sideboards compare favorably with any of those produced later by either Hepplewhite or Sheraton. Shearer made many different pieces of furniture, but he designed no chairs. His *Designs for Household Furniture* appeared in 1788, three years before Sheraton published his *Drawing Book*. He worked chiefly in mahogany and satinwood.

REFERENCE

English Furniture of the 18th Century, CLOUSTON.

SHERATON, THOMAS (1751-1806)

English cabinet-maker born at Stockton-on-Tees, where he remained until he went to London in 1790. Probably most of the furniture accredited to him was produced before his removal to London. His furniture was exquisite in shape, form, color and decoration. He delighted in inlays of rare woods and costly veneers; he used satinwood extensively and he was the champion and exponent of the straight line in furniture-making. His originality is chiefly evident in his chair designs. Sheraton published his *Cabinet-Maker and Upholsterer's Drawing Book* first in 1791, and again in 1793 and in 1802. During the last decade of the 18th century and the earlier years of the 19th, Sheraton's influence dominated the style of English and, of course, of American furniture of the best type. Sheraton was also a drawing master and a zealous Baptist. He preached in chapels of that sect and issued various religious publications, but financially he was a failure. During his later years, owing to his various ac-

tivities, perhaps, the high standard of his designs declined.

REFERENCE

Thos. Sheraton, ANTIQUES, Vol. 1, p. 25.

SKILLIN BROS. (JOHN and SIMEON)

Boston. Prominent wood carvers last part of 18th century. Carved the capitals on the Bulfinch front of the State House.

SKINNER, JOHN (1763-1813)

Pewterer at Boston.

SOLON, MARC LOUIS (1835-1913)

Noted ceramic artist and author. Worked at the Sèvres factory from 1862 to 1870. He then went to Minton's pottery at Stoke-on-Trent where he remained until 1904. He perfected the pâte-sur-pâte (q.v. PART 2) method of decoration to be seen on Minton ware. Solon was a talented designer and draughtsman, and he was the author of several books on pottery.

SOUMAINE, SAMUEL

Philadelphia silversmith of the middle 18th century.

SOUMAINE, SIMEON (1658-1750)

New York silversmith and maker of many fine pieces.

SOWER, CHRISTOPHER (1693- ?)

Pennsylvania clock-maker from 1734 to 1750. He was born in Germany and came to Philadelphia in 1724. A very gifted man, an author, printer, paper-maker, doctor and farmer, besides becoming a clock-maker. On his clocks he spelled his name Souers, but in his more learned callings it was Sower. He was proficient in each of his various trades and he was the first to print and publish the Scriptures in this country.

SPODE, JOSIAH (1733-1797)

The first of the three English potters of the same name is best known for his skill in under-glaze cream ware. After serving as an apprentice to Thomas Whieldon (q.v.) he began as a potter on Stoke-on-Trent, Staffordshire. He was a great copyist and made black basalt, jasper and stoneware, printed and enameled wares. He had a leaning toward Oriental subjects in his blue-printed ware and was the first to use the "willow pattern" on earthenware.

REFERENCE

Spode, FINE ARTS, March 1932.

SPODE, JOSIAH JR. (1754-1827)

The younger Spode introduced color on earthenware and on porcelain such as never before had been attempted on Staffordshire products. About 1800 he discovered that bone-ash, added to the porcelain ingredients, produced a body resembling true porcelain and his formula has since been used by all English porcelain factories. He also produced in 1805 a superior quality of earthenware with a white, dense body, closely approximating porcelain, which he called "stone china." In his decorations of porcelain Spode copied the styles of Dresden, Chelsea, Nantgarw, Swansea and other factories, but honestly used his own mark.

SPODE, JOSIAH 3rd (? -1833)

Succeeded Josiah, Junior, as head of the Spode factory in 1827. Associated with him in the management was William T. Copeland, the son of the William Copeland who was a partner of Josiah Spode, Junior, and at the death of Josiah, 3rd, control of the factory passed to William T. Copeland. He took as a partner Thomas Garrett and the business was conducted under that partnership name until 1847, after which it became "Copeland late Spode," for twenty years, and since, "W. T. Copeland and Sons."

SPRIMONT, NICHOLAS (1716-1771)

A silversmith of London whose name was entered at Goldsmiths' Hall in 1742. He was also actively identified with the Chelsea porcelain factory from about 1750 as a designer or modeler. Afterwards he became owner of the works until, owing to ill health, he sold the factory in 1769.

STEVENSON, ANDREW

Staffordshire potter of Cobridge. But little is known of his history. His best work was done for the American market and is confined principally to views of New York City and environs. The borders of his ware are decorated with flower wreaths and scrolls. In 1819, he sold his works to James Clews (q.v.) although there is evidence that he continued work as a potter for some years after that.

STEVENSON, RALPH

Another potter at Cobridge, Staffordshire, whose early history has been completely lost, but about twenty of his designs have been identified and these are highly prized by collectors. Much of his work was done for the American market, decorated with views of New York and Boston and identified by the oak leaf, also vine leaf, and acorn border.

REFERENCE

Old China Book, N. HUDSON MOORE.

STIEGEL, HENRY WILLIAM (1729-1785)

Called "Baron" Stiegel, largely at his own desire. Born (Heinrich Wilhelm) in Cologne, Germany, and came to Philadelphia in 1750 with his mother, a widow. He married in 1752, his first wife, Elizabeth Huber, the daughter of an iron manufacturer, and for a number of years was engaged in that business. In 1763 he started a glass-works for making window and bottle glass at Elizabeth Furnace, the site of the iron-works, but this factory was discontinued in 1765 when the new works started operation, a plant ten miles north which he had built and named Manheim. Stiegel brought skilled workmen from England and Germany and possibly from Italy. At first, this factory was also devoted chiefly to making bottles and window glass. In 1769 the plant was in full operation and his output, which was of superior quality, found a ready market in Philadelphia and in towns as far removed as New York and Boston. Stiegel glass was noted for its delicacy, its wonderful jewel-like colors and the beautiful designs. It was probably the most beautiful glass ever blown in the American colonies. He was the first American maker to attempt enameling on glass. Stiegel glass has been imitated by glass-makers ever since, and few collectors will now attribute any glass to Stiegel unless it is well authenticated. Owing to financial irregularities, which came to a head in 1774, his business was ruined and Stiegel died a poor man in 1785, perhaps largely due to his extravagant habits during the days of his prosperity. How he obtained the complimentary title of "Baron" is no mystery, as it was self-bestowed, but it was suited to the feudal luxury in which he lived before his failure. Noteworthy collections of Stiegel glass are to be seen at the Metropolitan Museum in New York and the Pennsylvania Museum in Philadelphia.

REFERENCES

Stiegel Glass, FREDERICK W. HUNTER; *Early American Craftsmen*, DYER; *A Portrait of Iron; Stiegel*, ANTIQUARIAN, June 1930.

SYNG, PHILIP (1703-1789)

The second of the name. His father

Philip (1676-1739), born in Cork, Ireland, came to Philadelphia in 1714 where he engaged in business as a silversmith. The son continued the business and by his energy and marked ability he took the lead of the silversmiths of that town. He was cultured, well-to-do and a personal friend of Benjamin Franklin. Syng made the inkstand on the Speaker's desk in the State House at Philadelphia where the Continental Congress met, and into this inkstand John Hancock dipped his pen before making his immortal signature on the Declaration of Independence, the other members following suit. George Washington also used the same inkstand in signing the adopted copy of the Constitution in the same hall in 1787.

T

TABER, ELNATHAN (1784-1854)

Native of New Bedford, Massachusetts, of Quaker parentage. He went to Roxbury and served as an apprentice to Simon Willard, afterwards engaging in clock-making on his own account. When Willard retired in 1839, Taber bought most of his tools and the goodwill of the business. His clocks equal in quality those of Willard.

TAYLOR, JOHN N. (1842- ?)

President of Knowles, Taylor and Knowles Co., of East Liverpool, Ohio, one of the largest producers of earthenware and tableware of the 19th century.

TERRY, ELI (1772-1852)

A leading American clock-maker of Plymouth, Connecticut. His first clock was a long-case with wooden works made by hand, as were all of his early clocks, in 1792, and it is still in good running order. In 1793 he began to manufacture clocks for sale, and 1797 was granted a patent for an improvement in clocks. He specialized on thirty-hour clocks of the shelf type with wooden works, for a number of years. In 1809 he formed a partnership with Seth Thomas and Silas Hoadley, which association lasted but one year. Many later prominent Connecticut clock-makers were apprentices of Terry at one time or another, before engaging in business on their own account. Mr. Terry seems to have occupied the same position with regard to Connecticut clock-makers that Wedgwood did to Staffordshire potters. He originated, they copied. His younger brother Samuel and his son Eli, Junior, were also clock-makers.

REFERENCE
Early American Craftsmen, WALTER A. DYER.

THOMAS, SETH (1785-1859)

Connecticut clock-maker, associated first with Eli Terry and Silas Hoadley. In 1812, he began business on his own account and acquired a fortune. He was not only a good mechanic but a clever business man as well. His early clocks had wood works and were of the shelf type, then very popular. In 1853 he organized the Seth Thomas Clock Company and the works are still in operation. After his death in 1859 the town of Plymouth was divided and that portion where the works was situated was named Thomaston in his honor.

TOFT, RALPH

A potter, brother of Thomas Toft. Specimens of his work dated 1676 and 1677 are in the British Museum.

TOFT, THOMAS

A pioneer Staffordshire potter of whom it may well be said that he has earned a foremost place in the history of British ceramics. Although but little is known of him personally, he is thought to have begun production about 1660. Between twenty-five and thirty dishes of his product are in various museums and collections. One is dated 1671. All are slip-decorated and are signed with his name.

TOMPION, THOMAS (1638-1713)

The "father of English clock-makers." He was born in Bedfordshire, a Quaker, and was admitted to the Clockmakers' Company in London in 1671. During his lifetime the English domestic clock developed from the "bird-cage" type into the tall-case clock, and for much of this development Tompion was respon-

sible. He invented the cylinder escapement, with horizontal wheel, improvements in striking clocks and the balance springs for watches. After his death his business was carried on by George Graham (q.v.), an associate for several years. Tompion was buried in Westminster Abbey.

TOPPAN, ABNER (1764-1836)

A Newburyport cabinet-maker, examples of whose furniture are now to be seen in the homes of families in that locality. He was a craftsman of good ability and prominent in local woodworking circles.

REFERENCE
ANTIQUES, June 1929.

TOWNSEND, JOB (1700-1765)

A cabinet-maker at Newport, Rhode Island. It is claimed by some authorities that he may have been the originator of the block-front design, usually credited to John Goddard.

REFERENCE
ANTIQUES, June 1937.

TOWNSEND, JOHN (1733-1809)

A cabinet-maker at Newport, Rhode Island, son of Christopher Townsend, and cousin of John Goddard. He made block-front furniture and is noted for some fine work in the Hepplewhite style.

REFERENCES
Metropolitan Museum Studies, 1928,

Part 1, p. 72; ANTIQUES, June 1937.

TRACY, EBENEZER (1744-1803)

Chair-maker of Norwich, Connecticut. He made a specialty of Windsor chairs, and there are many examples of these chairs with his brand E B TRACY burned in the bottom of the seat, surviving to the present time.

REFERENCE

ANTIQUES, Dec. 1936.

TRASK, ISRAEL (1786-1867)

Pewterer of Beverly, Massachusetts. He was active from about 1812 to 1842 and made whale-oil lamps, tea-pots, tankards and casters. Trask was one of the few pewter workers in this country who used chiseled decoration on his pieces. Israel's brother, Oliver (1792-1877), was also a pewterer of note.

REFERENCE

Israel Trask, ANTIQUES, Jan. 1924.

TRYON, ISAAC (1741-1823)

Cabinet-maker of Glastonbury, Connecticut, of good repute.

TUCKER, WILLIAM ELLIS (1800-1832)

The maker of the first American porcelain worthy of note. He began about 1825 in Philadelphia and his business grew rapidly. A great variety of domestic and ornamental wares, some of it an excellent copy of Sèvres ware, were made. After his death his partner, Joseph Hemphill, organized the American China Manufactory (q.v. PART 2).

REFERENCE

Footnote to Tucker History, ANTIQUES, Oct. 1936.

TUFFT, THOMAS (? -1793)

A Philadelphia cabinet-maker. His known work compares favorably with that of Gostelowe and Savery, both of Philadelphia.

REFERENCES

Blue Book, Philadelphia Furniture, HORNOR; *Thomas Tufft*, ANTIQUES, Oct. 1927 and March 1928.

TURNER, JOHN (1739-1786)

Master potter of Lane End, Staffordshire, contemporary with Wedgwood and associated with him in the working of some Cornwall clay pits. Turner started business in 1762, and in the production of unglazed stoneware he surpassed anything his contemporaries had done. He made jasper ware resembling porcelain, basalt and stoneware of cane color. His two sons, John, Jr., and William, succeeded to the business and carried it on until 1803.

TURNER, THOMAS (1749-1809)

English potter, employed in his early years at the Worcester porcelain factory where he became a skillful draughtsman and designer under Robert Hancock (q.v.) of that factory. In 1772 he went to Caughley and started there the manufacture of porcelain similar to the Worcester product, in which he was very successful. Turner introduced the famous under-glaze "willow pattern" decoration, and this blue and white table-ware became very popular. The Caughley factory was sold to Coalport in 1799.

V

VANDERBURGH, CORNELIUS (1652-1699)

Silversmith of New York. He ranked well among the craftsmen of the period and several examples of his work are in existence today. Together with Jacob Boelen (q.v.) he was appointed in 1695 as an officer to regulate weights and measures in New York.

VAN DYCK, PETER (1684-1750)

Silversmith of New York of Dutch descent. He was a craftsman of artistic gifts, surpassing in that respect most of his contemporaries. His son Richard continued the business after his father's death.

REFERENCE

ANTIQUES, May and June 1937.

VERNON, SAMUEL (1683-1737)

A famous silversmith of Newport, Rhode Island, who was also prominent in civic affairs. He produced a large quantity of silverware of superior quality. Vernon was highly esteemed in the community.

VOYEZ, JOHN

A French modeler employed in 1768 by Wedgwood, afterwards by H. Palmer. His work was of the classical order and his designs are to be found in the relief medallions of that period. His later work, among which are copies of Wedgwood models, is marked Voyez. The best known of his productions is the "Fair Hebe" jug made in 1788. Voyez was no doubt responsible, also, for many of the satyr-mask cups and jugs of that period.

W

WALL, DR. JOHN (1708-1776)

One of the founders of the Worcester Porcelain Works in 1751, and his name is closely identified with the first and by far the most important period of the history of that factory.

WALL, WILLIAM GUY (1792-1864?)

Born in Dublin, Ireland, and came to New York in 1818. He was a gifted artist and made many drawings of landscapes which were afterwards adopted by Staffordshire potters, notably Stevenson and Clews, as representative American scenes, for use on plates and other ware.

REFERENCE

William Guy Wall, ANTIQUES, July 1923.

WARE, MASKELL (1776-1855)

Maker of the Ware slat-back chairs, which business was continued by his sons.

WAYNE, WILLIAM (1730- ?)

One of a family of cabinet-makers of Wilmington, Delaware. He was a talented maker of highboys, secretaries, bureaus, etc. in the Chippendale style. Jacob Wayne (1760- ?) was an interpreter of the Hepplewhite and Sheraton styles.

WEDGWOOD FAMILY

There were numerous early Wedgwood potters before the time of Josiah, the most famous of the family. Gilbert Wedgwood was working in Burslem early in the 17th century. A puzzle jug made by John Wedgwood, great uncle of Josiah, is dated 1691. Thomas Wedgwood who died in 1671, son of Gilbert, and Doctor Thomas, his son, died 1739, were also potters. In 1740 Thomas and John, sons of Aaron, were potters at Burslem. Thomas was Josiah's father.

WEDGWOOD, JOSIAH (1730-1795)

He disputes with Palissy the title of "the world's greatest potter." "In a word, no other potter of modern times has so successfully welded into one harmonious whole, the prose and the poetry of ceramic art." He began business in 1749 with a capital of twenty pounds; in 1754 he formed a partnership with Thomas Whieldon, which continued for five years, and in 1759 began his career

alone at Burslem. In 1769 he established the village and works at Etruria, where he became wealthy and famous. With the patient industry of a practical potter, he had the foresight which enabled him to build up an important business which is still carried on by his descendants. During these years he was making white and cream (Queen's) ware, black basalt, red (rosso-antico) ware and jasper ware. In perfection and fineness, this last led them all. Although Wedgwood was constantly contriving new and improved methods, he patented but one, that of painting in encaustic colors. As a consequence of this practice, his product was copied by nearly all other potters. See WEDGWOOD WARE PART 2.

REFERENCES

Life of Josiah Wedgwood, METEYARD; *The Wedgwoods: Being a Life of Josiah Wedgwood*, JEWITT; *Josiah Wedgwood, Master-Potter*, CHURCH; *Josiah Wedgwood, Industrialist*, ANTIQUES, Aug. 1934.

WEDGWOOD, DR. THOMAS (? -1739)

Related to Josiah Wedgwood, himself a distinguished potter. He was the principal potter in Burslem, making salt-glaze and other wares. In 1731, Aaron Wood was one of his apprentices.

WHIELDON, THOMAS (? -1798)

One of the most distinguished of Staffordshire potters. He improved the older processes and wrought with them

ENGLISH SILVER KETTLE ON STAND AND TEAPOT, GEORGIAN PERIOD, 18TH CENTURY

ENGLISH SILVER FLUTED TUREEN AND COVER, LONDON, 1807

new kinds of ware. His solid agate-ware, his tortoise-shell and clouded wares have won him fame from both a technical and artistic standpoint. He began business as early as 1740 at Little Fenton. Josiah Spode was one of his apprentices. Josiah Wedgwood was a partner from 1754 to 1759. He was a man of mild and unassuming manners, but he left a permanent impression on the Staffordshire industry. The date of his birth is not known but he was a very aged man at the time of his death.

WHITELOCK, GEORGE (1780-1833)
Cabinet-maker of Wilmington, Delaware. Labeled pieces of his work indicate that he was a skillful craftsman.

REFERENCE
ANTIQUARIAN, Jan. 1930.

WHITNEY, ELI (1765-1825)
Famous for his invention of the cotton gin in 1794. He was born at Westboro, Massachusetts, and educated at Yale College. While on a plantation in Georgia, he invented his machine for separating the cotton seed from the fiber, which proved to be one of the most important inventions connected with the manufacture of cotton cloth. See COTTON GIN, PART 4.

WILDER, JOSHUA
Hingham, Massachusetts, most prolific maker of extant Grandmother's clocks.

WILL, HENRY
Pewterer of New York after the Revolution. His work is very rare and of a high order of merit.

WILL, JOHN
Pewterer of New York, active from 1751 to 1763.

WILL, WILLIAM (1742-1798)
Pewterer of Philadelphia. He made plates, basins, mugs, tea-pots, and spoons. Specimens of his work are very rare.

WILLARD, AARON (1757-1844)
Clock-maker and brother of Benjamin, Jr., and Simon, both clock-makers. His shop was located in Roxbury, near that of his brother Simon, and although his clocks do not rank as high in quality as those of his famous brother, next to Simon, Aaron was the most noted of the Willard family of clock-makers and in a business way he was the most successful. He retired from business in 1823.

WILLARD, AARON JR. (1783-1863)
Son of the foregoing. In 1823, he took over his father's business and continued it until 1850, when he retired. He originated the so-called "lyre clock."

WILLARD, ALEXANDER T. (1774-   )
Clock-maker, Ashby, Massachusetts, and a distant cousin of Simon Willard. He made tall clocks, chiefly with wooden works. The cases were usually of pine, sometimes of cherry, and many of

these clocks are still useful in recording the passage of time. His brother, Philander, was associated with him for a number of years. Philander made a curious gravity clock still in existence.

WILLARD, BENJAMIN JR. (1740-1803)

Clock-maker born at Grafton, Massachusetts, elder brother of Simon and Aaron and the first of the family to take up clock-making. Clocks made by him are marked Grafton (1764), Lexington (1768), or Roxbury (1771). So far as is known he made tall-case clocks only. He died in Baltimore.

WILLARD, SIMON (1753-1848)

Born in Grafton, Massachusetts, and the greatest clock-maker of this distinguished family. Just when he began to make clocks is not known, but he removed to Roxbury about 1788, and from that time his name led all the rest in the field of clock-making. His tall clocks were made between 1780 and 1802, and the so-called "banjo" clock was patented in 1801. It is said that he made more than five thousand clocks in his lifetime. The cases were usually made by Henry Willard of Roxbury or Charles Crehore of Dorchester, and the dials by Charles Bullard. The dials on Willard clocks were of wood or of iron painted with several coats, each rubbed down until the surface was like enamel. Willard was proud and sensitive, honest and diligent, but a poor business man. Although his improved timepiece (the banjo clock) was patented, he never protected himself against infringements, and it was not long before every clockmaker was making and selling it. Simon Willard sold his business in 1839 to Elnathan Taber (q.v.) and retired. At the time of his death he left less than five hundred dollars.

REFERENCES

Early American Craftsmen, WALTER A. DYER; *A History of Simon Willard, Inventor and Clockmaker*, JOHN W. WILLARD; *Clocks of Simon Willard*, ANTIQUES, Feb. 1922.

WILLARD, SIMON JR. (1795-1874)

He began to make clocks with his father and in 1828 he located at 9 Congress Street, Boston, where he remained until 1870. His astronomical regulator was standard time for all railroads in New England. His specialty was watches and chronometers, and although his name appears on the dials of some clocks, he never made them.

WILSON, ROBERT (? -1802)

English potter, associated at first with Humphrey Palmer. He introduced chalk into the body of cream ware, which served to whiten it. He made a copy of Wedgwood's copy of the famous Portland Vase with a gray body and cream-colored figures.

WINSLOW, EDWARD (1699-1753)

One of the greatest New England silversmiths and a member of a distinguished Colonial family. His work rivals that of Paul Revere, and his activities, aside from his craft, included many civic duties, military and judicial.

WINSLOW, KENELM (1599-1672)

Joiner in the Plymouth Colony, who came on the Mayflower, and one of the earliest names of furniture-workers in America.

WISTAR, CASPAR (1695-1752)

Wistar was born in Germany and came to this country in 1717. He started the first successful glass-making factory in America in 1739 in New Jersey, with the help of some skillful glass-makers from Europe. The settlement and the glass itself became known as Wistarberg (q.v. PART 3). After his death, his son Richard carried on the business for a while, then turned it over to a manager under whom it was continued until 1780, when the works were closed. The glass made there is among the rarest of American glass.

WOOD, AARON (1718-1785)

Staffordshire potter, brother of the elder Ralph Wood. Aaron Wood was one of the first to use cobalt blue on stoneware and he was noted as a block-cutter. This branch of the Wood family continued in the pottery business until well into the 19th century. One authority considers the Wood family to have been the most remarkable family in the history of English pottery.

WOOD, ENOCH (1759-1840)

Son of Aaron Wood, and began business for himself in 1784. He took James Caldwell as a partner in 1790, which continued until 1818, at which time his three sons became partners, under the name of Enoch Wood and Sons, which continued until the time of his death, and thereafter until 1846. Enoch Wood was one of the leading potters of his period, and as a modeler he ranks nearly equal to Ralph Wood in the making of Staffordshire figures. The bulk of his work was made for and sent to America. His favorite border was a sea-shell pattern.

REFERENCE

The Wood Family of Burslem, FRANK FALKNER.

WOOD, RALPH (1716-1772)

English potter noted for his Staffordshire figures; all known marked examples are in the under-glaze method. He produced the Toby Philpot (Fillpot) jug now in the British Museum, also the well-known "Vicar and Moses." The former was probably the original of a type that was afterwards imitated by all potters. Ralph Wood's work represents the highest point of achievement in Staffordshire figures.

WOOD, RALPH JR. (1748-1795)

He and his father were the first of the Staffordshire potters to impress their names on figure subjects. The son also adopted the practice of numbering his pieces. He was not as distinguished a figure designer as his father.

WREN, SIR CHRISTOPHER (1632-1723)

England's greatest architect, whose work marks in many respects the climax of classic style development in England. His indirect influence on interior decoration and furniture design and on the elevation of the popular taste in general can scarcely be overestimated. Together with Daniel Marot he designed and supervised the work at Hampton Court Palace. The great fire of London in 1666 gave him a great opportunity for the exercise of his genius, and from that time for forty years there was hardly an important building in or near London planned without his aid. St. Paul's Cathedral is his masterpiece, and he lies buried in its crypt.

PART VII

BIBLIOGRAPHY

BIBLIOGRAPHY

Part I

FURNITURE

AMERICAN

History of the American Clock Business for the Past 60 Years and Life of Chauncey Jerome Written by Himself, CHAUNCEY JEROME. F. C. Dayton, Jr., New Haven, Conn. (1860).

American Furniture and Decoration, Colonial and Federal, EDWARD S. HOLLOWAY. J. B. Lippincott Co., Philadelphia (1928).

Blue Book, Philadelphia Furniture, William Penn to George Washington, with Special Reference to the Philadelphia Chippendale-School, W. M. HORNOR, JR. Published by the author (1935).

Colonial Furniture in America (2 vols., 3rd ed.), LUKE V. LOCKWOOD. Charles Scribner's Sons, New York (1926).

Colonial Furniture of New England (new edition), DR. IRVING W. LYON. Houghton Mifflin Co., Boston (1924).

Connecticut Clockmakers of the 18th Century, PENROSE R. HOOPES. Edward Valentine Mitchell, Hartford, Conn. (1930).

Early American Craftsmen, WALTER A. DYER. The Century Co., New York (1915).

Early American Furniture, CHARLES OVER CORNELIUS. The Century Co., New York (1926).

Early American Furniture Makers, THOMAS H. ORMSBEE. Thomas Y. Crowell Co., New York (1935).

Furniture Masterpieces of Duncan Phyfe, CHARLES OVER CORNELIUS. Doubleday, Page & Co., New York (1922).

Furniture of Our Forefathers, The (2 vols.), ESTHER SINGLETON. Doubleday, Page & Co., New York (1919).

Furniture of the Pilgrim Century, WALLACE NUTTING. Old America Co., Framingham, Mass. (1924).

Furniture Treasury (Mostly of American Origin), (3 vols.), WALLACE NUTTING. Old America Co., Framingham, Mass. (1928-33).

Hadley Chest, The, CLAIR FRANKLIN LUTHER. Case, Lockwood & Brainard Co., Hartford, Conn. (1936).

Knowing, Collecting and Restoring Early American Furniture, HENRY H. TAYLOR. J. B. Lippincott Co., Philadelphia (1930).

Manual of the Furniture Arts & Crafts, A. JOHNSON & M. SIRONEN. A. P. Johnson Co. (1928).

Pine Furniture of Early New England, The, RUSSELL H. KETTELL. Doubleday, Doran & Co., New York (1929).

Practical Book of American Antiques, H. EBERLEIN and A. McCLURE. J. B.

Lippincott Co., Philadelphia (1928).

Quest of the Colonial, The, R. and E. SHACKLETON. The Century Co., New York (1907).

Shaker Furniture, E. D. and F. ANDREWS. The Macmillan Co., New York (1937).

Southern Antiques, PAUL H. BURROUGHS. Garrett & Massie, Inc., Richmond, Va. (1931).

Story of American Furniture, The, THOMAS H. ORMSBEE. The Macmillan Co., New York (1935).

A Windsor Handbook (American Windsors), WALLACE NUTTING. Published by the author (1917).

ENGLISH

Chippendale and His School, J. BLAKE and A. REVEIRS-HOPKINS. Frederick A. Stokes Co., New York (1913).

Chippendale Period in English Furniture, K. W. CLOUSTON. Edward Arnold, New York and London (1897).

Chippendale, Sheraton and Hepplewhite Furniture Designs, J. MUNRO BELL. Gibbings & Co., Ltd., London (1900).

Dictionary of English Furniture from the Middle Ages to the Late Georgian Period (3 vols.), P. MACQUOID AND R. EDWARDS. Charles Scribner's Sons, New York (1924-27).

Encyclopaedia of English Furniture, An, OLIVER BRACKETT. Ernest Benn, Ltd., London (1927).

English Domestic Clocks, H. CESCINSKY and M. WEBSTER. Geo. Routledge & Sons, Ltd., London (1913).

English Furniture, JOHN GLOAG. A. & C. Black, Ltd., London (1934).

English Furniture and Furniture Makers of the 18th Century, R. S. CLOUSTON. Clouston, Hurst & Blackett, London (1906).

English Furniture from Charles II to George II, R. W. SYMONDS. The Connoisseur, Ltd., London (1929).

English Furniture from Gothic to Sheraton, HERBERT CESCINSKY. Dean-Hicks Co., Grand Rapids, Mich. (1929).

English Furniture, Its Essentials and Characteristics Simply and Clearly Explained for the Student and Small Collector, JOHN C. ROGERS. Country Life, Ltd., London (1923).

English Furniture of the Cabriole Period, H. A. TIPPING. Cape, London (1922).

English Furniture of the 18th Century (3 vols.), HERBERT CESCINSKY. George Routledge & Sons, Ltd., London.

History of English Furniture (4 vols.), Age of Oak, Age of Walnut, Age of Mahogany, Age of Satinwood, PERCY MACQUOID. Lawrence & Bullen, London (1904-08).

Measured Drawings of Old Oak Furniture, J. W. HURRELL. B. T. Batsford, London (1902).

Old English Furniture of the 15th, 16th, 17th and 18th Centuries, G. OWEN WHEELER. Bazaar House, London (1924).

Old English Walnut and Lacquer Furniture, R. W. SYMONDS. Herbert Jenkins, Ltd., London (1923).

Period of Queen Anne, The, J. BLAKE and A. REVEIRS-HOPKINS. Frederick A. Stokes Co., New York (1911).

Present State of Old English Furniture, The, R. W. SYMONDS. Frederick A. Stokes Co., New York (1921).

Sheraton Period, (Designers from 1760 to 1820), J. BLAKE & A. REVEIRS-HOPKINS. Frederick A. Stokes Co., New York.

Tudor to Stuart, J. BLAKE & A. REVEIRS-HOPKINS. Frederick A. Stokes Co., New York (1911).

GENERAL

About Antiques, ELLA SHANNON BOWLES. J. B. Lippincott Co., Philadelphia (1929).

Antique Furniture, FRED W. BURGESS. G. P. Putnam's Sons, New York (1919).

Antiques, SARAH M. LOCKWOOD. Doubleday, Page & Co., New York (1925).

Antiques, Genuine and Spurious, FREDERICK LITCHFIELD. G. Bell & Sons, London (1924).

Antiques; Their Restoration and Preservation, ALFRED LUCAS. Arnold & Co., London (1924).

Manual of Buhl-Work and Marquetry, with Instructions, W. BEMROSE. Bemrose & Sons, London (1872).

Candle Days, MARION N. RAWSON. The Century Co., New York (1927).

Chats on Old Clocks, ARTHUR HAYDEN. T. Fisher Unwin, London (1918).

Chats on Old Furniture, ARTHUR HAYDEN. T. Fisher Unwin, London (1905).

Clock Book, Being a Description of Foreign and American Clocks, The, WALLACE NUTTING. The Old America Co., Framingham, Mass. (1924).

Collecting Antiques, WILLIAM G. MENZIES. Dodd, Mead & Co., New York (1928).

Collecting as a Pastime, CHARLES ROWED. Cassell & Co., London and New York (1920).

Collector's Manual, The, N. HUDSON MOORE. Frederick A. Stokes Co., New York (1906).

Decorative Styles and Periods in the Home, HELEN C. CANDEE. Frederick A. Stokes Co., New York (1906).

Domestic Utensils of Wood, 16th to 19th Century, OWEN EVAN-THOMAS. Published by the author, London (1932).

Dutch and Flemish Furniture, ESTHER SINGLETON. Hodder and Stoughton, Ltd., London (1907).

English and American Furniture, H. CESCINSKY AND G. HUNTER. Dean-Hicks Co., Grand Rapids, Mich. (1929).

First Steps in Collecting, GRACE M. VALLOIS. J. B. Lippincott Co., Philadelphia (1926).

French and English Furniture, ESTHER SINGLETON. McClure, Phillips & Co., New York (1903).

French Furniture, ANDRÉ SAGLIO. Charles Scribner's Sons, New York (1913).

Furniture, ESTHER SINGLETON. Duffield & Co., New York (1911).

Furniture Collector, The, EDWARD W. GREGORY. David McKay Co., Philadelphia (1923).

Furniture of the Olden Time, FRANCES CLARY MORSE. Macmillan Co., New York (1920).

Genuine Antique Furniture, ARTHUR DE BLES. Thomas Y. Crowell Co., New York (1929).

Handwrought Ancestors, MARION N. RAWSON. E. P. Dutton & Co., New York (1936).

Historic Wall-Papers, NANCY McCLELLAND. J. B. Lippincott Co., Philadelphia (1924).

How to Collect Old Furniture, FREDERICK LITCHFIELD. G. Bell & Sons, London (1904).

Illustrated History of Furniture, FREDERICK LITCHFIELD. Medici Society of America, Boston (1922).

Italian Furniture and Interiors, GEORGE LELAND HUNTER. Wm. Helburn, Inc., New York (1918).

Lure of the Antique, The, WALTER A. DYER. The Century Co., New York (1919).

Old Clock Book, N. HUDSON MOORE. Frederick A. Stokes Co., New York (1911).

Old Clocks and Watches and Their Makers (6th edition), FREDERICK J. BRITTEN. E. & F. N. Spon, Ltd., London (1904).

Old Furniture Book, with a Sketch of Past Days and Ways, N. HUDSON MOORE. Frederick A. Stokes Co., New York (1903).

Period Furniture Handbook, G. G. and F. GOULD. Dodd, Mead & Co., New York (1928).

Pleasures of Collecting, The, GARDNER TEALL. The Century Co., New York (1920).

Practical Book of Period Furniture, The, H. EBERLEIN AND A. McCLURE. J. B. Lippincott Co., Philadelphia (1914).

Practical Book of Italian, Spanish and Portuguese Furniture, H. EBERLEIN and R. RAMSDELL. J. B. Lippincott Co., Philadelphia (1927).

Wallpaper, Its History, Design and Use, PHYLLIS ACKERMAN. Frederick A. Stokes Co., New York (1923).

Part II

POTTERY AND PORCELAIN

AMERICAN AND ENGLISH

A B C of Collecting Old English China, The, J. F. BLACKER. Stanley Paul & Co., Ltd., London, 1930.

A B C of Collecting Old English Pottery, The, J. F. BLACKER. Stanley Paul & Co., Ltd., London (1930).

A B C of English Salt-Glaze Stoneware from

Dwight to Doulton, J. F. BLACKER. Stanley Paul & Co., Ltd., London (1930).

A B C of 19th Century English Ceramic Art, J. F. BLACKER. Stanley Paul & Co., Ltd., London (1930).

Anglo-American Pottery, EDWIN A. BARBER. Press of The Clayworker, Indianapolis, Ind. (1899).

Art of the Old English Potter, The, M. L. SOLON, New York (1886).

Artificial Soft Paste Porcelain, EDWIN A. BARBER. Penn. Museum, Philadelphia (1907).

Battersea Enamels, EGAN MEW. Medici Society, Ltd., London (1926).

Blue-China Book, The, ADA W. CAMEHL. E. P. Dutton & Co., New York (1916).

Bow, Chelsea and Derby Porcelain, WILLIAM BEMROSE. Bemrose & Sons, London (1898).

Bow Porcelain, FRANK HURLBUTT. G. Bell & Sons, Ltd., London (1926).

Bric-à-Brac Collector, The, H. LEWER and M. PERCIVAL. Dodd, Mead & Co., Inc., New York (1923).

Brief History of Old English Porcelain and Its Manufactories, A, M. L. SOLON. Bemrose & Sons, London (1903).

Bristol Porcelain, FRANK HURLBUTT. Medici Society, Ltd., London (1925).

Century of Potting in the City of Worcester, A, R. W. BINNS. Quaritch, London (1877).

Ceramic Art of Great Britain from Prehistoric Times to the Present Day, The, L. JEWITT. Charles Scribner's Sons, New York (1883).

Ceramics of Swansea and Nantgarw, The, WILLIAM TURNER. Bemrose & Sons (1897).

Chats on English China, ARTHUR HAYDEN. T. Fisher Unwin, London (1904).

Chats on Old Earthenware, ARTHUR HAYDEN. T. Fisher Unwin, London (1912).

Chats on Wedgwood Ware, HARRY BARNARD. Frederick A. Stokes Co., New York (1925).

Chelsea and Chelsea-Derby China, EGAN MEW. T. C. & E. C. Jack, London (1909).

Chelsea Porcelain, WILLIAM KING. Benn Bros., Ltd., London (1922).

Chelsea Porcelain Toys, G. E. BRYANT. Medici Society, Ltd., London (1925)

Cheyne Book of Chelsea China and Pottery, REGINALD BLUNT. Geoffrey Bles, London (1924).

China Collecting in America, ALICE MORSE EARLE. Charles Scribner's Sons, New York (1907).

China Collector, The; A Guide to the Porcelain of the English Factories, H. W. LEWER. Dodd, Mead & Co., New York (1914).

Collecting Old English Lustre, JEANNETTE R. HODGDON. The Southworth Press, Portland, Me. (1937).

Collecting Old Lustre Ware, W. BOSANKO. George H. Doran Co., New York (1916).

Early American Pottery and China, JOHN

SPARGO. The Century Co., New York (1926).

Earthenware Collector, The, G. W. RHEAD. Dodd, Mead & Co., New York (1920).

Encyclopedia of Ceramics, The, W. P. JERVIS. New York (1902).

English Delft Pottery, R. G. MUNDY. Herbert Jenkins, Ltd., London (1928).

English Earthenware and Stoneware, A. H. CHURCH. Chapman & Hall, Ltd., London (1885).

English Porcelain, A. H. CHURCH. Chapman & Hall, Ltd., London (1885).

English Porcelain Figures of the Eighteenth Century, WILLIAM KING. Medici Society, Ltd., London (1925).

English Pottery, B. RACKHAM AND H. READ. Ernest Benn, Ltd., London (1924).

First Century of English Porcelain, The, W. M. BINNS. Hurst & Blackett, Ltd., London (1906).

A Guide to the Knowledge of Pottery, Porcelain, and Other Objects of Vertu, HENRY G. BOHN. Bohn, London (1857).

Handbook of Marks on Pottery and Porcelain, W. BURTON AND R. HOBSON. The Macmillan Co., London and New York (1928).

Historical Notices of the Leeds Old Pottery, J. R. and F. KIDSON. Published by the authors, Leeds (1892).

History and Description of English Earthenware and Stoneware, WILLIAM BURTON. Cassell & Co., London (1904).

History and Description of English Porcelain, A (2 vols.), WILLIAM BURTON. Cassell & Co., New York and London (1902).

History of Pottery and Porcelain, Mediaeval and Modern, A, J. MARRYAT. Murray, London (1857).

History of the Ceramic Art, ALBERT JACQUEMART. S. Low, London (1873).

History of The Coalport Porcelain Works, L. JEWITT (1862).

Josiah Wedgwood and His Pottery, WILLIAM BURTON. Funk & Wagnalls Co., New York (1922).

Lead Glazed Pottery, EDWIN A. BARBER. Doubleday, Page & Co., New York (1907).

Liverpool Potteries, The, C. T. GATTY (1882).

Longton Hall Porcelain, WILLIAM BEMROSE. Bemrose & Sons, London (1906).

Lowestoft China, SIR W. W. R. SPELMAN. Jarrold, London (1905).

Makers of Black Basaltes, The, MAURICE H. GRANT. Blackwood, Edinburgh (1910).

Marks of American Potters, E. A. BARBER. Patterson & White Co., Philadelphia (1904).

Marks and Monograms on Pottery and Porcelain of the Renaissance and Modern Periods, WILLIAM CHAFFERS. Reeves & Turiner, London (1930).

Old Bow China, EGAN MEW. Dodd, Mead & Co., New York (1909).

Old Bristol Potteries, W. J. POUNTNEY. J. W. Arrowsmith, Ltd. (1920).

Old China Book, N. Hudson Moore. Frederick A. Stokes Co., New York (1935).

Old Derby China Factory, The: The Workmen and Their Productions, John Haslem.

Old Derby Porcelain and Its Artists-Workmen, Frank Hurlbutt. T. Werner Laurie, Ltd., London (1925).

Old English China, Mrs. W. Hodgson. G. Bell & Sons, Ltd., London (1913).

Old English China with American Views, Edwin A. Barber, Indianapolis (1899).

Old English Porcelain, W. B. Honey. Harcourt Brace & Co., New York (1928).

Old Leeds Ware, Henry B. Wilson.

Old Spode, T. G. Cannon. T. Werner Laurie, Ltd., London (1924).

Oriental Lowestoft, J. A. Lloyd Hyde. Charles Scribner's Sons, New York (1936).

Porcelain, William Burton. B. T. Batsford, Ltd., London (1906).

Porcelain, Edward Dillon. Methuen & Co., London (1904).

Porcelain of All Countries, R. L. Hobson. E. P. Dutton & Co., New York (1906).

Potters and Potteries of Bennington, John Spargo. Houghton Mifflin Co., Boston (1926).

Potters, Their Arts and Crafts, J. C. L. Sparkes and W. Gandy. Whittaker, New York (1897).

Pottery and Porcelain, Frederick Litchfield. A. & C. Black, Ltd., London (1912).

Pottery and Porcelain from the Earliest Times Down to the Philadelphia Exposition of 1876, Charles W. Elliott. D. Appleton Co., New York (1878).

Pottery and Porcelain of All Times and Nations, William C. Prime. Harper & Bros., New York (1878).

Pottery and Porcelain of Derbyshire, The, A. Wallis and W. Bemrose. Bemrose & Sons, London (1870).

Pottery and Porcelain of the United States, Edwin A. Barber. George P. Putnam's Sons, New York (1893).

Practical Book of Chinaware, The, H. Eberlein and R. Ramsdell. J. B. Lippincott Co., Philadelphia (1925).

Shenandoah Pottery, The, A. Rice and J. Stoudt. Shenandoah Publishing House, Strasburg, Va. (1929).

Spode and His Successors, Arthur Hayden. Cassell & Co., New York and London (1925).

Staffordshire Pottery and Its History, Josiah C. Wedgwood. McBride, Nast & Co., New York (1913).

Staffordshire Pots and Potters, G. W. and F. A. Rhead. Hutchinson & Co., London (1906).

Staffordshire Pottery Figures, Herbert Read. Houghton Mifflin Co., Boston (1929).

Story of Wedgwood, The (pamphlet), Josiah Wedgwood and Sons. New York (1930).

Tin Enamelled Pottery, Edwin A. Barber. Pennsylvania Museum, Philadelphia (1906).

Transfer Printing on Enamels, Porcelain & Pottery, William Turner. Chapman & Hall, Ltd., London (1907).

Two Centuries of Ceramic Art in Bristol, Hugh Owen. Bell and Daldy (1873).

Wedgwood and His Works, E. Meteyard. Bell & Daldy, London (1873).

Worcester Porcelain, R. L. Hobson. Quaritch, London (1910).

CONTINENTAL

A B C of Old Continental Pottery, J. F. Blacker. George W. Jacobs & Co., Philadelphia.

Chats on Royal Copenhagen Porcelain, Arthur Hayden. T. Fisher Unwin, London (1911).

How to Collect Continental China, C. H. Wylde. George Bell & Sons, London (1907).

Delftware, Dutch and English, N. Hudson Moore. Frederick A. Stokes Co., New York (1908).

Dresden China, W. B. Honey. A. & C. Black, Ltd., London (1934).

Dresden China, Egan Mew. Dodd, Mead & Co., New York (1909).

Dutch Pottery and Porcelain, W. P. Knowles. Charles Scribner's Sons, New York (1913).

Early Netherlands Maiolica, B. Rackham. Bles, London (1926).

French Pottery and Porcelain, Henri Frantz. Charles Scribner's Sons, New York.

Golden Age of European Porcelain, The, Dudley Leavitt Pickman. Published by the author (1936).

Hispano-Moresque Ware of the 15th Century, A. Van de Put. THE ART WORKERS' QUARTERLY (1904).

History and Description of French Porcelain, A, E. S. Auscher. Cassell & Co., New York and London (1905).

History and Description of Italian Majolica, A, M. L. Solon. Cassell & Co., New York and London (1907).

History and Description of the Old French Faïence, M. L. Solon. Cassell & Co., New York and London (1903).

Italian Ceramic Art, Henry Wallis. Quaritch, London (1902).

Majolica and Fayence, Arthur Beckwith. D. Appleton Co. (1877).

Porcelain, Oriental, Continental and British, R. L. Hobson. E. P. Dutton & Co., New York (1906).

Pottery and Porcelain (3 vols.), Emil Hannover. Charles Scribner's Sons, New York (1925).

Royal Sèvres China, Egan Mew. T. C. & E. C. Jack, London (1909).

Soft Porcelain of Sèvres, The, E. Garnier. Nimmo, London (1892).

ORIENTAL

Art of the Chinese Potter from the Han Dynasty to the End of the Ming, The, R. Hobson and A. Hetherington. Ernest Benn, Ltd., London (1923).

Chats on Oriental China, J. F. Blacker.

T. Fisher Unwin, London (1922).

Chinese Art, L. ASHTON AND B. GRAY. Hale, Cushman & Flint, Boston (1937).

Chinese Art (2 vols.), STEPHEN W. BUSHELL. Wyman, London (1906).

Chinese Porcelain, W. G. GULLAND. Chapman & Hall, London (1918).

Early Ceramic Wares of China, The, A. L. HETHERINGTON. Benn Bros., Ltd., London (1924).

Guide to the Later Chinese Porcelain; Periods of K'ang Hsi, Yung Chêng, and Ch'ien Lung, W. B. HONEY. South Kensington Museum, London (1927).

History and Description of Chinese Porcelain, A, WILLIAM C. MONKHOUSE. Cassell & Co., London (1901).

How to Identify Chinese Porcelain, W. HODGSON. Methuen & Co., London (1905).

Keramic Art of Japan, G. AUDSLEY and J. BOWES. Published by the authors, Liverpool (1875).

Later Ceramic Wares of China, The, R. L. HOBSON. Ernest Benn, Ltd., London (1925).

Old Chinese Porcelain, EGAN MEW. T. C. & E. C. Jack, London (1909).

Part III

GLASS

Adventures in Light and Color, CHARLES J. CONNICK. Random House, New York (1937).

American Bottles Old and New, WILLIAM S. WALBRIDGE. The Owens Bottle Co. (1920).

American Glassware, Old and New, EDWIN A. BARBER. Patterson & White Co., Philadelphia (1900).

Ancient Stained and Painted Glass, F. SYDNEY EDEN. University Press, Cambridge, Eng. (1933).

Cambridge Glass, 1818 to 1888, LURA W. WATKINS. Marshall Jones Co., Inc., Boston (1930).

Collecting Old Glass, English and Irish, SIR JAMES YOXALL. George H. Doran Co., New York (1916).

Collector's Guide of Flasks and Bottles, CHARLES McMURRAY. Published by the author, Dayton, Ohio (1927).

Early American Bottles and Flasks (2 vols.), VAN RENSSELAER. Transcript Printing Co., Peterboro, N. H. (1926).

Early American Glass, RHEA M. KNITTLE. The Century Co., New York (1927).

Early American Pressed Glass, RUTH WEBB LEE. Published by the author (1933).

Early Glass-Making in Virginia, MAUDE P. HULL. Jones Printing Co., Richmond, Va. (1933).

English Table Glass, PERCY BATE. George Newnes, Ltd., London (1905).

European Glass, WILFRED BUCKLEY. Ernest Benn, Ltd., London (1927).

Glass, EDWARD DILLON. G. P. Putnam's Sons, New York (1907).

Glass, GUSTAVUS A. EISEN and F. KOUCHAKJI. William Rudge, New York (1927).

Glass Collector, The, MACIVER PERCIVAL. Herbert Jenkins, Ltd., London (1918).

Glass-Making in England, HARRY J. POWELL. University Press, Cambridge (1923).

History of English and Irish Glass, The, W. A. THORPE. Medici Society, Ltd., London (1929).

History of Old English Glass, The, FRANCIS BUCKLEY (1925).

Irish Glass, M. S. DUDLEY WESTROPP. Herbert Jenkins, Ltd., London (1921).

Old English Glasses, ALBERT HARTSHORNE. Arnold, London (1897).

Old Glass and How to Collect It, J. SYDNEY LEWIS. J. B. Lippincott Co., Philadelphia (1916).

Old Glass, European and American, N. HUDSON MOORE. Frederick A. Stokes Co., New York (1924).

Old Irish Glass, MRS. GRAYDON STANNUS. The Connoisseur, London (1921).

Old Sandwich Glass (pamphlet), WILLIAM GERMAIN DOOLEY (1934).

Romance of Old Sandwich Glass, The, FRANK W. CHIPMAN. Sandwich Publishing Co., Sandwich, Mass. (1932).

Stained Glass, ALFRED WERCK. Nicholas L. Brown, New York (1922).

Stained Glass of the Middle Ages in England and France, H. ARNOLD and L. SAINT. A. & C. Black, Ltd., London (1925).

Stiegel Glass, FREDERICK W. HUNTER. Houghton Mifflin Co., Boston (1914).

Story of Sandwich Glass and Glass Works, The, FREDERICK T. IRWIN. Published by the author, Manchester, N. H. (1936).

Part IV

TEXTILES

CARPETS AND RUGS

Antique Rugs from the Near East, WILHELM BODE and E. KUEHNEL. E. Weyhe, New York (1922).

Chinese Carpets and Rugs, ADOLF HACKMACK. Librairie Française, Tientsin, China (1924).

Chinese Rug Book, The, MARY CHURCHILL RIPLEY. Frederick A. Stokes Co., New York (1927).

Collecting Hooked Rugs, E. WAUGH AND E. FOLEY. The Century Co., New York (1927).

Craft of Hand-Made Rugs, The, AMI M. HICKS. Robert M. McBride & Co., New York (1920).

European and American Carpets and Rugs, CORNELIA B. FARADAY. Dean-Hicks Co., Grand Rapids, Mich. (1929).

Handmade Rugs, ELLA SHANNON BOWLES.

Little, Brown & Co., Boston (1927).

Hand-Woven Carpets, Oriental and European (2 vols.), A. KENDRICK AND C. TATTERSALL. Benn Bros., Ltd., London (1922).

History of British Carpets from the Introduction of the Craft until the Present Day, A, C. E. C. TATTERSALL. F. Lewis, Ltd., London (1934).

Homecraft Rugs, LYDIA L. WALKER. Frederick A. Stokes Co., New York (1930).

Hooked Rug, The, WILLIAM W. KENT. Dodd, Mead & Co., New York (1930).

How to Identify Oriental Rugs, FFRIDA and A. T. WOLFE. T. Fisher Unwin, London (1927).

Oriental Rug, The, WILLIAM D. ELLWANGER. Dodd, Mead & Co., New York (1903).

Oriental Rug Book, The, MARY C. RIPLEY. Frederick A. Stokes Co., New York (1926).

Oriental Rugs, JOHN K. MUMFORD. Charles Scribner's Sons, New York (1901).

Oriental Rugs and Carpets, ARTHUR U. DILLEY. Charles Scribner's Sons, New York (1931).

Oriental Rugs, Antique and Modern, WALTER A. HAWLEY. John Lane Co., London (1913).

Practical Book of Oriental Rugs, The, G. GRIFFIN LEWIS. J. B. Lippincott Co., Philadelphia (1920).

Rugs, Oriental and Occidental, Antique and Modern, ROSA B. HOLT. A. C. McClurg & Co., Chicago (1927).

LACE

American Lace and Lace-Makers, EMILY C. VANDERPOEL. Yale University Press, New Haven, Conn (1924).

Chats on Old Lace and Needlework, MRS. E. L. LOWES. T. Fisher Unwin, London (1908).

History of Lace, A (4th ed.), MRS. BURY PALLISER. Low, Marston & Co., London (1902).

How to Know Laces, EDNA H. ROBERTS. Textile Publishing Co., New York (1925).

Lace and Embroidery Collector, The, MRS. R. E. HEAD. Dodd, Mead & Co., New York (1922).

Lace Book, The, JESSIE F. CAPLIN. The Macmillan Co., New York (1932).

Lace Book, The, N. HUDSON MOORE. Frederick A. Stokes Co., New York (1904).

Lace Guide for Makers and Collectors, A, GERTRUDE WHITING. E. P. Dutton & Co., New York (1920).

Lace in the Making with Bobbins and Needle, MARGARET L. BROOKE. Boni and Liveright, New York (1925).

Seven Centuries of Lace, MRS. JOHN H. POLLEN. Heinemann, London (1908).

NEEDLEWORK

American Samplers, E. BOLTON AND E. COE. Mass. Society of Colonial Dames, Boston (1921).

Art in Needlework, L. DAY and M.

BUCKLE. B. T. Batsford, Ltd., London (1900).

Book of Old Embroidery, A, ALBERT F. KENDRICK. The Studio, Ltd., London (1921).

Development of Embroidery in America, The, CANDACE WHEELER. Harper & Bros., New York (1921).

Dictionary of Needlework, The, S. CAULFIELD and B. SAWARD. L. Upton Gill, London (1885).

Elementary Embroidery, MARY SYMONDS (ANTROBUS) and L. PREECE. Hogg, London (1915).

Embroidery and Needlework, GLADYS W. FRY. Sir Isaac Pitman & Sons, Ltd., London (1936).

Embroidery and Tapestry Weaving, MRS. A. H. CHRISTIE. Sir Isaac Pitman & Sons, Ltd., London (1928).

Embroidery Book, ANNE K. ARTHUR. The Macmillan Co.

English Embroidery, A. F. KENDRICK. George Newnes, Ltd., London (1904).

English Needlework, A. F. KENDRICK. A. & C. Black, Ltd., London (1933).

Note on Stitchery, A, L. PESEL and E. NEWBERRY. Part of A Book of Old Embroidery (q.v.).

Popular Weaving and Embroidery in Spain, MILDRED STAPLEY (BYNE). William Helburn, Inc., New York (1924).

Samplers and Tapestry Embroideries, MARCUS B. HUISH. Longmans, Green & Co., London (1913).

TAPESTRIES

Bayeux Tapestry, The, FRANK R. FOWKE. Arundel Society, London (1875).

Elizabethan Sheldon Tapestries, JOHN HUMPHRIES. Oxford University Press (1928).

Handbook to the Teniers Tapestries, H. C. MARILLIER. Oxford University Press, London (1932).

History of Tapestry from the Earliest Times until the Present Day, A, W. G. THOMSON. Hodder & Stoughton, Ltd., London (1930).

Practical Book of Tapestries, The, GEORGE LELAND HUNTER. J. B. LIPPINCOTT Co., Philadelphia (1929).

Tapestries: Their Origin, History & Renaissance, GEORGE LELAND HUNTER. John Lane Co., New York (1912).

Tapestry Book, The, HELEN C. CANDEE. Frederick A. Stokes Co., New York (1935).

Tapestry, the Mirror of Civilization, PHYLLIS ACKERMAN. Oxford University Press, New York (1933).

Tapestry Weaving in England from the Earliest Times to the End of the 18th Century, W. G. THOMSON. B. T. Batsford, Ltd., London (1914).

MISCELLANEOUS

Book of Hand-Woven Coverlets, ELIZA C. HALL. Little, Brown & Co., Boston, (1912).

Chintz Book, The, MacIVER PERCIVAL. Frederick A. Stokes Co., New York (1923).

Decorative Textiles, GEORGE LELAND HUN-
TER. J. B. Lippincott Co., Philadelphia (1918).

Dyes and Dyeing, CHARLES E. PELLEW
(VISCOUNT EXMOUTH). McBride, Nast
& Co., New York (1913).

Early American Textiles, FRANCES LITTLE.
The Century Co., New York (1931).

Handicraft Art of Weaving, THOMAS WOOD-
HOUSE. Hodder & Stoughton, London
(1921).

Hand-Loom Weaving, MATTIE PHIPPS TODD.
Rand McNally & Co., Chicago
(1914).

Historic Textile Fabrics, RICHARD GLAZIER.
B. T. Batsford, Ltd., London (1923).

Homespun Handicrafts, ELLA SHANNON
BOWLES. J. B. Lippincott Co., Philadelphia (1931).

Old Patchwork Quilts and the Women Who
Made Them, RUTH E. FINLEY. J. B.

Lippincott Co., Philadelphia (1929).

Painted and Printed Fabrics, H. CLOUZOT
AND F. MORRIS. Metropolitan Museum, New York (1927).

Quilts; Their Story and How to Make Them,
MARIE D. WEBSTER. Doubleday,
Page & Co., New York (1915).

Romance of French Weaving, The, PAUL
RODIER. Frederick A. Stokes Co.,
New York (1931).

Romance of the Patchwork Quilt in America,
The, C. HALL AND R. KRETSINGER.
Caxton Printers, Ltd., Caldwell,
Idaho (1935).

Shuttle-Craft Book of American Hand-Weaving, MARY M. ATWATER. The Macmillan Co., New York (1928).

Weaving with Small Appliances, LUTHER
HOOPER. Sir Isaac Pitman & Sons,
Ltd., London (1922-25).

Part V

MISCELLANEOUS METALS

Book of Sun-Dials, The, MARGARET GATTY.
G. Bell & Sons, London (1900).

Chats on Old Copper and Brass, FRED W.
BURGESS. T. Fisher Unwin, London
(1914).

Colonial Lighting, ARTHUR H. HAYWARD.
Little, Brown & Co., Boston (1927).

Early American Wrought Iron (3 vols.),
ALBERT H. SONN. Charles Scribner's
Sons, New York (1928).

Early Chinese Bronzes, ALBERT J. KOOP.
Ernest Benn, Ltd., London (1924).

Encyclopedia of Iron Work, OTTO HOEVER.
Ernest Benn, Ltd., London (1927).

English Iron Work of the 17th and 18th
Centuries, J. S. GARDNER. B. T. Batsford, Ltd., London (1911).

English Metal Work, W. TWOPENY. John
Lane Co., New York (1904).

Iron and Brass Implements of the English and
American Home, J. SEYMOUR LINDSAY.
Medici Society of America, Boston
(1927).

Old Pewter, Brass, Copper, & Sheffield Plate,
N. HUDSON MOORE. Frederick A.

Stokes Co., New York (1906).

Silver: Pewter: Sheffield Plate, FRED. W. BURGESS. George Routledge & Sons, Ltd., London (1921).

Story of Snuff and Snuff Boxes, MATTOON M. CURTIS. Liveright Publishing Co., New York (1935).

Wine, Spirit and Sauce Labels of the 18th and 19th Centuries, H. C. DENT. Hunt, Norwich, England (1933).

PEWTER

American Pewter, J. B. KERFOOT. Houghton Mifflin Co., Boston (1925).

Chats on Old Pewter, H. J. L. J. MASSÉ. T. Fisher Unwin, London (1928).

Irish Pewterers, H. COTTERELL AND M. WESTROPP (1917).

National Types of Old Pewter, H. H. COTTERELL. ANTIQUES, INC. (1925).

New Pewter Marks and Old Pewter Ware, C. A. MARKHAM. Charles Scribner's Sons, New York (1928).

Old Pewter, MALCOLM BELL. Charles Scribner's Sons, New York (1913).

Old Pewter, Its Makers and Marks in England, Scotland and Ireland, H. H. COTTERELL. B. T. Batsford, Ltd., London (1929).

Pewter and the Amateur Collector, EDWARDS J. GALE. Charles Scribner's Sons, New York (1910).

Pewter Collector, The, H. J. L. J. MASSÉ. Herbert Jenkins, Ltd., London (1921).

Pewter Design and Construction, WILLIAM

H. VARNUM. Bruce Publishing Co., Milwaukee, Wis. (1926).

Pewter Down the Ages, H. H. COTTERELL. Houghton Mifflin Co., Boston (1932).

Pewter Plate, H. J. L. J. MASSÉ. Geo. Bell & Sons, Ltd., London (1904).

Pewter Work, FREDERICK R. SMITH. Sir Isaac Pitman & Sons, Ltd., London (1930).

Rhode Island Pewterers and Their Work, CHARLES A. CALDER. Johnson & Co., Providence, R. I. (1924).

Some Notes on American Pewterers, LOUIS G. MYERS. Country Life, Ltd., London (1926).

SILVER

American Church Silver of the 17th and 18th Centuries, Museum of Fine Arts, Boston (1911).

American Silver of the 17th and 18th Centuries, C. LOUISE AVERY. Metropolitan Museum, New York (1920).

American Silversmiths and Their Marks, STEPHEN G. C. ENSKO. Robert Ensko, Inc. (1937).

Apostle Spoons, Their Evolution from Earlier Types, and the Emblems Used by the Silversmiths for the Apostles, CHARLES G. RUPERT. Oxford University Press (1931).

Chats on Old Sheffield Plate, ARTHUR HAYDEN. T. Fisher Unwin, London (1920).

Chats on Old Silver, ARTHUR HAYDEN. T. Fisher Unwin, London (1915).

Domestic Silver of Great Britain and Ireland,

EDWARD WENHAM. Oxford University Press, London (1932).

Early American Silver, C. LOUISE AVERY. The Century Co., New York (1930).

Early American Silver Marks, JAMES GRAHAM, JR. (1936).

Early Silver of Connecticut and Its Makers, GEORGE M. CURTIS. International Silver Co. (1913).

English Goldsmiths and Their Marks, SIR CHARLES J. JACKSON. The Macmillan Co., London (1921).

Goldsmiths' and Silversmiths' Work, NELSON DAWSON. G. P. Putnam's Sons, New York (1907).

Guide to Old French Plate, A, LOUIS CARRÉ. Chapman & Hall, Ltd., London (1931).

Hall Marks on Gold and Silver Plate (9th edition), WILLIAM CHAFFERS. Reeves & Turner, London (1905).

Historic Silver of the Colonies and Its Makers, FRANCIS H. BIGELOW. The Macmillan Co., New York (1917).

History of Old Sheffield Plate, A, FREDERICK BRADBURY. The Macmillan Co., London (1912).

Illustrated History of English Plate, Ecclesiastic and Secular, An (2 vols.), SIR CHARLES J. JACKSON. Country Life, Ltd., London (1911).

List of Early American Silversmiths and Their Marks, A, HOLLIS FRENCH. Walpole Society, New York (1917).

Maryland Silversmiths, 1715-1830, J. PLEASANTS AND H. SILL. Lord Baltimore Press, Baltimore, Md. (1930).

Old English Plate Marks, WILFRED J. CRIPPS. John Murray, London (1901).

Old English Silver, W. W. WATTS. Ernest Benn, Ltd., London (1924).

Old French Plate, WILFRED J. CRIPPS. Murray, London (1880).

Old London Silver, Its History, Its Makers and Its Marks, MONTAGUE HOWARD. Charles Scribner's Sons, New York (1903).

Old Plate, Ecclesiastical, Decorative and Domestic; Its Makers and Marks, JOHN HENRY BUCK. The Gorham Mfg. Co., Providence, R. I. (1903).

Old Sheffield Plate, JULIA W. TORREY. Houghton Mifflin Co., Boston (1918).

Old Silver and Old Sheffield Plate, HOWARD P. OKIE. Doubleday, Doran & Co., New York (1928).

Old Silver of American Churches, E. ALFRED JONES. Arden Press, Letchworth, England (1913).

Old Silver of Europe and America from Early Times to the Nineteenth Century, E. ALFRED JONES. J. B. Lippincott Co., Philadelphia (1928).

Old Silver Spoons of England, NORMAN GASK. Herbert Jenkins, Ltd., London (1926).

Sheffield Plate, HENRY NEWTON VEITCH. George Bell & Sons, London (1908).

Sheffield Plate, BERTIE WYLLIE. Charles Scribner's Sons, New York (1913).

Silver and Sheffield Plate Collector, W. A. YOUNG. Dodd, Mead & Co., New York (1919).

Silversmiths of Utica, GEORGE B. and MINNIE W. CUTTEN (1937).

Part VI

BIOGRAPHY

Adam, Robert, and His Brothers, J. SWAR-BRICK. B. T. Batsford, Ltd., London (1915).

Adams, William, An Old English Potter, WILLIAM TURNER. Chapman & Hall, Ltd., London (1904).

Chippendale, Thomas, OLIVER BRACKETT. Hodder & Stoughton, Ltd., London (1924).

Coney, John, Silversmith, H. F. CLARKE. Houghton Mifflin Co., Boston (1932).

Dummer, Jeremiah, Colonial Craftsman and Merchant, 1645-1718, H. CLARKE AND H. FOOTE. Houghton Mifflin Co., Boston (1935).

Gibbons, Grinling, and the Woodwork of His Age, H. A. TIPPING. Country Life, Ltd., London (1914).

Hancock, Robert, and His Work, A. R. BALLANTYNE. London (1885).

Jones, Inigo, and Others, Designs of, INIGO JONES, and Others. Ware, London (1757?).

McIntire, Samuel, His Life and Work, The Wood-Carver of Salem, F. COUSINS AND P. RILEY. Little, Brown & Co., Boston (1916).

McIntire, Samuel, Carver, and the Sandersons, Early Salem Cabinet Makers, MABEL M. SWAN. Essex Institute, Salem, Mass. (1934).

Palissy, Bernard, PHILIPPE BURTY. Libraire de l'Art, Paris (1886).

Palissy the Potter, HENRY MORLEY. Boston, Ticknor (1853).

Revere, Paul, and His Engraving, WILLIAM L. ANDREWS. Charles Scribner's Sons, New York (1901).

Revere, Life of Colonel Paul, E. H. Goss. J. G. Cupples, Boston (1891).

Savery of Philadelphia, Life of William, FRANCIS R. TAYLOR. The Macmillan Co., New York (1925).

Wedgwood, Josiah, Master-Potter, A. H. CHURCH. Seeley & Co., London (1903).

Wedgwood, The Life of Josiah, from His Private Correspondence and Family Papers, ELIZA METEYARD. Hurst & Blackett, Ltd., London (1865).

Wedgwoods, The: Being a Life of Josiah Wedgwood, L. JEWITT. Virtue Bros. & Co., London (1865).

Willard, Simon, Inventor and Clockmaker, A History of, JOHN WARE WILLARD. E. O. Cockayne, Boston (1911).

Wood Family of Burslem, The, FRANK FALKNER. Chapman & Hall, Ltd., London (1912).

BIBLIOGRAPHY

AUTHORS

	Part		
ACKERMAN, PHYLLIS	(IV)	Tapestry, The Mirror of Civilization	1933
ACKERMAN, PHYLLIS	(I)	Wallpaper, Its History, Design and Use	1923
ANDREWS, E. D. AND F.	(I)	Shaker Furniture	1937
ANDREWS, WILLIAM L.	(VI)	Paul Revere and His Engraving	1901
ANTROBUS, MARY (SYMONDS) AND PREECE, L. See SYMONDS, MARY, AND PREECE, L.			
ARNOLD, H. AND SAINT, L.	(III)	Stained Glass of the Middle Ages in England and France	1925
ARTHUR, ANNE KNOX	(IV)	Embroidery Book	
ASHTON, L. AND GRAY, B.	(II)	Chinese Art	1937
ATWATER, MARY M.	(IV)	Shuttle-Craft Book of American Hand Weaving	1905
AUDSLEY, G. AND BOWES, J.	(II)	Keramic Art of Japan	1875
AUSCHER, E. S.	(II)	A History and Description of French Porcelain	
AVERY, C. LOUISE	(V)	American Silver of the 17th and 18th Centuries	1920
AVERY, C. LOUISE	(V)	Early American Silver	1930
BALLANTYNE, A. R.	(VI)	Robert Hancock and His Work	1885
BARBER, EDWIN ATLEE	(III)	American Glassware, Old and New	1925
BARBER, EDWIN ATLEE	(II)	Anglo-American Pottery	1899
BARBER, EDWIN ATLEE	(II)	Artificial Soft Paste Porcelain	1907
BARBER, EDWIN ATLEE	(II)	Lead Glazed Pottery	1907
BARBER, EDWIN ATLEE	(II)	Marks of American Potters	1904
BARBER, EDWIN ATLEE	(II)	Old English China with American Views	1899
BARBER, EDWIN ATLEE	(II)	Pottery and Porcelain of the U. S.	1893
BARBER, EDWIN ATLEE	(II)	The Ceramic Collectors' Glossary	1914
BARBER, EDWIN ATLEE	(II)	Tin Enamelled Pottery	1906
BARNARD, HARRY	(II)	Chats on Wedgwood Ware	1925
BATE, PERCY	(III)	English Table Glass	1905
BECKWITH, ARTHUR	(II)	Majolica and Fayence	1877
BELL, J. MUNRO	(I)	Chippendale, Sheraton and Hepplewhite Furniture Designs	1900
BELL, MALCOLM	(V)	Old Pewter	1913

PART

Bowles, Ella Shannon	(IV)	Handmade Rugs	1927
Bowles, Ella Shannon	(IV)	Homespun Handicrafts	1931
Brackett, Oliver	(I)	An Encyclopædia of English Furniture	1927
Brackett, Oliver	(VI)	Thomas Chippendale	1927
Bradbury, Frederick	(V)	A History of Old Sheffield Plate	1912
Britten, Frederick, J.	(I)	Old Clocks and Watches and Their Makers	1904
Brooke, Margaret L.	(IV)	Lace in the Making with Bobbins and Needle	1923
Bryant, G. E.	(II)	Chelsea Porcelain Toys	1925
Buck, John Henry	(V)	Old Plate, Ecclesiastical, Decorative and Domestic, Its Makers and Marks	1903
Buckley, Francis	(III)	The History of Old English Glass	1925
Buckley, Wilfred	(III)	European Glass	1927
Burgess, Fred. W.	(I)	Antique Furniture	1919
Burgess, Fred. W.	(V)	Chats on Old Copper and Brass	1914
Burgess, Fred. W.	(V)	Silver: Pewter: Sheffield Plate	1921
Burroughs, Paul H.	(I)	Southern Antiques	1931
Burton, William	(II)	History and Description of English Earthenware and Stoneware	1904
Burton, William	(II)	History and Description of English Porcelain	1902
Burton, William	(II)	Porcelain	1906
Burton, William	(II)	Josiah Wedgwood and His Pottery	1922
Burton, W. and Hobson, R.	(II)	Handbook of Marks on Pottery and Porcelain	1928
Burty, Philippe	(VI)	Bernard Palissy	1886
Bushell, Stephen W.	(II)	Chinese Art—2 Vols.	1906
Byne, Mildred (Stapley).	See Stapley, Mildred.		
Calder, Charles A.	(V)	Rhode Island Pewterers and Their Work	1924
Camehl, Ada W.	(II)	The Blue-China Book	1916
Candee, Helen C.	(I)	Decorative Styles and Periods in the Home	1906
Candee, Helen C.	(IV)	The Tapestry Book	1935
Cannon, T. G.	(II)	Old Spode	1924
Caplin, Jessie F.	(IV)	The Lace Book	1932
Carré, Louis	(V)	A Guide to Old French Plate	1931
Caulfield, S. and Saward, B.	(IV)	The Dictionary of Needlework	1885
Cescinsky, Herbert	(I)	English Furniture from Gothic to Sheraton	1929
Cescinsky, Herbert	(I)	English Furniture of the 18th Century	1915

PART

DAY, L. AND BUCKLE, M.	(IV)	*Art in Needlework*	1900
DENT, H. C.	(V)	*Wine, Spirit and Sauce Labels of the 18th and 19th Centuries*	1933
DILLEY, ARTHUR U.	(IV)	*Oriental Rugs and Carpets*	1931
DILLON, EDWARD	(III)	*Glass*	1907
DILLON, EDWARD	(II)	*Porcelain*	1904
DOOLEY, WILLIAM GERMAIN	(III)	*Old Sandwich Glass*	1934
DYER, WALTER A.	(I)	*Early American Craftsmen*	1915
DYER, WALTER A.	(I)	*The Lure of the Antique*	1919
EARLE, ALICE MORSE	(II)	*China Collecting in America*	1907
EBERLEIN, H. AND RAMS- DELL, R.	(I)	*Practical Book of Italian, Spanish and Portuguese Furniture*	1927
EBERLEIN, H. AND McCLURE, A.	(I)	*Practical Book of Period Furniture*	1914 1914
EBERLEIN, H. AND McCLURE, A.	(I)	*Practical Book of American Antiques*	1928
EBERLEIN, H. AND RAMS- DELL, R.	(II)	*Practical Book of Chinaware*	1925
EDEN, F. SYDNEY	(III)	*Ancient Stained and Painted Glass*	1933
EISEN, GUSTAVUS A. AND KOUCHAKJI, F.	(III)	*Glass*	1927
ELLIOTT, CHARLES W.	(II)	*Pottery and Porcelain from the Earliest Times Down to the Philadelphia Exposition of 1876*	1878
ELLWANGER, WILLIAM D.	(IV)	*The Oriental Rug*	1903
ENSKO, STEPHEN G. C.	(V)	*American Silversmiths and Their Marks*	1937
EVAN-THOMAS, OWEN	(I)	*Domestic Utensils of Wood, 16th to 19th Century*	1932
FALKNER, FRANK	(VI)	*The Wood Family of Burslem*	1912
FARADAY, CORNELIA B.	(IV)	*European and American Carpets and Rugs*	1929
FINLEY, RUTH E.	(IV)	*Old Patchwork Quilts and the Women Who Made Them*	1929
FOWKE, FRANK R.	(IV)	*The Bayeux Tapestry*	1913
FRANTZ, HENRI	(II)	*French Pottery and Porcelain*	
FRENCH, HOLLIS	(V)	*A List of Early American Silversmiths and Their Marks*	1917
FRY, GLADYS W.	(IV)	*Embroidery and Needlework*	1936

	PART		
HOBSON, R. L.	(II)	The Later Ceramic Wares of China	1925
HOBSON, R. L.	(II)	Porcelain of All Countries	1906
HOBSON, R. L.	(II)	Worcester Porcelain	1910
HOBSON, R. AND HETHERINGTON, A.	(II)	The Art of the Chinese Potter from the Han Dynasty to the End of the Ming	1923
HODGDON, JEANNETTE R.	(II)	Collecting Old English Lustre	1937
HODGSON, W. MRS.	(II)	How to Identify Old Chinese Porcelain	1905
HODGSON, W. MRS.	(II)	Old English China	1913
HOEVER, OTTO	(V)	Encyclopedia of Iron Work	1927
HOLLOWAY, EDWARD S.	(I)	American Furniture and Decoration, Colonial and Federal	1928
HOLT, R. B.	(IV)	Rugs, Oriental and Occidental, Antique and Modern	1901
HONEY, W. B.	(II)	Dresden China	1934
HONEY, W. B.	(II)	Guide to the Later Chinese Porcelain; Periods of K'ang Hsi, Yung Chêng, and Ch'ien Lung	1927
HONEY, W. B.	(II)	Old English Porcelain	1928
HOOPER, LUTHER	(IV)	Weaving with Small Appliances	1922
HOOPES, PENROSE R.	(I)	Connecticut Clockmakers of the 18th Century	1930
HORNOR, W. M., JR.	(I)	Blue Book, Philadelphia Furniture, William Penn to George Washington, with Special Reference to the Philadelphia-Chippendale School	1935
HOWARD, MONTAGUE	(V)	Old London Silver, Its History, Its Makers and Its Marks	1903
HUISH, MARCUS B.	(IV)	Samplers and Tapestry Embroideries	1913
HULL, MAUDE P.	(III)	Early Glass-Making in Virginia	1933
HUMPHREYS, JOHN	(III)	Elizabethan Sheldon Tapestries	1929
HUNTER, FREDERICK W.	(III)	Stiegel Glass	1914
HUNTER, GEORGE LELAND	(IV)	Decorative Textiles	1918
HUNTER, GEORGE LELAND	(I)	Italian Furniture and Interiors	1918
HUNTER, GEORGE LELAND	(IV)	The Practical Book of Tapestries	1929
HUNTER, GEORGE LELAND	(IV)	Tapestries: Their Origin, History and Renaissance	1912
HURLBUTT, FRANK	(II)	Bow Porcelain	1926

	Part		
Koop, Albert J.	(V)	*Early Chinese Bronzes*	1924
Lee, Ruth Webb	(III)	*Early American Pressed Glass*	1933
Lewer, H. W.	(II)	*The China Collector; A Guide to the Porcelain of the English Factories*	1914
Lewer, H. and Percival, M.	(II)	*The Bric-à-Brac Collector*	1923
Lewis, G. Griffin	(IV)	*The Practical Book of Oriental Rugs*	1920
Lewis, J. Sidney	(III)	*Old Glass and How to Collect It*	1916
Lindsay, J. Seymour	(V)	*Iron and Brass Implements of the English and American Home*	1927
Litchfield, Frederick	(I)	*Antiques, Genuine and Spurious*	1924
Litchfield, Frederick	(I)	*How to Collect Old Furniture*	1904
Litchfield, Frederick	(I)	*Illustrated History of Furniture*	1922
Litchfield, Frederick	(II)	*Pottery and Porcelain*	1912
Little, Frances	(IV)	*Early American Textiles*	1931
Lockwood, Luke V.	(I)	*Colonial Furniture in America*	1926
Lockwood, Sarah M.	(I)	*Antiques*	1925
Lowes, Mrs. E. L.	(IV)	*Chats on Old Lace and Needlework*	1908
Lucas, Alfred	(I)	*Antiques; Their Restoration and Preservation*	1924
Luther, Clair F.	(I)	*The Hadley Chest*	1936
Lyon, Dr. Irving W.	(I)	*Colonial Furniture of New England*	1925
Macquoid, Percy	(I)	*History of English Furniture—4 Vols.*	1904–08
Macquoid, P. and Edwards, R.	(I)	*Dictionary of English Furniture from the Middle Ages to the Late Georgian Period—3 Vols.*	1924–27
Marillier, H. C.	(IV)	*Handbook to the Teniers Tapestries*	1932
Markham, C. A.	(V)	*New Pewter Marks and Old Pewter Ware*	1928
Marryat, J.	(II)	*A History of Pottery and Porcelain, Medieval and Modern*	1857
Massé, H. J. L. J.	(V)	*Chats on Old Pewter*	1928
Massé, H. J. L. J.	(V)	*Pewter Plate*	1904
Massé, H. J. L. J.	(V)	*The Pewter Collector*	1921
McClelland, Nancy	(I)	*Historic Wall-Papers*	1924
McMurray, Charles	(III)	*Collectors' Guide of Flasks and Bottles*	
Menzies, William G.	(I)	*Collecting Antiques*	1928
Meteyard, Eliza	(VI)	*The Life of Josiah Wedgwood from His Private Correspondence and Family Papers*	1865

	PART		
PERCIVAL, MAC IVER	(IV)	*The Chintz Book*	1923
PERCIVAL, MAC IVER	(III)	*The Glass Collector*	1918
PESEL, L. AND NEWBERRY, E.	(IV)	*A Note on Stitchery*	1921
PICKMAN, DUDLEY LEAVITT	(II)	*The Golden Age of European Porcelain*	1936
PLEASANTS, J. AND SILL, H.	(V)	*Maryland Silversmiths, 1715-1830*	1930
POLLEN, MRS. JOHN H.	(IV)	*Seven Centuries of Lace*	1908
POUNTNEY, W. J.	(II)	*Old Bristol Potteries*	1920
POWELL, HARRY J.	(III)	*Glass-Making in England*	1923
PRIME, WILLIAM C.	(II)	*Pottery and Porcelain of All Times and Nations*	1878
RACKHAM, BERNARD	(II)	*Early Netherlands Maiolica*	1926
RACKHAM, B. AND READ, H.	(II)	*English Pottery*	1924
RAWSON, MARION N.	(I)	*Candle Days*	1927
RAWSON, MARION N.	(I)	*Handwrought Ancestors*	1936
READ, HERBERT	(II)	*Staffordshire Pottery Figures*	1929
RHEAD, G. W.	(II)	*The Earthenware Collector*	1920
RHEAD, G. W.	(II)	*Staffordshire Pots and Potters*	1906
RICE, A. AND STOUDT, J.	(II)	*The Shenandoah Pottery*	1929
RIPLEY, MARY C.	(IV)	*The Chinese Rug Book*	1927
RIPLEY, MARY C.	(IV)	*The Oriental Rug Book*	1904
ROBERTS, E. H.	(IV)	*How to Know Laces*	1921
RODIER, PAUL	(IV)	*The Romance of French Weaving*	1931
ROGERS, JOHN C.	(I)	*English Furniture, Its Essentials and Characteristics Simply and Clearly Explained for the Student and Small Collector*	1923
ROWED, CHARLES A.	(I)	*Collecting as a Pastime*	1920
RUPERT, CHARLES G.	(V)	*Apostle Spoons, Their Evolution from Earlier Types, and the Emblems Used by the Silversmiths for the Apostles*	1931
SAGLIO, ANDRÉ	(I)	*French Furniture*	1913
SHACKLETON, R. AND E.	(I)	*The Quest of the Colonial*	1907
SINGLETON, ESTHER	(I)	*Dutch and Flemish Furniture*	1907
SINGLETON, ESTHER	(I)	*French and English Furniture*	1903
SINGLETON, ESTHER	(I)	*Furniture*	1911
SINGLETON, ESTHER	(I)	*The Furniture of Our Forefathers*	1919
SMITH, FREDERICK R.	(V)	*Pewter Work*	1930
SOLON, MARC LOUIS	(II)	*The Art of the Old English Potter*	1883

		PART		
TURNER, WILLIAM	(II)	Transfer Printing on Enamels, Porcelain and Pottery		1907
TURNER, WILLIAM	(VI)	William Adams, an Old English Potter		1904
TWOPENY, W.	(V)	English Metal Work		1904
VALLOIS, GRACE M.	(I)	First Steps in Collecting		1926
VANDERPOEL, EMILY N.	(IV)	American Lace and Lace-Makers		1924
VAN DE PUT, A.	(II)	Hispano-Moresque Ware of the 15th Century		1904
VAN RENSSELAER, STEPHEN	(III)	Early American Bottles and Flasks		1926
VARNUM, WILLIAM H.	(V)	Pewter Design and Construction		1926
VEITCH, HENRY N.	(V)	Sheffield Plate		1908
WALBRIDGE, WILLIAM S.	(III)	American Bottles Old and New		1920
WALKER, LYDIA L.	(IV)	Homecraft Rugs		1930
WALLIS, A. AND BEMROSE, W.	(II)	The Pottery and Porcelain of Derbyshire		1870
WALLIS, H.	(II)	Italian Ceramic Art		1902
WATKINS, LURA W.	(III)	Cambridge Glass, 1818 to 1888		1930
WATTS, W. W.	(V)	Old English Silver		1924
WAUGH, E. AND FOLEY, E.	(IV)	Collecting Hooked Rugs		1927
WEBSTER, MARIE D.	(IV)	Quilts, Their Story and How to Make Them		1915
WEDGWOOD, JOSIAH C.	(II)	Staffordshire Pottery and Its History		1913
WENHAM, EDWARD	(V)	Domestic Silver of Great Britain and Ireland		1932
WERCK, ALFRED	(III)	Stained Glass		1922
WESTROPP, M. S. DUDLEY	(III)	Irish Glass		1921
WHEELER, CANDACE	(IV)	The Development of Embroidery in America		1921
WHEELER, G. OWEN	(I)	Old English Furniture of the 15th, 16th, 17th and 18th Centuries		1924
WHITING, GERTRUDE	(IV)	A Lace Guide for Makers and Collectors		1920
WILLARD, JOHN W.	(VI)	A History of Simon Willard, Inventor and Clockmaker		1911
WILSON, HENRY B.	(II)	Old Leeds Ware		
WOLFE, F. AND A.	(IV)	How to Identify Oriental Rugs		1927
WOODHOUSE, THOMAS	(IV)	Handicraft Art of Weaving		1921
WYLDE, C. H.	(II)	How to Collect Continental China		1907
WYLLIE, BERTIE	(V)	Sheffield Plate		1913
YOUNG, JENNIE J.	(II)	The Ceramic Art		1878
YOUNG, W. A.	(V)	Silver and Sheffield Plate Collector		1919
YOXALL, SIR JAMES	(III)	Collecting Old Glass, English and Irish		1916

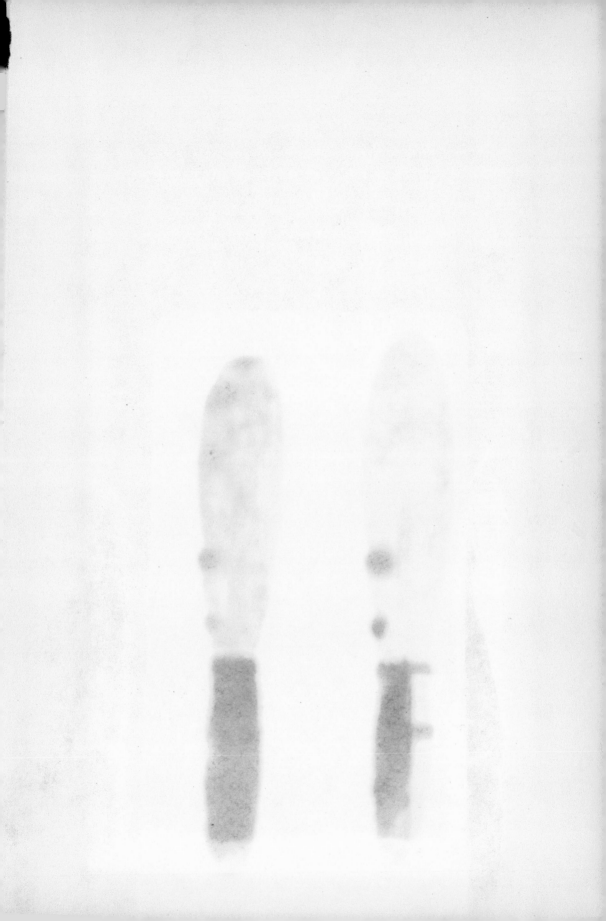